A Journey Through Life:
CHOSEN

Father Luke Zimmer, SS. CC.

Queenship
PUBLISHING COMPANY
P.O Box 42028 Santa Barbara, CA 93140-2028
(800) 647-9882 • (805) 957-4893 • Fax: (805) 957-1631

© 1997 Queenship Publishing

Library of Congress #: 97-067358

Published by:
 Queenship Publishing
 P.O. Box 42028
 Santa Barbara, CA 93140-2028
 (800) 647-9882 • (805) 957-4893 • Fax: (805) 957-1631

Printed in the United States of America

ISBN: 1-57918-000-0

iv

ACKNOWLEDGMENTS

First of all, I would like to take the opportunity to thank all those who have contributed in any way to this book, such as my family, friends and colleagues. Each person in my life has helped me become the person that I am today. I am very grateful to these people because God has blessed me tremendously through them.

I would also like to thank Pat Jersin for transcribing my audio tapes. Without her help, I would have never been able to finish this book. I would also like to thank Queenship Publishing Company for their support by publishing this book.

CONTENTS

PART II

PREFACE

A Journey Through Life: Chosen

Many people have asked me over the years to update my book, *Chosen*. Many of these people have been deeply moved by my book for a variety of reasons. Some people just found *Chosen* to be interesting, while others found *Chosen* to be inspiring. Most of the people who have read *Chosen* also say that they have been moved by the Holy Spirit to live a life of holiness. This is the reason why I decided to divide *A Journey Through Life: Chosen* into two parts: Part One is *Chosen*, while Part Two begins in 1974 and ends in 1996.

1. Part One

There is nothing new in Part One: *Chosen* because I believe many people have been touched with the way it is. Hopefully, those people who have never read *Chosen* will find Part One to be very enriching and inspiring. As for those people who have already read *Chosen*, I hope they will re-read it so that they may refresh themselves.

2. Part Two

In Part Two, I decided to write my book in chronological order. The reason is because so many events have touched me in a variety of ways. Often times, these events have given me greater insight into the spiritual life, which is why throughout *A Journey Through Life: Chosen*, certain themes will keep reappearing. In fact, when we journey through life, we constantly need reminding along the way. As I always say, repetition is the beginning of wisdom. And throughout this book, I repeat various themes so that the people reading the book can also learn and relearn.

Along with the many events that have happened to me since *Chosen*, I also go into great detail in regards to pilgrimages, Renewal Weeks and annual retreats. Hopefully, these places and times of reflection will be very insightful to those who have been on pilgrimages or Renewal Weeks with me. As for the annual retreats, these times of reflection have always been a source of great grace.

Also in Part Two, I respond to various accusations that have been brought against me. Often times, people have accused me of being a fraud, a magician or a person who works with Satan. Some people have accused me of being ignorant and a gullible peasant who always reads into things. Other people have accused me of being a madman, who is hysterical and possibly schizophrenic. Naturally, I totally disagree with each of these accusations. Likewise, if none of these accusations are true, then there must be a rational explanation that will explain all these accusations. The answer, of course, is that God's grace transforms those whom He loves into Jesus Christ so that they may intimately imitate the Son of God. Ultimately, this means to suffer persecution, misunderstanding and even rejection. In this suffering, I believe that each person can know, love and serve God better when he or she is carrying the Cross. This is why I often talk about surrender, forgiveness and relationships with God, others and self.

PART I

Reason for Writing This Book

In the Spring of 1974 I was on my way to Rome to attend a meeting at the International Institute of the Heart of Jesus. I stopped en route to spend a week on the East Coast, in Fairhaven, Massachusetts. I did this because I wanted to see some of the Fathers of our Congregation.

One day, when I was visiting one of our Fathers, at St. Mary's Church, in North Fairhaven, I received a long distance telephone call. The call came from Mother Mary John Dominic, Prioress of the Contemplative Dominican Order, living at the Monastery of the Mother of God, in West Springfield, Massachusetts. She had called to ask me if I would come to visit the Monastery and speak with the Sisters. But I told her that it would be impossible, since I was on my way to Rome and had only one more day to spend in Massachusetts before I would be on my way.

She told me that one of our Fathers, Father Ducey, had an aunt in the Convent there. It happens I knew Bill quite well. We were in the Seminary together and he was one year behind me. That night, as we were going home, we went past Sacred Heart Parish, in North Fairhaven, and there Bill stood outside. I stopped and told him about the conversation I'd had with Mother Mary John Dominic. When he heard this, he said "Well, I don't have anything to do tomorrow. I'll take you there. I'd be glad to drive you to the convent." I agreed that I would go and we went, the next day, to visit the Sisters.

While I was there, I was given the privilege of speaking with the Sisters in the Community room. I talked to them about our Congregation. I also spoke to them about the Rosary and my own

Rosary devotion, hoping that they would be encouraged to continue to pray the Rosary and to have an even deeper love for our Blessed Mother. Since these Sisters have Perpetual Adoration of the Blessed Sacrament, I hoped, too, that they would also be encouraged to pray the Rosary while they were in prayer before the Blessed Sacrament.

After leaving the Monastery, we went back to Fairhaven and, the following morning, I went on my way to Rome, not giving another thought to my visit with the Sisters.

When I arrived home in California, I received a letter from Sister, asking me if I would consider the possibility of writing the story of my life. In a return letter, I told her that, no, I would not write the story of my life, that I felt very negatively about this, that I did not think that it was my duty to even make such a decision and that the only way I would do it would be if I was asked to do so by my Superiors. I figured that would be the end of that.

A few weeks went by and then Sister wrote a letter to Father Provincial. She originally addressed the letter to Father Harold Meyer, thinking that he was my Provincial. The letter found its way to the desk of Father Harold Whelan, who, in actuality, was and still is my Provincial. She expressed in it the feeling that many people would be inspired, much good could come from letting people know the manner in which God has worked in my soul.

After reading the letter, Father Whelan called me into his office and told me about it. He questioned me, "How do you feel about it? What do you think? Would you like to write the story of your life?" I answered, "Not really," explaining to him that I felt very hesitant about the whole idea. His reply was, "You are to do it."

My reasons for not wishing to write about my life were many, and at the time I thought them quite valid. I thought that many people would consider me to be proud and boasting, were I to tell the things that God has done in my soul. I felt that I would risk much suffering, that it might easily be rejected or ridiculed. I could be thought of as a crack-pot or a "Holy Joe."

Father Whelan understood these sentiments and, even as he ordered me to write, expressed some of the same thoughts. He said, "Usually people have their lives written after they are dead, not before they die." And, at that time, I agreed. This is exactly how I felt, but I began to reflect on the fact that nowadays, more and more, people are writing about their lives, the things that God has given to them, as a witness to God's Grace. Father Patrick Peyton has written about his life, and his mission to promote Family Prayer. Thomas Merton has written about his life, as a Contemplative Monk, called upon to break his silence through his pen to bring a greater awareness of contemplative prayer into the world. There are many, many more that I could mention.

And then I realized that, to remain silent, thinking that this is humility, is a false way of thinking which we should overcome. We cannot just pass over the things that God does in our lives as if they did not happen. I think, at times, we *do* have a responsibility to share what has happened in our lives, the experiences that we have received and the Graces and gifts that God has given. It is a grave responsibility. We *must* share these with others, especially today. We live in a time when people need more than ever to be shown that God *does* exist, that He does choose people, at times, and give them a special mission in life.

To be chosen, in this way, does not make any one person great or extraordinary, in his own right. This, in itself, does not make that person a saint. What it does mean is that God can choose whomever He will for whatever He wishes. Usually, when He is working with souls and He has a special mission to be performed, God chooses the lowly. We know this from His life, when He was on earth. He walked with sinners, He talked with sinners, He ate with sinners and, for this, He was accused by the Pharisees and Sadducees.

And so, God continues, in the same manner today. He chooses sinners, still, to carry out His designs. His reason for doing this is to make us realize that, of ourselves, we are nothing. We can *do* nothing, without Him. We are weak and *He* is the One Who is strong. He wishes us to become strong, through Him and in Him, in order that He may glorify Himself. He uses these weak instruments to confound the strong so that, through the events that take place in the life of that person, it is *God* who shines through, it is *God's* work which is manifested — not the individual, not the person whom He chooses to use.

This is what I hope, in relating the story of my life, will shine through: that God is the One to be praised and honored, God is the One to be glorified, and no one else. Like St. Paul, *we* can glory in our weakness and in the folly of loving God, because it is through our weakness and through our folly that we gain the strength of God. It is God, alone, Who helps us to live the life that He wishes us to live.

I hope that relating the story of my life will inspire many people, that many sinners will be encouraged and inspired to become strong, with the help of God, to overcome their weaknesses. It is my hope that they will realize that God loves them and that He is willing to accept them, to embrace them, and to draw them into an intimate union with Him. It is with these thoughts that I now begin to tell the story of my life.

CHAPTER 1

EARLY YEARS

I was born on August 3, 1923, on a small farm of but 80 acres, at Lake Five, Wisconsin, the fifth child of Jacob and Catherine Zimmer.

My Dad

My father was a very poor man who worked hard and whose life showed strong evidence that he felt great responsibility toward his family and his God. I feel that my father was a deeply religious, even saintly, person. He began each day of his life by turning to God and directing toward Him one simple prayer — "All in Your Honor."

The very words of this prayer are eloquent evidence of the depth of his feelings about his God. I never heard him use God's name in vain. I never heard him tell a dirty joke or speak ill of others. I never saw him drink to excess. In fact, he seldom took any liquor whatever, because he was very conscious of his responsibility to support his children and my Mom and, also, of his responsibility toward society.

His religion was a way of life for him which he lived very, very fully. It was more to him than just going to Church on Sunday, although we most certainly did go to Church on Sunday, as a family. We observed all the laws of the Church and we prayed together as a family, saying the Family Rosary each evening. But it was far more than just outward devotion that mattered to my father. His faith was his whole way of life.

In the early years of our childhood, while we were so poor, he did have one weakness in that he was inclined to be a bit too care-

Mom and Dad

All the family - excluding Joe
Girls - Laura, Mary, Pat and Cathy

The five boys - Joe, Ro, Jim, Ben and Larry   *Doctor Joe*

ful with regard to money. He would express concern each time my mother helped the poor or gave money or an extra meal to beggars who would come to our door. He was always a little afraid that he would not have enough money to maintain our home and take care of our family's needs. In later years, though, he more than made up for this. He became a very generous man who would often help others, even to building their houses for them, using his time and talent without expecting to be paid.

But in those days we not only did not have any of the luxuries of life, we sometimes had not even the necessities of life. We did not have the modern conveniences enjoyed by others in our neighborhood. We had no electricity, running water, or plumbing in the house. We had only the barest necessities for carrying on the work on the farm. Our machinery was old and we had horses to do most of the work in the fields, no tractor, no modern equipment.

For clothing we had mostly hand-me-downs. Dad was not able to buy new clothes for each of us. He even had to save for a long time just to buy clothing for himself or Mom. Often people would feel sorry for us and give us clothes that they no longer needed. They also brought food to help us. I think these things accounted for Dad's concern over money. It must have been very hard for him to accept these gifts of charity from others because he had come from a rich family and to go from riches to poverty is not an easy thing.

My Mom

My Mom was also a deeply spiritual person. If she did have any outstanding fault at all, in the eyes of a growing son, it was, perhaps, that she got angry very quickly. She corrected us severely, spanked us often and would often yell at us. Yet who can really blame her for this when she had so many children under foot?

But she lived a truly Christian life and was very charitable, always finding time to be concerned over the poor, the sick, and the suffering. Her heart would always go out to all these people so that many people came to her for solutions to their problems, knowing that they could talk to her and that she would always find time to listen.

Her life was full of trials and constant hardship. She had to work hard in primitive conditions. She had to do the washing with an old run down washing machine, which caused her much grief — more grief than it should have. Each week the washing had to be done. This meant carrying water into the house, heating it, and then getting a cranky old engine started. It was quite a chore to have to endure every week amid the mountains of other chores that fill the life of a woman who lives on a farm.

She had to do all the sewing for our clothes. This seldom meant cutting a garment out of a nice, new piece of material. More often than not, it meant mending old clothes, when they were torn, or making over the clothes that had been given to us by others. This required far greater expertise and patience than if she had been fortunate enough to have new material for every garment she was called upon to make. We really didn't mind having to wear hand-me-downs or old second hand clothes. It just didn't make that much difference to us. We knew that we had to wear our best when we went to school or to Church. We weren't allowed to go off from the house like people often do today. We dressed for our farm work and our daily chores like many people do for Church today. Times have certainly changed!

My Mother also had to do the canning. She had to put up many vegetables and much fruit for the long winter months, so that we would have sufficient food in the house when the winter storms came. And, when the cold weather arrived, she was always very concerned over us. She did her job well.

All of this is merely to point out the type of life which we led. Many people today think that growing up in this manner, living with hand-me-downs and not having every desire satisfied will leave a scar on a person's life. They use this as an argument against having large families. I don't agree with this way of thinking at all. It didn't leave any scars on our lives. I think we came through our family life quite well and there were nine of us children. We certainly had a happy home life. There was much love in our home. All the possessions of the world can't match that. And my parents never allowed worldly deprivations to become an excuse to stop loving God, each other, or us children. They knew what was really important in this life.

Born With A Deformity

I came into this world with a club foot. My left foot turned backwards and this needed to be corrected. My father was worried about the expense and so he argued against it for a while. He hoped that perhaps, through massaging and working with it, the foot could be straightened out by itself. Naturally this wasn't successful because it simply is not the way to go about it.

My Mom insisted that I should be taken to a doctor. In the end she won out and I was taken. This required many trips to both the doctor and the hospital. The leg had to be broken and put into a cast repeatedly until it finally straightened out. Obviously this caused me a good deal of pain. One can only imagine the pain that their sympathy caused my parents to feel, or the patience that was required of them in coping with the heavy casts and incessant crying on my part that was brought about by all of this.

But finally the leg was straight, although, even until this day, the leg is weak. The ankle is also very weak. My left leg is shorter than the right and smaller, although this is not terribly noticeable to others. Parents today have a tendency to question the wisdom of bringing a child into the world with a birth defect. Well, I am certainly grateful that my parents did not feel that way! And I am also very grateful to my Mother for insisting that the leg be straight-

After my cure

ened, that I have the necessary operations, so as to prevent me from having any serious deformity throughout my life.

During the first few years of my life I was also extremely ill, hovering many times between life and death. My parents were told that what was happening was that the white corpuscles in my bloodstream were "eating up" the red corpuscles. What this means in today's terminology is that I had leukemia.

Grandma

During this time my Grandmother lived with Mom and Dad and she often used to take care of me. She was a wonderfully giving person who would spend hours sitting with me in a rocking chair. I had very curly hair and she would spend much time brushing it, talking to me and singing to me. She was also spending that time praying for me, that I would get better and one day be well. She prayed that I would one day be a priest. Even though I was such a tiny youngster at the time, I can still remember her rocking me so lovingly.

One day we learned that she had cancer and would have to undergo surgery. To have an operation in those days was not the easy thing that it is today, and so she suffered a great deal. She came through it, though, and came home. I was only three years old and, when she cam home, I can remember running to the door and saying, "Oh, Grandma, you didn't die! You didn't die! You came back to us!" It made her very happy to see how much I loved her and she continued, even after so much suffering, to rock me and help to take care of me.

Earlier, before I was three years old, because of my illness and so many surgeries to straighten my leg, I used to cry quite a bit. It was often necessary for someone to walk the floor with me at night in order for anyone in the house to get any sleep at all. My Mom would walk the floor with me one night, my Grandma the next night, and my Dad the next. My Dad didn't think that I ought to be doing all that crying and he didn't relish giving up his sleep to walk with me. One night he gruffed out the words, "If he doesn't stop all that crying, I'm going to throw him out in the snow!" My Mom just looked up at him very calmly and said, "Maybe he'll be a priest someday. Then it will all be worth it." Dad snorted back, "Yeah, sure. And I suppose he'll be the Pope, too!" Mom still enjoys telling us all this story and we always get a good laugh out of it.

Eventually Grandma's strength gave way and she died. I can still remember the morning when she died. I had been upstairs sleeping because it was very early in the morning, around 7:30. I heard them say that Grandma had died and I came down and saw that she was dead. Later the undertaker came with the hearse and took her away. That is my last memory of my Grandma on this earth. I don't remember the funeral because I don't think I was allowed to go.

But she has always remained a vivid image in my memory and I have felt her influence throughout my life. I know that I owe much to her, through her prayers and intercession, for my vocation and later on in life.

Finally the day came when I left infancy, with all its illnesses and surgeries, behind me and it was time for me to go to school. I attended a one-room grammar school which had all eight grades. We had only one teacher.

My first teacher was Miss Snow. Later on, she became Mrs. Andrew Ennis. She was a wonderful teacher, quite serious, even at times perhaps too serious. She was young, not necessarily beautiful in a physical sense, but her personality was truly beautiful. She didn't have an easy time of it trying to teach us. There were older boys in the class and they were anything but docile. They teased her, played pranks on her, and, in general, made her life miserable at times.

Nevertheless, she managed to stay with us for a good six years and she imparted a great deal of good sound knowledge to our education. It was during that time that she changed from being a Christian non-Catholic to being a Christian Catholic. Her pleasing and pleasant personality was the sort that leaves its mark on students. She was a very good soul.

After she left we had another teacher whose name was Miss Burke. She was a beautiful, young Irish woman and was my teacher for my seventh and eighth grade years. She was jovial and kind and created a happy atmosphere that made school an interesting place in which to be. She started each day off with dancing. It set a happy tone for the entire day and made this period of time beautiful for me.

School teacher Miss Burke and my sister Pat

Puppy Love

It was during this time that I had my first real crush on a girl and I suppose this added to the happiness I enjoyed during those last years of grammar school. Her name was Maureen and she had blue eyes and red hair. When you are young and smitten by your "first love," you are convinced it's the "real thing." I fancied this a real, deep love life in my youthful innocence. She loved me, too, so there was much rapport between us, complete with all the fluttering of hearts and pulling at the heartstrings that accompanies the puppy love of that age.

To people so young this seems a very serious thing, even though it may seem silly and foolish to the adult world. It's an important part of growing up, an experience we all must go through.

One always remembers these first experiences with much affection in later life. I think Maureen was a wonderful person. If God had intended my life to take a different turn, perhaps I might have married her one day. Who knows? But it wasn't intended to turn out that way.

Actually I consider it a serious mistake for people to get deeply entangled at so young an age. It is, after all, just puppy love. It's no wonder that, if taken more seriously than it ought to be, it can lead to a dog's life. You can't really understand love at that age. Yet today we see youngsters, at that same age, involved with these infatuations and being allowed to let them go far beyond the innocent affection which I experienced.

This stage is, as I said, a part of the lives of all people, a reality that we should all think about and learn to understand so as to be better able to help our young people to grow gracefully through these years. We should provide the wisdom and understanding they need to guide them through this time without becoming entangled in such a way as to damage their later years.

Our School

I guess today people might laugh at the mention of a one-room school. People nowadays think they belong to the middle ages or primitive times. I can't help but wonder, though, looking at all the fancy paraphernalia and modern equipment in today's schools. Do we really need all that in order to give a good education? I don't think so! Granted we were a small school and today's schools must deal with larger numbers of children. We were never more than eighteen nor less than thirteen during the time I attended grammar school.

But, from that school, there came two doctors, a psychiatrist, a veterinarian, two nurses, two teachers, an engineer, and myself, a priest. They say, "The proof of the pudding is in the eating thereof," and I don't think we did too badly. We were able to take our places among the best of students in high school and, later on, in universities.

It's not the paraphernalia, the latest inventions, the greatest technology that's going to give the kids a truly good education. It is rather a dedication on the part of the teachers. And it's a willingness to *be* educated, to go forward, on the part of the students.

I do feel that one thing was definitely in our favor and that was that the students were serious minded. They wanted an education and knew that it was a joy and a pleasure to prepare oneself for life, to learn about the world and what was going on and how to get along in it. I don't think today's schools could have improved on our education.

Religious Training

We received our religious training, for the most part, through the good example of our parents. Religion meant far more to them than just an outward attempt at devotion. Their faith in God was lived in every fiber of their beings. Yet there were also in our lives the external signs of devotion that make up a definite part of Faith. We were taught to develop a great love for God, for our Blessed Mother, for the Rosary, for our Church, for the pope and for priests. We all had great respect for priests.

During my grammar school days we also had formal religious instructions. This amounted to only fifteen minutes, once a week during the school months. We would walk over to the Church, a mile and a half away, for these classes and then our parish priest, Father William Restle, would come down and give us our instruction. He had to split the group into different sections so as to spend fifteen minutes with each one. In this way, we learned about our Faith.

We didn't learn a great deal about our religion, only the bare necessities. I feel that I hardly knew my religion at all. We learned about it more through living it because the actual formal knowledge was so sadly lacking. This was not due to a lack of interest on the part of the priest or my parents. It was due, in part, to the hard life of the farm community, where there was always so much work waiting to be done and seldom much time to sit down for anything.

I think that this happens still in many families today. People lead active lives, religion is not really learned, and it is not understood correctly and appreciated as it should be. I think, though, that in most lives today there is far less reason to have

My first Holy Communion

this happen. If time can be found for Little League and for Scouting and for PTA and whatever else, then time could be found for parents to teach their children about God. Very few children today are required to do so many chores that there is no time left over for this.

Proper Sex Education Necessary

There is still another area in which children should be given a great deal more help and instruction. This is in regard to the teachings about sex. I realize that today there is an over-emphasis on the subject and that they are teaching about sex in schools. Still, I do not feel that they are giving proper instruction about sex today any more than they did in my day. The only difference is that the subject is more openly discussed.

In my day our parents never really spoke about that question. They never explained anything to us and so we did not learn anything at all about sex from them. Our parish priest also never spoke about these things. We therefore had no way to get this training from the proper source.

We did learn from others. We were observant. We knew from watching animals, how their young came into the world and of course we were able to deduce from this the manner in which children came into the world, so that, by the age of eight, I knew this much. But, what I did *not* know was the teaching of Jesus Christ about this great and beautiful gift that God has given to us. I learned from the wrong sources and, naturally, I learned the wrong things.

Sex — A Gift From God

It is a tremendously beautiful gift that God has given to us, to be co-creative with Him in bringing life into the world. This gift should be used only by a husband and wife. When they do, it is something very great, beautiful and wonderful. The body is not dirty, nor sex dirty or wrong. It is only the misuse of it that is wrong. God does not create evil. God creates only good and it is God Who created this great power within man.

There are two great drives within man. The first is the desire to preserve his life, to stay alive and to live. This is within all men and is the greatest urge within him. The other is the urge to reproduce himself. This drive is also in all men. It is one which has a strong wish to be satisfied. However, we must learn to control this drive so that we do not misuse this gift that God has given to us, this *trust* that God has given to men.

If we do no learn correctly, if we are not told the beauty of its proper use, the temptations we will run into to use it improperly and the consequences thereof, it becomes very easy to fall into the habit of misusing this gift. Knowledge, in itself, about the nature of sex is not enough. It is necessary that one be taught the need for self-discipline. We must be taught how to avoid temptations, the reasons why we should do so, and the way to keep and preserve intact this beautiful gift that God has given to us, so that we will know how to use it only as God wishes. If we do not receive this instruction, we are left prey to all manner of pitfalls and temptations.

Parents' Duty To Teach Sex Education

This instruction should, primarily, come from the parents. It should not be abrogated, shirked, or turned over to others. It is the responsibility of the parents to instruct their children on this subject in such a manner as to allow them to *appreciate* the beauty of God's plan for mankind in bestowing upon him the privilege of participating with Him in the creation of life. The instruction provided by the school systems is most certainly not sufficient. In most cases it is no more than a mechanics course on the subject, with no thought or appreciation of the morality, the beauty, the principal purpose for which the gift of sex was created.

Since, in my parents' day, sex was never openly discussed, their hesitancy to speak of the subject was an understandable thing. But, in our day, this is not the case. There is no excuse in today's world for parents, through negligence or embarrassment, to overlook this serious responsibility to their children. The devil is doing a pretty good job of exploiting his ideas on the subject. Surely God's plan in the use of sex deserves, at the very least, "equal time" with the world's and the devil's ideas about its use!

Because of my ignorance, I must admit that I misused this gift. I honestly did not know that it offended God for me to do so. That may sound strange to most people.

We Have A Free Will

But really, when you stop and think about it, maybe it isn't so strange, after all. How many of today's young people, engaged in sexual misbehavior, really know and understand that what they are doing is wrong? How many connect the misuse of sex with God's laws? Or would they argue, "It's human nature. It's instinct. You can't help it" Of course, they are wrong. We are not men of instinct. We are men of reason. We have a free will and we *can* learn right from wrong — *if* we are told.

This was especially true in my case. I am the sort of person who must be *told*, "This is wrong. That is right." At least I was at that time. If no one told me, then I simply did not know, and I acted accordingly, from the time I was thirteen, until the time when I was twenty years old.

We Are Responsible For Our Actions

Once in a while, it occurred to me that it might be wrong. But I refrained from asking questions, out of embarrassment, thinking, "What if I am wrong? What will people say? What will they think of me?" And thus I rationalized with myself, thinking, "If others do it, then it can't be wrong. Else they wouldn't do it." Well, I was very wrong in that respect and I was very naive. I didn't know much about people and human nature. I was far too idealistic. Today I am more of a realist than I was at that time.

I also refrained from raising any serious questions because I perhaps subconsciously figured that, if I found out that my way of acting was wrong, then I would have to stop — and maybe I did not wish to do so. So I continued to act as I did, without too much effort on my part to find out the truth. I excused myself with the fact that I was also busy with my farm work and my high school work and so I never took time to sit down and read and study as I should have done. Later on, I got this opportunity and I did find out the correct things, as I shall explain later.

A Journey Through Life: Chosen

CHAPTER 2

HIGH SCHOOL DAYS
AND AFTER

When I went to high school I took the easiest course because I didn't feel that I was going to go into any particular profession and I didn't know just what I wanted to do in life. I had no ideal or goal in mind, except perhaps to go back and work on the farm. I did want to get married. I wanted a large family, too. I just figured that I'd get through school as fast and as easy as I could and worry about what to do with my life later on.

What Vocation To Follow?

In my senior year I began to think occasionally about the priesthood. The reason for this was because of something that happened during the summer preceding my last year in high school. My aunt, Sister Mary Bernard, and my great-aunt, Sister Mary Clementine, came for a home visit and they spent five days with us. It was the first time that they had been permitted to do this. I watched them while they were with us and their religious garb intrigued me. They would get up very early every morning and I would see them walking out on the lawn and saying their prayers. They would eat very little, talk less. They were preaching a sermon in silence. I began to think that maybe God wanted me to be a priest. These thoughts kept coming back to me, off and on, during that entire summer.

One Sunday in particular, these thoughts were especially persistent. I had been keeping score for a baseball team during that summer. One Sunday we were on the playground right next to the pastor's house. I could not help but think, all that afternoon, as I watched his house, "What is Father doing? What type of life does he really have? Is he happy? Does he pray a lot? What does he *do*?" And I knew I had an attraction toward that life. I wished I could go and talk to him about it, but I was too shy and I just didn't do anything about it.

These thoughts persisted for a good while after that. But, each time they returned, I would always start to think, "How can I be a priest?" I had no knowledge of Latin. I hadn't taken Latin because I'd figured it would be too hard. I didn't have any money. I thought that, to go to a seminary, you needed a lot of money to pay for the education. I didn't realize that, if you had a vocation, you could go through free, that you didn't have to worry about the money. And then, too, I told myself, "What about the problem with the girls? I like them." After all, I wanted to get married, so I just decided that I did not have a vocation and pushed it out of my mind. I figured the best thing to do was just to continue as I had been, for the time being.

After I graduated from high school I stayed on my Father's farm and continued to run it. I had been helping gradually more and more ever since I'd turned thirteen. We lost all our cattle that year and my Dad had to go back to working as a carpenter in order to support the family. My brothers had to go out and get jobs and I had to start taking over the work of the farm. My younger brother, who was just eleven at the time, helped and the two of us did most of the work. By the time I had graduated from highschool, I had reached the point where I could do most of the work on the farm.

In the beginning it was a great joy and a pleasure to stay home and do the work on the farm. It was hard work, manly work, but it was very challenging and rewarding work, in itself. Still there came a day when I realized that I could not spend the rest of my life this way. It just wasn't right for me.

If I stayed right where I was, I could envision nothing but a state where money was always going out while we never really got anything back for it. I began to reason that I could never possibly support a family this way. We would always be in debt. I could see no possibility that anything really worthwhile could ever develop for me from what I was doing and the way I was living. I felt that, possibly, I ought to be doing something different, but I didn't know just what it would be at the time.

CHAPTER 3

JOINING THE ARMY AIR CORPS AND SICKNESS

The war was on and I had a deferment from the draft board, but one day I got to talking to our mailman, who was on the draft board. I asked him if it would be possible for me to enlist in the service, in spite of the deferment. He said I certainly could and that he would be happy to make arrangements so that I could, if I really wanted to.

I told him to go ahead and make the arrangements. I had reached a point where I knew I had to do something to change the course of my life and this seemed like it. I didn't tell my Dad what I'd done because I didn't dare. I was too afraid of what he might say.

Finally the letter came, asking me to report for my physical. When I did and passed, I was sworn into the Army Air Corps. I was overjoyed. I came back home to tell my parents that I was going into the service. The finality of having been sworn in gave me the courage to face them.

How I Broke The News To My Parents

We happened to have neighbors visiting with us that night. We were all sitting around the table, playing cards and laughing, when I blurted out, "I am going into the service." My Dad just sat and looked at me for a moment. He didn't want me to go but he knew it was already too late.

His voice had an almost pleading tone when he said, "Now what am I going to do?" In the brazen stupidity of youth, I neither knew nor cared that I was laying a heavier burden of worry on my Father's shoulders. I didn't even think about what I was saying, as I sullenly retorted, "Well, you can go to Hell!" Then I did realize what I had said. My Dad didn't say a word back to me. His only reaction was to sit there, pale and hurt looking. Maybe he said nothing because others were present. Maybe he was just too shocked to answer me. I guess he didn't know what to say to me and I guess he knew it wasn't the right time to say anything to me, watching my attitude, the way I must have looked, and the way I said things.

But, like a flash, the thoughts came to my mind. "Do you really mean this? Do you really want your Dad to go to Hell?" And it was as if I saw Hell and I knew there was a Hell and I knew there was a Devil. And so, I said to God, "No. No. I don't mean that. I don't want anything to happen to my Father. Rather it should happen to me — and never to my Dad."

Of course, I still had to go to the service, but I was very sorry for ever having said a thing like that.

I Become Ill

A few nights before my departure, the same people were back playing cards again. It was a gathering to say farewell to me. I had accidentally bumped my leg, while cleaning out the chicken house, and I had developed a very sore and painful leg. All evening, while I was trying to play cards, the pain persisted and grew worse. Finally, I felt as though I were going to pass out. I decided I'd better walk outside and get some fresh air. After a while, I came back into the house and began playing cards, but I felt faint, just as before.

I remember getting out the words, "I am going —" That was the last thing I said. I fell over and, when I awoke, there were people standing all around me. I heard someone say, "Get a priest." Another said, "No, get a doctor." As soon as I could speak, I told them what was wrong. When they could see that I was conscious, they said, "O.K., we don't need to call a priest, but we will still have to call a doctor." And so they did.

When the doctor came and looked at me, he discovered that I had phlebitis, a blood clot in the leg. It had developed from my having bumped the leg a few days before. A piece of it must have gone to my heart and that was what had caused me to pass out. I guess I am lucky that I ever regained consciousness.

The doctor prescribed some medicine and told me to stay in bed and put a heating pad on my leg. He promised to come back the next day. I did as he'd told me and fell asleep, not realizing that the heating pad was defective. By the next morning, it had burned through to the bone.

When I awoke, the blood clot was gone, but the leg was so badly burned that I had to take care of it for many, many weeks. The doctor made arrangements with the army so that I wouldn't have to report right away and I stayed home for another two weeks, hoping to get my leg into shape.

Reporting For Duty

Finally I was able to report to the service. My Mom made the trip with me to Ft. Sheridan, in Great Lakes, Illinois. We spent the time at Great Lakes having our clothes issued to us, getting our hair cut, being involved with orientation, tests, and what have you. Finally, we were ready to disembark for the place where we were to spend our "boot camp."

Sick Again

It started to rain while we were waiting for the train. It was damp, cold, and dreary, a real wet, spring-like day. I wasn't feeling too well and I felt my throat getting sore, so I decided to lay down after I got on the train.

I awoke in the middle of the night with terrible pain in my legs and all I could think was, "That clot must be back again." I told one of the soldiers what I thought was happening and he went to the person in charge and told him what was wrong. When they came back, they told me that, when we arrived in Kansas City the next day, I'd better let a doctor take a look at me.

At noon, the next day, the doctor came in to see me. He quickly decided that the best thing to do would be to take me to the hospital. The next thing I knew, I was being unceremoniously loaded onto a stretcher and taken in a van to Ft. Leavenworth Hospital, where I spent the next sixty-one days.

The doctors began to examine me and, after many tests during the next few days, it was discovered that I had rheumatic fever. Knowing nothing at all about the disease, I was relieved when they told me what was wrong with me. I told myself, "Now it won't be so bad. I'll get back on my feet in no time and be as strong and healthy as I've always been." I was soon to discover that I was sadly mistaken. The days lingered on into weeks and the weeks into months, before I was finally well and could go on my way. It was during that hospital stay that I again started thinking about becoming a priest.

Fr. Luke's family farm where he grew up.

CHAPTER 4

MY VOCATION
IN LIFE IS DECIDED

It was during that interval that I received a letter from my youngest brother, explaining that my second oldest brother was planning to be married. He was going to marry a Christian non-Catholic. I had nothing against non-Catholics. Many of them were my friends and I thought that they were dear, wonderful people, but I did not think it was wise for people getting married to have a mixed marriage. I felt that Catholics should marry Catholics, non-Catholics should marry non-Catholics, so that there would be harmony and peace in the home, with no fighting over religion. Children should be raised in one faith and given a chance to live this way so as not to have them confused.

I decided right then and there that I would become a priest. The same objections as before still taunted me — no money, no Latin, and I still liked girls. So I told God, "O.K., I *will* be a priest. But You'll have to see to it that I can learn sufficient Latin. If You'll do that then I'll give up the idea of getting married and I'll give myself completely and totally to You."

I decided that I would do this, in reparation, so that my sister-in-law would be converted, become a Catholic, and there would be one faith in the house and family. This is the offering that I made and, from that time on, I never again doubted that I had a vocation.

That was the occasion that it took to make me solidify my ideas and definitely decide that it was the right thing for me to do, but it was a firm decision and it began to reflect in all my actions from that moment on.

Boot Camp

After being in the hospital for sixty-one days, I was permitted to go to Texas to begin my "boot camp." When I got there, the group I had started out with was just finishing up and here I was, just coming in. I'd missed training with them and had to start all over again. All this accomplished for me was to add a mood of dejection to the weakness I still felt from having just left the hospital. I still wasn't feeling at all well.

Actually the doctors didn't even want me to start my basic training right away. But, somehow, my papers got mixed up and I was put into basic training immediately. I kept up with the training right along with everybody else, but I felt weak and faint the whole time. Many times I just didn't think I was going to make it, but I was determined to do so and I did, right up until the very end of the basic training.

Sickness Returns

What was happening was that I was having another attack of rheumatic fever. I didn't want anybody to find out about it so I kept silent. I was assigned to cooking duty as we went into one of our final exercises, toward the end of basic training.

We were out on bivouac, walking back seventeen miles and carrying a full pack. The awful weakness and feeling of faintness persisted and grew worse until I finally had to tell the sergeant about it. He just said, "Go ahead and march. You can make it. Nothing's going to happen to you." So I decided I would walk back with everybody.

After about an hour, we had our first break and I sat down. It was decidedly the wrong thing to do, because, when I stood up, my feet were so swollen and sore that I could barely walk. I decided that I'd better not sit down and rest from then on when we took a break and so I just kept on going without stopping, until we got back to the barracks.

When we got back, we had some time off, but the only thing I wanted to do was to go to bed. I wasn't hungry, so I went to bed immediately. The next morning I knew I had to go to the doctor. My foot was badly swollen. When he saw me, he put me right back in the hospital.

In The Hospital Again

And so, here I was, back in the hospital a second time. The first time 'round, they had given us sulfa drugs to try and counteract the rheumatic fever. It had no effect, whatsoever, so this time when I came in, they were giving us twenty-one aspirins a day for it. For the next few days I felt like I was on a "cheap drunk." The beds would spin 'round and 'round. I couldn't figure out what was going on and why it was so hard to wake up. I was sleepy all the time and I could just barely hear the nurse coming down the aisle from many beds down. By the time she would get to me I would be just awake enough to take medicine or food, when it was given to me. I just couldn't seem to feel "with it."

Finally it hit me, "It must be the medicine that's causing this!" and so I quit taking the medicine. I just hid it under the pillow and, within a few days, the motion and the feeling of seasickness disappeared. I kept the pills hidden during the day when they came in to change the bed or do anything for me so that they would not find them. Then, at night, when I was able to get up and hop down to the bathroom, I would just flush them down the toilet. I never took any more of the pills and I began to feel better just by staying in bed. The pain left and I knew I was beginning to get well.

Experiment With Penicillin

Then they decided to conduct an experiment. They decided they would give us a shot of penicillin every three hours for fifteen days, day and night. They chose the two who had been the longest in the hospital and the last two who had come into the hospital with this illness. I happened to be the last one in, so I was one of the ones chosen for the experiment.

We learned very quickly that penicillin had no effect on rheumatic fever at all. It might prevent an attack of rheumatic fever, but, once you have an attack, it doesn't do anything at all to help you get over it. All we got out of that experiment was a few more aches and pains from the "shots."

I remained there in the hospital until they decided to move me to a hospital in Tucson. Before they could move me, I had an attack of appendicitis and had to have surgery for that. A few days following the surgery, they decided I was well enough to move and I was taken by stretcher to a plane bound for Tucson, Arizona, where I stayed for a good little while in the last part of 1944.

At The Hospital In Tucson

I remember coming into the ward and the first thing that happened was that the man next to me wanted to show me some dirty pictures. Since I had decided to be a priest, I didn't feel that I should be looking at things like that and I told him so. I simply said, "I don't look at those," and he just sat there looking sort of surprised and didn't say a word. But, I found out that, later on, this had a tremendous effect on him. He had defected from the Church and was no longer even going to Mass. He had been a big football player and, when he got rheumatic fever and was left so weak and helpless with it, he felt that God was treating him unfairly. He was trying to "strike back" by not practicing his faith.

Later on, after I left the service and was discharged, he straightened himself out and got back to the Church. He wrote me a beautiful letter about it, thanking me for this incident. My having refused to look at those pictures had made a tremendous impression on him. It made him take a look at himself and realize what he was doing and that it was wrong.

Witnessing For God

News got around that I was a Catholic and people started coming around to ask questions about the Faith. A few came to ridicule, but it didn't bother me. I was very happy to have the opportunity to talk about my Faith.

Talking about my Faith also made me painfully aware of my lack of knowledge about it. I just didn't know *anything* and I knew that this had to be rectified, that I *had* to do something about it.

Holy Hour Once a Week

After I'd been in the hospital awhile, I got well enough to go out on a pass once a week. For me, that meant going for a Holy Hour, in Tucson, at the Benedictine Sisters of Perpetual Adoration of the Blessed Sacrament Sanctuary, and this is where I would go every Thursday night, just to participate in this Holy Hour.

One night, as I was walking out from the Holy Hour, I noticed some literature, the magazine that the Benedictine Sisters put out from Clyde, Missouri. It was called *Tabernacle and Purgatory*. There was also a little leaflet on the Scapular Devotion and, in this way, I learned more about our Blessed Mother and discovered what the Scapular Devotion really meant.

Discharged From The Service

At this point, the service decided that they could not take the risk of keeping me any longer. Rheumatic fever can re-occur repeatedly and the danger is always there of having it ruin one's health completely or even cause death. I have seen others who suffered greatly, whose hearts were damaged, and some who even did die from the disease. Knowing this, I considered myself pretty lucky to be permitted to go home.

Going Home

On my way home, I took the train through the southern route to Wisconsin. There was a little boy on the train, traveling with his Mother. They were on their way to a reunion with the Father. I had the privilege of taking care of him most of the way. It was a great pleasure and, once again, the desire to have a family of my own came back. I quickly set it aside because I had told God that I wanted to be a priest and I meant it. I wasn't going to change my mind.

Sick At Home

It was in the middle of winter and coming from the beautiful weather in Tucson to the stormy cold weather in Wisconsin was a drastic change. I got home and was there only a very short time when I had another attack of rheumatic fever. This time it really hit me hard. I had joint involvement throughout all of my body, except for my neck. I was completely immobile for many days and nights.

The pain was just unreal. If someone so much as walked across the floor, the vibration was enough to make me scream with pain.

My Mother waited on me, hand and foot, took care of me and stayed up nights with me. My Dad also watched at my bedside and my younger brother and sisters all helped to watch at my side and take care of me.

One day my brother, who was studying to be a doctor, came home and explained to me just what the dangers of rheumatic fever amounted to. He told me that this was a long, drawn-out process. Now I finally realized the full impact of this sickness. Before this time I'd thought that it was just a passing thing, soon to be over with, and that I would be up and around and able to go about my business. Now I realized that this was not to be the case.

I became so ill that a priest was called and he gave me the Last Sacraments. They thought I would surely die, but I managed to "weather the storm." I think the thing that kept me alive, during all that time, was my tremendous desire to be a priest.

I remember one occasion in particular. One afternoon a neighbor came to visit. He couldn't walk very well. He used a cane and, to sit down, he had to hold on to something to steady himself. He made the mistake of grabbing my foot and I nearly came right out of that bed, in spite of the fact that I had been unable to move. The pain was that intense. It felt as though someone had stabbed me in the back, over and over again. Sharp stabs of pain jolted through my body again and again.

Until that point I had been able to speak normally. After this happened, I was so weak from the whole ordeal that I couldn't even whisper. I heard the man's wife say to my Mother, "Why, he won't live. He's suffering too much." But I knew that God would let me live to be a priest — at least that was my hope and my prayer.

Gradually I began to get a little better. I had become so weak that I couldn't even lift an empty glass. I had to remain on my back most of this time. It's a good thing that it was during the winter months, or I would have been covered with bed sores to add to my misery.

Finally, toward spring, I was able to roll over on my side for a little while. I would get completely out of breath and all tired out, then I would have to go back to my original position. Since I now realized what a long, drawn-out affair this was going to be, I began to pray more.

CHAPTER 5

SUFFERING CAN BE TURNED INTO JOY

The Value of Suffering

One day, as I was looking at the Crucifix which hung on the wall across from my bed, I saw Christ on that Crucifix and I said, "Who am I to be above the Master? He suffered so much and He was innocent. He never did anything wrong in His life. Certainly I can suffer and offer my sufferings with Him to the Father for others." And this is what I did. Then suffering took on deeper meaning. I realized, at that moment, that Jesus Christ was an all-loving God. I realized that He loved me with an unconditional love, He loved me just as I was.

What a tremendous realization! What a tremendous experience, to find out and really understand that Jesus Christ is truly our Brother! He is our God! He loves us and He gave His life for us! He shed His Blood for us! He gave His *all* for *us*! He gave His Church for us! These thoughts just overwhelmed me and for many days I thought about just that. I could think of nothing else.

I never asked the question, "Why me, Lord? Why did I have to suffer?" I thanked God that I never asked that question. To me it was a simple matter of accepting and seeing the value of suffering and offering it up to God.

Learning About God Through Prayer

I began to learn my Religion by looking at the Cross, meditating and thinking about God, and by saying the Rosary. I would picture in my mind all the different details that took place in each mystery.

The Annunciation

I would picture the Angel coming to Mary, the conversation that they had, the response of Mary, what this all meant, and how the Holy Spirit formed Christ in Mary and our redemption actually began at that moment.

Visitation

I pictured Mary going to visit Elizabeth, greeting Elizabeth, what happened, the response between them, the stay that they had together, her return to Nazareth, her home town, Joseph's trial, when he saw her, the concern he suffered, the conversation he had with the Angel, the way he obeyed and took Mary as his wife and took her into his home, taking care of her and being a true foster father to Jesus and a true husband to Mary.

Birth Of Christ

Later on, they made their trip to Bethlehem. I pictured the circumstances of the birth of Christ, the Angels coming to the shepherds, the shepherds coming to adore Christ, the Magi coming, their visit with Herod on the way, their warning to return by another route, Joseph's warning to take the Holy Family and flee to Egypt, and I could picture each detail of all these things.

Presentation — Offering In The Temple

Then they went to the Temple and the old man, Simeon, came and saw them and took Christ in his hands and offered Him to the Father, prophesying about Christ, about Mary, about the way in which her Heart would be pierced with a sword of sorrow, the prophetess, Anna, her words and what she did. Finally, their suffering, while they were in Egypt, the trip back to Nazareth, their life there.

Finding Jesus In The Temple

Then, the next time we see them is in the Temple, when Jesus was twelve years old and they lost Him, the things that happened, how they searched for Him, found Him in the Temple, listened to His questions and answers with the doctors, their amazement at His knowledge of the things of God and the conversation between Jesus and Mary.

Agony In The Garden

Next I would think about the Sorrowful Mysteries, Jesus, in the Garden of Gethsemane, suffering after He had been with the Apostles in the upper room and instituted His Church, the Priesthood, the Blessed Sacrament, His fearful and frightened pleading with His Father to be merciful and let this Chalice of suffering pass from Him, yet resigned to the Will of God the Father, His finding the Apostles asleep and asking them to come and pray and watch with Him. But they fell asleep again and did not participate. Then Judas came, Christ was captured and led away, put into prison, questioned by Caiphas, treated harshly, taken to the Temple, where Pilate sent Him to Herod and Christ remained silent when a robe of mockery was put about His shoulders and He was brought back to Pilate again. The people demanded crucifixion for Him and Pilate washed his hands and gave the condemnation sentence.

Way Of The Cross

Then He walked the Way of the Cross to Calvary, met His Mother and, when He saw her, He suffered with her. This gave me strength, yet it deepened my own suffering, because I knew that my own Mother watched me suffer. Interior suffering is far greater than exterior. I knew it must have been the same with Jesus. It gave me greater understanding of Jesus' suffering, the longing He had for the salvation of souls, how He wished to alleviate suffering, yet had to go through such intense suffering in order to bring about the happy conclusion of His mission. I recalled how His Mother went with Him, giving Him courage to continue, standing beneath the Cross, watching Him suffer and die.

Crucifixion

I watched Him being nailed to the Cross, dying, the words that He spoke, the meaning of these words. I kept going over them all in my mind, again and again, seeing how they signified the tremendously deep love that Jesus had for us. And, all the while, I learned still more about my Religion.

Resurrection

Lastly, I meditated on the Glorious Mysteries. I thought about Christ, rising from the dead, that one day we, too, will rise from the dead with Him, His meeting with the Apostles after His Resurrection, the gift of hearing Confessions, the power to forgive sins, the *command* to forgive sins.

Ascension Into Heaven

Then came His Ascension into Heaven, the Glory that He got from His Father. I pictured what went on in Heaven, when He came home and that He is there now, as a Mediator, with God the Father. He's an Intercessor. He's the One Who will offer prayers to the Father. He said He would come again.

Descent Of The Holy Spirit

He said, also, that He would send the Holy Spirit. He told the Apostles to wait and pray and they did, with Mary, His Mother, beside them. Then the Holy Spirit came upon them and they went out and preached the message of Christ and, just as Christ promised, they knew that the Holy Spirit would bring to their minds all that He had taught them so that they could go forward and preach this message to the whole world. This is exactly what they did.

To Be An Apostle

I dwelt on what it means to be an Apostle. I feel that it is one who is called by God, one who has been given the same mission that Christ received, one who must share this with others, one who must preach this, no matter what the cost, no matter what the price, no matter how much suffering, no matter even if they are killed like the Apostles were. They must still be willing to carry their cross and bring this message to the whole world. This gave me greater courage to continue in my desire to be a priest and to carry out this work for God, once I became one.

Assumption Of Mary Into Heaven

Then I thought about Mary's life, how it ended, how she died, how she was assumed into Heaven. We do not know this from Scripture, but we do know this from the teachings of the Church, the Traditions of the Church. We cannot help but see how fitting it was that, since she did not participate in the fall of man, she would not have the stain of sin upon her soul at any time, that she was immaculately conceived, free from sin, that she *should* have the reward, the privilege, the gift of having her body assumed and re-united to her soul to be in Heaven, with her Son, her God.

Mary's Relationship To The Blessed Trinity

She was intimately associated with the Triune Persons by reason of the very fact that she was chosen by God to be the Mother of Jesus, to be a real daughter to the Father, to be the Spouse of the Holy Spirit. There is a deep, intimate relationship between the Blessed Mother and the Blessed Trinity.

Queen Of Heaven And Earth

In the last mystery, the Coronation, she is given her rightful place as the Mother of Christ and the Mother of all men and the Queen of Angels and men. She is the highest, next to God. She is not God, she is still a creature. She is like the moon, in comparison to the sun. We have great love and respect for her, but we do not ever offer her worship nor would she accept it. We respect her, because she is our Mother. We love her and we ask her to intercede for us.

If we can ask people in this life to pray for us, then how logical to ask her. And why can't we also ask the saints, since they are the special friends of God and are with God and can pray for us and intercede for us? Why *can't* we ask them, if we can ask people in our world to pray for us, to help us? This is what we mean when we turn to them.

So, I learned many, many things by saying the Rosary, day in and day out, all fifteen decades. I thought about all that these different Mysteries meant in the spiritual life. They really came alive for me and gave me great joy and deepened my understanding of their meaning. I got much happiness out of praying my Rosary for the honor and glory of God. And, by thinking about each Mystery deeply, applying it to my own life, I learned much more about Scripture, more than if I had just read it. I learned how God really loves us, Jesus really loves us.

Learning About God Through Reading

I spent much time each day reading books on the lives of the saints. I would read through pamphlets and I would say many other prayers. Every day I would say the Litany of the Sacred Heart, the Litany of the Holy Name, the Litany of the Blessed Mother, or any other beautiful prayer that I could get hold of. Of course, I found out later on that these things were not necessary. It is more necessary to meditate and to talk to God and to be aware that we are with God. I felt that saying the Rosary was the best way for me to do this and I derived much benefit from saying the Rosary in this manner.

Little Rose Ferron

The first book that I received, after I was ill, was given to me by a friend. It was called, *She Wears a Crown of Thorns*, the life of Little Rose Ferron, by Father Boyer. I know that she is not recognized by the Church as a saint. Many feel that she was not a person who will ever be canonized. I could not help, in reading that book, but feel that here was a person who loved God, who suffered for God and who was filled with charity for others.

The family had fifteen children and each one was dedicated to a Mystery of the Rosary. Little Rose was number ten, dedicated to the Crucifixion. It was not surprising then that, in her life, she followed the Cross of Christ, carried that Cross, and participated in the sufferings of that Cross. Christ let her bear the marks of His suffering in her body, her hands, her feet, her side, her head, just as St. Francis of Assisi did, many years ago, just as Padre Pio and Therese Neumann of more modern times.

I didn't know of any of those things before I read that book, so it was sort of an eye opener for me to realize that God could choose someone and give such tremendous gifts as these to anyone here on earth. I know that these special gifts did not make her a special person. What made her so beautiful was her tremendous, heroic life of Christian living, her purity, her fortitude, her courage, her humility, her obedience to all her spiritual advisors, the leaders of the Church, priests, pastors, and the Bishop. She had tremendous power with God in the conversion of sinners, to bring them back to God, to help them to make peace with God. She prayed for them, she interceded for them, she paid the price for them and they responded, with an open heart to God's gifts and graces, when He gave them, and they made their peace with God.

She was an instrument of reconciliation, just as Jesus was. He was the greatest person of reconciliation and we, also, must be instruments of reconciliation. We will do that, if we are Christlike. I feel that she was Christ-like. She taught me this lesson and she taught me the beauty of trying to do the Will of God.

Suffering is not a curse. Our nature naturally rebels against it and we do not like to suffer, but suffering can be accepted and offered for the conversion of other people. God made this necessary in the economy of salvation. It is through suffering that many graces are given and so we should never say, "Why do I have to suffer?" We should say we are privileged to suffer with Christ. We do not look for it, but, when it enters our lives, we accept it and we use it for God's honor and glory. We *can* pray to suffer, if we are willing to carry the Cross, whatever God may wish to give, but we should not *inflict* punishment, we should not *inflict* suffering upon ourselves. We should do only what God wishes us to do. If we are given an illness or a suffering, then we should accept it and have the right attitude of mind about it. Then we will be filled with peace, joy and happiness, in spite of physical pain, mental pain, emotional upsets, spiritual problems or dryness, or what have you. We can have that real deep love, peace, satisfaction, joy and happiness that God gives to people who learn this tremendous lesson.

So my suffering then was not suffering any longer, because it had a mission. I had a joy in doing this for God and for others. I felt that this was one way I could contribute to help spread the message of Christ throughout the world, right from my own sick bed. I finished reading this book in the spring of 1945.

Other Reading Material

Then I decided to read again the magazine, *Tabernacle and Purgatory* and the Scapular Devotion leaflet I had picked up when I was still in the service. I decided to use some of the money that I received from the Government, as disability compensation, to give gift subscriptions to different people among my relatives and friends. For many months I sent five new subscriptions in each month. It cost a good bit and maybe I should have used the money for my family or for the poor, but, at the time, this is how I saw fit to use the money and I did so.

After awhile the Sisters sent me, as a gift, a box of all their booklets and a Crucifix. I didn't get a chance to look at them right away. I was reading other books and studying them, especially the lives of saints, such as St. Francis of Assisi, St. Francis Xavier, Maria Goretti. I read also about Fatima and Jacinta. It was the first time that I had heard about Fatima and I read avidly with the story leaving a deep impression on me.

The book that most impressed me was the one about St. Francis Xavier. Here was a real saint. When he was young, he was worldly, he was intelligent, he was not religious. It took another saint to change him. This was St. Ignatius. He would always say to him, "Francis, what does it profit a man to gain the world and suffer the loss of his soul?" This would make Francis very angry and bitter against Ignatius. Finally Grace triumphed and Francis gave in and became a priest, a great missionary, and a tremendous saint.

CHAPTER 6

A REAL CONVERSION
OF HEART

Learning The Truth

On December 3, 1945, the Feast of St. Francis Xavier, I was reading my brother's religion book. While I was reading, I came across the section concerning morality and sex. Suddenly, for the first time, I discovered the teaching of the Church in this regard. Here I was, twenty-one years old and only now learning these things. I read avidly and, because, as I read, I began to realize that I had misused this gift, I cried like a baby. I realized that I had done something that was contrary to God's wishes.

Christ's Love For Us

I had no guilt feelings about this. I knew that, since I hadn't been aware of any wrongdoing, I was guilty of no sin. Still I felt that I wanted to speak of it in Confession, and so, when Father Restle came, I told him.

He had to sit there, next to me, in a chair, while I told him these things. When he was ready to leave, he looked at me and I could see a look of hurt in his eyes. Yet there was also a look of love and compassion as well. I thought about the time when Christ had looked at Peter, after Peter had denied Him three times — when Christ looked into his eyes — how Peter must have felt! How loving and forgiving must the eyes of Christ have been!

Plea For Help

I asked Jesus, at that moment, to give me the Grace never to offend Him in this way again. I asked His help because I knew that, without it, I could do nothing. I knew that the temptations to commit this sin would be very strong and I wanted nothing ever to stand in the way of a complete and total giving of myself to God.

Temptations Continue

I was tempted severely, many times, not only then, but also down through the years. But God showed me the way to conquer, to overcome temptations, by putting complete trust in Him, relying always on *His* strength. He showed me how to pray and to ask for help in such ways as repeating short prayers again and again, such as, "Jesus, Mary, and Joseph." Then, when temptations approach, you are praying, instantly and instinctively and you can conquer.

Gradual Learning Process

Perhaps, to many, it will seem foolish that I would share this particular aspect of my life, but it is most important to me to do so because I learned such a tremendous and valuable lesson in all of this and I would like it to be shared as well. I learned the importance of helping others so that they will not make these same mistakes. I learned the grave necessity of teaching young people properly in this area so that they will know not to offend Him in this manner and will be drawn closer to Him and desire to learn more about Him.

It took me a long time to learn these things. God was indeed patient and long-suffering with me. But, little by little, my mind began to be opened and I began to see things more clearly and to understand more about the spiritual life. I began to realize that much more is involved than just keeping a set of rules. It is a matter of *showing* our love. Because, if we truly love, we will not want ever to do anything that is displeasing to God or will keep us away from Him. Our love will grow so strong that we will want nothing more than to be in His Presence always, showing and proving our love for Him.

Be Single-Minded

We must learn to be single-minded, to keep our minds entirely upon God. In this way, we will do away with the things that might lead us away from Him. This is the most important aspect of the lesson that I learned on that day. I gained, at that moment, a much deeper insight into the things of God, His tender love and mercy, and it strengthened my spiritual life and deepened my prayer life as I continued to pray after that time.

CHAPTER 7

THE COURSE OF MY LIFE CHANGED THROUGH ST. LOUIS de MONTFORT'S DEVOTION TO MARY

As I mentioned earlier, the Benedictine Sisters had sent me a box filled with some wonderful booklets. Shortly after making this Confession, I decided to begin reading these booklets. I picked different ones at random, until I came to the one called, *The Secret of Mary*, by St. Louis de Montfort.

I read every word, captivated by it, and decided that I would consecrate my life to Mary, in this manner. As I made all the preparations, I recalled that April 28th was the day on which St. Louis de Montfort died and I figured this would be a good day for me to make my consecration to Mary.

Consecration To Mary, As A Child

Every day, for a month, I prepared myself. I wrote out my Consecration, on the night before, April 27. Then, the next morning, the first thing I did was to read the Act of Consecration — and I meant every word — and I signed the paper.

Holy Spirit To Be My Guide

I did not intend to consecrate myself as a slave, as St. Louis de Montfort explains, but more as a child. I did not intend to live the *letter* of the devotion, but rather the *spirit* of the devotion. I wanted the Holy Spirit to guide me, correct me, protect me, and lead me, so that I would not get bogged down in incidental and accidental things to spiritual living. In that way we will live with the freedom of the *children* of God. And so I asked the Holy Spirit, after having made and signed the Consecration, if He would take over and guide me and help me in living this life that I was giving to Him.

Mary Brings Us To Christ

Immediately I was filled with a deep love for our Blessed Mother. I had loved her always, throughout all my life, but now this love was magnified so that I could see clearly her role in the spiritual life, that she is to help to bring us to Jesus, and that she does so and quickly. She helped me to know Christ, to love Christ, to feel Christ in my life. I knew He was with me. I knew of this tremendous love that He had for me, even more than I'd ever realized before. Each day my love was deepened and strengthened.

Transformation Of One's Outlook

It seemed like a veil was taken from my eyes. Before it was like watching a play on a stage with the curtains drawn. We see only vaguely and hear only partially. We do not get the full impact of what is going on. It seems to me that we are looking at things from man's point of view and not from God's viewpoint. Then, all of a sudden, the curtains are drawn and we see things the way He sees them. We judge things the way He judges. And everything takes on a new meaning. All creation, every person in the world, the whole world takes on new meaning and we now realize that life is really worth living. This is exactly what happened to me. This is just what I felt like I was going through.

Jesus Leads Us To The Father

I had a tremendous longing for Jesus. The words of Jesus, in the Gospel, kept coming back very clearly. He said, "The Father and I will come to You," and He led me to the Father and a great love and devotion to the Father developed within me. This was a tremendous happening in my life, something more than I had ever before experienced. Everything in my life became Father-centered, so that I did all through Mary, with Christ, in Christ, offering everything to the Father.

Sends The Holy Spirit

He then said, in the words of the Gospel, "I will ask the Father and He will send to you the Holy Spirit." We experience this, we know this, and what does it mean? I think it means being Baptized in the Spirit, becoming more aware of the Spirit working in one's life and the purpose of the Spirit in one's life — to form Christ in us, to make us Christ-like, to make us a *beloved son or a beloved daughter of God the Father*, and I actually *experienced* this.

Living In Union With The Triune God

Within the next two or three months all these different things transpired in my life and I began to live always in the Presence of God. At this point we can make a terrible mistake. We can think that we are holy, that we are sanctified, that we have reached the summit, that we are better than others, but this is not true! What this really means is that we are just beginning to understand, to live and to realize the deep, intimate relationship of spiritual living between each Person of the Blessed Trinity and the Soul. This is what I experienced. This is what happened in my life, the *knowledge* of this deep relationship.

Time Of Searching

During this time, I knew that I wanted to be a priest, but I became very confused. I knew that I wanted to be a Religious, but

I didn't know which way to turn. Since I didn't have religious train-ing, I didn't know too much about religious orders. I knew very little about Diocesan priests, but not too much even about them, and so I just didn't know where to turn for information.

I did know that I wanted to be a "Religious" priest (a priest belonging to an order as opposed to a Diocesan priest). My broth-ers, because they were going to Marquette, told me I should be a Jesuit. I thought about it, before this Consecration, and had been more or less resigned to the thought that maybe this was what God wanted. But, as soon as I made the Consecration, everything be-came topsy-turvy and I just didn't know where I should go or what I should do.

Congregation I Wanted

Finally I knew that I wanted to join a Congregation that had devotion to the Sacred Heart of Jesus, to the Immaculate Heart of Mary, to St. Joseph, and with Adoration of the Blessed Sacrament — not exposed, but kept in the Tabernacles, and one which had missions and preaching.

The next four months were therefore a time of deep suffering and trial for me. I wrote to the Benedictine Sisters, in Clyde, Mis-souri, and asked them for information, if such a congregation as I had in mind did indeed exist. They wrote back and told me to con-sider the Benedictine Order and they sent literature on this Order, but I did not want to join the Benedictines, after reading their ma-terial. I knew that is not where God wanted me to be. I had to wait awhile longer in order to find out where God wanted me to be in the religious life.

I knew one thing — that I wanted to be a Religious priest. One thing only was concrete in my mind, that I wanted to give myself as a Religious with vows, living a stable life. I did not know then that, when you entered the Religious life, you might be moving about in different places, even have the rules relaxed and be able to come back home to visit. These were things I did not think about at the time. I was ready to give myself completely and totally to God, whatever He wished me to do, wherever He wished me to go.

Night Adoration

After I made the Consecration to Mary, on April 28, 1946, I also tried to develop a deeper prayer life. I discovered other pamphlets which I had not as yet read and I picked up a booklet on night adoration in the home. I read that and decided to make night adoration in the home, which I did every week, from two until three o'clock in the morning. I kept this up, even after I got out of the sick bed and went to Marquette University. Little did I realize that the one who began that work, Father Mateo, was a member of the Congregation of the Sacred Hearts of Jesus and Mary. There was nothing in that little booklet to indicate that he was from this Congregation, except for the initials after his name, and I didn't know what those meant.

Enthronement Of Sacred Heart In The Home

I also read the booklet called *The Enthronement of the Sacred Heart in The Home*. I definitely wanted to have this in our home, because this is a natural outcome of the Consecration to Jesus through Mary. The growth in this devotion to Mary leads you to Christ and you fall in love with God, with Christ. You wish to have Him as your King and to be always present as King of your home. You develop a deep love for Him in the Blessed Sacrament. You also have great devotion to His Sacred Heart.

I asked my Mother if we could have the Enthronement of the Sacred Heart in the Home, and she consented. We set the date for July 7, which also happened to be the date of the canonization of Mother Cabrini. Mother Cabrini was a missionary sister, who founded the Order, the Missionary Sisters of the Sacred Heart. She had a great devotion to the Sacred Heart.

One day my doctor friend came to visit and he said, "What are you doing still in bed?" He also said, "You know, what you really need is to have your tonsils out. I'll take them out for you. I'll go back to my office and check my schedule to see when you can come in and have it done." So he went into the office and checked, but he found out that his schedule was completely filled until the mid-summer. That would be right in the middle of the polio season and he said he couldn't risk taking them out then, because of the danger of getting polio being so critical.

The risk of having the rheumatic fever return, after the polio season was past, was also great. It began to look as though I was destined to spend another entire year in bed. I didn't want this because I was yearning to begin to study to be a priest. I didn't really know when I could actually begin because I was still very weak. I still could only get out of bed for just a very short time each day and that with great difficulty and hardship, because I tired so quickly.

Sacred Heart Grants A Favor

On July 7, 1946, the day Mother Cabrini was canonized, we had our Enthronement. Father Trost, our new pastor, came and had dinner with us. After dinner, at two o'clock, we had the ceremony of the Enthronement of the Sacred Heart in the Home. While the ceremony was in process, I said to Mother Cabrini, "If I am to be a priest, you see to it that I get my tonsils out and can begin my studies. You had a great devotion to the Sacred Heart, so you intercede with Him. Then, if I am not intended to be a priest, I will know by not having this request answered."

At five o'clock that evening, Dr. Robert Purtell called and said that I was to come into the hospital and that he would perform the operation the next morning. A lady who was to be operated on had canceled her surgery and so I took her place. I had my tonsils out the next morning. I sat in the office, rather than going to the hospital. I had a local anesthetic and was very much awake, trying to cooperate with the doctor so as to let him get his instruments way down into my throat, without my gagging too much. He did a very excellent job of removing them.

CHAPTER 8

DISCOVERING THE CONGREGATION GOD WANTED ME TO JOIN

After the tonsils were out, I gradually improved until I was well enough to travel. I decided I would visit a buddy of mine, Robert Phillips, who lived in Chicago Heights. He had also had rheumatic fever, but he had a much more severe case than I did. He didn't have to stay in bed as long as I did, but his heart was damaged more than mine had been.

I decided to spend a few days with him, figuring that the trip would be a good way to test my physical strength after my long illness. Toward the end of August, I finally felt really strong enough to make the trip. I didn't feel any weakness at all while I was on that trip. While I was there, he decided to show me the Church he went to and the school he had attended as a young boy.

God's Instrument — Sister Belane

We began our tour and, as we were walking past the fifth grade room, I noticed that there was writing on the board about the Hearts of Jesus and Mary. Something happened within me all at once. A great surge of happiness filled my soul at the sight of those words and I blurted out, "*That's* what I want. *That's* what I am looking for!" There was a Sister at the back of the room, Sister Belane, a Franciscan Sister. She was dusting and, when she heard this, she stopped her work and came up to me and said, "You are to join the Congregation of the Sacred Hearts of Jesus and Mary and Perpetual Adoration of the Blessed Sacrament."

I was rather startled at this sudden outburst from her, but she was so enthused that she began taking me all over the school, where we met other Sisters and, to each one, she would introduce me as the future Father Luke, of the Congregation of the Sacred Heart of Jesus and Mary, the one who would take the place of Father Luke Golla.

I was just dumbfounded at all this and I did not believe a word she was saying. In fact, I was thinking to myself that she must be as "nutty as a fruitcake." She made me promise to write to her and she gave me her name and address. She said, "Make sure, now, that you write to me. This is what you are to do, you are to join *this* Congregation. This Congregation is your vocation." I figured, "Well, I'll just go along with her and see what happens." And, after we left, I began to think over what had happened and to think, "Well, gee. Maybe God *is* calling me to this Congregation. Maybe this *is* the one He wants me to be in." I decided that I would make a novena to St. Anne, and to St. Jude.

Answer To Novena Prayer

I began that novena on the last day of August and finished it on the eighth of September. On the night of the eight of September, I am not sure if I was awake or sleeping, but the Sacred Heart appeared to me. When He came, He did not say a word, but I knew that He did want me to join this Congregation, that this was definitely the place where He wanted me to be. When I awoke, I said, "O.K., I will find out about this Congregation."

Now I was terribly drawn to it and I knew, at that moment, that this is where I did belong. I never wavered in this decision during all the time from then until I actually did join the Congregation.

I wrote to Sister Belane, telling her what I had seen. She became very upset and startled because she did not believe in visions and extraordinary things from God happening in the lives of everyday people. She wrote back and told me to write to the Sacred Hearts Fathers and to explain everything and get the information I needed from them, so I wrote to one of the Fathers.

A Time Of Trial

I waited for awhile and soon a letter arrived. It was a two-page letter. It said that I should forget about the Congregation, that I did not have a vocation, my health was not good enough, because I had been sick for two and a half years and, besides, the vision that I'd had classified me as a fanatic. They most emphatically did not feel that I had a vocation to their Congregation. As big as I was, I cried for two days, but I did *not* for one moment, doubt that God wanted me.

I Am Certain Now — This Is Where God Wants Me!

I sent the letter to Sister Belane and she was also upset about it. Then she decided to go ahead and write to obtain literature about the Congregation for me. When she finally received it and sent it along to me, it was pretty close to Thanksgiving time. When I opened the booklet and read it, I knew it was exactly what I was looking for. The picture on the front of the booklet was exactly what I had seen one day, while kneeling in prayer before the Blessed Sacrament. I saw myself as the priest in the picture, offering Mass. The whole world was offering their prayers to the Father, with Christ, in the Mass. This really attracted me because it symbolized the life that I was trying to live. I thought, "This is definitely what God wants!" When I re-read the booklet, everything, point by point, was what I was looking for and I had no doubt at all that this was the Congregation for me, that this was where God wanted me to be.

I knew nothing more about the Congregation, not even that Father Damien, the leper priest, was one of our priests. It was only later on that I found out anything about our founder, Father Joseph Coudrin. I was truly uneducated about all these things. Later on, when I finally did go to the Congregation, I had to learn many things that most of the others were long since familiar with.

CHAPTER 9

MARQUETTE UNIVERSITY

By this time I had already begun my training toward the priesthood, at Marquette University. My tuition was paid for by the G.I. Bill. I was able to get full benefits from this. I took a six-hour long test and the results showed that the life I had chosen was definitely suited for me. They showed that I should be a social worker and this fit in exactly with the life of a priest.

Subjects Taken

Then I had to begin to study. This is where I began my Latin, Philosophy, English, Mathematics, History, Religion, etc. I had previously begun to prepare, just a little, in Latin. My sister, Mary, going to Hartford High, took Latin. When she came home, she taught me what she had learned in school and, in that way, I had learned quite a bit about Latin before I actually began the classes at Marquette University.

We had a very strict taskmaster for a teacher. He was a wonderful man and I liked him very much. It was a small class and he drilled us very strenuously so that we got a good basic foundation. It got to the point where, when I went home, I could close my eyes and hear him speaking and going through the whole class. In that way, I was able to learn the Latin quite easily.

Daily Schedule

I spent two years at Marquette. While I was there, I joined the Sodality. I had a definite schedule worked out for my life. I would rise very early, attend Mass and receive Holy Communion. I went to Confession every week, I said my Rosary and prayed much. From Mass, I went to have my breakfast and then made the Stations of the Cross, in the little Chapel, at Johnson Hall. Then I would begin my day's classes. At noon I would attend another Mass and then go and lead the Rosary in the Chapel for any students who might want to participate. Afterwards, I would have my lunch. Then either class or studying. If I had the afternoon off, I would go home and study. In the evening, all of us living in that house went out together for dinner and then we came back and studied again. Then I said some more prayers before I went to bed. I still continued my night adoration all the time I was at Marquette University.

Helping The Needy

My extra activities, outside of studies, consisted of visiting the sick or poor. I tried to help them, to bring food to them, insofar as my budget would allow. I gave much time to two women, in particular, who needed a great deal of help. One had been a nurse and was quite ill; the other was on drugs and was very sickly.

Teaching Youngsters

I also participated in the C.C.D. program at our own Church. Each week I would drive out to our area, to Lake Five, and give young people their classes. I was able to inspire them to make night adoration at least once a month, but the parents objected. They thought that their children needed their rest, so they chose an earlier hour so that they could have the Holy Hour without losing their sleep. Actually, one hour a month is really nothing, if you are giving your time in this way to God. The benefits they would have received would have been much greater than the sleep that they got. Choosing an earlier hour prevented them from making a real sacrifice. Nevertheless, I was very happy to get them to pray and make reparation for sinners and for the good of the world. I also encouraged them to have the Enthronement of the Sacred Heart in the Home and we carried out this program throughout the time I was at Marquette University.

I had as spiritual director during that time, Father George Ganss, S.J., who was very wonderful. He never once tried to direct me into the Jesuits or into another Order. He saw that God definitely wanted me in the Congregation of the Sacred Hearts of Jesus and Mary and that that is where I belonged.

After I had finished two years of study and two summer courses, he told me that it was time that I joined the Congregation. He said, "Get going and join the Order. If you don't, a truck might come along and hit you." And so I had my physical and obtained all my application papers. Dr. Purtell gave me the physical and he gave me a high recommendation, saying that I was perfectly O.K., as far as the rheumatic fever was concerned. My heart had stabilized and I was ready to participate in the seminary life.

I entered the Seminary in the beginning of September or late August of 1948. I traveled by train to Fairhaven, Massachusetts and, since I hadn't known how long the trip would take, I arrived a day early. I was greeted with much confusion and bustling in the Novitiate. They were getting things ready for our arrival. They didn't have the beds ready yet so the Novice Master, Father Meldan McGoohan, a real tough Irishman, let me sleep in his room. I slept in his bed that night and he slept on a cot. The next day, one of the novices said to me, "You will soon be made to forget what he did. He won't even think about the favor that he did for you tonight. He's going to be plenty tough with you, so I wish you luck."

CHAPTER 10

RELIGIOUS LIFE BEGINS

Novitiate Life Begins

The next day the Novitiate officially began. It began with an eight-day retreat, given by Father Eugene Robitaille, SS.CC., the Assistant Novice Master, at the time. There were thirteen novices that had arrived.

Before the retreat started we went to the Chapel. It was a beautiful, calm evening. The sun was shining through the stained glass windows and the bottom windows were open. It was altogether a pleasant, quiet and peaceful atmosphere.

I decided that I would say the prayer of St. Michael, the Archangel and ask him and the other Angels to cast out any evil influence of the devil that might be in the area or in the Chapel. I said the prayer and immediately there was a terrible sound. The whole building shook and the windows slammed shut. Nobody knew what was happening. I knew, though, that the devil was being chased out. Many may laugh at this, but I am sure that is exactly what took place.

The First Retreat In Religious Life

The retreat was very beautiful. During its course, God said to me, "This is where I want you to be," and I was assured by Him that this was my vocation.

On the sixth day, two of our novices left, one in the morning and one in the afternoon. This really shocked me. I had never thought that anybody, after giving themselves to God, could just pick up and leave, especially so quickly, without giving it a chance and thinking things through. It seemed to me that they had wasted their whole effort in coming and I could not fully understand their leaving for a long time.

Taking Of Religious Name

At the beginning of our Novitiate, as soon as our retreat was over, we had to have new names. This was to signify that we were changing our way of life from the world to the dedication of religious living. It stood for a complete and total break. In the Old Testament, whenever God gave a person a new mission, He would always change their name for them and this was the Scriptural basis for this.

I was asked what name I wanted and I said, "Luke." My name had been Bernard before entering the Seminary. There had been another novice who wanted the name I had chosen, but he was one of the ones who left during the retreat and so I was able to have the name I chose. He was older than me and, since we were ranked according to birthdate, he would have had first preference in choosing a name.

Meditation Followed

We began each day with meditation, followed by Mass. During the day there was the Office to be said, classes to attend, and work. We quickly settled into a routine. The meditation period was very painful for me because I had been used to thinking on my own about God, saying my Rosary and meditating on the Mysteries, thinking about the Gospel passages, and applying them to my own life. It had become a real intimate love relationship with God, talking to Him, telling Him that I loved Him. This new form of meditation sort of "went against the grain" with me and I didn't like it at all. The method used was to read a passage in a book, sit in silence thinking about it for ten minutes, then read another, think again, read again, and think about what was read. This would go on for thirty to forty-five minutes. Sometimes our Novice Master would call on us to make our meditation aloud, to tell what passages read meant and so forth. This is not the proper way to teach meditation and I found it distracting and a hindrance to prayer instead of a help. I felt that it was going backwards, which it was. I no longer needed the book, no longer needed a prop for prayer. Just a word or a glance was sufficient to make me have a real conversation with God, from which acts of love, reparation and thanksgiving would flow from my heart and mind.

But, as I worked, I was able to get back to the meditation that I was used to and then my whole day would become a true union with God, throughout that year.

Trying To Share Religious Experiences

I made the mistake during that year of sharing some of my life with others. At that time you were considered proud or arrogant to be talking or sharing with others about such things, but I didn't even know that these things were not given to everybody, because I was so naive. God only did this for me because I was so unlearned about my religion and it was necessary for Him to point the way for me because of my lack of knowledge, my lack of Faith.

I needed these signposts and guidelines more than others and that is why He condescended to give these things to me. It didn't make me greater than anyone else and I was not special because of them. This is just the way God found it necessary to deal with my soul. I thought that He dealt this way with everyone, but I soon found out the hard way that this was not true. My Novice Master became very angry with me because he felt that I should not be talking about these things. He thought that I was setting myself up as a saint, thinking that I was something special, someone chosen for a great mission. He gave me a lecture that I never forgot. As a result, I clammed up and did not speak any longer of the things that took place within my soul and in my spiritual life, except to my spiritual director. Even now it is very difficult for me to open up and speak of this and yet I feel that we must share these things at times for the good of others.

As I said before, we must do this in order to let people know that God does work with souls and how He works with souls and why He does these things, so that people don't just go through life thinking that God does not care about anybody or anything.

I finally came to the end of my Novitiate. Father Meldan McGoohan had been transferred in August, on my birthday, and so we were under Father Kevin O'Brien for the last month of our Novitiate.

I particularly want to relate this next story because I think it has significance.

The night before our profession of vows, we went to bed but I wasn't able to sleep. From around ten o'clock on I had the feeling of another presence in my cell. Our cells were tiny, just room enough for a bed, a chair and our few personal belongings, with hooks for hanging up our clothes.

Tempted By The Devil

I felt the terrible presence of the devil. He was in my cell and I couldn't rid myself of the feeling of his being there. This went on all during the night. I remained awake the entire night and toward morning the devil began to tempt and taunt me. He ridiculed me, saying that I wasn't worthy to be a Religious, that I should give up the whole idea, and that I was the worst of sinners because of my past life. He told me that I was the most terrible sinner in the whole world and that I should not go through with taking my vows. He told me that I still had time to change my mind, to walk out, if I wanted to.

Finally, he said that in order to prove what he was saying to be true, two black dogs would enter the Church the next day, during my profession. I didn't know what to do about what he had said. I just stayed awake all during the night.

The next morning we had Mass. We went first to the Chapel for meditation and then the Mass was said by Father Eugene Robitaille. Then we began to get ready for our profession which was to be at ten o'clock, at St. Joseph's Church in Fairhaven. Before we left, Father Eugene said to me, "You look very pale, is anything wrong?" I said no because I didn't want to tell him what had happened during the night, even though I had been going to him for spiritual guidance throughout the Novitiate.

We went over to the Church and the profession ceremony began. Father William Condon, the Provincial, was seated on a chair.

He rose, read the ceremonies, and gave a sermon. After the sermon, he sat down again and we began the actual taking of our vows. When the one just ahead of me went up to take his vows, a neighbor's two black dogs came into the Church and walked up the center aisle!

I nearly fainted. Just for a moment, I didn't know quite what to do, whether to run out or to go forward and take my vows. Then I decided. I told myself, "I am certainly not going to let the devil stop me. I won't let him win his game." I went forward, placed my hands in the provincial's, and made the vows. Then I went over to the Gospel Book and said, "So help me, God, and His Holy Gospel."

The perspiration was literally rolling down my face. It happened that a picture was taken for the *Standard Times*, in New Bedford, right at that moment. When the picture appeared in the paper the next day, you could see the drops of water coming down my face.

After leaving the ceremony, we went outside and had a celebration, but I couldn't help but remember the things the devil had said to me, and what had happened. He had also said that, because of me, many souls would be lost, especially those of the youth. It hurt me and troubled me somewhat for many days, though I never mentioned it to anyone at the time. I just kept it to myself and wondered about it.

Home On Vacation

The Congregation had initiated a new policy which permitted us to go home for vacations, and so I was permitted to leave shortly after my profession, to spend a few days at home. When I had entered, it had been with the idea that I would never again see my parents or brothers and sisters or relatives. I had expected to leave and that would be it.

Reflections On What Had Happened

When my Mother had learned that I was going to be a priest, she had tried to talk me into becoming a Diocesan priest. She would say, "Wouldn't it be nice if you could come home?" She just couldn't understand at first that it was God Who wanted me to be in this Congregation, and that I had to listen to Him. When we are deciding about our vocation we must always listen to what God wants and not to what our parents or other people might prefer.

Father Trost always teased me whenever we met. He would say, "You ought to be a Diocesan priest," and I would say, "I want to be a Religious priest." Then he would say, "Why do you want to be a *Religious* priest? Why don't you be a *Catholic* priest?" It was a joke between us, and, for the next few years, whenever we met, this is the bantering that would go on between us. He was a wonderful priest, and I had great fun talking to him. He had a really nice sense of humor. He also helped me in many, many ways during those years.

But, of course, I *did* have to go off to Massachusetts and join the Congregation that God wanted me in. Naturally, when I came home after taking my vows, I had my habit. I was very proud of my habit and I still am. Many people today try to say that wearing it means that we have cut ourselves off from the world, that it indicates that we do not care about the people of the world.

This is ridiculous; our habit is distinctive. It gives a witness to our commitment to the Religious life. It's a sign to the whole world that we have given ourselves to God. We should be happy to wear it just as people in other professions are proud to wear their uniforms. Why shouldn't *we* also be proud to wear *our* habit to show forth our witness to God? I would never want to give up my habit.

When we wear the habit, it is a distinctive way of letting people know what Congregation we belong to, and I am certainly not ashamed of our Congregation. I am, on the contrary, very proud of it. I think it has everything that the world needs for our day, for our times. It did when I joined it, and it does still, even today.

CHAPTER 11

SEMINARY LIFE

From my home I reported to the Major Seminary in Washington, D.C., where we had our Philosophy and Theology. I was put into Philosophy and spent one year studying it, but then I was able to skip the other year because of the Philosophy I'd had at Marquette University. Then I was put into first year Theology, which I enjoyed very much. The teachers were good, when we first came into the Seminary, and I learned much from them.

Community Life

Our seminary life (we were 24) was a real community life. We shared with one another, worked with one another, played with one another, and we prayed together. It was a very real and happy family. Sure, we had our "ups and downs," our problems, our teasing and arguments sometimes, but, on the whole, I think we had a very happy seminary community life. I wouldn't trade it for anything in the world. It was like a family to me, and I grew to love all the seminarians and priests, everything about the Seminary.

I learned many things during this time, especially about God. We had the same format for meditation as we had in the Novitiate, and, again, I did not care for that, so these two years it was necessary to struggle through those times.

Adoration Of The Blessed Sacrament

During recreation or work periods, I could always revert back to my other form of meditation, talking to God and being with

God. What made me the most happy was being able to spend a half hour every day before the Blessed Sacrament, in prayer alone, talking to God in the Blessed Sacrament. Once a week, one hour during the night, I also had that privilege. I never felt the schedule was a burden or simply something that I had to do because a bell rang. I always, during the whole seminary training, went to the spiritual exercises because of my wanting to go, because of my love for God, because of the deep conviction that I was doing God's Will. Therefore it was a joy to perform all the spiritual exercises and I never missed a one unless I was sick. This was seldom, because I was almost never sick in the Seminary. And so a deeper union with God developed and I enjoyed being there.

Studying in Rome

When I finished the second year in the Seminary, I was asked to go to Rome to continue my studies there. I was afraid, mainly because I felt I didn't know enough Latin to be able to pick up what they were saying when they spoke it in the classes. Classes in Rome are conducted a lot differently than the ones in the United States. In the United States, there are questions and answers and discussions between the teachers and the students. A good rapport develops and they make sure you have understood everything before going on. But in Rome, you just had a professor come in, give a lecture, and walk out. It's all in Latin, and you just sit there and you either get it or you don't.

It took quite a while for me to grasp what they were saying, but finally I did. I got to the point where I could understand, and I took Hebrew and Canon Law. I took my test for Hebrew and passed it. I took my test for Canon Law, and passed it also.

During the middle of the year, I got another attack of rheumatic fever. One day we were out for a Christmas celebration. We had to walk through the rain and the cold, and it affected me immediately because of the dampness and lack of warm clothing. I had to be taken to the hospital, where I spent three weeks. I had to miss my classes and studies, and it was a terrible ordeal because I was anxious to get back and study. Also, my heart began to be affected, and I had pains in the chest.

Finally the doctors told me I could go home. The pain and the swelling disappeared, and the effects of the rheumatic fever were gone. When I began to go to classes again, I had to leave a half hour earlier than everyone else just so that I could get to school on time. I had to walk very slowly because of my illness.

Meditations As I Liked It

It was really a chore to carry on. It was not an easy thing, physically, but spiritually speaking, it was a very beautiful year which I would not want to trade for anything in the world. I was able to talk to God in my own way, and to meditate and really pray correctly as I had always done. I used the statue that was behind the Altar, the statue of Jesus and Mary, for my meditation during that whole year. It depicts Mary, pointing to her Heart with one hand, while the other hand points to Jesus, who is blessing the world. It told me the story of my vocation, the whole meaning of our Congregation, the purpose of our life, offering everything through Mary, to Christ, living with Christ and offering everything to the Father. In this way, the world would be blessed, it would be sanctified. These were my thoughts during that time.

Close Union With Christ

My life also became more Mass-centered. The Mass and Christ in the Blessed Sacrament had more meaning. My love for Him deepened, and my time spent with Him was lengthened. I spent more time in prayer, in a real deep union with Him. It was easy to do this because of the type of life we were living.

God seemed to spoil me, granting me every request, even the littlest detail. Prayers were answered lovingly and tenderly. I will speak about this a little and go back a few years, in order to show you what happened in regard to my prayer life.

My Aunt Cured

It began with my aunt. I heard that she was going to have a baby in 1948. She had a tumor at the same time which was growing and would deform the baby completely, if not removed. If the tumor were removed, it would mean taking the life of the baby. They just didn't know what to do. They wrote to me about all this, and I asked the Little Flower of the Child Jesus to cure her. One day, when I was in Latin class, all of a sudden, I smelled a beautiful rose scent. I looked around to see if any of the girls were wearing perfume. I thought I was smelling perfume rather than this rose smell. Then the thought came to me that my aunt was cured.

After class was over, I went to the Chapel to say the Rosary as I always did every noon. While I was saying the Rosary, the smell came back, even stronger. Again it said to me, "Your aunt is cured. Everything is O.K." And then I said, "If this is true (I was always a doubting Thomas), I want a rose to *prove* that my aunt is cured." I had to have proof for everything.

I went on with the rest of my day and the next morning I went to Mass, as usual. I went to breakfast and came back to the Chapel to begin my Stations of the Cross. I knelt down in the back of the Chapel, and nobody else was there. Finally, I began making the Stations of the Cross, and, when I finished, came back to the same place. When I came back to that spot there was a *rose* on the seat. The rose was not a fresh one, but an old and dried one.

I took the rose in my hand, and it had the same smell that I had noticed the day before. I took it with me and put it in my pocket, carrying it around with me for the rest of the day. Finally, I went home and put it on a dresser in my room. Just then I heard my brother, Joe, coming home.

I greatly admired him. He went through the service, and was a crew chief in the Army Air Corps. He worked on the B-29s and spent a lot of time doing mechanical work. Then, after he ended his service, he came home and began studying to be a doctor, an entirely different field than what he had been working in. All of us in the family always have admired the strength and courage that he had in doing all this.

As I saw him coming, I hid the rose. He came into the room and immediately said, "What's that beautiful smell?" And so, I told him the story about our aunt, and what had happened, but I added, "We still don't know for sure."

He exploded at me, "Oh, you of little faith! Why do you doubt? You've got your proof. Why don't you just thank God? Starting tomorrow, I'll go to Mass with you every day and we'll thank God for this, and that's that!"

A few days later, we received a letter from our aunt saying that she was cured. She had proof of this from the doctor. The child was O.K., and was not in any danger. Later on, the child was born, on August 5, 1948. She was born normal and perfectly healthy, and my aunt is still living today and has not had any more ill effects from any tumor in that area. I was asked to be the Godfather to this young baby, and I gladly consented. This is one of the last things I did before joining the Congregation. I went to Nebraska and was the Godfather of Mary Anne Schaefer.

Death of Father Peter Brooks, S.J.

There were other such things that happened while I was at Marquette University. This next incident was not in the nature of a request being answered, but it is simply another indication of the way that God has worked in my life. One day, in 1948, I was walking past the Chapel, and I noticed the President, Father Peter Brooks, S.J., saying prayers in the Chapel. I was told, by God, to tell him to prepare well, that within nine days he was going home. I knew immediately that this meant that he was going to die, but, since this was the first time anything like this happened to me, I was hesitant. I said, "What would he think if I were to come in and say such a thing? I would be laughed at and not taken seriously. I'd be considered to be a nut." So, out of human respect, I said nothing. I did not go in and tell him. In the meantime, during those nine days, I got the mumps and had to go home from my studies.

I spent my time out at the farm with my Mom and Dad, and the rest of the family. I was listening one day to the radio, and heard the news that Father Peter Brook, S.J., the President of Marquette University, had died from a heart attack. I counted back and it had been just nine days from the time that I had been told to tell him about this, but I never told anyone about it. It bothered me a great deal that I did not do what I was asked to do by God.

Accident, My Cousin's Illness, And Neighbor's Death

Another thing that happened was that I "saw" my cousin get sick. I knew that he was ill and in danger, and so I prayed for him. He had a ruptured spleen, and it was removed, but he recovered. Still another incident happened concerning one of our neighbors, who was a non-Catholic. He always drove very fast. I was driving past the tavern at Lake Five one day, when the thought came to me that he was in danger, that he was going to be in a terrible car accident, and be killed. I asked God, "Don't let that happen. Please let him live. Give him the grace to be converted and become a Catholic before he dies. Don't let anything happen to him. It doesn't make any difference what happens to the car, but protect him." A short time later, he had an accident. The car was completely de-molished, but the only thing that happened to him was that he was thrown into the back seat, and his shoes came off.

Nothing was wrong with him that time, and he was preserved safely. One would have hoped that this would teach him a lesson, and that he would afterwards drive more carefully. Unfortunately, that was not to be the case. I was told by God on another occasion that this man was going to have another accident, but that this time he would be killed. I prayed that this would not happen, but God said this is the time. I prayed that he would be sorry for his sins and that God would take him home to heaven. It happened that he did have a terrible accident, and was killed as I had seen.

Death Of Neighbors Living In Wisconsin

Then, while I was in Rome, I was told by God that a young man was going to die that night and that I should pray for him. I did so, praying that he would be ready to die and meet his God. But I also argued with God and said, "Why don't You take his father? His father is much older, he is in his 80s. Surely this young man has his whole life ahead of him. Why do You have to take him?" But God said, "This is the time." And so I prayed for him. That night he had a heart attack and died. He was alone and had not a soul with him.

Another neighbor had had a stroke, and couldn't walk too well; the one who visited me and had to grab onto something to sit down.

He was also going to die. I was told this, so I prayed for him, that everything would go well with him. Still another neighbor ran out of gas and went to the station to get more. He was bringing the gas can back toward the car, and, while I was in Rome, I "saw" him do this. I knew that a car was going to hit him and kill him. I knew that he needed prayers, so I prayed for him that he would be able to die in peace with God. He was hit by a car, and did die immediately.

Another neighbor of mine was on a road, driving, and I saw him come to the end of the road. His car was still going fast, and I knew that he was going to be killed, so I prayed for him, that he would be able to make peace with God before he died.

My Father's Accident

One night, I saw my father going home and coming to the intersection where he makes a left turn to go toward home. I saw another car coming toward him, hitting him, and him flying from the car. Again, I prayed that he would be unharmed, that the car would be demolished, but he would be O.K., and that is exactly what happened.

You can call it ESP, premonition, clairvoyance, or what have you. I just don't know. I am simply relating things as they happened.

Death Of A Religious Brother

Still another incident happened after I became a priest. I knew that a certain Brother was in danger, and that he was going to die. I, myself, had a longing for death, also. But I was told that he was going to die, and so I prayed for him. I thought that I really ought to get to a telephone and call the Superior and let him know that this Brother was in danger, but, again, out of human respect, I did nothing. The next day I was told that this Brother had died that night, and I was very upset that I hadn't called.

Then, when I was Superior at Bishop Amat High School, one of our priests came and asked if he could go out. I said, "Yes," but, as he left, I had the feeling that he was going to be in an accident, but with our car. After he went out, I immediately went to the recreation room and asked, "Did Father take one of our cars?" They said, "No, he went off with another student who graduated, and they went to a movie." So, I thought, "That's good. He'll be all right."

I went back to my work again, but the thought returned so I prayed that he would be all right. Father came back that night from the movie, and, taking one of our cars, he went over to the house of this young man. The young man had some religious problems and he wanted to talk them out. When Father was on the way home, he fell asleep and hit a light pole, and landed in the hospital, with his skull fractured so you could just lift it right up. He didn't look like he was going to make it. Then I blessed him, and he got well rather quickly, surprisingly so. Things like this do take place in my life.

Small Desires Satisfied

But, to get back to my stay in Rome, as I said, even the slightest desires were answered. For instance, one day I had a strong desire for some pancakes. I said, "Even if I only had two of the pancakes like my Mother makes, I would be very happy." When I came down that morning, there were two pancakes on my plate, just like my Mom makes, and nobody else had any. Another time I wanted to hear the whippoorwill whistle or call again. The next morning there was a whippoorwill singing away very strongly and beautifully right outside my room and it satisfied my desire.

Spiritual Growth

During that time I developed a great love for Jesus in the Blessed Sacrament. I had a tremendous longing to go to Communion all during the day and to be with Him in Communion. I also developed a deep longing to die and to be with him in Heaven, to be absorbed, as St. Paul tells us. Naturally, we cannot do that. We must wait for what God wants and live the life God wishes us to live. But this was building up within me until I reached the point where I constantly lived in the Presence of God, and felt this Presence of God within me. This lasted throughout the Rome visit, through many, many years, and even until now, today.

Examinations

Finally came the end of the year, and time to take our examinations. I had missed quite a bit because of my illness, and felt I wasn't prepared, but I intended to do my best. When I got to the room for the questioning, there were several professors to question us on various phases of Theology and Scripture. The questioning began and something happened to me. My mind just went completely blank. A psychologist might say it was fear. They might have many explanations for it, but this is what did happen. I just couldn't think of one thing until the examination was over, then I was able to speak in Latin again. But, during that time, everything just went blank, and so I naturally did not pass that test.

Summer Vacation

Then I went on my summer vacation. We were going up to Holland, and Father Cyprian went with us. We went by train through Italy, France, and Belgium. We stopped off in Belgium, and went to the Motherhouse where we saw Father Damien's museum.

Learning More About Our Founder

We also learned more about our Founder, Father Joseph Coudrin. What a tremendous person he was. He was God's "Underground Man." For the first ten years of his priestly life, he worked during the French Revolution, in disguise, carrying on the work of a priest very successfully. He was responsible for many priests coming back to their ministry, and he had many narrow escapes. His life was one of real heroism. After the Revolution was over, he began our Congregation. It is interesting to note that, while he was in the seminary, he had a great devotion to Our Lady, the Blessed Mother, and to the Sacred Heart. It was through the devotion to St. Louis de Montfort that he developed his spiritual life, and it was used in starting our Congregation. It was based on that and the A.A., which was the *Cor Unum,* the One Heart, which was the devotion to the Sacred Heart, but also intimately connected with the Heart of Mary. So he was trained for his calling even before he entered the seminary. He was a farm boy, and it seems that he was quite brilliant, but he had to learn things from God more than he did from studying or from other people. This is how he prepared for his work of starting our Congregation.

Father Damien, as we know, was one of the greatest of all men of Charity. He gave his life to work with the lepers. There are many books on his life, so it is easy to know about him, to find out about him and to learn, through reading of him, more about our Congregation. He lived our life, the spiritual life, the way it should be lived. I learned a good bit more about our Congregation while I was in Belgium.

Rheumatic Fever Returns

Then we went to Holland, where we stayed for quite awhile. While I was in Holland, I again got another attack of rheumatic fever. This was a terrible ordeal. We went to visit the Trappist Monastery one day. Again we walked and, as in Rome, we got caught in the rain. When we got there I felt very bad. My leg hurt, and they told me I didn't look too good, so maybe I ought to lie down. I did and, when they came to see me, I couldn't move because my leg was too swollen. I had some good luck because they were delivering coal that day to the Monastery. They loaded me on that truck and drove me back to our headquarters, the Provincial house in Holland. I crawled upstairs and went to bed, and stayed there until the swelling disappeared. Meanwhile, I kept on studying and preparing. I felt that I had to take that test over, back in Rome, and continue with my studies. It was not meant to be that way. As I recuperated, I was able to do little odd jobs around the house, and to keep up with my prayer life and deep union with God.

Learning A Lesson

Finally we had to go back to Belgium, but, before we went to Belgium, the Fathers wanted to treat us to a good time, so they took us to a celebration. This celebration takes place annually in Holland, and people come from all over Holland for it. The young and the strong go sixty kilometers from the city of Nijmegan. The ones who are not so strong go forty kilometers, and the ones who are very young go only thirty kilometers. Then they have three days in which to march back into town. As they come in, they are playing their songs. They are dressed according to the section of the country from which they come, and they are having a gay and happy time.

As they were walking in, I was watching and enjoying it, but the thought came to my mind, "I wonder how many of these people really understand the meaning of life? How many of them are really on their way to be with God? They seem to make a great sacrifice just to get a bouquet of flowers and a little medal for finishing the trek into this city." And so I had the tremendous desire to preach to them and to let them know the meaning of life. Naturally, that was impossible. I couldn't speak Dutch, and so I felt frustrated. Yet the desire kept welling up within me. I would have liked to go to all the countries of the whole world and tell them about the love of God, and preach the message of Christ. Then God said to me, "You *can* help everybody in the whole world." And I asked Him, "How? *How* can I do that?" The answer was, "Become a saint! Become a saint!"

And then I realized that, by becoming a saint, we do affect the lives of every person in the whole world. Our vocation is one of love, to love God, to love our fellow man. And, in loving, becoming a victim of love, as the Little Flower was, we can bring about the spiritual well-being of the whole world. I had an enormous message taught to me that day. It is something I'll never forget, something that has been with me all these years. From there we went on to Belgium.

Final Profession Of Vows

While I was in Belgium, I had to prepare for my final vows. I took my final vows on September eighth, rather than the fourteenth of September, as I was supposed to do. While I had been in Rome, I had begun to wonder, "Well, gee. Does God really want me to take these vows, and continue on?" And I said to the Little Flower, "If God really wants this, you better see to it that I take my vows on the eighth of September. It's the day that you were permitted to take your vows." I felt that this would be a nice way of making my final profession to God. I did not say anything to anyone about this. One day my Superior in Rome called me and said, "We will have to get a dispensation for you." And I said, "What for?" He answered, "A six-day dispensation so that you can take your vows on September 8th, when the Brothers in Belgium take their vows. That way we won't have to have two ceremonies. You can have your ceremony with them." Of course that was fine with me. He obtained the dispension and, when I got to Belgium, I prepared for this profession and took my vows on September 8, 1952.

During the profession, we always lay down and put the funeral pall over us to signify that we are dead to the world, that we are to live this new, dedicated life. While I was laying there, I really felt alone. I felt, if death is like this, it must be terrible. I just felt abandoned by God and by everyone.

I didn't have anybody there except Father Superior, whom I knew in Rome, and one Brother, who was with me in Rome. Otherwise, everyone else was a complete stranger. During the profession, Father Gerald de Becker gave the talk, speaking a few words in English for me, congratulating me and wishing me well, and then continuing with the ceremony.

After the ceremony was over, Father Superior, in Rome, informed me that my Provincial wanted me to return to the United States, without any questions asked. I went back to Rome, packed my things, and returned to the United States.

Back In The U.S.A.

When I got back, I was rather weak yet, from the illness I'd had in Holland. I could not do very much strenuous work, so I was permitted to work in the office of the Enthronement Center. This gave me much time to myself, and I really was able to talk to God, and further develop an intimate union with Him.

During this time, the last part of my seminary training, the classes were just plain torture. There was only one class that I really enjoyed. This was Moral Theology, given by Father Vincent Davis. I thought he was a born teacher. He made class lively with his jokes, but also interesting. He taught us a great deal about moral problems and questions of the day. But the other classes just seemed to drag on and on. I was able to read Latin at the rate of about forty pages an hour, with no difficulty, and I was way ahead of the class. They could only cover two or three pages a day, and it was most boring for me to sit through. Nevertheless, I didn't say anything, but just sat there and took it all in.

During that time, I worked out questions and answers for all the phases of moral and dogmatic Theology that could be asked of us on our final examinations, by a board of the professors. We always had to take these Canonical tests before we could be permitted to be ordained. I worked out all of these things and Brother Jeremiah Casey, who was my classmate, typed them up for everybody, and they used this to prepare for the examinations for many years after that.

Helping Others

Also during this time, I was tutoring others, helping with any problems they had in their studies. Before any major test, I would draw up a list of questions that I thought the professors would ask, and we'd have bull sessions together to go over all of these things. Most of the time, these were the questions that were asked, and everybody was prepared to answer them. I did feel a sort of accomplishment in the seminary in that way, and I also liked being back with the rules and the seminary atmosphere. I don't see anything wrong with the way we lived our life at that time. It was a time of deepening our knowledge, our love, and our union with God.

Ordination

Mom, Dad and Myself

Dr. Jim and Myself

CHAPTER 12

THE PRIESTHOOD

In June of 1954, it came time for my ordination. My parents and some of my brothers and sisters came to Washington, D.C. for the ordination. On the night before I was ordained, I again could not sleep. I was wondering if I was doing the right thing. I guess we all go through that. We think about what it means to be a religious priest, to give oneself completely to God, without any strings attached — all the implications. In the end, I decided, "I am going to be a priest, and that is that." I knew it was the right thing for me to do.

Ordination At The National Shrine

The next day, June 5th, we had the ceremony and I was ordained at the site of the National Shrine of the Immaculate Conception. The Shrine was not yet built at that time. We still had only the crypt and the basement part, but I was ordained there. I always had a great longing and love for our Blessed Mother, especially under that title, so I was very happy to have the privilege of being ordained in that shrine.

Our stay in Washington, D.C. was helpful in many ways, because we were able to go to various lectures given at the University. We also were able to attend different plays and social activities among different Religious communities. I always had good rapport with the Josephites and the Benedictine Sisters. I got to know all the other Religious communities in the area quite well.

After our ordination, we came back to the seminary and had our festivities and celebrations. Then, the next day, I was to say the

Community Mass for the seminarians. I did this and also stayed for Father Jeremiah's Mass. Then I started on my trip back to Wisconsin. I drove as far as Indiana, the first night, where I stayed until the next morning. I then went to the Convent, where Sister Belane lived, in Mishawaka, and I said a Mass for her, because she was instrumental in pointing out to me where I belonged. I wanted to thank God, with her present, for this great favor.

After the Mass was over, she finally explained to me why she knew I was the one to go to this Congregation. She told me that the night before she met me, she had received word from Germany that her brother had been killed.

She had been expelled from Germany by Hitler, along with her whole community. Her parents starved to death during the war. Her brothers and sisters suffered greatly. One of her brothers had turned against God. She had prayed for twenty-five years that he would be a priest, but it seemed that he had a deaf ear. Then, the night before she met me, she had received word that he had been killed, shot through the heart by the Communists.

And so, she went to Christ, in the Blessed Sacrament, and said to Him, "I've prayed all this time and look what happens." She felt that her brother was lost, and so she asked God to send someone to take his place, someone who had devotion to the Sacred Heart, someone who would be a priest. When I had mentioned what I did about the Hearts of Jesus and Mary, she knew immediately that I was the one to take her brother's place. She referred to me always, from then on, as her brother. It deepened my admiration for her that she waited until this moment to tell me of this.

She had to live her spiritual life, her religious life, completely on blind faith. Something of this nature was rather unusual to take place in her life. She offered all her prayers for many, many years for me. I think it was through her prayers that I was able to become a priest, receive the many graces and gifts that God bestowed upon me, and become a spoiled child of the Sacred Hearts.

Hearing My First Confessions

Next, I continued on to Wisconsin, and the first confessions that I heard were the First Confessions of the little ones of my own parish, who were preparing for their First Holy Communion. This was quite an experience.

My First Public Mass

Then I had my first Mass, in my parish, on the Feast of St. Anthony, June 13th. It was also the Feast of the Blessed Trinity. I was ordained on the vigil of the Holy Spirit, and I always had a special devotion to the Holy Spirit and, naturally, to the Triune God, and I asked them to bless my work, my life, and my priesthood, and make it fruitful. For, without His grace, without His help, we can do nothing, and we are nothing. We just beat the air with fruitless toil. But, with His help, then much good can come.

A Priest Forever

These were my thoughts after I was ordained. When you're ordained, you look in the mirror, and you don't feel or look any different, yet you are deeply aware that you are a priest, a priest forever. I knew what I was doing when I entered the seminary. I knew that, when I took my vows, I gave myself to God, that I was to be single-minded and give my life to Him, and live a celibate life. I knew that, when I stepped forward, I was deciding, of my own free will, to become a priest. I was old enough to know what I was doing. I had many years to make up my mind, to decide what to do. I could have left at any time. The doors were always open for me to leave and yet, I took this step and I am a priest forever. This is a great privilege.

This is how I look upon it. I think the priesthood is a very beautiful calling, a tremendous vocation, a great life. I want to live it and I do live it. We have to remember that we are fragile, that we have a weak human nature, and can fall by the wayside, just like anybody else. Priests are tempted just like anybody else, can give up, just like anybody else. But, if we pray, then we have God's help, and we remain humble and will not turn our backs upon God.

I will not walk away from God, I will continue to do my work for God. In saying this, I am not judging anyone. I am just saying that God will do for us, if we continually pray and stay close to

Him. I think that this is one thing that priests today must realize more fully. They must really dedicate themselves to a life of prayer and a life of union with God, in order to remain faithful to Him.

When we first become a priest, we are in the "honeymoon" stage of our priesthood, just like when people get married. They're elated, joyful, happy. We experience the same thing in being able to say Mass, and to understand what we are doing.

When I first said Mass, the song, "He's Got The Whole World In His Hands" was popular, and all I could think of when I held Christ was, "I've got the whole world in my hands." This is really true. He's the Creator of the world, with the Father, and so we hold the Maker of the world. Therefore, we have the whole world right in our own hands, being able to touch Christ, and to realize that He is there, although we do not see Him! But He is actually there, under the appearance of bread and wine, and they change into the Body and Blood of Jesus Christ — and they do this by our words. "This is my Body" and "This is my Blood"! What a tremendous Grace that we have, to be able to say these words and have these things happen.

But we have to live by Faith, and we know that these things will happen only because Jesus said they would. That is what we believe, that is what we accept. And so the Mass takes on enormous meaning for us at that time. It should always have this meaning, every time we say Mass. And, when I have said Mass, down through the years, this is exactly what is taking place. I am always aware of the tremendous dignity and power of the Mass. Being a priest is not dull. It's a marvelous thing to be a priest.

My first Mass was very, very beautiful. Father Restle, the former Pastor, did the preaching. Father Trost was on the Altar with me, master-of-ceremonies, and my cousin, who was studying to be a priest, was there.

Prayer Necessary For Vocations

We have seven priests and about twenty-five Sisters in the Religious life from three generations in my family. I feel that my vocation was brought about through the prayers of my Grandmother, but also through the prayers of Sister Mary Clementine. She prayed that from each of her brothers' and sisters' families someone would go, either to the Convent, or to the priesthood, or to the brother-hood, and she was successful in her prayers. They were answered.

She also wanted this to continue on into the next generation, and I happened to be one of the ones chosen. So I am sure that it is through the prayers of others that vocations are given. And I think that, when there is a lack of vocations, it's because people don't pray. Jesus said, "Pray, therefore, that I send laborers for the harvest, because the harvest is ripe, but the laborers are few." And so we definitely should pray for vocations, and pray hard.

Someone *has* to pray for God to give this vocation. Before He called His Apostles, Jesus prayed, and it's the same thing. People in the Church should *pray* for vocations to the priesthood, brother-hood, and sisterhood, and pray unceasingly that we get holy priests, brothers, and sisters who are dedicated completely and totally to God and the things of God, and well-being of the world. This means bringing God's message to the world, God's principles to the world, so that the world will be Christianized, so that the problems that it has will be solved.

CHAPTER 13

FIRST YEARS AS A PRIEST

Temptation To Change To Trappist Life

After I was ordained, I still had a few more studies to finish because I had missed a few courses as a result of my year in Rome. I still had to study the tract on Grace for Dogmatic Theology, and a few things about the Sacraments and Moral Theology. And so, I spent about twelve weeks studying these things in the Seminary.

During that time, I also had a desire to be a Trappist. This came to my mind repeatedly during the Novitiate, and I kept putting it out of my mind. Then the thoughts came back during the seminary days at Washington, and at various times just before I was ordained. Again, I put them out of my mind. After I was a priest, these thoughts returned.

Still I tried to ignore them and continue in my work. I was assigned to be vocation director of our Congregation, and all the while these thoughts kept returning, so I decided to settle the question once and for all. I drove up to Spencer, Massachusetts and talked to the Trappists. They questioned me and told me that I should come immediately, that I should wait no longer, that I did seem to have a vocation there.

I then went to speak with one of our Fathers, Father Clement Kilgoar, who was then my spiritual director. I explained to him what I was thinking and he said, "No, I will not permit it. You do not have the vocation to be a Trappist. You will remain in the Congregation. You have been called here, and you will live this life."

Therefore, I gave up all ideas of joining the Trappists and, since that time, the idea of becoming a Trappist has never come back. This proves that sometimes the devil inspires the desire for us to change vocations, to go from one Congregation to another, or one life to another. We have to be very careful. We should follow the advice of our spiritual director. If God is really calling us to live a different life, then He will inspire us to think continually about this for many, many years. Finally our spiritual director will see that this is what must be done. In my case, immediately after speaking to my spiritual director, the temptation was gone. I followed his advice and it went away. This shows that it was not from God, that God did not want it, and that He wanted me to remain a member of the Congregation of the Sacred Hearts of Jesus and Mary.

Vocation Director

I began my work as a vocation director. I traveled much, preached often, went to many places, wrote many letters, and worked very hard in carrying out my work. But I always said all of my prayers, no matter what time of day, or what happened during the day. I always was very conscientiously faithful to my spiritual exercises. This sometimes required great sacrifice, but I felt it was necessary.

Learning Process

I was alone most of the time while I was traveling, and so I could talk to God for hours and hours, thinking about Him constantly, and therefore a deeper spiritual life developed as I was going about this work. It was not an easy task to carry out this vocation work, because we were not known sufficiently, and I had to more or less feel my way along.

Financial Pinch

It was also not easy from a financial standpoint, because I turned in my weekend work and Mass stipends to the Novitiate so I seldom had much money for carrying out the work. One time, I had to travel to Philadelphia and Washington, D.C. from Fairhaven, Massachusetts. I had $13 in my pocket, and I did not ask for any money to do the work. I just left and went on the trip. I was gone for three weeks, and, when I came back, I still had $5. People were always very good and generous along the way. They gave donations, food, and help, and I would try to stay in rectories overnight.

Learning More About Priests' Living

When you come into a rectory, you hear the pastor's story about the parish, and about the curates and, in the evening, you hear just the opposite story. Then you hear the associate's story about the pastor, and about the parish. When you get a steady diet of this you begin to realize just what the priesthood is like across our country. I visited many rectories and heard many things in the first few years of my priestly life. Sometimes it was not an easy or pleasant situation I found myself in, having to listen to all these complaints about what was going on, but, for the most part, I felt that the priests were quite good and dedicated. They were really paternal and charitable, and went out of their way to be nice to me, and to give approval to anything I would try to do for the students.

Family Visiting

To go to the family and speak to them was rather difficult. There was always a barrier. They didn't want their children to become priests, brothers, or sisters, so I always had to find a way in which to get into the home. Finally, I discovered that the best way to approach a family was to try to have the Enthronement of the Sacred Heart in the home. In doing that, I had time to socialize with them, and talk to them. Then, on another occasion, I could come and we could talk about the vocation of their son or daughter. In that way, I could easily establish a rapport, so as to really find out whether there was a vocation. I didn't learn this until toward the end of my term as vocational director. I wish I'd learned it in the beginning, because I am sure much more fruitful work could have been accomplished.

15-Decade Rosary

One day, when I was driving along doing my vocation work, on June 14, 1955, God told me to say the fifteen-decade Rosary every day until I died. I said, "That's impossible. You know what I do every day." And then I went through my schedule with Him, as if He didn't know. I explained all my prayer life, my traveling, everything. And I said, "Well, how on God's earth can I ever fit in the fifteen-decade Rosary?" I told Him it was just impossible.

Again, He said to me, "You are to say the fifteen-decade Rosary every day until you die." And so, I said to Him, "O.K., if that's what You want, You give me a fifteen-decade Rosary." Little did I realize that, the very next day, it would happen.

The next day, I had an appointment with Little Rose Ferron's sister, Flora. I came to her home at one o'clock, and rang the doorbell, and there was no answer. I went back to the car and prayed the Rosary and meditated. At two o'clock, I came back and rang the bell again. Still no answer. I went back and prayed another Rosary, and meditated some more. At three o'clock, I came back and rang the bell — no answer — I went back out and prayed still *another* Rosary, and said my Office for the rest of the day, and anticipated for the next day. At four o'clock, when I returned, there was still no answer, so I decided to give up and go home. As I was coming down the stairs, a lady drove up and said, "Father, they must be home because their car is in the driveway. I have a pass key. I used to take care of Little Rose. I will go in and see what has happened." She went in and found out that they had fallen asleep and didn't hear me.

Then they all came down and were sitting around the table, and I asked Flora, in the course of the conversation, if she had anything of Little Rose's that she could give to me. Flora said, "No, I can't think of anything." Then the lady who had let me in said, "Father, I have something." I asked what it was, and she said, "I'll go home and get it."

A half hour later, she came back and said, "Here, Father, I feel I must give this to you. I don't know why, but I do." Then she gave me a fifteen-decade Rosary, and told me that Little Rose made it. Our Lord had blessed it, and she gave it to her as a gift in reward for helping to take care of her. Now she said, "I want you to have it."

Chosen — An Instrument To Cure People

I took the Rosary and went back to Fairhaven, Massachusetts. On my way, I was thinking of what happened, and God also told me that He was going to use me to cure people. Immediately it came to my mind, "No, I can't do that. First of all, I'm not worthy because of the past life that I lived. You just cannot choose me for that." Yet He said He would use me to cure people.

Sister Scholastica Reagen and Fr. Luke at St. Joseph Monastery.

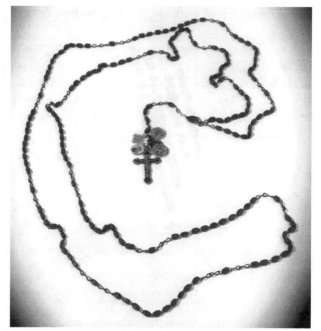

15 decade Rosary

Crucifix with relic of true Cross

CHAPTER 14

CHOSEN — AS INSTRUMENT OF GOD

Again I doubted the message, and I said, "If that is the case, then I want a relic of the True Cross, to prove this." Being chosen for this was frightening to me. All I could envision was people coming from all over and demanding my time. Some would come out of curiosity, some with belief, others just to ridicule. I rejected the whole idea as being too repugnant to me, and I just didn't want this to happen.

But then, after thinking about it awhile, I said, "Well, if You really want me to do this, then I *do* want a relic of the True Cross, to assure me that this is what You really want." I continued on my way home, thinking about all that had happened during the day, receiving the Rosary and what Our Lord had told me. When I got back to the Novitiate, I told my Spiritual Director, who was Father Eugene Robitaille at the time, about what had happened.

I showed him the Rosary. It had a very strong rose scent, and he told me to take it and place it in a glass of water overnight, to see if the scent had been put on it or if there was a Heavenly origin for it. The next morning, when I got up, I said Mass. After Mass was over, I went up and got the Rosary. It had a stronger rose scent than when we had put it in the water.

I did not speak about this to many people. I very seldom spoke about it. I tried to keep this a secret as much as possible, because I felt it was necessary to keep it a secret, especially after the treatment I had received during my Novitiate days. I did not want that ever again to be repeated.

Again, I acted out of human respect. This is one of my greatest faults, worrying about what people will say, what people will think, and so I just kept my mouth shut and didn't say anything.

Receiving The Relic Of The True Cross

I had to give mission collection talks in Wisconsin, and it was necessary to drive to get there. I took another young person with me. As we were driving through Mt. Vernon, Ohio, I decided to thank a man who had prayed for me when I was sick. He prayed that I would get well and become a priest, and, since we were going through his town, it would be an act of courtesy to stop by and thank him.

We went to his place, but he did not want to let us in because his mother was ill. She had had a heart attack just a few days earlier, and he thought it might upset her. But, when he found out why I was there, and that I didn't want to take too much of his time, he said to come in. I went in and, while I was there, he showed me a room he had in his home, a Chapel, where he had the Stations of the Cross, and various things from the Holy Land. He explained all this to me, and, all of a sudden, he stopped and said, "Father, you are the one."

I looked at him as if he was a little wacky. Then he went into the next room, and, when he came back, he gave me a Crucifix. He said that there was a relic of the True Cross in the Crucifix, and he gave me the papers, the documents, to prove that it was from Rome. He told me these words, "You are to bless people who are sick. If God wants to cure them, He will. If not, they will receive special Graces to suffer in a resigned way. And, even if a person is not sick and you bless them with this Crucifix, they will receive special blessings."

I thanked him, but I did not tell him what God had told me on the fifteenth of June. This was on June 29th, 1955, the Feast of St. Peter and Paul. I continued on my journey to Wisconsin, and, while I was in Wisconsin I gave a talk in the parish where my cousin was living.

The First Cure After Blessing

My cousin told me that one of her best friends was sick, and asked if I would go to visit her. I decided I would and, while I was there, I blessed her with the relic of the True Cross. I prayed that either she would die on the fifteenth of August, or be cured. She'd had her kidney removed, and her incision wasn't healing. She'd had a very bad time. On the fifteenth day of August, she was cured. She got her health back, got up and did her work, and she has had many children since. God was very good to her.

Ulcer Cure

When I was at the parish that weekend, the pastor hemorrhaged from ulcers, and begged me to stay for the week and help him. But I had an appointment the next day in Dubuque, Iowa, and I didn't feel that I could stay. I told him that I couldn't stay, but I'd give him a blessing instead. He might have thought, "Big deal!" Of course, what I meant was that I would give him a blessing, hoping he'd be cured. I didn't tell him about the relic, just gave him the blessing and went on my way. I found out later on that he was cured, right on the spot, and able to continue and carry on his work without any difficulty. God was very, very good.

Bishop Aided

I drove back to Fairhaven, Massachusetts, after I had finished my work in the Midwest. When I came back, there was a bishop from Ireland visiting there. He had just had an operation and he felt very ill. I called him aside and explained to him that I didn't feel worthy to bless him with the relic, but I said, "Bless yourself with it." He did and, the next day, he felt well enough to go out and play eighteen holes of golf. When I saw him the next night, he burst out, "Father, it worked! It worked!" I just put my finger up to my lips and he said, "I understand," and he didn't say anything more about it. But he received the strength to be well and I am very pleased with this.

Spinal Meningitis

There was a young boy in our parish who had an attack of spinal meningitis. The day before this, I was telling the janitor, who was a friend of mine, about the relic. I didn't know why I was telling him and I said so. I told him, "I simply feel that I have to tell you these things." The next morning, he told me about this young boy, Paul Mello, who had spinal meningitis.

I told him, "This afternoon, I'll go over with you and we'll visit him in the hospital." And so we did. I went over and blessed him. Nothing happened. The next day I went back in the morning and blessed him again. Still nothing happened. I went back in the afternoon and blessed him, and this time he was cured. The doctors kept him in the hospital a little while longer, just to make sure, but he was cured. Today he is married. I just happened to see him recently, when I was on my way to Rome, and he is very strong and healthy. It was a wonderful gift that God gave to him.

There was another youngster, a little girl. She had a birthday and her family didn't have any celebration. Well, she wanted to have a celebration, and so she ran home and lit a candle. Nobody else was with her, and she went toward the window. The curtains caught fire, and then her dress. They heard her screaming from downstairs, and someone ran up and threw a blanket around her, and rolled her down the stairs. This saved her life, but her body was burned from her knees up over her ears — ninety-five percent of her body. Even her ears fell off because they were so badly burned.

Her face was completely burned. Her whole body was burned. They had to take her to the hospital, and there she was wrapped in gauze. When I saw her, she looked like she was a mummy. She remained that way for many days, and I went and blessed her every day. Finally they took away these rags, these "winding sheets." Then you could see the charred black scars and scabs all over her body. Then they had to peel all this off. When you looked, you could see into her abdomen, her intestines and everything.

It was an ugly sight. You could even smell her when you came into the hospital, from many corridors away. The hospital was filled with this burnt and putrid odor. But I went to visit her every day and blessed her. They said it would take many years for her to rehabilitate herself and have the skin grow back on. The skin grew back almost miraculously, on most of her body, except for her face. They tried to graft skin onto her face, and it just wouldn't take. They would get it on too tight, and have to take it off again.

At last, the skin did reappear on her face, but she had some scar marks and they had to rebuild her ears. I always teased her and said they were going to give her rabbit ears. We got to know one another quite well.

Psychologically, she adjusted within ten months, and was well on her way to recovery. Today she is married, and is a very wonderful person. She recently had a baby girl. She has concern and compassion for everyone, especially for anyone who has to suffer. She is a great pleasure to meet and to talk with. She learned much from her experience, as we all must.

Diabetes

Then I went to Washington, D.C. and visited a woman who had her leg amputated. She had diabetes, and her spirits were quite low. I tried to cheer her up and I gave her a blessing, hoping that she would snap out of it. When I came downstairs, they told me that there was another person, a little boy, in the house who also had diabetes. I blessed everyone in the house, and little did I realize that the little boy would be cured. He was cured on the spot.

Leukemia

The next person was a friend of mine who had leukemia. I went to school with him, and I blessed him. I learned that on his way to the Mayo Clinic in Rochester, he felt that he was cured. He was, and we praise God for that.

Cancer

I blessed a lady with leukemia, and her leukemia was cured. Later, when I was assigned to Bishop Amat High School, in La Puente, California, a young boy, seven years old, was brought to me by the Sisters. He had cancer of the mouth and throat, and the doctors could do nothing more for him. I blessed him. I visited him later, and blessed him and he was completely cured from this cancer. He still lives, healthy and strong. He is living in Gardena, California.

Cancer Cure

While I was Dean of Discipline at this same high school, a boy came in one day and said that he had to go home and take his youngest brother and his mother to the doctor. I asked him what was the matter, and he told me that his brother had cancer. I asked how old the child was, and he told me that he was only a baby. I laughed at him and said, "That's impossible. Little babies don't get cancer." He replied, "The specialist said so. You can call my Mom and see that I'm telling the truth." Then I said, "O.K., I'll believe you, but I want you to do one thing. You tell your mother to bring that baby to me tonight." I explained about the Crucifix and he did bring the baby back. I blessed the little boy and told the Mother to bring him back in nine days. I blessed him once again, and he was cured.

Brain Tumor And Spinal Meningitis

I blessed two people with brain tumors and they were cured. One of the coach's daughters had spinal meningitis. I went with him to the hospital and blessed the child, and, when we came back and watched through the glass that separated the rooms from us, she was cured, right before our eyes, in about twenty minutes.

Cancer — Not Cured

There was one man who had cancer of the face and he was not cured, but he was given the resignation to accept his death. He was a non-Catholic.

Brain Tumor

Another person had a brain tumor, and was living in Texas. I was living in Hawaii, and had no way of reaching him, and so I just prayed and blessed him from where I was, and he was cured of the brain tumor.

Cancer

I said Mass in the home of another woman, living in Hawaii. She had cancer of the stomach and a big sore on her knees. I blessed her, during that Mass, and, the next morning, all these things had disappeared.

Leukemia — Not Cured

Another young boy, living in Hawaii, had leukemia. I blessed him and prayed that he would be cured, but nothing happened. Then I started praying that, if God was going to take him in death, He would give me a sign. Finally, on November 21st, the Feast of the Presentation of the Blessed Mother, he got worse and I knew that he was going to die.

I began to pray then that he would have a happy death, that he'd go directly from this life into Heaven. On December 8th, he again took another turn for the worse. I visited him every day in the hospital and blessed him. On December 16th, I came to see him and he was happy and joyful, up and around and reading. I thought, "Well, gee, did I make a mistake?" He seemed to be getting along so well. When I came back, the next morning, he was in a coma. He never came out of that coma and he died on December 18th, at five minutes to five.

I woke up where I was sleeping, and it was as if he came to my room and thanked me for my prayers. I knew he was there and that he had died. I got up immediately and went over to the Church and prayed and said Mass. Then I called the hospital and it was confirmed that he had died. I never told his mother about this. They were very poor and suffering greatly. It was really a sad situation, and I felt very badly about this, but there was nothing more that I could do.

God Cures — Not Man

And so, you see, it's not every time I pray for people or bless them that they will be cured. Some are, some are not. Some are cured immediately, some after time. It proves that God is the One Who cures people, no one else. We should not become elated or think that we are great or better than anyone else if we have this power, if God gives this power. He is only using us as an instrument to bring about these cures in the lives of people.

It calls to mind the words Our Lord said, in regard to people who cured. He said, when they died and came up to Heaven, "I do not know you." And they said, "Didn't we cure people in Your Name? Didn't we prophesy in Your Name?" And He said, "I never knew you." There's always the danger of thinking that we are causing these cures, of becoming arrogant or proud and taking this to ourselves. It's just not that way at all. We don't cause cures. Not ever. It's just that God rewards our Faith when He cures people, the ones He wants to have cured. The others will have to not be cured. He knows what is best. He knows why they're suffering, not only for the good of their own souls, but for the good of others.

Right Attitude About Suffering Most Helpful

Many ask why they are suffering. Suffering can make us very selfish and self-centered. It can make us repugnant to others. We can complain about ourselves, talk about ourselves constantly.

Or, we can be just the opposite, be happy and cheerful, praising God and thanking Him that we are considered worthy to suffer with Him and to offer our sufferings for others and bring blessings and Graces upon the world.

When we are suffering, we should realize that we are participating in the mission of Christ, in the sufferings of Christ. We can offer this and carry the Cross for the good of the whole world. This will bring many Graces upon our families, relatives, friends, the ones we witness to by showing how to suffer in a proper way, not being discouraged or displeased. It can bring blessings on ourselves, too.

And, if we have no suffering, then it gives us a chance to be more prayerful, more charitable. When we wait on people who are suffering, we are actually waiting on Christ. We are helping that person to carry his cross and we are, therefore, like Simon of Cyrene, and Christ is the One who is suffering in that person. This is how we should look upon it.

Not that suffering is great, in itself. It is not. It is an evil, in itself, the result of sin. It is not the result of our sins, but from the very fact that sin was committed. Suffering came into the world through sin, and will remain in the world until the end of time. This is a mystery of suffering, that it can bring great good to the world.

My Sister, A Person With Retardation

I know this from my own suffering and from the suffering of my family. There has never been a year when we did not have some major sickness in our family, since 1944. My younger sister, Catherine, is a retarded person, retarded to the level of an eighth grader. When she was young, she had spinal meningitis, though we did not realize it at the time. There was no way of getting to a doctor because we had a terrible storm at the time. We had to use snow shoes and walk four miles over to the doctor and tell him what the symptoms were. He would give us medicine and we would bring it back and give it to her until finally she got well, but her mind was affected and she became a retarded person.

We didn't realize this until much later. She developed physically just like everyone else, and she didn't show any signs of retardation through grammar school years, because her level was the eighth grade. She was able to do all her work and she was going along very well until she got into high school. Then we discovered that there was something wrong.

When we had tests made in the clinic, given to her by my brothers, we found out that she'd had spinal meningitis when she was young and that her retardation was traceable to that time. It was a cross to accept and to carry. She has to carry that cross, even to this day. She's left out of many things in life, but still, she is useful in life. She is able to help other people, older people. She's in a nursing home. She waits on them, delivers the mail, waits on the table, and so forth. And in this way, she is able to do something that is useful, even if she cannot get married and have a family of her own. Her life is well worthwhile.

That's what we have to realize in regard to people who are retarded or have physical suffering. There is tremendous worth in the soul of that person, and these are things that we must learn as we go through life.

Suffering A Mystery

I talk to many people who do not want to accept suffering. They think that God has to cure every person who is suffering, that He has to hear and answer every prayer that we send up to Him in regard to this healing. That is not God's way. God still knows what is best for each person, and we should be willing to accept this. We must never become "puffed up" if God does happen to use us for these things. God runs the show, and God is the One Who will use us as He sees fit, when He sees fit.

Do Will Of God

In the beginning, I was quiet about all this, but now I really don't care any more. If people come, well, so be it. But they must realize that they should not ever build up false hopes. They can ask God to cure, but we must always use the proper means first. That is what God gave us doctors for. We must take the advice of the doctor, take the medicine that the doctor prescribes, and then we have a right to ask to be cured, if it is God's will to do so. Always, though, we must tell Him, "Whatever You wish, so be it." God gives us the Grace to suffer in a proper way, for His honor and glory, if He wishes us to do so.

I could speak of many other cures and healings, but I think that enough has been mentioned to show what God has done in my life. This is what I have to witness to, and to live, and to accept, and to believe. It is important to overcome the fault of acting out of human respect. I will begin to act this way more and more, from now on. I am no longer afraid to speak of these things that God has done in my life.

CHAPTER 15

PARISH WORK

When I finished my vocational work, I was assigned to St. Joseph's Parish in Fairhaven, Massachusetts. At that time we just received our obedience, our Provincial called us in and told us, "This is what you are going to do." No questions were asked, and there was no conversation or discussion about whether you liked this assignment or not. You just obeyed. I never knew why I was transferred from the vocational work to be an assistant in a parish. I did like the vocation work, and I gave my best and my all to it. And then, when I was transferred to St. Joseph's without an explanation, it did hurt a bit, but I knew that I had to give myself to the work of the parish with the same zeal and the same effort.

New Dimension In My Priesthood

And so, I did just that. I was at St. Joseph's Parish, in Fairhaven, for a little over two years. I was able to help and become friends to many people. Many are still my friends today. The young people were constantly with me, mainly because I was young at the time. I love children. I think they are very great. They're very lovable and loving, innocent and trusting, faithful and obedient. I love to work with children, especially with teenagers.

Book Work

During the day I had to take care of the books and other work that really should have been done by other people. Nevertheless, it gave me time to really talk to God, to be in union with God. I continued my prayer life as I had in my vocation work. I said my fifteen-decade Rosary every day, and I prayed for the people of that parish congregation.

Some Problems

The parish was not deeply spiritual. It had many problems. We had a school, and the children were wonderful and showed great respect. The teachers were quite strict, a little too strict, I thought. Sometimes I would go over to try to help with the discipline, but I would never strike a child. I had them take a ruler and come up before the class. Then I would put out my hand and tell them to hit me. They would rather have taken a beating than to do so. Many of them just broke out crying, and they did not want to do that, but they would change and start to behave afterwards. Then I was told by the pastor that I should not go over to the school any more, that Father Regis would take care of it, and that was that. I never went over to the school again.

Painting The School

While I was there I had to take over the parish while the pastor was gone. He said that he wanted the school painted, and that we were going to have volunteers to paint the school. It ended up that the teenagers and myself did most of the work, along with the people who were in the Boy Scouts. They were so wonderful that I gave them a steak dinner when everything was painted and we were all done.

Only A Few Help

I learned from that that we should never rely on volunteers to do a project in a parish, because the work always falls on the shoulders of the few. Only the few are dedicated and give of themselves completely all the time. The majority do not, and so it's not fair to the few who do. I figured that, from then on, we should rely on hired help, paid with money from the treasury, where everybody contributes, for any work that had to be done. The amount of money coming into that parish, though, was very small. We were still trying to live in the 1860 level, thinking that you can run a parish with that amount of money. It was impossible. It had to be increased.

Drive For Financing A High School

We also had a drive for a high school. This was rather repugnant. We had to preach to the people and tell them to give money for that high school. One Sunday, I gave a sermon and I used the example of the man in the Gospel, who built his barns and had a lot of money, and filled his granaries. Then he built more and said now he could relax because he was so well off. Then God said, "You fool, this night I demand your soul of you." I used that example about people constantly building up their money and not using it for the honor and glory of God. I asked people to help with this project.

There happened to be one man in Church that day who very seldom came to Church. But he happened to come that Sunday, and he happened to be the sort of person I was thinking about. He owned a greenhouse and, the next day, one of our Fathers went to visit him. He said, "What is that young whippersnapper priest trying to do? Doesn't he know that I had to sacrifice and give the price of a new suit toward this high school?" He went on ranting and raving and then finally he told Father that now he could sit back and relax. He was giving out his work to other people so that he could enjoy himself. He had enough money now.

It happened that that night he had a heart attack and Father was called to the morgue to give the Last Sacraments. The new suit he received was really for his funeral. This really struck me hard because I'd used that example in the sermon the day before, and he had complained so much about it. Father told me all about it and, here he was dead, just like in the Gospel. It taught me a lesson. I continued on in the parish, and we had a successful drive for the high school. The collections picked up, too, though we did not preach for money for them.

Giving Service

I prayed, worked, and gave service to others, and I tried to visit their homes. However, I did not have too much time. Many people came to us. We were always working on marriage cases, rectifying them. We rectified at least three marriages every month. We had convert classes. We had to give separate classes for this. We had a C.C.D. program, too, and so my time was taken up almost completely in the ministering of the parish, without going to the homes that I would have liked.

Change Of Assignment

Finally, at the end of two years, or perhaps a little more, I was called in by the Provincial, and he said, "I want you to be the director of a new seminary, in Winona, Minnesota." Again, no questions asked. I was told to go, and that was that. He also told me that he wanted me to go out and look over the property, and get it ready for the coming of the class.

Furnishing The House

I drove with three young teenagers out to Winona. When I arrived, it was to find only a dinky, little house, which most people would use for two children.

I furnished the house. On the porch area I had to put bunk beds, one on top of the other. We had six people living there. We had to put lockers there and in the two rooms upstairs. We were four to a room, and it was very crowded. We had a total of fourteen students. I used my room as an office, a bedroom, and a storage room for the Chapel. We also had a Chapel. I set that up. I had some kneelers made, and bought a washer and dryer, and set them up in another area, the kitchen area. Every single space, in each room, was used to the full.

Those two years were very happy ones. We had to live in close quarters, with many privations, and we took our meals over at the college, but the students could snack at our place and do their studying there. I saw to it that things were running smoothly, and worked with the architect to try and arrange for the building of a seminary so as to have a minor seminary in that area.

I believe that, when one is given a job to do, he should be allowed to run that job without any outside influence. He should be both willing and able to do so or he should not be appointed in the first place. It was the wish of the Provincial and his council that they decide each detail concerning the building that was to be done. My own suggestions were misinterpreted and thought to mean that I wanted to "run the whole show." This wasn't the case at all. I only wanted to do the work that I felt that I had been assigned to take care of. But after I received a letter saying that I was not to do anything further in regard to the building, I made no further contacts with the architect. Though it was difficult for me to carry on my work in this fashion, and I began to feel like no more than an extra spoke on a wheel, nonetheless, I did so.

New Assignment Again

The Provincial came out, made his visit and told me that I was doing a good job, and that he was very happy with everything. Then, very shortly thereafter, I received a letter saying that I had been transferred and was to be a teacher in La Puente, California. Once again, without any explanation, just, "You go and that's it." And that is what I did. I obeyed.

CHAPTER 16

ASSIGNMENT IN CALIFORNIA

I went to California and taught French, Latin, and History for the first two years. The second two years, I was made the counselor of the school for the boys and so I gave up teaching History, and taught just one class each of French and Latin, and I also taught some Religion. The last two years I was there I was made dean of discipline and dean of study for the boys. I taught only one class, a Religion class, during that time.

Those were happy and fruitful years, during which I was able to pray much and stay close to God. They were work-filled years, too. As dean of discipline, I had to play a game and be an actor, which was not easy. I am not that strict or that tough by nature with kids, so it was a really traumatic experience to have to go through. I'd have to eat many Rolaids to settle my stomach, but otherwise, I did enjoy the work.

Purpose Of A Catholic High School

I do feel that a Catholic high school must teach and give a good solid foundation in Religion. What good is their training, their education, if they don't have a good, solid foundation? I felt that they were not getting this in many instances, because many left the high school and later became drop-outs from their Religion. It was something that happened in the 1960s, I know. It happened in every school throughout our country, but, again, I wonder if we did not stress the right things or if our curriculum was really providing the proper religious instruction for that level. There are many questions unanswered and unsolved.

Crisis Of Faith

The Faith of students should be deepened in high school, not destroyed or weakened. And I've seen so much of that. Maybe it's just a sign of the times, a crisis of the times, that people are going through, that caused this to happen. Nevertheless, it's something that causes me much worry and concern. We know that the Vatican Council took place and that what happened in the time since, with regard to teachers and students, is that there is great confusion, much doubt and criticism, in regard to Faith. The students are the ones who are really suffering from all this.

Teenagers Need Leaders

My stay at Bishop Amat was a good experience for me. It helped me much in my own spiritual life, and deepened my understanding of people, especially teenagers. I know that the majority of teenagers are very good, wonderful people. We should not look down on them or criticize them too much. We should be the guides and the leaders, the ones who listen, the ones who help them to develop correctly, in all phases of their lives. They have much to offer. They are the future of our country, the future of our world, the future of our Church. We have to have great faith in them. I believe that many of them are well-qualified to be the leaders in the world of tomorrow.

Desire To Fulfill Real Mission In Life

All during the time I was in Seminary, while I was vocational director, as a priest in a parish, a superior in a seminary, a teacher at Bishop Amat, and also, in the last three years, the Superior of the Religious Community, I felt that God wanted me to do something different, something in relation to the Consecration that I made in 1946. I always felt that He was calling me to share this with the world as I saw and lived it. I did not know when, where, or how this could be brought about, but it was always there in the back of my mind.

I was therefore watching for the opportunity to begin and, when I was made Superior, the thought was still in my mind. I never tried to force my ideas on anyone, never really spoke about them to anyone. I did sometimes speak about these different things to my Religion classes, without saying why I was teaching these ideas. It was, more or less, the building of a foundation of my own idea, of how they could be shared with others. It was a learning process for me.

Turmoil In Community Living

After Vatican II, I saw what was beginning to happen in Community life, and in religious living, and I did not like what I saw. The lack of prayer life, on the part of my Congregations, the lack of praying together, with everybody going his own way, was disturbing to see. Communities were more like a motel, where you came in and slept during the night; a service station where you ate together, and that's about all the Community life amounted to. It was said that you could have camaraderie in the recreation periods and talking to one another, and that was supposed to be sufficient. But prayer life was sadly neglected. I did not believe then, and I still do not believe, that the religious life is meant to be lived this way. I believe that we are all called to live a life of community praying, praying together, *supporting* one another in our prayer life.

Since I saw this happening while I was Superior, I knew that I was responsible for the Community. One day I will answer to God. Perhaps I was not strict enough, in correcting different things that I did see. I just let things go many times. I did correct different ones at different times, but, on other things, maybe I should have been a little stricter.

I felt that I had to live the life myself, as I saw it, and to do penance for the Community. As a result, I got up every morning at a quarter to four, and spent the time before the Blessed Sacrament in prayer from then until 7:30, when I went over to the school. I did this for a period of two years, the last two years that I was Superior, without anyone in the Community knowing what I was doing.

I believe that our Congregation is a wonderful Congregation. It was founded to pray for sinners of the world, to ask God to be merciful to them, and we are able to do this through adoration of the Blessed Sacrament. We are also to spread devotion to the Sacred Hearts of Jesus and Mary. If we do not do this, then I begin to wonder, do we have the right to exist?

CHAPTER 17

NEW ENDEAVORS

I did not wish to be Superior any longer, and I said so. I expressed my desire to my Superior to preach and spend time spreading the message of God, giving retreats and missions, and, hopefully, beginning the work that I felt God was calling me to do. I wished to call people to devote their lives to Christ through Mary, as I had been living this since April 28, 1946. I did not know fully yet just how I would present this to people.

I still had to think about this for many hours, weeks, and months and to develop these ideas in my mind so that I could begin to properly teach people, so that it would be acceptable, and people would be willing to live this type of life. And so, I expressed my desire to the Superiors, and they respected my wishes, even though the majority of the members of the house wanted me to have a second term as Superior.

Assigned To Hawaii

I was told that I would be permitted to begin, and that Father Dominic Crewe was being assigned with me to begin the mission work. But, before it could get off the ground, I received a letter from Rome, where the Provincials were meeting. They had been talking among themselves, and our Irish Provincial wanted Father Dominic Crewe to be the Novice-Master in Ireland. So, Father McCarthy, who is the Provincial out East, said, "If I give you Father Dominic Crewe, I want Father Brendon Commisky to teach in the Seminary and to come from Ireland to go to our Major Seminary in New Hampshire." It was agreed upon. That left me free, but with no assistant to help in carrying on the work that I had proposed to do.

Joe Dowling, who was the Vice Provincial of our area, did not know what then to do in my case. To give retreats and so forth alone is quite difficult. It really would be overworking oneself, so to start a mission with only one would seem sort of useless.

Then Father Harold Meyer, from Hawaii, who was present, asked that they send me over to Hawaii and have me teach in the Seminary for one year, on a loan basis. This is what was decided. I received a letter stating so when I was in Wisconsin, on my vacation. Father Dowling wrote to me stating that I had been assigned to Hawaii to teach in the Seminary.

Well, I objected. I told them that I did not feel that I should be going to teach in the Seminary in Hawaii, and that I didn't feel qualified to teach the subjects they wanted me to teach. They said I would not be teaching Latin because they had a Latin teacher. The only courses open to teach were English, History, and, naturally, Religion.

In the end, I wrote back and said reluctantly that I would accept. I would teach a course in English, a course in History, and then the rest would be Religion for the whole Seminary department. This is what I was permitted to do. This was actually a blessing in disguise, though I didn't realize it at the time.

A New, Quiet Way Of Life

When I went to Hawaii, my life was very different. The atmosphere was tremendously different from that of the thriving and busy high school, where we had 1,600 students and I was in charge of 800 boys. This was a Seminary, where we had only twenty some students. The contrast was a drastic one. I welcomed the peace and quiet, the docility of the students, and the location of the Seminary, right on the ocean. My room was only a hundred yards from the beach. It was a beautiful area and an equally beautiful beach, but I could not swim because of the repeated attacks of rheumatic fever. Every time I went on the beach, my pains would come back very rapidly and forcefully, so I just stayed clear of the water.

We had a very small property, yet it was adequate for the size of the Seminary, and the number of students we had. It was a pleasure to spend the year with them. It was a whole year's treat for me. I taught my classes and spent the rest of my time reading, studying, and trying to learn to play the guitar. I never succeeded in doing that, because I didn't have anybody to teach me, and I was not that musically inclined that I could learn correctly.

Giving Retreats

On the weekends, I would go up to Schofield Barracks to help out at the Army installation with Mass and Confessions. The year went by quite rapidly. I got to know all the Fathers and, at the end of the year, I was asked to give the retreat for the Fathers, the Brothers, and the Sisters. It seemed to be acceptable. Naturally, I preached quite strongly and emphasized that the deep spiritual life is the important role in the life of the Religious. I stressed again the elements which set our Congregation apart from other Religious orders. I truly enjoyed giving those retreats.

Family Home Missions

I was only there on a loan basis, and I knew that I could not go back to California to begin preaching by myself, so I looked around and finally decided that I would work in the Family Home Missions. Father Gerard Christopher, one of our priests, was stationed in a parish, but he'd always had the idea that he'd like to say Mass in homes, with a dialogue with the people, and I had, more or less, the same idea. I decided that this might be an excellent way to begin the work of the Apostolate in some way, and to begin to formulate my ideas on how to get this across to people. So I said that I would pursue this.

We went to see our Provincial and explained what we had in mind, and he gave permission. We went next to the Bishop, and he also gave permission to begin this work. So, for the next three years we spent time in Hawaii, going from parish to parish, having groups formed where we would have six to ten families present for Mass in the home, with discussion after Mass. We would come back to these same people once a week, for four to six weeks, depending on the parish. Sometimes it wasn't for that long. We had a very flexible program, but, on every night, we had a different group and were in a different home and area in the parish. It proved to be very interesting, and I think it was successful. I wrote a book about this called *The Family Home Missions*.

During the first week we would talk about the changes in the Church, the reason for the changes — why the Church changes some things and doesn't change others. We had some very lively discussions. It was a means of educating people, mainly in the movement of the Church as the Church was progressing and beginning to implement the documents after Vatican Council II.

The second week we spoke about the husband-wife relationship. The third week, the parent-child relationship. The fourth week was family, school, Church, society relationships. I explained all this in the book that I wrote and many people find the book enjoyable to read.

This book was not the work that I intended originally to do. Nevertheless, in it, I speak about the morals of our day, the questions and problems that need answers and solutions. I feel that the only solution is the answer found in the teachings of the Church and Christianity. This is what that book is about and it also explains the work that we did in Hawaii during those three years.

In the summertime, we naturally didn't do this work, because it was very difficult to carry out during the summer. So I was free to help out in parishes or give retreats or go back to the mainland and do other work. One summer, in 1969, I decided to give a retreat or a mission to the lepers and I wrote to the Chaplain and told him that I was willing to come and to give this mission, and that I did not want any money. The only thing I wanted was their prayers. He gave me permission to come.

Molokai — Home Of Lepers

This was not the first time that I had gone there. I went there in 1967, for the first time, to make my own retreat. When you walk into the settlement, the first thing that hits you, like a tidal wave, is the utter and total silence of the place. You begin to wonder, "Why is it so quiet?" Then you realize the reason. It's because there are no children. Children are what make the world go around, and, if we do not have children, it is a very dull, drab, and dreary place. There were no teenagers either, and I realized then, very quickly, the importance of children, the importance of teenagers. I've worked with children all my life, all my priestly life, and it was quite a contrast to come into a situation like this.

Leprosy

The people, naturally, are deformed. There are two different types of leprosy. One is non-contagious, or at least that's the broad way of explaining it. In the non-contagious stage, the body is deformed in the hands, the feet, and the face. The rest of the body seems to be free from any deformity or ill effect of the leprosy, although its victims are very susceptible to other diseases and suffer greatly because of this.

The other type, the contagious type, is where they get sores all over their bodies. They get a very high fever, and it's very painful, in the beginning. Then, as the sore dries up, it just falls off. Before too long, the complete structure of the face is gone. They lose their ears, nose, eyelashes, and eyelids. Their faces completely disintegrate. It's good that they are blind, so that they cannot see your reaction. The other parts of their bodies are also affected. Many times they do not have any hands or feet, and they have to be taken care of completely by nurses and doctors, and they are hospitalized and can no longer remain in a home.

Living Conditions

When you go into a settlement, you see that each leper who can take care of himself has his own home. Sometimes they are married and live together as husband and wife, and are able to cook for themselves and take care of their gardens and so on. They can read, have the radio and T.V. and all the modern conveniences of life. The government takes care of them. They get a pension, after they've been working a certain number of years in the settlement. They have a fairly good life and can lead a nearly normal life now, because sulfa drugs can cause the disease to be arrested. But, if they stop taking the sulfa drugs, or, if at any time the sulfa drug no longer has effect on their bodies, the disease may again manifest itself and begin to progress within two years.

Most of the people there were elderly. When I was giving the mission, I found out that many of them were no longer going to Church. I visited them in their homes and asked them why. I visited everyone in the settlement. Many said that they knew that they were doing wrong, but that they would probably live a long life and would come back to God in their own good time. They felt that they had a chance to receive the mercy of God at any time they wished, and so they were sinning by presumption. Rather than living a good, solid, dedicated Christian life, they were just drifting along in life, letting their lives be wasted.

Meeting A Saint

When I went to the hospital, I met one especially beautiful soul. Her name was Maria Tanya, a Japanese leper, and a Catholic. She was quite striking to see. You saw before you a miserably deformed person and yet you knew at once that there was something different about her. A Rosary hung from her neck. She had the worst type of leprosy in its most advanced stages. I spoke to her and said that I wanted her to pray for me. I told her what I wanted to do, the work of spreading the special mission that I felt God wanted me to carry out, and she promised that she would pray. She had already been praying for many, many years.

She had been suffering like this for eighteen years, praying for priests all the while. She would say one Rosary after another, and she would take the stumps of her hands and push the Rosary between her teeth. That is the way she counted the beads, and she would do this nine times a day, for priests. She dedicated her whole life to praying for priests, to sacrificing her life for them. She was a very saintly soul. You could not help but feel this when you were in her presence, this great union that she had with God, this great love that she had for God. She did not have to speak because her whole being spoke for her. She gave a real witness to the world right there from that hospital bed. Though she was seen by only a few people, her influence on the world was tremendous. I feel that her influence on my own life has been momentous, and that the prayers that she said for me were very powerful and swiftly answered.

Needing An Operation

I had a physical ailment when I was doing my work in Hawaii. The last few months before I went to Molokai to give the lepers their mission, we worked in Blessed Sacrament Parish. One night I was giving a Mass, and I thought that I had perspired a lot that night. Actually, I was bleeding from the rectum, because I had hemorrhoids, a very painful type, and it was agony to go through the day with this ailment. I discovered that what I had thought was perspiration was, instead, blood. After that, I would have to take a pillow along with me while I carried out the work of the Family Home Missions.

I did not wish to have my surgery in Hawaii, because I wanted to finish the work of the year and give the mission for the lepers. Then I wanted to go to the mainland and have my brother take care of it. When I got home, my brother was at a convention in Boston, so I knew I couldn't wait there for him. I had to get back to California, so I went there and had the operation.

The night before the surgery, the anesthesiologist came in to talk to me, and said that it was going to be a very painful operation. After he left, I said to God, "O.K., I'll be perfectly willing to accept any suffering involved in this, and I offer it for the salvation of souls." But, when I had the operation and was recovering, I discovered that I didn't have any pain. It seems that, at times, God simply wants us to accept and to offer up the pain and suffering that we might have and that this is sufficient. Then He takes away the pain. That's exactly what happened with this ailment.

The doctor couldn't understand why I had no pain. One doctor, who was not a Catholic, came in and told me that, "It must be because you are very close to God that you do not have this pain." He was very moved by all this and he gave me a book about God working in souls, and helping people to suffer. I appreciated this very much.

I Decide — Go To Rome!

While I was in the hospital, Father Dowling, my Vice Provincial, and the Provincial from the East, Father Fintan, came and told me they would like me to go to Rome to study the Spirituality of Vatican II, under Father Ricardo Lombardi, the Jesuit priest who has the Better World Movement. This meant taking a ten-week course, and that I would be out of Hawaii for the ten weeks, leaving Father Christopher alone to work in the parish.

I replied that I did not think that I would want to go. First of all, I didn't want to study any longer. I figured, "What's the sense? Why should I even bother?" But then, during the night, I couldn't sleep. Around two o'clock, the idea came to me, "Maybe now is the time to see the Holy Father and find out what he thinks about this mission that I feel God has given to me; to see whether it is really from God, and if I can get the blessing of the Holy Father."

Made A Pilgrimage

And so, I made up my mind that I would go. I decided that, instead of just flying over from California, straight to Rome and back, I would go to Ireland and through France, making a real pilgrimage out of the trip. By taking the train from Paris to all the other places in France that I wanted to see, and then to Rome, I would be able to do this for only $4 more than just flying straight to Rome, and this is exactly what I did.

East Coast And Ireland

I went by myself on this pilgrimage. I flew to the East Coast, spent a week there, and visited all the Fathers, renewing old acquaintances. It was good to see everyone. From there I went to Ireland. While I was in Ireland, I visited the grave of Father Meldan, who had died on July 6th.

I had known when Father Meldan died. I was at home, in Adoration before the Blessed Sacrament, in my Parish Church, when I was told that he was sick and that he had died. Actually, I hadn't known the circumstances, but, when I got back to the Community, I found out that he had had a stroke and died shortly thereafter, the same day, within a few hours. I had just prayed for him, that he would go straight to Heaven. I went to his grave, mainly because I always had a tremendous respect for him, and I knew he was a just and a holy Religious. I wanted him to intercede for me, that I might obtain an audience with the Holy Father, and to pray that the work of the Apostolate would succeed and be for the honor and glory of God, and for the good of our Congregation.

After I did that, I spent a few days in Ireland, visiting the Fathers and the Seminary, and the Sisters, and traveling through Ireland, seeing the beauty of the country. I was really impressed with the country, with the friendliness of the people and the type of life that they were leading at the time, the rustic quiet life, not like the hustle and bustle in America!

France

I finally got over to France. I flew on a Sunday, after saying Mass in the morning. I had written ahead that I was coming, and I was hoping that the Fathers would meet me there, but, when I landed in Paris, there was no one there. I found out that my luggage had been damaged, and I had to buy a new bag and transfer my things into it. In the process, I left my Breviary on the counter. I caught a taxi and got over to the Provincial House. I was telling them who I was and why I was there when, all of a sudden, I remembered that I didn't have my Breviary. I explained to the Superior that my Breviary was gone, and asked him if he would take me back to the station, which he did. When we got there, I found the Breviary, which was most fortunate.

Then I said, "Since we're here, how close are the Sisters?" The Sisters' Community is on Picus Street. It is actually where our Congregation was founded. It is the place where our Founder saw, in a vision, that he would begin. He and Mother Foundress are buried in the cemetery, right next to this building. I wanted to go to the Founder's and Foundress' graves.

Prayed That The Apostolate Would Become
A Part Of Our Congregation

I asked him to take me there, and he consented. I prayed before their graves, and I asked the Founder and Foundress to pray for me, and to intercede for me, and to help me to obtain the audience with the Holy Father, that the blessing of God would be upon the Apostolate, and that I would know what to do, and that it would become a part of our Congregation, hoping that it would be accepted, without too much difficulty, by our Congregation.

Lisieux — A Place I Love

From there, the next day, the Father Procurator and another Father were so kind as to drive me to Lisieux, to the Little Flower's Shrine. I always had a great devotion to the Little Flower. I think she's a magnificent, magnanimous soul. She gives us the guidelines for leading real God-like lives. I think that she has much to offer for our present day spirituality. If we would just be humble enough to be childlike as she was. She always had a tremendous love for priests. She had also a great love for the missions. She was made Patroness of the Missions, and she was constantly concerned about the people who were estranged from God.

She prayed constantly for reconciliation and for renewal, and so she is a person who can help us in our Apostolate. That's the reason I went there and asked her help. I said Mass next to her body, her grave, and asked her help during my prayer and adoration in that Shrine.

After that we had dinner in a restaurant, and then later went to visit the graves of the parents of the Little Flower. I prayed to both of them for help also. They were a great family. They gave all their children to God, either in death or the Religious life. They were saintly people themselves, and I felt that they were in Heaven and could easily be turned to. Since they were the Father and Mother of children, I felt that they could understand the life of a young person. I bared my soul to them and asked their help. Then I came back to Paris and had dinner at night with the Fathers. I spoke to the former Superior General, Father John of the Heart of Jesus Elbee, SS.CC., who was a very saintly person.

Paray-le-Monial

From Paris, we went the next morning by train to Paray-le-Monial. I arrived in Paray-le-Monial at two o'clock in the afternoon, and I asked the Sisters if I could say Mass. They said yes, and so I said Mass right next to the place where St. Margaret Mary is buried, asking her help to obtain the blessings of God upon what I was trying to do, and to see the Holy Father.

After I finished with Mass, I went around Paray and visited different places and the religious museum that was present. I went to the Church where Father Columbriere is buried. I went there deliberately because I was told by a priest to go to his grave, to kneel and ask for his wisdom in guiding other souls. So I went to the place where he is buried. I was quite shocked, because what I found was just the skeleton. His body was broken up and laid with the trunk part first, the legs over that, and the arms over that, with the skull right on top. It was a glass cage and that's all that you could see. I prayed to him, also, and asked the same favors of him.

From there, I went back to the hotel where I stayed overnight. The next morning, I said Mass early, at the Altar where Our Lord appeared to St. Margaret Mary, and gave her the mission of spreading the devotion to the Sacred Heart throughout the world. He told her that, because she was so humble and lowly, the lowliest of all creatures, He chose her. He could have chosen anybody, but it seems that, when He chooses anyone for a mission, He always chooses the one least suspected, and she was the one.

She was told at one time to do Penance for the lack of charity among the Sisters of her Community. As a result, she had to tell them this, and they didn't like it at all. They actually beat her up physically that night because they resented what she had said. They did not accept her well at all.

It would be a wonderful thing to read her life, to realize what she really had to go through, and discover what a great saint she truly was. She only lived for forty-three years, to carry out her mission, yet her impact upon the world was felt for many, many years, and still is felt today, although today it is not felt as much as it should be.

While I was there, I offered myself completely and totally to God during that Mass. It seemed to me that God did accept what I offered, and it seemed that the whole Heavenly Court, all the Angels and the Saints, gathered with me and prayed for me, offering me to God, the Father, with Christ, through Mary, and in the Holy Spirit. I felt God's Presence very, very forcefully and it stayed with me.

Lourdes

From there, I proceeded on to Lourdes by train. I was supposed to arrive in Lourdes in the middle of the night, but I said to God, "I want to get there early, at least by seven o'clock, so that I can find a place to stay and, hopefully, meet one of our Fathers." Father Eugene Robitaille was going to Rome, and I was hoping to meet him and continue on my journey with him.

I got good train connections with only a five-minute interval between trains, and arrived in Lourdes by seven o'clock in the evening. I went to the hotel where I was hoping to find Father Eugene Robitaille, but I found that he had not come there. I asked if I could have a room, and they said they were all filled. They did phone around and found out that there was a room in another hotel, which I took. The reason there was such a lack of space was because it was around the Feast of the Holy Rosary and there were 40,000 people there.

The next morning, I said Mass in the Chapel. After I finished Mass, I went to the Mass of the Sick, where they had many priests and some Bishops and a Cardinal saying Mass, because of it being the Feast of the Holy Rosary. They had many thousands of people laying around on stretchers and in wheelchairs, just waiting to be cured, if possible. I saw the Mass and heard the sermons, and watched them bless the sick and give the Last Sacraments to the sick.

Finally, after two hours, I went over to the side shrine, where the Blessed Mother appeared to St. Bernadette. I wanted to get in there to say my fifteen-decade Rosary in that Shrine. The guards had blocked it off, but a Bishop came up and tapped one of the guards on the shoulder and said, "Let Father in." I went in and said my fifteen-decade Rosary, again asking the help of the Blessed Mother to let me see the Pope and let everything work out properly. I said that I would dedicate this work to her and asked her protection in this.

Then I visited other parts of the Shrine and area, and finally went back into town, where they were selling many souvenirs. I just browsed around all the different shops, killing time, waiting to get on a train, and go on to Rome. That night I got on the train.

Trip To Rome

I had a long ride and, during the night, there was a commotion. It seems that this one person from India was afraid of being attacked by a group of young boys who were taking dope. They were really making a lot of noise, talking loudly, and taunting him. The wife came to my compartment and asked if anyone knew how to speak English. I said that I could, and she told me to come with her to the other compartment, which I did. When I got there, the teenagers saw me and immediately quieted down, and sat down and behaved themselves. They finally went to sleep.

I talked with the man from India, and he was a very learned person, a very religious, spiritual man. I was quite edified by the life that he was living. I told him why I was going to Rome. It got to be about two in the morning, and I figured there would be no more trouble, so I went back to my compartment, where I tried to get a little sleep. I was not too successful.

About four o'clock, I heard an ungodly scream, and was wondering what had happened. Immediately, I jumped up and ran back to the other compartment, thinking that it was the young people, that they had awakened and were becoming vicious again. I soon found out that this was not true. It was a man who was just putting on a show. He really wasn't ill, but he was pretending that he was. What he wanted was to get off the train, so he was telling everybody, crying out loudly, that he was dying and that he needed a doctor, and that he needed help. He was pounding his bare chest and bending over in pain. This went on for some time, until the conductor came and saw him. At the next town, he let him off and gave him his baggage. As soon as he got his baggage and was off the train, he walked away as if nothing had happened. It was quite a mystery to me.

The train continued all that day, and arrived in Rome about ten o'clock at night. Just before we arrived in Rome, I looked across the compartment, and there was a man sitting there trying to sleep. I looked up at his luggage and noticed the address of our Fathers, and that he was going to Rome. I said to him in Latin, "Who are you? Where are you going? Are you a priest?" He answered, "Yes. I am going to the General House of the Fathers of the Sacred Hearts of Jesus and Mary." I told him that was my destination also. I said, "I am a priest of the Sacred Hearts." He replied, "I, also am one."

He didn't look that way, because he wasn't dressed as a priest. I was very surprised. Because he was going to the same place, and was expected, the Fathers met him at the depot and I was able to go with him right to the house.

Home At Last

When I got to the house, I was able to say Mass. I hadn't said Mass yet that day, and I never miss a Mass unless I absolutely have to. Actually, I've never missed Mass in my priestly life, except for the time I was in the hospital for the hemorrhoid operation for four days, and on one other day I had the flu. In twenty years' time, these are the only days that I have ever missed Mass. When I am on vacation, no matter where I am, I always make sure that I can say Mass. I feel that this is the greatest privilege that a priest has, the greatest act that we can perform, that is, to offer up the Holy Sacrifice of the Mass. We are offering an act of adoration, of love, of worship, of thanksgiving, of reparation, and an act of petition to God the Father. We are uniting ourselves with Christ, and all the whole Mystical Body is praying with Christ at one Mass. It's not just a meal, it's more than that. It's a Sacrifice and a Sacrament. It just should be the center of a priest's life and something that we should try to live every moment of our lives. We should be in union with Christ at each Mass that is being celebrated throughout the world. It's the *whole* Mystical Body of Christ praying, the Angels and saints in Heaven, the souls in Purgatory, and all the people on earth. We can unite all of this and offer if all to God.

This is what Mass means to me. I would never miss Mass, unless God demanded it of me through sickness. That's the only way that I will ever miss Mass. I think that the priest who deliberately does not say Mass, doesn't understand what his priesthood is, or what the Mass is all about. He needs to deepen his life and prayer life to really understand what is taking place, that this is something very tremendous, the greatest act he can perform in his whole life.

There is nothing greater in the world that a priest can do. Even forgiving sins does not equal the offering of a Mass. The Mass is the fulfilling of our priesthood to the full. And, naturally, we have the privilege of receiving Christ, in the Blessed Sacrament, where He comes within us, Body, Blood, Soul, and Divinity. There is an encounter where He transforms us and He makes us more like unto Him, giving us His strength and His courage and His life, and developing us, making us grow more in union with God. All this is what the Mass means to me.

I asked again for help from our Founder, because I was saying Mass at the Altar that he had always used. Then, the next day, Brother Gabriel, a very wonderful brother, drove me out to the place, Rocca di Papa, where we were to take this course.

Movement For A Better World

The course was given under the guidance of Father Lombardi and the Better World Team, made up of four different people from the United States. They were Sister Patricia, Sister Alice, a Franciscan, Father George Ninterman, a Dominican, and a Jesuit priest, Father John Comey. People from throughout the world came for this gathering, about a hundred and twenty. They didn't expect that many, but it was an opportunity to meet people from every continent in the world, and it was a broadening experience, for which I was very happy.

Father Lombardi was a tremendous person with great charisma. God has really blessed him to have great insights into spiritual living, and it was very wonderful to hear him. Also, the different experts from the various Theological departments and universities came to give lectures at this meeting. Even Father Arrupe, the Jesuit Superior, came to give a talk to us.

I derived much from this gathering in Rocca di Papa, and I am sure that it did influence my thinking very much from that time on. It helped me in becoming a little more tolerant of people, and understanding them and their viewpoints. I learned more about how to accept others' viewpoints, rather than just clinging to my own. While I know that I have a right to say what I think, and to live as I see fit, I also have to learn to respect the rights of others, that they have the same right, and I may not infringe upon it, although we can learn from each other. St. Paul tells us to reject the bad and take the good.

We learn what is good and what is bad by comparing it to the teachings of Christ, deciding whether or not it is according to them. We pray for the discernment of the Spirit. This is a very difficult thing. We can make many mistakes, be tricked by the devil, and, by our own weakness, our own prejudice, our own pre-judgments, we can destroy this atmosphere of acceptance. It is therefore very important to be open to the Spirit and the Will of God, and be willing to learn from others. We have to judge and weigh things and see whether we wish to make them a part of our life or not, then, ultimately, we make that decision and have to live by it.

Father John Comey was the member of the team whose job it was to "shake us down" and make us think and look into ourselves, to see where we were going, and what our ideas were, to make us come to grips with ourselves. He was more like the "blockbuster" type. He did a good job of being and doing just what he was supposed to.

Father Ninterman was very spiritual. He had a deep Scriptural basis for everything that he said. The most lasting impressions that I received were from him. I think that he gave a magnificent exposition of spirituality.

I did not care much for the presentations made by the two women. Not because they were women, but simply because I didn't care for their style, or the way they presented their material. However, they did add much to the team and I learned also from them.

Visit From A Friend

I had been in Rocca di Papa only a few days when I received a telephone call from Sister Placida, a Benedictine Sister. She grew up with me at Lake Five, during the latter years of my childhood. I got to know the family quite well, so she was a good friend. I wrote to her when she went to Los Angeles to work, and kept up the correspondence when she joined the Benedictines.

She was in Rome, on a vacation, and was with a group who were going to have an audience with the Holy Father the next day. She was very excited, and she told me, "I am going to see the Holy Father!" The way she described it, I thought she was having a private audience, while actually she was having a general audience of the sort where she would be standing in front and the Pope would come down and greet various people. She just happened to be one of the ones he would greet.

When he came to her, she gave him my picture and said, "Here is a picture of Father Luke Zimmer," and she went on to tell him about the work I wished to do. She handed him a small booklet describing the work, and said to him, "Promise, promise, promise to see him!"

He said, "I will try," and he gave the picture and the booklet to his Secretary, Bishop Jacques Maritain, and she said, "See to this," and then the audience was over. She came to where I was staying and told me about this, terribly excited. I thought, "This is great. Perhaps now obtaining an audience with the Holy Father will be easy."

I Ask A Friend For Help

Still, I knew something concrete had to be done, and so the first opportunity I had, I went to Rome and visited a friend of mine, a Jesuit priest. He worked in the Apostleship of Prayer Office, and I asked him to present my work, which I had written, to the Holy Father. I explained that the reason I wasn't going through my own Congregation was because the Superior General was up in France making a visit, and I didn't know when to expect him home.

I should actually have gone to Father Cyprian and had him do it, but since I knew the other Father, I asked him instead. He turned it in to the Holy Office and I went back to another week's work at Rocca di Papa. Then, on another weekend, a priest for whom I am spiritual director came to Rome. He knew Cardinal Larrona, and we had an audience with him. He said he would do everything possible to try to get me an audience with the Holy Father. He personally went over twice to make this request, but was told that it should be done through the Superior General of our Order.

Visit At Padre Pio's Grave

Since I still didn't know when the Superior General was coming home, I went up to Father Pio's place and prayed before his grave. I said Mass there in the evening, and again the next morning.

It was quite an experience to see the effect that he still has on people. When his picture was brought out, the people just went wild, and surged forward to venerate it. I didn't think this was quite proper, but who are we to judge? And his Confessional — people would just come and stand and watch at that Confessional for hours.

The Brother took us all around and showed us everything. I wanted to see Father Pio's room and I said so. The Brother said, "We are not supposed to allow that." I said, "I've waited seventeen years to see this and I want to see." And so, he said, "O.K." He went to his Superior and the Superior said, "Tomorrow morning, after your Mass, you may have permission to come." I did, and when we went to his room, I saw where he lived, his bed, his chair that he used to sit on to say Rosary upon Rosary, far into the hours of the night and early morning. He always made the statement that, if he didn't say fifteen decades of the Rosary every day, he considered his day wasted. Many times he said as many as forty Rosaries a day.

That sounds impossible to us, but he was a very saintly man. He slept only a very little, and had many hours' time to pray. He did hear Confessions during the day. He said his Mass early in the morning and he spent a lot of his time in prayer. I saw the place where he received the stigmata in the choir loft and the Crucifix from which the rays came to penetrate his body. They told us about many different things that happened to him, and that there were miracles being granted, through his intercession, after his death.

The Night He Died

When I was in Hawaii, on the night that he died, I knew that he had died. God had told me and, the next day, I saw the write-up in the paper. Another time, when he became very ill, I was told to pray for him, that he was very sick. I did, and I asked my spiritual director, "Is anything wrong with Father Pio? Did you notice anything in the papers about him?" He said no, and I said, "Well, I was told I had to pray for him, that he has been sick." Three weeks later, we found out that he had been very sick, and then he got well again and continued on with his work.

As always, right up to the very end, he did his work. It was only on the very last day that he got weak and died. It was after his fiftieth anniversary of having the stigmata in his hands and the wound in his side. I realize that this did not make him a saint. It was the heroic life of virtue, not the gifts that were given to him. The bilocation, the gift of curing people, the gift of reading souls, the stigmata, the suffering with Christ, didn't make him a saint at all. It was his real deep union of life and prayer with God.

That is what makes a person a saint, and this is what makes Padre Pio a saint. I definitely believe he is a saint, and I think that one day we will see him canonized. His cause is already introduced in Rome. There are many, many miracles granted through his intercession.

Visit To Assisi

On another weekend, I went up to Assisi. I also have a special love for St. Francis and St. Clare, because I was Baptized on the Feast of St. Clare, the 12th of August. I went through the Monastery afterwards and saw where she slept, ate, and lived, and where she held the Blessed Sacrament against the Saracens. All the while we were going around, Brother was picking flowers and taking different things from the various places. When we finished and were ready to leave, he gave each one of us a flower. He gave the other people a white flower, and, when it came my turn, it was a red rose. He said, "I want you to have this." Well, that had a great significance to me, although I did not tell him. It meant much to me because it seems that whenever great favors are given to me, I receive flowers like that, a red rose or a yellow rose. At that time there were more red roses than yellow ones. I left there and went through all of Assisi during that day. I enjoyed the places where St. Francis had been and went down to the Church where he was buried and saw that. The next morning, I said Mass there. He's buried on top of a pillar, and there are four altars around the pillar. There were four of us priests, and so each one said a Mass at a separate Altar that morning. I offered it, asking St. Francis and St. Clare to intercede and to help me to see the Pope, and to get the blessings of God upon my work, and the blessings of the Pope upon my work.

Pope Paul VI, Sister of Bishop Helmsing and Sr. Placida, O.S.B.

Audience with Pope Paul VI

CHAPTER 18

AUDIENCE WITH POPE PAUL VI

When I returned from Assisi, I learned that the Superior General was home. I went to him and explained what had happened with regard to Sister Placida, and that I would like to see the Pope. He told me to write what I had told him, what Sister had done, and what the Pope had said. Then he told me that he would write a letter and send it to the Pope's Secretary. When all that had been written, I sent in the letter, and went back for some more of the training at Rocca di Papa, on the Spirituality of Vatican II.

Since we didn't hear anything from the Holy See, I figured, "We'll give it one more try." I had one more weekend off, and I went in and said to Father Cyprian, "Please take me to see the Secretary of the Pope." He said, "O.K., but we'd better take a copy of that letter, so he'll know what we are there for."

We went into the office and, when we got there, the Bishop was not in. They told us that he would not be in for at least two hours. Father Cyprian wanted to go home. He said, "We can't just sit around and wait for two hours." I didn't want to go home and I said so. I asked him, "Let's give it just five more minutes." Then I leaned back and prayed to the Blessed Mother and said, "We want to get to see the Bishop. Please get him here in five minutes."

Bishop's Reaction

Within five minutes, he walked in. He apologized for keeping us waiting, and asked us what he could do for us. Father Cyprian gave him the letter that we had sent to the Pope. He looked at it, read it, and began to criticize and ridicule me. He said, "So, you're a mystic!" I protested, "That is not what the letter says." Then he began to tear me apart, sentence by sentence until he made me feel like a big fool. Finally I became quite impatient and I told him, "I've got to see the Pope," and he said, "Everybody's got to see the Pope." I countered with, "I've got something to tell him." He retorted again, "Everybody's got something to tell him." I said, "I've got something *special* to tell him." Weakening just a little, he said, "Well, what do you have to tell him that's so special?"

I told him what I had in mind, and he asked me if I had told this to the Pope. I told him, of course not, that, if I *had* told this to the Pope, then I wouldn't need to see him. At last he said, "O.K., I'll be fair with you. You go and write what you told me. Then we will give it to the Pope, and the Pope, himself, will make the decision whether he's going to see you or not. If he says 'no,' then the answer is 'no.' If he says 'yes,' then I will have nothing more to say."

God Speaks Loud And Clear Through Others

I went from there and had dinner with Father Duran and Father Heston, who later became Archbishop Heston. We were gathered around the table talking. Monsignor Heston did not know that I wanted to see the Pope, but the conversation drifted to the way in which to see him. He said, "If you want to see the Pope, this is what you have to do. You should write a letter saying, 'I'd love to see Your Holiness, and have a private audience with you, but I am only a simple priest and don't deserve any consideration, so certainly that's impossible. I would be happy, though, if this could happen. But I will even be pleased if I could have a semi-private audience, where other people are gathered, just so I could talk to you. I know that even that is a great favor to be granted. I'll even be willing to accept a general audience, provided I can speak to you, standing in front of all the crowd and speaking with you.'" He told us, "You are going to get the first one, if you ask in this manner." I said to myself, "God is speaking to me — loud and clear!"

I went home and wrote what the Bishop had told me to write, and used the information the Monsignor had described, adding a little note saying that I wanted to have a picture with His Holiness, so that I could send it to my aged parents. Then I turned the letter in.

I went back to Rocca di Papa to continue the course, and found out that Father Cyprian had written to Father Jacques Maritain, the Bishop, and said to him that he had asked for an audience for one of our Bishops from Peru, and they had refused; they had asked for an audience for one of our Bishops from Chile, who was living in our house at the time, and he had also been refused. Now he said, "I am asking for an audience for Father Luke Zimmer, and I will not take no for an answer. I want that audience on December 10th, and I want the ticket for it on the night of December 9th."

When I heard this, I said to myself, "That just blew everything. Now I certainly will *not* get the audience with the Holy Father." On the night of December 9th, I was waiting for a call from the General House, saying that I had the audience. At four o'clock, when they usually deliver the tickets, there was no call. Six o'clock came and there was no call. Again the same at eight o'clock. Finally, we went in for dinner and I just gave up. I said, "Well, it's impossible. It's all finished now. It will never happen." Yet, deep in my heart, I knew that it *would* happen, that my prayers would be answered.

We Have The Audience With Pope Paul VI

Then there was a telephone call. The message was that we had received a call from the Vatican, and that the audience I had was with Father General and myself, on December 17th. That was it. It was only for us two, so I knew immediately that it was a private audience that I had.

Then the devil really worked me over. He made me think, "What if the Pope gets sick? Then you're just going to miss out, anyway." The next week was just a terrible ordeal of anguished suffering and waiting.

On the night before I was to go to Rome, the 15th of December, I got the flu. I felt very sick, but I fought it and, when they came to pick me up, they told me that Father General also had the flu, and they didn't know whether he could go along with me for the audience. When I got back, I immediately went up to Father General's room and he said, "Oh, I am so sick. I don't think I can go." And I said, "But you have to. It'll only take a little while." But he told me, "You don't know this. You don't know the Vatican. You'll have to wait in an empty, cold room for hours before the Pope will even get to us."

Then I suggested that we go late, and get there barely before twelve thirty, when we had our appointment. We'd have plenty of time and we'd hope that the room would be warm. He promised to let me know the next morning. I went down to the Chapel then, and prayed to the Sacred Heart, "Now everything has been arranged. Please let it go through, and don't let anything happen. Let the Superior General be well and strong enough to go through with this, and let me be strong enough not to be so sick that I can't carry on, and please don't let the Pope catch any of this sickness from us." I prayed for half an hour this way.

You Are Not To Talk To The Pope

The next morning, I heard Father General coughing, and I knew he was up. After the Mass was over, he leaned across the dressing table in the Sacristy and said, "Be ready to leave at twenty minutes to twelve." And, at twenty minutes to twelve, I was ready. We went to the Vatican and went into the room, and it was nice and warm. We had just time enough to take off our coats, and our name was called. We went in for the audience, and, as we were going to the door, the Bishop came up to me and said, "You are not to talk to the Pope." I was startled at this. After all, this had been my whole purpose in coming here. While we were waiting, there were two Sisters with the Pope. We were half way up the room, and waiting our turn, when I turned to Father General and said, "What am I going to do?" He answered, "Don't mind the Bishop. Go ahead and speak. The Pope certainly will not know why we are here. He has had the general audience and the semi-private audiences, now the private audiences. Certainly, he will not remember why you are here, so just go ahead and speak."

We went up to the Pope. It was our turn. The Pope reached out his hand to me, and I was startled at this. I had figured he would shake hands with the General first. I shook my head and pointed to the Father General, and the Pope just shook his head and put out his hand again, and shook hands with me. Then he shook hands with Father General, who introduced himself in Italian. He said, "Oh, you speak Italian." The Father General said, "Yes, I speak Italian." Then he said, "Here is Father Luke Zimmer."

The Holy Father Remembers

As soon as he mentioned my name, the Pope leaned forward and said, "From Honolulu." Then the Pope explained what I was doing, what I was hoping to do, point by point. He showed that he knew, and that he remembered what I was there for. Afterwards he said, "I thank you. And I thank you for being faithful to Jesus Christ. I thank you for being faithful to your priesthood. I bless you. I bless your work. I bless anyone who will help you in your work." Then I asked him, "Could I have permission to start this Apostolate?" He said, "I will give the permission, according to what the Superiors decide. If they decide that you are to do this work, I give my wholehearted permission."

What he was saying was the same thing that Pope Leo XII told the Little Flower. That, if the Superiors are willing, everything else goes. If the Superiors are willing, then it is from God. And so, this is what the message was.

Little Flower Helps Me!

Now I turned to the Little Flower and prayed. "I received the same answer as you, and so I put everything into your hands, and I ask you to help me to obtain the Superior's permission to do this work."

Then the Pope gave us some souvenirs, and gave me a blessing, and I kissed his ring again, and left. As we were leaving, the Bishop came up and said, "Boy, you sure talked a long time to the Pope, and the Pope also talked a long time to you." I answered, "Yes, and thank you very, very much." He said nothing more, and we left.

We went home and were sick for three days. Both of us got up in the morning and said Mass, and then went right back to bed. I said my other prayers also, but the rest of the day I stayed in bed.

I wanted to be well enough to travel so I could go back to the United States. First of all, I wanted to stop in Fatima and thank God for the blessings and graces that had been given, and for the privilege of seeing the Holy Father. This had been a part of my pilgrimage plan from the beginning.

Problem In Going To Fatima

As I left Rome, flying to Madrid, I was constantly coughing, and still continued to do so for many weeks afterwards. When I got to Madrid, the plane was delayed for at least seven hours, and I did not know why. Finally, I learned that the fog had closed in the Lisbon airport, and we could not get into Portugal. They wanted us to go to a hotel. This would mean missing Fatima, so I said to the Blessed Mother, "O.K., if you don't want me to go, that's all right with me. I'll just have to make arrangements to fly to the United States from Madrid instead of going to Lisbon. But, if you really want me to be there, and to thank God for what He had done, you make the arrangements so we can get there."

Then we were told that we were to board the plane, because the fog had lifted. Within thirty-five minutes we landed in Lisbon. The Fathers had known that I was coming, but, because the plane was delayed, they were not there to meet me, and I had to get a taxi to go to our house. I was very happy to finally get to the home of our Fathers. I was very pleased because I knew many of them. I had seen them in Holland before, and many of them were from Holland, so I felt very much at home with them.

The next day, they were planning to take me to Fatima. I was told that I really should take a train with the seminarians, so I could go early and get to Fatima and back all in one day. But, when I awoke the next morning, there was a note under my door. I read it and it said, "Sleep later, because Father Superior has other means of getting to Fatima."

When it was ten o'clock and I was ready to go, I found out that Salazar's chauffeur had his limousine there, and he drove me to Fatima. It was quite a wonderful experience to go through the countryside up to Fatima and to continue to that great Basilica.

Prayer Answered

I wanted to say Mass while I was in Fatima, at Jacinta's Altar. Father Superior told me that I could say Mass at Francesco's Altar, and so I went into the Sacristy and said I wanted to say Mass there, if it would be possible. I was told, yes, it would be possible, but not at Francesco's Altar, because it was going to be used. I would have to use Jacinta's Altar. And so, I got my wish. I said Mass and I prayed to both Jacinta and Francesco to thank God for me for the favors that I had received, and for being able to see the Pope.

Impression When Seeing The Pope

I was so pleased and happy to see the Pope, but I could see that he was filled with great sorrow. I could see in his eyes the suffering, yet also, the love and tenderness. The humble attitude that he had made you feel that he listened to you as though no one else in the whole world, nothing else in the whole world, mattered. He spoke to you directly, as if all the problems of the world were gone, and it was just the most important thing in the world that he was doing in his life right now. That is the impression that he gave to me.

He was very different from Pius XII. I saw Pius XII on seven occasions. On one occasion, I spoke to him. When he looked at you, he looked right through you. He was a very spiritual, tall, and aristocratic person. There was a striking contrast between the two of them. While I was in Fatima, I thanked God for the great favors received, and I prayed to Our Lady of Fatima to help me to implement this work that I wanted to carry out in the future, for the whole world. After saying Mass, I spent an hour in adoration, and then we had dinner and drove back to Lisbon.

Mary Helps Again

When I got to Lisbon, I found out that my plane ticket had been canceled by TWA, and there was no way of getting back to the United States. I called them to ask what the trouble was, and they said the flight had simply been canceled. I told them that I couldn't just sit around waiting for another plane, and that I wanted to switch to another to get back to the United States. There was one seat left on Pan Am, and they booked me for that. I went back to the mainland and arrived at the same time as I would have with TWA. I only had to let the people know that I was coming on a different flight, and with Pan Am, rather than TWA.

I was very fortunate because, as we left Portugal, the fog was coming in and closing that airport, and after I landed in Boston, a strong snow storm closed that airport, too. I went on to Fairhaven, Massachusetts, and stayed there for a short time, before continuing on to California, and finally, to Hawaii.

I returned to Hawaii because I had promised that I would continue to work in the Family Home Missions program until the end of June, 1971. We had several different parishes already scheduled until that time. Then I wanted to begin the work on the Apostolate of Christian Renewal.

CHAPTER 19

WRITING MY BOOKS

(A) The Family Home Missions

During the last six weeks, while I was in Kauai, I decided to write the book which I mentioned before, the first book that I wrote, *The Family Home Missions.* One day, when I was almost finished with this book, a young lady came and, as she watched what I was doing, she told me that she had a major in English, that she had a Master's degree, and that she would be very willing to correct the manuscript. I thought that this would be an excellent opportunity to have this done, and I agreed.

This young lady expressed the desire to become a Catholic, and, also a Sister, but I found out that she could not possibly become a Sister, because of previous marriage entanglements and so forth. It was even doubtful whether she could become a Catholic. Nevertheless, she took the manuscript and corrected it. When she brought it back, I noticed that she had done a very good job of correcting it. On various points that appealed to her, she had written on the margin such things as "Right on" and "Out of Sight."

She was also planning to type the manuscript for me, but just before she began, she heard that one of her friends had taken an overdose of drugs, and died. She was quite upset over this, and as a result, she herself started taking drugs. From then on, she was "out of it" and I knew that she could not finish the work on the manuscript, so I asked her to return it to me.

She thought I was being very ruthless in doing this. I wasn't harsh or anything with her. I just told her that I would like to have the manuscript back, because I had to leave soon and I didn't know whether I would see her again (or if I would ever see the manuscript again, if she continued on in the condition she was putting herself into). She gave me a good tongue lashing, but I did get the manuscript back.

I flew from Kauai to Oahu, and, before leaving for the mainland, I visited another friend of mine. In the process of my explaining what had happened, this lady decided that she would offer to take care of the manuscript and have it typed. She said her daughter wasn't doing anything that summer, and that it would be a good thing for her to be occupied with. I figured it would be safe with them, and so I left the manuscript with them, and went on to the mainland, thinking that everything would work out with it.

(B) Apostolic Renewal

When I arrived on the mainland, I went to St. Genevieve's Parish to help out there, and I began to write my second book, *Apostolic Renewal*. I was in the parish for over a month and, since I had much of the material gathered, it was mostly a matter of typing it and rearranging and putting it into order. Previously, the lady in Hawaii whose daughter was planning to type the manuscript for *Family Home Missions* had wanted to help write *Apostolic Renewal*, but she had reached a certain point and been unable to go any further. I don't know the reason why, but she could not continue and so, at the time, I hadn't known just what to do about it.

The first eighty pages were submitted to several different publishers, and they all came back rejected. I sent it to the Provincial out East, and he read it and said it was too traditional, intransigent, and pre-Vatican II. He didn't think it was correct or that I should even bother with it. I didn't tell him that she had written this part. Then, later, I was told by the Provincial that I should write the book myself, so I decided to go ahead and do it on my own. I did use some of the material which had been written by this lady, and it helped to make the writing of the book a lot easier.

In writing that book, I would think about the material far into the night, until around two o'clock in the morning, deciding what I was going to say. Then I would get up, say my prayers, and begin to write and try to put onto paper what I'd thought about before. But, many times, what came out of the typewriter was completely different from what I had previously planned. The thoughts just seemed to flow easily and come very quickly, so that the book was able to be completed within a month and a half.

I didn't finish it while I was at St. Genevieve's. I went on vacation, back to Wisconsin, and it is there that I finished the work. This book was written to help people to deepen their spiritual lives, to understand more fully what I mean by the Apostolate of Christian Renewal.

While I was in Wisconsin, I thought about the fact that the manuscript had also to be typed. A friend of mine, Marian Anheuser, made arrangements with another woman to type it professionally for me. She paid for this work, and I was very grateful. It was a great sacrifice, I am sure, on her part. It was also a great act of Charity. I was very appreciative for everything that she did.

In the meantime, I was still waiting for the first book. I received no word at all. Finally, I decided to call them, only to be told by them that they hadn't even started.

Study Of Renewal

I was supposed to travel throughout the United States, studying the differing phases of renewal that were going on in various areas. I told these people to please try to do everything possible to get it done by the time I came back, so that it would be waiting for me in Wisconsin. I went then to a number of places, Dayton, Ohio, Massachusetts, Michigan, etc. I visited the "House of Prayer," in Michigan and the Pentecostal Movement, known as the Charismatic Movement, in Wisconsin. I saw much that was going on in the world with regard to renewal, but not one of the programs was like what I was planning and hoped to establish. I made up my mind that I definitely had to go on my own and continue the work as I saw fit.

Problem Developed

When I arrived back in Wisconsin, there still was no manuscript from Hawaii. I called the people again and they still hadn't done anything with it. They promised to have it to me within ten days. I had nowhere else to go so I just stayed home for those ten days, waiting and waiting for this to arrive. Nothing happened. In the end, I wrote them a special delivery air mail letter, and told them that I had counted on them, and that I wanted the manuscript as soon as possible. When I came back from Nebraska, the manuscript was there, but nothing had been done with it. This really left me very discouraged. One of my greatest weaknesses is impatience. Writing these books certainly helped me to try to cultivate patience with people and learn that we must try to understand their problems, that they are busy, too, and cannot just drop everything and do things right away, even though they might like to. Still, I know the importance of this work and that is why I was so concerned. It made me think of a lesson I learned when I was a young boy.

I Learned A Lesson Over Again

When I was in grammar school, we read a story one time about a meadowlark. One day she went off for the day. When she came back, the little larks were all excited and upset, saying that people had visited the field and said that it was time to harvest the crop. The farmer was talking with the people, and they were saying that they came to help him to do the work. He said, "O.K., we'll begin tomorrow." And so they said, "We'll have to move. We've got to get out of here." The mother lark said, "We don't have to go yet. We have plenty of time. We'll just wait another week."

Another week went by and then the farmer came out and looked at the field. This time his relatives were with him, and they said, "We'll come and help you harvest the crop." The mother bird came back that night and the little birds told her what had happened. They were all excited again, and said, "Now we'll definitely have to get out of here." But the mother lark said, "No, we'll just wait a little while yet."

Another week went by and the farmer came out and looked at the crop, and was walking along and said, "Well, *I've* got to get this grain cut now and get my work done!" When the meadowlark came home that night and the little larks said to her that the farmer said he was going to cut the crops, the mother bird said, "Well, *now* it's time to move." The moral of the lesson is that if you really want something done, you have to do it yourself. This lesson is brought home to me over and over again, in dealing with people.

Be Willing To Be Hurt

Not that people are bad, or that they don't mean well. It's just that they say they want to do a thing, then something comes up and they never get around to it; or, maybe they just don't think it's that important, and so they procrastinate and put it off and put it off. In the meantime, you're sitting and waiting, and nothing is taking place. And so, I learned my lesson. And yet, I have to learn it again and again, because I really trust people, and take them at their word. When they say they are going to do a thing, I take them at their word and think they mean it. Not only that, when they say they are going to do a thing for the Apostolate, or for God, I believe that they are completely and totally dedicated to carrying this out. I find out that human nature is just not that way, always. As a result, I get hurt many times.

And yet, I still have faith in human nature. If I would just go into a hole and carry on my work on my own, and not let other people help; if I did not want other people to help, or ask them to help, then certainly nothing would be done, either. We must take the risk of having people say no to us, or that they don't want any part of what we are doing. We must also take the risk of having them say yes, and not really intend to do what they say they will. On the other hand, we meet people who *are* completely and totally dedicated, who give of themselves completely, are willing to do anything, who do almost too much, so that we risk asking too much of them. That's something we must also be careful of, that we not be overbearing or too demanding. We must not ask too much of people who are generous, though I am sure, that of such people, nothing would be considered by them to be too much. They really are dedicated, and give of themselves completely to God, and to the work of God, and are interested in what is to be done. We can always count on such people.

See Best In People

We must see the best in *all* people. We must not condemn or look down on people because they may have weaknesses. If we are let down by people, because they have weaknesses, then we must forgive them, continue to pray for them, and wish them well. We should never act in such a way as to cause people to feel guilty or rejected if they have been unable or unwilling to keep promises they have made to us.

Forgive And Forget

This is how I feel, and when I work with people, or like them, it is forever. I never hold grudges against people, no matter what they may do to me, say about me, even if they cause great suffering in my life. Still, I will wish them well, and be always willing to work with them again, should they ever wish to offer again to do anything in our work, in God's work. As Christ was forgiving, so must we also be.

Man Proposes But God Disposes

What I had originally hoped to do, in beginning the work of the Apostolate, was to go to Rome and set up headquarters there. I would have liked to have spent a period of two years learning Spanish and French before actually beginning the work. However, when I made that request, it was rejected as being too premature. It was felt that the work might not be accepted on a worldwide basis, by different nationalities or countries. I was told that I should begin the work in the United States, on a limited basis, so as to let it prove itself, and in that way find out if it was truly from God, and therefore worthwhile.

A question was raised by one of the Fathers that perhaps they were dealing with a person who was an *"Illuminati,"* one who is under an illusion, who merely thinks that he has a mission from God, but, in reality, does not have a mission at all. It was also asked whether I was really the right person to do this work. These questions hurt a little bit. We don't like to think that members of our own Congregation might think that we're just a "nut" or a "fly-by-night," when we know that we have based our mission on a lifelong, thought-out, prayed-over decision; but, of course, they didn't have knowledge of my background or life, so perhaps this explains why such statements were made.

Father General misunderstood my reasons for wanting to come to Rome. He thought that I was trying to supplant the work of the Enthronement, and that was the farthest thing from my mind. I definitely believe in the Enthronement, and consider it a natural outgrowth of the work of the Apostolate. The Enthronement is a part of the work of the Apostolate. The Apostolate is intended to be the foundation, to prepare people to live the Christ-like life. It is an indoctrination in living the Christian life, a *way* of life. This must also be lived by people who have the Enthronement. What good does it do for the family to have the Enthronement, to hang a picture of the Sacred Heart in their homes, if they do not understand what they are doing, if there is no Christian life whatsoever in the home? It must be understood. It must be lived. It must be practiced. And that is the role of the Apostolate in the life of the individual.

The Apostolate is a Covenant made between the individual and God. The natural outgrowth of the individual commitment to Christ will be for the person to try to involve the family and inspire them to be drawn toward making the same commitment. Then the family will be ready for the Enthronement, which is the Covenant made between the family and God.

When a Congregation is given one mission, it does not mean that all the work of that Congregation must, from then on, be geared to that work alone, without allowing for God to give any other mission to any other member of the Congregation. God can choose anyone He wishes to carry out a mission for Him. And, just as a flower is first a bud and then gradually opens out, He can give a mission whose purpose is only gradually made known or "opened" to the eyes of man.

When the work of the Enthronement was first begun, the family was a far more tightly knit structure. Today, society has so weakened the family circle that it has become vitally important to first reach the individual person. We cannot possibly hope to reach a whole family while its members are all suffering from spiritual anemia. Once the prayer life, the spiritual life, of the individual members of a family has been developed and deepened, then they will wholeheartedly desire that Christ be Enthroned as the Head of that family.

Nonetheless, my ideas were misunderstood, and my work was seen as something completely opposite to the work of the Enthronement. I was, therefore, not permitted to come to Rome. I had also wished to take a family from Hawaii to Rome to help with the work. The family had sufficient money that they could have taken care of their own needs. They would have only a token salary, and they could have been an asset to the Superior General Council and their administrative work.

But that is not what God wanted. God was speaking to me through my Superiors in a very loud and clear voice, and I, therefore, never complained or tried to counter against the decision that they made. I knew then that I must prove my work, that it was from God, by carrying it out in the United States.

Next the question arose, should it be done in Hawaii, or should it be done on the mainland? I wrote a letter to Father Meyer in Hawaii, and he wrote back that, since so many things seemed to point to that direction, he felt that the work should begin on the mainland, and that it ought to begin in California. He also said that they were not in a position to give approbation to the work because I was not one of their subjects, I was a member of the Province of California, and therefore the approbation should come from my own Provincial. He said, as well, that they could not give me any financial aid whatsoever. Actually, I never expected that.

I called Father Dowling and read the letter to him, and I said, "I'd rather begin the work here in California, under these conditions. What do you think?" His answer was, "You make the decision." And so I did. I went back to Hawaii, packed by belongings, retyped my *Family Home Missions* book, which took about ten days, and then I came back to the mainland and began the work of the Apostolate.

Permission Given By My Superiors

When I returned to the mainland, I was told by my Superiors that I may do the work, but that I should not ask for any financial aid. They would be unable to help, nor did they really have a place for me to stay. I went to the residence at Bishop Amat High School, where I'd lived when I was Superior, and I was allowed to stay and work from there.

Permission From Archbishop Manning

However, before I began the work of the Apostolate of Christian Renewal here in the United States, I went to Archbishop Timothy Manning, and he gave me permission to do this work. He said, "I want you to write what you are doing, and wish to do, and submit it to me. I will then give you written approbation for this work." I replied, "That's really not necessary. Your word is good enough for me." But he said, "I want it that way." I did as he asked, and he gave me written approbation, toward the end of 1971, in a beautiful letter which I include here, to show how I then had the opportunity to do the work in this Archdiocese.

(The Cardinal's letter)

December 2, 1971

Reverend Luke Zimmer, SS.CC.
Fathers of the Sacred Heart
14341 Fairgrove Avenue
La Puente, California 91746

Dear Father Zimmer:

This letter is written in response to your recent visit, and to the recording of that visit in your letter of November 26th, 1971.

Let me say at the outset, with emphasis, that the purpose of the Apostolate of Christian Renewal is entirely praiseworthy and meriting of full approbation. It is entirely within the guidelines of the Vatican Council and subsequent documents. I pray that your Apostolate will have every success.

The long-term proposals involving a "pious union," and other projects, I think should be reviewed in a progress report. I would request, therefore, that a year hence you confer with me about these matters.

It would be my hope also that some direction should be given to our teen-agers. They are waiting for challenge and I think that a challenge of reparation would be a whole mission field for them. They must be the apostles to their own peer group.

May God bless you, your dedication and your work.

Very sincerely yours,

Timothy Manning
Archbishop of Los Angeles

Seeking An Opportunity To Preach

I didn't have a penny. People did give me a few dollars, now and then, so that I could buy gas, and I borrowed a car from the Community at Bishop Amat. I visited all the retreat houses in the Archdiocese of Los Angeles, and asked them if I could give retreats, but they told me that their schedule was completely booked for the year 1972, and that it was impossible to fit me into their schedule.

I didn't know what else to do, so I turned to the pastors I knew, and asked them if they would give me a chance to preach at all the Masses, and to have workshops, to begin the Apostolate. The first parish in which I began was St. Louis of France, in La Puente, where Father James Mulcahy gave me the opportunity to begin. I started giving conferences in the parishes, and also in homes, in different areas. I would follow the same format that I had used in Hawaii, for the Family Home Missions. By this, I mean that I had the same group come once a week, for different weeks. I had different groups every night of the week, so that I had five workshops going on at one time.

Prayer Answered — I Get A Car

I knew that I would need a car before I got too far under way. I was tying up the Community car, and I knew that it was a great sacrifice for them. It would not be a good idea for me to constantly ask to have the use of the car. I didn't know where to go, what to do, or how to get the money to acquire one. I called a few people, and just asked them to pray. I said, "I don't want you to give money, but just pray that we will get money to carry out this work."

Once, when I was in Nebraska, I had blessed a lady who had cancer, and she had been cured through the use of the relic of the True Cross. God cured her, but she had remembered me, and thought about me for many years. She wanted to contact me, and to give a donation to whatever I was doing. My aunt contacted me and told me about this, and she got my address and gave it to the lady. The next thing I knew, I received a check from the lady for my work, which came as a complete surprise. Then other donations came, from other people, smaller donations, a hundred dollars, twenty-five, twenty, ten, five dollars at a time. And, when I went to pay for the car, I found that I had exactly enough money to pay for the '72 Maverick, the insurance, the license plate, right to the penny. No more. And that is how I got the car I needed.

I Wrote My Third Book —
The Apostolate Of Christian Renewal

The Apostolate began to grow, to increase. During the day, I had some time on my hands, and so I decided to write another book. I wrote this book because I wanted people who were joining the Apostolate to have a handbook, or reference, so as to deepen their knowledge of what I was trying to do, and what the Apostolate was all about. Therefore, I sat down, wrote the book, and took it to a printer in Los Angeles, and asked about having it printed. I was told that it would be printed in two to three weeks' time, but again I had to have patience.

Aid Given Again

It was spring election time. They had to print all the ballots, and so they did that first, before getting to my work. When finally they go to it, they told me that what I owed them must be paid within two weeks, at which time I would be receiving the books. I was $1,170 short of having the amount needed. Again, I didn't know where to turn, so once again I called up various people and told them, "Do not send money, but just pray that we get sufficient money to pay for the printing of the book."

I had ten thousand copies printed and, within forty-eight hours, we had $1,215. I asked myself, "Why the extra money? How come that came in?" Well, when I went to pick up the books, I found out that there was an additional charge for some expenses involved with the covers of the books, which the printer had previously neglected to tell me about. That is where the extra money was needed. I was very grateful and it gave me great Faith and joy to know that now God was really blessing this work, and that He definitely wanted the Apostolate for the world.

Publishers Accept My Books

As I continued with the workshops, this book sold very rapidly. Within less than a year, all ten thousand copies ran out. I could have had them reprinted, but I wanted a publisher to take over so that they would stand the expense of printing and publicizing it, and so that it would spread farther than my own little area where I was working. Finally, I sent it to Alba House, in New York. They accepted both *The Apostolate of Christian Renewal* and *Apostolic Renewal*. They did not accept *The Family Home Missions*. For what reason, they never stated, but, anyway, they sent this book back.

Then I contacted Vantage Press and they are the ones who took over that book. I did not know at the time that when printers take a book, it takes at least a year or longer to get it printed. They have to send us the galley proofs again and again, so that we may read and correct them, until they are finally correct. The initial work would seem very slipshod to the eye that is inexperienced with regard to the ways of printers. It is most amazing to me that books turn out without mistakes, or at least with very few mistakes, in the final product. It was another aspect of the learning process for me. But, at last, the books were all out, and are now for sale so that people can purchase them.

CHAPTER 20

ROSARY PILGRIMAGE
TO THE HOLY LAND

In August of 1972, I was given the privilege of going to the Holy Land. I was a chaplain for Father Peyton's Rosary Pilgrimage to the Holy Land. I had always wanted to go to the Holy Land, but I never thought that it would happen. This gave me an opportunity to fulfill one of my long-felt desires, and I was very pleased to be able to participate in this pilgrimage.

First I flew to the East Coast, and visited the Fathers. Then I went to New York, where I met the other pilgrims, coming from different parts of the United States. I was very fortunate in having my brother, Doctor James Zimmer, his wife, and my two nephews with us on the trip.

Arrival In Israel

We had a very pleasant flight over, and, when we landed, it was toward evening. Finally, we got to the hotel and got settled. I was able to say Mass at the hotel that night for the people who came with us. As I have said before, I definitely believe that a priest should say Mass every day, no matter where he is, no matter what he has been doing, whether he is on vacation, tour, or pilgrimage. We must always be willing to make that sacrifice because I believe that Mass is the most beautiful and the most important act that we can perform during the day.

Bethlehem

The next morning, we took a bus and went out to Bethlehem, and on beyond Bethlehem, into the fields to the alleged actual spot where the Angels appeared to the Shepherds. I said Mass there, out in the Chapel. The thoughts that I had, at that moment, were very profound and deep, and full of awe. To think that I was in the Holy Land, and that I had the privilege of saying Mass where the Angels came and announced the birth of Christ!

I thought about the shepherds, these simple people, uneducated, and yet the ones who were chosen by God to be the first to have the news announced to them. And they left their flocks and went to Bethlehem, and found Jesus in the Manger.

Later on in the day, we went to Bethlehem, to the place where Jesus was born. There is a Church built over the spot where Christ was born. You go down through a little corridor, down some stairs, and into the section where Christ was born. Of course, today, it is

Fr. Patrick Peyton and Myself

quite ornate. People from different countries have donated material to make it look very beautiful and attractive. Yet, to me, that distracts from the tremendous event that took place at that spot — the actual birth of Christ, Our Lord.

We saw how the Blessed Mother took Christ and turned to her right and placed Him in the Manger, where the animals were. We were told by the guide that there were actually three sections to that cave now, but in the time of Christ, it was only one complete cave. It has since been partitioned off into the three different sections.

The Bible Came Through Christ's Church

The first section you come into is the place where Christ was born. Then you have to go through a passage, and work your way around to the second part, which is where St. Jerome spent many years of his life, copying the Bible. This makes you realize that the Bible came down from God, through the hands of the Jewish people, and through the Church. The first Evangelists and the Apostles wrote the Bible, and it is the property of the Church, and has been preserved and kept, down through the centuries, by the Church. If we had not done so, the world would not have the Bible.

The word of God and the accounts of God's life and Christ's life here on earth are a tremendous treasure that we have received from God. It is important to become really familiar with that beautiful Book of God, and to study it more thoroughly and make it a part of our lives.

In the last section of the cave, there is a place where the Holy Innocents are buried, the ones who were killed when Herod wanted to destroy Christ. You cannot help but be filled with respect in realizing the tremendous historical event that took place here.

We left Bethlehem and went to some souvenir shops and bought a few things, and then went back to the hotel. In the afternoon, we were taken through various sections of Jerusalem, the pool of Bethsaida, the Pool of Siloe, and the older section of Jerusalem. We saw the Wailing Wall, which was quite interesting. It was a very beautiful first day.

Nazareth

We also had the privilege of traveling up to Nazareth. It deeply impressed upon us the tremendous sacrifice made by Mary in coming to see Elizabeth, to see the rugged terrain of this country. When you read in the Gospel that she hurried up over the hill country, you have no idea that this is a great distance, and that she had to travel over many hills. Nazareth is on top of a mountain, and she had to come down that mountain into a beautiful valley, the valley of Gesureth, for about fifteen miles. The next distance, of about sixty miles, is nothing but mountains, hills, and sand, all over the place. No matter where you look, that's all you see.

You see some floating shepherds out there, and you wonder where they will ever get any food for their flocks of sheep or goats or camels. You see the poorest of the poor, the destitute, in these people, and your heart goes out to them. They live just day by day, and you wonder how they make a living, how they manage to struggle along. You can see easily how there would be bandits, as described in the Scriptures, robbers who would waylay you. Even today, this could happen.

Jerusalem

When you come nearer to Jerusalem, you see mountains with rock, no matter where you look you see terraced hills, where they have the vineyards, the olive trees, and the other fruit bearing trees. All this makes you realize that here is a rugged country, a very insignificant, poor, down-trodden country, where people have to really work hard in order to make a living, and yet God chose for His people to be in that place.

Prison In The Time Of Christ

From there we went through most of the city of Jerusalem. We saw the place where Caiphas lived, and where Christ was put in prison. We saw the two different types of prisons that existed in the time of Christ. There was an open area, where people were chained to the wall. This was also the place where they were flagellated. We saw the torture section, where people would be whipped, as according to the Jewish custom, thirty-nine lashes. They would say forty lashes, minus one. There was a place where the people would have to put their heads and their hands through a stone opening, which would hold them securely, while they were being whipped.

Then you look into another section of the prison, where there was a dungeon-like area. People had to be lowered down and put into this room. That is what is described in the Scriptures, that the man was lowered down, and this is where Christ was placed, while He was waiting for His trial. And then, finally, you know what happened. He was questioned and He answered the High Priest. They decided that He had blasphemed, and so they decided to punish Him by delivering Him to be scourged.

The Upper Room

We also saw the replica of the upper room. It certainly was not the upper room, because most of the places where Christ lived, or walked, or saw, were destroyed by the invading forces from outside the country, down through the centuries, especially around 70 A.D. Most of these places were destroyed so that they can only say, "Perhaps this is where it all happened," but they are not definitely sure.

Way Of The Cross

We saw the place where the Temple used to be, and Herod's place, where Christ was condemned and carried the Cross. We followed the Way of the Cross, and visited all the different basilicas, where He was crucified, where He was buried, where He rose from the dead. I had the privilege of saying Mass there. I also had the privilege of saying Mass in Nazareth, while we were there, and in Bethlehem.

Traveling Through Israel

I said Mass in a different place every day, as according to the schedule which was worked out by the Rosary Crusade. I also said Mass on the Mount of the Beatitudes. It was enlightening. I read the Sermon of the Mount that day, and it had deep meaning for me.

We also crossed the Lake of Timerius, or the Lake of Galilee. I don't think it was in the same type of boat that Christ used in His day, but it was still quite an experience. For every place that we went, whether it was to the Wall of Jacob, to Jerico, the Dead Sea, the Hill of Temptation, Mt. Tabor, any of these areas, it naturally brought back the memories of Scriptural passages, and it just came to life for me. It had more meaning for me, and, since then, my meditations on the Rosary have been enriched tremendously. I hope that many people will get the opportunity to go to the Holy Land and to walk in the land where Christ walked and saw.

You can feel the holiness of the place, in spite of the tension, hardships, and difficulties of the people who live there. We had an Arab guide, who was a Catholic, and I was most surprised to find out that ninety percent of the people in Bethlehem were Catholics, and that many Arabs in that section of the world were Catholics. It was quite a revealing fact to me, an interesting note to learn.

Beggars

We were treated very well by the Israelite people. One thing that you do notice, as soon as you come into the area, is that you are constantly being asked for donations from the young Arab children, mainly because they have a hard life, and they are trying to get ahead. They want to have help and they really do need help. Nevertheless, the tourists are very generous, perhaps much too generous, so that these children make pests of themselves. After a few days, you get sick and tired of it, and you hope that they will stop badgering you about giving money. You know that they have to live, and that they need a livelihood, but you would also like to have quiet and peace, when you are walking through the Holy Land.

Carried The Blessed Sacrament

I had the privilege of carrying the Blessed Sacrament, while I was on this pilgrimage. I had permission from my Confessor to do this, and so Christ was going to all the different places that He went to when He was a young boy and a young man, the places where He preached and taught and cured. That, too, was great for me. I did this because we have to make Adoration every day in our Congregation, and it is very difficult to do this when you travel to far distant places. If you're in the Holy Land, for instance, there are constant interruptions and immense crowds so that it is almost impossible to have a moment with yourself and with Christ. Carrying the Blessed Sacrament gave me an opportunity to really be with Christ.

I know that we have Christ in our hearts and souls, and that I live in the Presence of God. I feel the Presence of God at all times, but it is a wonderful thing to have Christ in the Blessed Sacrament, in His Resurrected Body, to be able to carry Him with me, to be able to turn my mind to Him, and realize that He is with me, and to be able to adore Him. I can offer up my thanksgiving and reparation to Him in this way — thanks for all the Graces, and reparation for my sins and the sins of others. I pray for all the people I see and meet and ask Jesus to bless each one of them, as I go along in my journey.

And so, it's not just for safekeeping that I carry the Blessed Sacrament, but out of respect, love, and reverence for Jesus, that I want to give Him this adoration. I do not want to ever miss my Adoration, as a Religious of the Congregation of the Sacred Hearts of Jesus and Mary. Many people might laugh at me for doing this, but I feel very strongly about it. I think that this is why we are called to be Religious of the Sacred Hearts, to make this Reparation before Jesus, in the Blessed Sacrament. It is a great privilege for us and a great honor. This is the way I look upon it, and this is why I carry the Blessed Sacrament. Jesus said He will not leave us orphans. Well, I don't want to be an orphan. I want to have Him with me, even though I know I have Him in my heart.

Encountering Christ

While I was in the Holy Land, there was one place in particular that I found especially impressive and enjoyable. It was a beautiful spot. That was the city of Emmaus. We all know that, after Christ died and rose from the dead, the disciples from Emmaus were walking down the road, when He joined them, just as they were talking about Him. They were downcast, sad, and disappointed. They thought that Christ had been the Messiah and yet their hopes had been shattered, because He had been crucified.

He asked them, "What are you discussing, on the way?" They turned to Him and said, "Are you the only stranger in Jerusalem? Do you not know what has happened?" Then they told him about Jesus, and what their expectation had been. He began to explain the Scriptures to them. He started with the Old Testament, and proved that the Messiah had come, that the Messiah had to suffer, and that he was quite different than what they had expected. He was not to be a military king or leader upon the earth, or a worldly king, to throw off the yoke of the Roman Empire. His was to be a kingdom of souls, a kingdom of the mind, a kingdom of the heart, a kingdom here on earth and in Heaven.

He told us that the Kingdom of God is within us, when He was on earth. He came to establish this kingdom on earth, His Church, to guide people and to help them to come to Him and to love Him. He explained all these different things to them and, when they reached the town where they stayed, it was late. They said, "Come on in and stay with us." And, when they were there, they offered Him supper, and, while they were sitting down, He took bread and broke it and they recognized Him instantly, in the breaking of the bread. We can perhaps rightly say that Jesus offered His first Mass, after rising from the dead, in that place.

These were my thoughts, when I was at that spot, when I was in the upper room. I realized that here was the place where Christ instituted the Blessed Sacrament, where He instituted the Priesthood, and He showed His humility, His loyalty, His charity, His love for the disciples, as He washed their feet as the symbol of what they were to do — to serve others.

Here at Emmaus, He offered this sacrificial banquet, right here at the supper table, with the two disciples from Emmaus, and then He disappeared, as soon as they recognized Him. And they said to each other, "Were not our hearts burning, when He was explaining things to us? Were they not filled with joy?"

That is exactly what happens to us when we realize who Christ is. And I think that, when we come to the realization of Who Christ is, it is like Peter, James, and John, on Mt. Tabor, when, all of a sudden, Christ was transfigured before them. We actually understand Who He is and so we fall in love with Him! We understand that He is the God-Man, and what He represents and all that this means, and we *must* fall in love with Him, and wish to follow Him.

Then the two disciples went back to Jerusalem and told the Apostles what they had seen, and what Christ had told them, and they were all filled with joy, peace and happiness. That's exactly what should happen in our lives. After we have found Christ in our own lives, we should find great joy in wanting to tell others about Him. The Christian life was never meant to be a dull, dreary, or dragged out life.

CHAPTER 21

DAD'S DEATH

While I was going home from Emmaus, back to Jerusalem on a bus, I was filled with thoughts about my Mom and Dad. I love my Father and Mother very much, as I love my whole family, every one of them. I love my spiritual family, as well. I was praying, on this occasion, just for Mom and Dad. I prayed to God, that if Dad would have to suffer long or have to go to a rest home, where Mom could no longer take care of him, or if they would have to move away from the farm which Dad loved so much, please God, take him home.

And I prayed, that when Mom's time came, the same thing would happen for her, that she would not have to suffer any loneliness, or being away from what she always wanted, what she really liked, because her life was so hard, throughout all the years. She had many privations, and yet she had many consolations also. She enjoyed great joy in seeing her children be raised and get into different fields or professions, and to succeed in their chosen fields, yet her heart was touched by many heartbreaks, in seeing the sickness, sufferings, problems, trials, and tribulations that came into the lives of many of us in our family. These all caused her much sorrow, concern and suffering, yet they deepened her prayer life. Her principles are unwavering and she is a person of deep charity and love.

We left Jerusalem, soon after the trip to Emmaus, and flew back to the United States. When we arrived in the United States, I decided to go out East and visit there for another week, before going home. I was only there three days when I had the feeling

Dad's Funeral

that I should go home. I didn't know why. I had not ever had this type of feeling before, but I felt an urgency about it, so that I didn't question or hesitate. I just decided to take the next plane to go home.

When I arrived in Milwaukee, I went to my brother, Doctor Jim's home. I had dinner with him, and, after dinner, he said he would take me to Larry's place so I could pick up Larry's car and go on home from there. And I answered, "No, not tonight. Please, you take me home." He did, and when we got home, Dad was in bed and he said, "Thank God that you are home. Thank God that you are safe." Jim gave him the little souvenir that he had bought for him in the Holy Land. It was a Jacob's Well. He showed it to him, and Dad was very pleased with this. Then we went out to another room.

We heard some commotion and went back to the bedroom, and there Dad had had a stroke, a massive stroke, although we didn't realize this at the time. He was praying very diligently at that moment. You could see that, and read the words on his lips. I immediately ran upstairs and got the Holy Oils and came downstairs and gave him the Last Sacraments.

Jim watched him for awhile and he seemed to be resting. Actually, he had gone into a coma, and we didn't realize it. The next morning, we realized this was more serious than we had thought the night before. We called my brother, Jim, and he said he'd arrange to have him come to the hospital. He sent out the ambulance, and then the waiting began.

Dad actually lasted for another eight days, but he never came out of the coma enough to speak to us. One day he did open his eyes and smile and he seemed to recognize us, but he never spoke. We were there with him, praying for him. I prayed very hard that he would die quickly. We gave instructions to the doctor and nurses that they were not to use any extraordinary means to keep him alive, that they were to let nature take its course, keep him comfortable, and let God decide when he was to die.

Naturally, we may never use anything or cause anyone to die before their time. We may not take life, but that does not mean that we have to prolong life unreasonably. We can use the ordinary means, prescribe the necessary medication, but we don't have to go to extremes to make people stay alive for just a few more days. It's really not necessary.

On Wednesday, we received a call that Dad was slipping away fast. We went in and found that they had used these extraordinary means to keep him going, anyway. They pounded his chest and all that, to get his heart going again, and then he lived for another three days. I had to leave to go and give a retreat in Detroit, on Christian Renewal, at the Blue Army Center, so I prayed earnestly that God would take him quickly, so that I would be able to be home for the funeral.

On Saturday morning, he died, and on the following Monday, Labor Day, we had the funeral. We had it rather quickly, because it was easier to have all the people come, since it was a holiday weekend.

I took charge and made all the arrangements for the whole funeral. It was rather difficult for me, but I did it. I was O.K. until I was to say a few words after the Mass, and then it was just a little too much, and I really cried, the tears flowing freely.

But I do thank God for taking him in this way. He had a beautiful funeral, the singing was magnificent. They sang, "I Am The

Resurrection And The Life." My brother, Joe, participated in the Mass. He read the first reading, and the responsorial psalm. There were the three priests who had been in our parish, down through the years, Father Restle, for fourteen years, Father Trost, for eleven, and Father McLaughlin, for many years, the longest of the three.

Dad's funeral was the first in the new church in our parish. It was a very wonderful feeling the way this funeral was done. My own Provincial, Father Harold Whelan, some of my brother priests, Father Larkin, Father LaBrecque, and Father Petrie, all came. It was a tribute from our Congregation to have members present for my Dad's funeral. All in all, it was a very happy occasion.

We will meet our Dad again, at the Resurrection, and even before that, when we die ourselves. One day we will all be together in Heaven with him.

CHAPTER 22

APOSTOLATE SPREADS

After the funeral, I returned to California to resume the work of the Apostolate of Christian Renewal. The work spread slowly, but surely and gradually. I was still the only one working on it, but it was picking up, and I knew that we would soon need our own place or "Center" from which to work. I learned that there was a home for sale in Hacienda Heights that seemed ideal. Buying it would have meant that I'd go into debt for about $60,000. I had only $5,000 to pay down on it, and I actually needed at least another $5,000. They wanted $10,000 paid down, but I wasn't told this at first, and only found out about it later.

We Get A New Center

I knew, in my heart, that I would not be able to handle such a debt. The interest alone would have been outrageous. It would have snowed us under, and we would have been stopped in our tracks, before we even got started. I went to the Cardinal and explained what I wanted to do, and asked his blessing for this. He said, "It's best not for you to do this. You're only getting into debt, and there is no need for that because I have a place that you would be able to use, and you don't have to pay any rent for at least a year. You can work from there and make your Center in that place."

I was most grateful to him. It turned out to be a very beautiful home, a perfect center. We have a place where we are able to have Mass, we have offices, and sufficient room to live, for the time being. We have been living there for a year and a half now, but it is

Ann Gouveia, 94 years old, and Father Reed

Fr. Luke - Silver Jubilee of religious profession

beginning to be inadequate. We will need some other place in the very near future. I am sure we will have to have different headquarters eventually. It is a very nice and most enjoyable place, though, for now, and I am sure we are going to stay there for yet a little while.

Father Barrett, W.F., Joins Us

In April of 1973, Father Kevin Barrett, a White Father, joined our staff. He had been thinking, for a long time, about joining the Congregation of the Sacred Hearts of Jesus and Mary. When he first wrote to Father Larkin about coming and joining our Congregation, he was working in the mission fields for the White Fathers, over in Zambia. One day, when he was passing through California, Father Larkin gave me a letter from Father Barrett and said, "You answer this." I did, and, in the course of the correspondence, I found out that Father Kevin wanted to do the same type of work that we were doing in the Apostolate of Christian Renewal, and that he was definitely very interested in joining the Congregation of the Sacred Hearts of Jesus and Mary.

He is adamant about the importance of living the life of the Congregation, as the Founder intended it to be lived, and in accordance with Vatican Council II. The Second Vatican Council says that our Communities are to go back to the Charisma of the Founder, the ideals and the ideas of the Founder, to try to put them into practice and, also, to base our life on the Gospels and to carry this out in our daily living. He definitely had this in mind, when he finally came and decided to join us. It was a great blessing that he did come. He has a great talent, a tremendous talent, to work in drawing cartoons. He did this for a living before he joined the Seminary. He worked for CBS, drawing cartoons for various TV programs. Now he could use this to great advantage for God.

When he came, we decided to put out a little magazine, four times a year. We call it *The Christian Renewal News*. Father does all the art work in it. He also has done art work for booklets on abortion, adoption, pornography, sex education, euthanasia, and he is currently planning a booklet for Renewal and the Holy Year. He is very gifted and talented and we are very happy to have him with us. We certainly hope, that if God wants him to be a member of our Congregation, he will join us, in our Congregation, in the near future.

Sally Wood, Fr. Finbarr and Fr. Luke

Fr. Luke with Mrs. Shipstad, a strong supporter

Father Finbarr Devine, SS.CC., Joins The Staff

Shortly after Father Barrett's arrival, another priest, who had been teaching at Bishop Amat High School, decided that he wanted a deeper spiritual life, and to be able to work with people in a different manner than teaching. He also came to live with us. I didn't ever ask him to join us. I just said that, if he wanted to work with us, to go right ahead, whatever he saw fit to do. He definitely is beginning to get involved. He has tremendous work ahead of him.

He has worked out a beautiful program of renewal for elementary schools. In the fall, he's going to be doing that work, almost exclusively. He also is involved in the Charismatic Movement. He has deepened his own spiritual life in this manner, and I am sure that he will be a great asset, and bring many graces and blessings upon young people and upon all the people in the Archdiocese.

Publish Our Own Magazine

We decided to send out the little magazine that we put out, *The Christian Renewal News,* free, to every bishop, to the pastors of every parish, to convents, hospitals, religious communities, Catholic grammar schools and high schools, all across the country. Naturally, every member of the Apostolate of Christian Renewal also receives a free issue. It costs us a great deal of money to send out each issue, around $2,500. That means a total expenditure of around $10,000 a year, just to send out this magazine. I am sure that the cost will probably go up, as the years go by, if we continue to send out this magazine.

We hope that priests, brothers, and sisters will read this magazine, and that it will help them to know about the Apostolate, what we are trying to do, the aims and the goals of the Apostolate. It is another means of making the Apostolate known.

Conferences On Cassettes

Another thing we have done is to put the Conferences that I have given on cassettes. We have put ten different talks on five tapes. A sixth tape in the set, which we call our "Six-Pack," contains thirteen songs written and sung by Mark Greer. We sell this "Six-Pack" for $24.95. We're hoping that many people will order these talks. They can use them for their families, or for group gatherings in their homes. In this way, they can share this message with others and help them to understand the religious life better, and to deepen their understanding of their Commitment and the way they should be living in following Christ.

This, then, is the manner in which the work has progressed, so far. We have also received a grant from a corporation which enabled us to send the cassettes to every bishop in the United States, and also to every contemplative religious order. The reason for sending them to the Bishops is that we want them to know about the Apostolate, that this work is going on. Hopefully, they will sponsor it, and try to implement it in their own dioceses and archdiocese.

We sent them to the contemplative religious orders, because we want their prayers. We *need* their prayers. In order to carry out any work, we need prayers. We feel that the prayers of contemplative Orders are very, very powerful and beneficial. With their prayers, they can enter into our work, the work of carrying out the Apostolate.

It's God's Work

Actually, it isn't our work, it's God's work. This was brought home to me very forcefully one day. I was attending a meeting of the International Institute of the Heart of Jesus. A lady asked me to see if her husband would give us a grant to carry out this work. I was bashful about doing so. I'd rather die than ask for money, but she kept on insisting. I also wanted the International Institute of the Heart of Jesus to incorporate more devotion to the Blessed Mother, and her Immaculate Heart, into the work that we would be fostering. And so, I went up to this man and talked to him about putting Mary into the fore in the work, but I didn't mention anything about the money.

As I was walking away from him, headed toward my sister-in-law, who was to pick me up and take me to her home, God said to me, "You fool! This is not *your* work. This is *my* work. You may not feel embarrassed, and you should not feel ashamed to ask anybody for aid in carrying out this work. It gives the people

who do give money to it an opportunity to receive many blessings and graces from Me."

That drew me up short. It made me realize that, subconsciously,
I must have thought that it was my work. This was a terrible fault
in my character. I should have really whole-heartedly said, "This
is *God's* work." So, if I say "my" work, or "our" work, I really
mean it is God's work.

This man did give the grant, so that I could carry out the work
of sending the tapes as mentioned, and so that some of the expenses of the Center could be taken care of. It was also used to set
up an Enthronement Office of the Sacred Heart in our Center. This
is appropriate, because the Enthronement work is part and parcel
of the work of the Apostolate. It is not just something aside from
the Apostolate. It is an integral part of it. This is as it should be. It
is sad that this has not always been understood in all places where
we have done the work of the Apostolate.

A Journey Through Life: Chosen

CHAPTER 23

A PROBLEM DEVELOPS

I wanted to have an Apostolate office in Milwaukee and to set it up in conjunction with the Enthronement Center. In carrying out the work, the Sister in charge unfortunately pushed the work of the Apostolate in such a way as to make people in the area feel that she was not taking care of any of the Enthronement work.

Enthronement And The Apostolate

People who join the Apostolate usually follow this very quickly by having the Enthronement of the Sacred Heart in their homes. The work of the Enthronement is therefore benefited and fostered. An argument was raised against our work that this was not the case. This was absolutely false. However, I was told that we could not remain in the Enthronement building. We then had to separate the Enthronement from the Apostolate work.

Received An Ultimatum

The Bishop had given permission for us to be there, and to work there, but the people who wanted the Enthronement only went to the Bishop and complained. Naturally, he told them that we should work it out among ourselves. He did not want to get involved in the argument, and he did not do so. I was issued the ultimatum that both Apostolates, the Enthronement, and the Apostolate of Christian Renewal, could not remain in the same Center.

I was told that if I would get rid of the Sister in charge, I could remain. I could not do that. I could not abandon her. I decided to have her leave the Center and it was my idea to set up a small office, and, in that way, at least be able to carry on the work of the Apostolate in the Archdiocese of Milwaukee. It didn't work out that way, at that time. It turned out to be nothing but a thorn in my side.

Inactivity

Actually, what has happened since, is that the Enthronement Center has become a place where they simply pick up the mail. No activity has been going on in there since we left. I hope that soon there will be an increase of the work of the Enthronement, so that it will not continue to be only done in dribs and drabs.

Our own Apostolate work also came almost to a complete stand-still. The priest-moderator, a Diocesan priest who was appointed by the Bishop to carry on the work there, felt that the Bishop ought to give us an office to work from. Sister said that she wouldn't continue, unless Father stayed on the job. Therefore, nothing much was done for a time. The situation was a great source of sorrow to me. Perhaps I was at fault indirectly for this situation. Maybe I didn't explain fully enough to everyone involved just what the purpose of the Apostolate is.

Was I At Fault?

I didn't say more in the beginning for several reasons. I know from past experience that, when people are involved with a work, they tend to become so enthused and filled with zeal that they talk of nothing else. They give no one else a chance to talk about anything else either, and they leave one with the impression that they think they are the only ones doing any important work. I did not wish to appear this way. Also, many of my ideas, with regard to spreading the work of the Apostolate, simply did not "gel" all at once.

After I'd written my books and given Conferences for awhile, my ideas changed and deepened. I could see different insights, and was able to help to make the Apostolate better than in the beginning. Until that time, I did not speak, even to the Fathers of my own Congregation, at any great length about this work.

The Apostolate And Members Of Our Congregation

I did have one opportunity to do so. That was at the Provincial Council meeting. In June of 1972, we had our Retreat and Chapter meeting, when we talked about the rules that we would live by. I was given the opportunity then to explain to them what the Apostolate was. I explained why I joined the Congregation, why I thought God called me to do this work, and what I planned to do in the future. I explained that I would use the money that was given to me to carry out the work of the Apostolate, and that I would not ever incur financial responsibility on the part of the Congregation toward this work. I also said that I would not ever try to bring embarrassment on my Congregation, because of the work, because I love it and think it is a tremendous Congregation.

They took a vote and gave me permission to begin, as I had outlined my plan to them. Very few of the Fathers in our Province are as yet involved. Perhaps they don't yet understand the work I am doing or are still a little suspicious of it. This could be why they are holding back the support I would like them to give to it. Nevertheless, I respect their opinions and I do like each member of the Congregation. They are doing wonderful work, each in his own Apostolate. I cannot expect them to drop everything and join in the work of the Apostolate and become a member of the preaching there. I do not at all intend such a thing. One thing only I would wish to have from them. That is the support of their prayers and their interest. A greater understanding always creates an easier atmosphere for carrying out our work.

My Character Is Strengthened

One thing has happened since that time. I have gotten over my weakness or fault of "human respect." For many years, I didn't carry out this work or suggest that I had this work to do. I mentioned the treatment that I received in the Novitiate, and that I didn't wish to go through the same experience again. I became quiet, hesitant, and did not wish to speak out or act forcefully. It was only after I saw the Pope and received his blessing and the Grace from this audience, that I had the fortitude to go out and do the work. Now I no longer care what other people think. I know that God wants this work to be done, and I will do it as long as I can.

If the Superiors should ever say stop, then of course I would have to stop. But I don't see how that could every happen. After the books have been written and published, after twenty-five hundred people have become involved, and it has spread throughout both the United States and the rest of the world, the magazine is going, the cassettes are done, and the work of the Apostolate is beginning to expand ever more rapidly, I don't see why they would ever wish to step in and say, "Now stop everything." Nevertheless, I know they could do this and I would be obedient. God could even step in and stop it now. I could die any minute and the work, as far as my involvement is concerned, would stop. God can do what He wants, when He wants, where He wants and as long as He wants. This is the attitude that we should always have. If God really does want the work to continue, it will go on. If it is God's work, then nothing can stop it. If it is man's work, nothing will make it go on. Sooner or later, it would stop.

God Gives Mission

In the eyes of the Church, a few years is not sufficient time to see whether something is from God or not. It must be tested by time for many, many years. Sometimes God gives a Mission or an Apostolate, a certain work to be done, and it might be for only a certain era of the Church's existence. It might be for only twenty, fifty, or a hundred years, or it could be something that is to be carried on forever, for always. I do not know whether this work is something that is meant to be temporary, or if it is something that is to have a permanent nature. I hope and pray that it will be permanent, but only God knows.

Apostolate Transforms People

Maybe its purpose is to serve as a way of bringing about renewal and reconciliation in the Church. I hope that this is the case.

We see many movements in the Church today, all valid and very beneficial to the people. People all work in different ways and respond to different ideas, and therefore there is a valid reason to have the various different movements. Many will say, "There are so many movements in the Church. Why have another one?" That is the reason. We must try to touch all people in the way that they can best be reached.

I do feel that this Apostolate is going to benefit many. I know, from the use of the tapes, from the books, and from the conferences, that we have touched souls and that people have been transformed. I have seen the changes in lives. I have seen non-Catholics become Catholics. I have seen non-practicing Catholics come back to their Faith. I have seen lukewarm Catholics become zealous, and I have seen zealous Catholics deepened their spiritual lives still more. It is meant to deepen people's spiritual lives and their commitment to God.

A Movement, Never An Organization

And so, I do feel that this is a valid movement. I call it a "movement," because I do not want it to be just another organization. I do not want it to interfere with any organization. It is meant to supplement them, to embellish them. It is to give people a deeper spirituality in their organizations, so that they can become vibrant and get really involved. This is why I have started the Apostolate, and why I feel that the Apostolate is something that is God-given. It is something that God wants, and I am willing to give the rest of my life to it. God could even make me sick, so that I'd become inactive. Then I would carry on the work of the Apostolate through my suffering.

Priests Should Get Involved

What I am hoping and praying for is that many priests will become involved in this, that they will take the challenge, and that they will take the time to work with people, and will never become discouraged or frustrated. So many times, we want instant success. We want to have people understand immediately and live as we feel is the best way for the Christian life to be lived. But we must be long-suffering and patient with people. We should try to help them to understand, even if we have only a small group, it is well worth working with them. If we reach even five or ten in a parish, we can transform a parish within five years. It's the overall result that we are looking for.

"By their fruits, you will know them." If the Holy Spirit brings forth the gifts that St. Paul speaks about, Charity, Joy, Peace, Fortitude, Courage, Meekness, Kindness, Tenderness, all these things, then it certainly has to be from God. As I said, if we get only a few people to live this, to understand this, to try to become saints, it will be well worth it.

Spiritual Directors Needed

I would like to see more priests become spiritual directors, real guides in spirituality. That means knowing, practicing, and living asceticism and mysticism themselves. They must experience this before they can share it with others. I'm hoping that, in their lives, they will share this with others, that they will take the Apostolate to them, that they will become a part of it, so that they can help others to make it a part of their lives.

Brothers And Sisters Invited To Join

I would also like to see the Brothers and the Sisters in Religious Orders do the same thing. I would like to see different leaders among the lay people, who would be inclined to share these things with others, to help others, to give workshops or conferences in homes, by using the tapes or what have you, so that we can bring about a true renewal.

CHAPTER 24

THE HOLY YEAR
AND THE APOSTOLATE

The Holy Year

I was most pleased and happy that the Holy Father proclaimed a Holy Year, with the theme of Interior Renewal and Reconciliation. In June of 1972, when the tenth anniversary of his Papacy took place, I sent him copies of my book and I wrote him a letter, congratulating him. At the time, there was a clamor for his resignation. I stated in the letter that I hoped he would not resign, that he'd have sufficient health to carry on and continue to do the work he was doing.

I also stated in the letter that I hoped that the Holy Year theme would be the Interior Renewal of Man. I am not so naive as to think that what I wrote could have caused the Pope to decide to use that theme; however, when he did officially proclaim, on May 9, 1973, that there would be a Holy Year, he declared that the theme was to be the Interior Renewal of Man and Reconciliation. I was most elated!

Interior Renewal

I was so pleased because I knew that now this was the way in which the Apostolate could be spread. It would grow through the Holy Year, because the Apostolate's goal was exactly the same. My books have the same theme running throughout the whole work.

177

This interior renewal of man means to "put on Christ," as St. Paul tells us. We cannot do that unless we know and love Christ.

I feel that, in order to know and love Christ, we must have a deep love for Mary, because she brings us to Christ. Once we know and love Christ, He has said, "The Father and I will come to you," and we will experience this in our lives. He said, "I will ask the Spirit and He will come to you." And that is the beginning of a real interior renewal. From this deep union of love for God flows naturally the reconciliation.

Reconciliation

When there is a deep union with God, there is a reconciliation between man and God, between soul and God. We know that there is a need for reconciliation between man and man. When you are at peace with God, then you wish to be at peace with your fellow man. You look upon him as a brother in Christ, and so you go out to him, give of yourself to him, and share with him, hoping for the best for him. You work for this. This is what we are trying to accomplish in the Apostolate of Christian Renewal.

Planned Renewal Center

I would like eventually to have a permanent Renewal Center. This would not have to be very large, but it would require space enough for at least a dozen or so priests. It should have a Chapel, conference rooms where people could come to receive spiritual guidance, offices for handling correspondence, and a shipping and receiving center. We would also need the natural facilities (kitchen, bathrooms, etc.), that are to be expected with living quarters.

This Center would act as a sort of "home base," or "main artery," for other, smaller Centers throughout the world. It would be a place where priests, brothers, sisters, and lay people could come to spiritually renew themselves, if they wished, and then go out and spread the work of the Apostolate to all of the people in the world.

It would be ideal to have at least several priests living in this Center at all times. Theirs would be a multiple purpose. They would, of course, handle the immediate work connected with the Apostolate

The Morse clan

Ann Holcomb with Helena Maxfield who offered her life for apostolate.

Cissie Morse - Victim soul

179

in the area proximate to the Center. They would handle correspondence, they would provide spiritual guidance, especially for priests and Religious wishing to devote themselves to the spread of the Apostolate. And, most important of all, in their religious community life, within the Center itself, they would provide a strong spiritual "task force" of prayers for the spiritual welfare and needs of all those connected in any way with the Apostolate.

It would be a Center where people could come and visit, to meditate, study on their own. People could deepen their love for God. What I'm hoping for is that Vatican II can be completely implemented, as the Pope and the Bishops foresaw, not the way we might want, or other people might want, but in the way that is for the good of the Church.

I want to do this work for, in, and through the Church, not outside the Church, or against the Church, but completely in harmony with the hierarchy. We should all be united and work together for the honor and glory of God. This is what I've dedicated my life to. I pray that God will help me to carry on this work for Him.

People Are Beautiful

We have many wonderful people in the work of the Apostolate. One family, in particular, is the Morse family. They have ten living children, and one who has died. This one child had bone cancer. She accepted the suffering from this, and offered it to God. She took no pain-killing drugs, so that her mind would be clear, and so that she could make a gift of her suffering to God, in reparation for the crime of abortion. She understood the meaning of life very, very well. This is explained in a book, written by her mother, called *Cissie, Sweet Child Of Grace*. This book is also available. This family has been one of my main supports in regard to praying. Whenever I need or want anything, I ask them to pray, and they do a very quick job. God answers their prayers very quickly.

Another wonderful person that I met was Helena Maxfield. She, too, had cancer, and she offered her life, also without taking the pain-killing drugs. She offered her suffering for the work of the Apostolate. She also died, and I am sure that both she and Cissie are interceding for us, from Heaven.

Still another tremendous person was the Japanese leper woman, in Molokai, who had been praying and sacrificing for us. I know that she has the same power in Heaven, and that she is able to help us, too.

There are many other wonderful, wonderful people who are going all out to carry out the work of the Apostolate, who give of their talents, their time, their energy, and even their money, to carry out this work. I am most grateful to all of them.

We Live And Do Our Work Through Donations

We do not have any fees or meetings, as such, in the Apostolate. It is possible to prepare oneself completely by the use of the books and thereby become a member of the Apostolate. I will never make an appeal for money, through the mail, because I feel that the majority of the people in this world receive sufficient appeals from many sources. However, I am most grateful for any donation that is given. We are a tax-exempt organization, we are incorporated, federally and state-wise, so that any donation that is given can be tax deductible. I hope that many foundations and companies and people of means will come to our aid, to carry out this plan of work which we envision.

I do feel that God wants this. It is only a matter of when and where to really begin. I would like to establish the Center in Southern California. I ask everyone who reads this book to pray for this work, and every Mass I say is being offered for all our benefactors, for every member of the Apostolate, their families, relatives, or friends, for the spread of the Apostolate, and for the good of the Church, the cause of Christ. I ask you to help in any way you wish.

CHAPTER 25

NEED OF SPIRITUALITY

We see people, on the one hand, searching for spirituality. They will do everything possible in order to learn about God, to experience God. On the other hand, we see people repressing the Spirit. We see them turning against God, becoming angry with Him, abandoning Him, not believing in Him, rejecting Him. We also see those who militate against Him, and who, in all claims, are practical atheists.

We have to strive to overcome these things. We have repressed spirituality too long. That is our modern neurosis. We must become spiritual people. I have many people come to me and ask, "Teach us how to pray," or "How do you pray?" In the past, I think that we were secret Apostles. We kept all these things to ourselves. Now is the time when we must speak out and show people how to pray.

How To Pray

I think the first thing we must do is to go to Scripture and read the account of the time when the Apostles came to Jesus and said, "Teach us how to pray." We see that Jesus immediately points out that we should pray for the honor and glory of God. He said we should address, "Our Father who art in Heaven" and "hallowed be His name" and "that His kingdom should come."

God Comes First

In other words, Jesus put God first. And, in our prayers, we must also put Him first. We must recognize the place of God in our lives, in our spirituality. It's not just man to man. It's not just a horizontal phase of giving service to man. It is also an elevating of our minds, hearts, and souls to Almighty God, recognizing that, without Him, we are nothing, we can do nothing.

Pray From The Heart

Once we have recognized and accepted this, we can begin to pray correctly. However, we should not be like the Pharisees. We know that the Pharisees claimed to have great faith. They *claimed* to have a deep sense of religion. They *claimed* that they prayed, that they gave ten percent of their money to the poor, that they fasted. But, what did our Lord say to them?

He said, "You hypocrites! You pray with your lips, but your heart is far from me. You are like whited sepulchers, filled with dead man's bones. You have cleaned the outside of the cup, but the inside is dirty." He also said that they loved to preach in the Synagogues and to pray in the prominent places, just so that they could be seen by men. He said that they extended their phylacteries and that they placed burdens upon other men, instead of trying to uplift them, that they multiplied their prayers, their sacrifices, and their offerings, and that all this was displeasing to God.

We Are Sinners

They really were not praising God. God was not the One Whom they were honoring. They were really honoring only themselves. They were putting on a good show for other people, for the praise of other people, so that they would be considered holy. We must be, instead, like the Publican, like the humble sinner, and say, "Lord, be merciful to me, the sinner." That is recognizing the fact that we *are* sinners, and then our prayers will be heard.

Realize The Presence Of God

When we pray, we should put ourselves in the Presence of God, think of what we are doing, realizing that God is with us, realizing that God loves us with an unconditional love. He loves us as we are, and we should open our hearts to Him, tell Him of our weakness, our sinfulness, our need for Him. He will come quickly to our aid.

Formal Prayers Insufficient

It is not enough just to pray formal prayers, meaning prayers that have been written by others, or by ourselves, or to read one novena after another. All these things are very good, and many people have sanctified themselves in this way. The reason for this is that they were God-loving people who loved their fellow man, and, when they prayed, it was with attention, devotion, and meaning. They realized what they were doing, Who they were addressing, and it left an impact, an impression upon their souls. They became transformed, and they really loved God. We cannot say that they have lived a useless life. If they were just to read the prayers for prayer's sake, it is a different story. Then we know that they did not do so correctly, we can see that they were only babies in the spiritual life.

Meditation

Still, many have deepened their spiritual lives and reached a deep union with God by following this method of prayer. I feel, however, that this is not sufficient. We should deepen our prayer life still more. We should advance to the next form of praying, which is meditation. This is not just thinking. Many people feel that, if they do not think about the different things of God, then they are not praying. Real prayer is loving, and that comes from the *will*, and not from the *intellect*.

We must learn to love, and not worry about what happens within the intellect. I feel that we should take a book, if we need one, to begin our meditation. On the night before, we should read a passage from this book. I consider the Bible to be the best book for this purpose. We don't pick it up just to read it. Anyone can read a Bible or other book, and it will not necessarily leave a lasting impression upon them, or change them. It will not necessarily help them to come closer to God, to live a life of love for God, and their fellow man. If they study a subject and obtain a knowledge of that subject, so that they can quote Scripture passages at random with facility and ease, it is not really prayer.

It does not follow that they have understood and that it has penetrated their souls. We must first learn to give ourselves totally to God, to give our hearts to Him, then the Scriptures will take on meaning, and we will encounter Christ. When we encounter Christ, we experience what happened to Peter, James, and John, when they went with Him to Mt. Tabor and He was transfigured before them, and they saw Him in all His dazzling brightness. The whiteness of His garments filled them with awe, respect, and fear. We know what then happened. We heard the Father say, "This is my beloved Son, in Whom I am well pleased."

Realize Who Christ Is

I think *we* must come to that realization. When we finally realize Who Christ is, we see Him in a different way, and we can never remain the same. But, even if we come to understand Him and recognize Him, encounter Him as the Resurrected Christ, the all-loving Person, still the glimmer of His Divinity shines through but seldom. Most of the time we see Him, as the Apostles saw Him, in His humanity.

Like Us, Except Without Sin

I think it is important to understand this, to accept Jesus Christ as God and man, to realize that He had a human nature, and that He was like us in everything but sin. St. Paul tells us that. He had all the experiences of any human person. By this, I mean that He ate, drank, was tired, suffered disappointments, felt rejected, lonely, also joy, happiness, and peace. He was tempted in every way that we are tempted. He suffered, and terribly, so we cannot say that Jesus cannot understand human nature or our lot in life. He went through it, and, since He did, He identified Himself with us, He knows us, He cares for us, He loves us!

Ask

And this is the all important thing. Because He loved us, He gave His life for us, shed His Blood for us, did many other things for us. His gifts are there for us, just for the asking. He said, "Ask and you shall receive. Seek and you shall find. Knock and it shall be opened to you." He said that everyone should ask — everyone! It doesn't make any difference who we are, what we are, we should ask.

Give Yourself To Him

Many people feel that they are not worthy to address God, to talk and to pray to God. We will never be worthy. We should just give ourselves to Him as we are. Then *He* will begin to transform us, to help us, to change us, and to make us like unto Himself. This is the process that our prayer life should follow.

Count Your Blessings

In meditating, it would be well to read a passage, to study it, and to pray about it. Then we should tell God of our love, and thank Him for the many things He has given to us. We have much for which to be thankful. If we were to sit down and write out the things for which we ought to be thankful, I am sure that we would be quite surprised at the number of gifts, talents, and Graces that God has given to us. We can count our blessings, especially here in America. We have much from God. Since we have been given so much, we owe God much, and we should share with others.

Share With Others

God said, "I have given you freely, give to others freely." If He has given us riches, then we should share them with others. We are not an island, we cannot just keep these things for ourselves. I think that, in praying, we will come to this conclusion.

Praying is not only kneeling before God, pouring out our hearts. It's more. We should pray in union with every soul that lives now, or ever has lived on the earth, so that our prayer touches both God and the whole Mystical Body at the same time. To that end, I composed a "Mystical Mass Prayer," while I was working in the Family Home Missions in Hawaii. I share it here in order to point out the manner in which our prayer should be a time of union both with God and with our brother and sister in Christ.

The Mystical Mass Prayer

Saint Michael, the Archangel, defend us in battle; be our safe-guard against the wickedness and snares of the devil. May God rebuke him we humbly pray; and do you, Prince of the heavenly host, by the power of God, cast into hell Satan and all the evil spirits, who wander through the world seeking the ruin of souls.

Most Sacred Heart of Jesus, have mercy on us. (Three times)

I wish to invite each angel and saint in heaven and soul in purgatory to pray with me and for me.

Eternal Father, I offer to You through the Immaculate and Sor-rowful Heart of Mary, in the Holy Spirit, the Body, Blood, Soul, and Divinity of Your Divine Son Jesus from all the altars through-out the world at each Holy Mass which is celebrated on this day and every day until the end of time.

To each Mass, I wish to unite everything that took place in the lives of Jesus, Mary, and Joseph while they lived on earth (think of the things in detail or just in general), and their existence in heaven for all eternity. I wish to unite everything which took place in the life of each angel in Heaven (creation, trial, victory, glory, and joy in Heaven — honor and glory given to God); all that took place in the life of each of the saints in Heaven while they were living on earth, after death, and the glory they give to You in Heaven (offer all their prayers, sufferings, trials, successes, failures, and faults). I wish to unite to each Mass everything which took place in the life of each person in purgatory, their life on earth; after death, their suffering in purgatory, and the happiness they will have in Heaven. To each Mass I wish to unite everything which happens in the life of each person who is living and will live until the end of time. To each Mass I wish to unite the glory of all creation. Finally, I wish to unite myself with Christ in each Mass which I offer to You. Take me and do with me what You wish, when You wish, as long as You wish. Give me the serenity to accept the things I cannot change, the courage to change the things I can, and the wisdom to know the difference.

Help me to love You, my God, with my whole heart and soul, with all my strength and mind. I wish to accept the type of death You wish me to die — when, where, how, and why!

Let each Holy Mass be an act of love and adoration which I wish to offer to You, God the Father, since You are our God, our Creator, and our Father — *my* Father! To You, God the Son, since You are God, our Redeemer, Mediator, King, Judge and Brother — *my* Brother! To You, God the Holy Spirit, since You are our God, our Advocate, our Helper, our Sanctifier — *my* Holy Spirit!

Let each Holy Mass be an Act of Thanksgiving for all the gifts and graces given to each person and each one who will exist, especially for...

Let each Holy Mass be an act of reparation for all the sins that have, are, and will be committed until the end of the world, especially sins of ingratitude, indifference, disbelief, unbelief, swearing, cursing, blasphemy, sacrilege, anger, hatred, murder, and all sins of impurity.

From each Mass, O Triune God, I ask You to bless my Father, Mother, Sisters, Brothers, Relatives, Friends, and especially.....

Bless the Holy Father, Cardinals, Bishops, Priests, Nuns, Brothers, Seminarians, and all aspiring to the service of God, especially... and may more and more aspire to God's service.

Bless the poor, the sick, the dying, and the poor souls in Purgatory.

Bless and cure ...

Let each Holy Mass be a petition for peace, and for an increase of Faith, Hope, and Love.

Help Others

We must go out from our prayers and help others. I think this is an important thing to remember.

Pray More

We, in America, pray far too little. We should pray much more. I feel that, for Religious, priests, brothers, and sisters, three to five hours a day should be spent in prayer, before the Blessed Sacrament. Many will say, "We don't have the time. We have to help so many people." Actually I think, if we would analyze our lives, check to see how much time we really waste, how much time we think we are busy, when actually we are not, then we could find much more time for our prayer life. I think that lack of prayer is one of the main reasons why our work is not as effective as it should be. We do not pray nearly enough. Even if it means giving up some of our time to sleep, some of the time that we spend eating, some of our time spent in our own personal recreation, we will learn more and our work will be more fruitful, if we spend our time before Jesus in the Blessed Sacrament.

Not Enough Time!

I also feel that our lay people must be willing to pray more. I am sure that many people feel that they have too many things to do, and they do not have time to pray, but how much time is wasted before the TV? How much time is spent in illicit pleasure seeking or recreation? It's a matter of putting priorities in their proper place, putting first things first, and coming to God.

Excuse Ourselves Easily

We know that Our Lord invited people to a banquet and very few came. He told the people to go out into the highways and by-ways and bring them, but there was always an excuse as to why they could not come. We use the same "cop-out," the same excuses. We do not want to be near God, because, when we are near to God, we will have to change. We can never remain the same and we really don't want to have to change.

Lead A Good Life

Many will now object and say, "Well, I want God. I want a life that is good and wholesome." We also hear that pagans lead a good life. Do you not often hear the expression, "He's not a Christian, but he's a good man, or a good woman." But that's not *spiritual* goodness. There is much more to life than that, it's deeper than that. We must have a spiritual motivation, a spiritual reason for our lives. I feel that, in our prayer life, we will learn to understand this. We will learn to put our priorities in the proper place, and to realize that we are *privileged* to be able to give ourselves to God in prayer.

The Way To Meditate

In our prayer life, in our families and in our homes, it would be well to spend at least fifteen to thirty minutes a day in meditation. When we prepare to meditate, we ought first to take a passage from the Bible or another book, even a phrase from a prayer, such as the Our Father, and read it. Then, if a phrase strikes us, has deep meaning for us, we should stop and repeat it again and again until we can no longer say it. Then, just rest in silence before God and you will have reached a depth in your prayer life. You will be praying correctly.

You will find, in praying thus, that there will come a time when you will no longer need any book or "prop." You will be able to simply speak to God in your own way. The words will flow from you easily, rapidly, joyfully, peacefully. You will have a great joy in your heart at being able to be in the Presence of God. We must also realize that it will not always be this way.

If nothing seems to come from your prayer life, you cannot seem to get started, or to have this experience in praying, stop and go back to the book. Perhaps you have done something that has caused you to lose the ability to pray in this way. If that is the case, go back and begin again. If still you find that the book is not helpful, that you still can no longer pray in this manner, then you may be being called to pray in a deeper way. You must not give up. This is where many people make a grave mistake. They say they can no longer pray and they just cut their prayer life out. They make the greatest mistake of their lives!

Waste Your Time!

At this point, you are being called to a higher form of prayer. You are being asked to surrender yourself totally to God. You should have within your heart a great desire to pray, a desire to be with

God, even though you cannot, even though it is painful and you feel that you are wasting your time — accomplishing nothing. Well, waste your time! Stay there. Give yourself to God and be satisfied simply with being in the Presence of God. Your *heart* is speaking to God just by reason of the fact that you *want* to give yourself to God. You are praying with your will. If you can learn this, you will pray well.

Need The Holy Spirit

We must remember one thing more, and this is that Our Lord *wants* us to pray. He wants us to ask for certain things. There are some things for which we need to pray. Sometimes people are very sluggish in regard to religion. They do not care for their prayer life. They think that they might become *too* holy. They do not seem to think that this is proper. It is not for them. They think that those who pray are just wasting their time. They laugh at them and ridicule them. What is needed in the lives of such as these is the power of the Holy Spirit, who is indeed needed in *all* our lives.

Ask For Coming Of The Holy Spirit

We must pray for this. Jesus Christ said that we should pray, and that He would send the Holy Spirit. We should pray with faith, realizing that what we ask will be given to us, if it is the Will of God. It is certainly God's Will for the Holy Spirit to work within our souls, because it is the work of the Holy Spirit to form Christ within us, to make us a beloved son or daughter of God the Father. God wants the Holy Spirit to work in our lives, and this is what we should ask for. We should pray for it repeatedly, time and time again, and then we should wait for Him to come.

Wait For Holy Spirit

Wait for Him to come. It may take some time. We should be patient and persevering. We should continue to ask and to wait until God, in His own good time, will enlighten us, will send the Holy Spirit more forcefully into our lives so that He can work in us.

Aware Of Holy Spirit

When we have the Holy Spirit working in our lives, we are aware of this. There is an added dimension in our lives. Our prayer life will necessarily deepen, because it is He Who is guiding, protecting, and watching over us. He is helping us, and we must give ourselves to Him completely. In this, perseverance is the most important thing. God will give to us anything that will help and benefit our spiritual life, anything that will further the kingdom of God on earth, God will give to us. And so we should ask, we should not hesitate, we should believe.

Lesson In Faith

Jesus taught the lesson of faith many times when He was talking with the Apostles. There is one occasion that is especially outstanding. That is when He was walking along one day, and was hungry. He saw a fig tree, and He went up to it. We are told in Scripture that it was not the time for figs, and He found no figs on the tree. He went away but He cursed the tree as He was leaving. On the way back, Peter said, "Lord, look at the tree You cursed. It withered up and died." And what did Our Lord say? He said to Peter and the other Apostles, "If you do not waver, if you believe in your heart, you will do greater things. You will say to the mountains, 'rise,' and they will go into the sea. If you believe, it will be done. If you doubt, it will not take place."

We cannot just say, "Lord, do this thing, or that thing," and, when it doesn't immediately happen, say, "Well, I thought as much." We are showing doubt with this attitude. But, if we really believe, in our hearts, and if what we ask is for God's honor and glory, then we will definitely receive what is best for us.

Discern The Spirit

We must learn the proper things for which to pray. We must discern the Spirit. We must desire that which God wants. Not everything that we might wish to have or that the world wants is what God wants. We do not really need everything that we think we must have. God knows what is best for us. God knows our needs. Therefore, we need to discern the Spirit, pray to the Holy Spirit, so that we may know what God wants in our life and follow God's Will.

God's Will To Be Followed

That is not always easy to know, but we must pray to know it, and then be willing to accept that God's Will be done in our lives. We cannot pray for material pleasures alone. We cannot pray simply for our own comfort and worldly ease. God will never answer such a prayer, because the world is the enemy of God. They are not compatible. The things of the world are not what God wants for us.

God wants us for Himself, and God wants us to use the things of the world for His honor and glory, not just for our own ease, our own sinfulness. And so we must persevere in our praying to discern the Spirit.

Persevere

Christ tells us that a lady came and asked some things from a man, and he would not have any regard for God or for man but, because of her persistence, he gave her the things that she wanted. Another time, Our Lord was walking along, and a woman came after Him. She kept on pestering Him to cure her daughter. The Apostles got angry and said, "Why don't You send her away?" He did not, and He rebuked them, and granted to this woman what she asked. It was her perseverance and Faith that moved Him.

The Faith that is shown by many people, such as the woman who bled for twelve years, will touch His Heart. She said, "If only I touch the hem of His garment, I will be cured." And when she did, Christ said, "Who touched me?" Then the woman came up and confessed, and He said, "Because of your great faith, you have been healed."

Faith and perseverance are very important in our prayer life. Still another thing which is important is an upright intention. We must purify our intentions, again bringing home the importance of the discernment of the Spirit.

Consolation In Prayer

Sometimes we will have consolation, but it seems it's only a glimmer, at times. We feel that we have a glimpse of Christ, as the Apostles did, on Mt. Tabor, in the Transfiguration, and we feel the tremendous love that overpowers us, takes hold of us, and we cannot but be satiated with this tremendous outpouring of God's love in our hearts. This is a warm, glowing feeling that comes over our whole being, and we can say with Peter, "Lord, it is good for us to be here." We are filled with greater love and dedication and conviction for what we are doing. This happens to us in our prayer life from time to time.

Generally speaking, our lives will run on a smooth, steady course, joy-filled in the knowledge that we are doing the Will of God, and living in the Presence of God. We *feel* the Presence of God, no matter what we are doing, where we are going. This is before our minds and our hearts at all times.

Desolation In Prayer

There may be moments of desolation, moments of dryness, when we feel that we cannot truly pray. There are many reasons that might cause this. First of all, it could be our own lack of generosity. We may cause it by our own faults. We may become filled with the spirit of the world or an attachment to creatures or things, and, in this way, lose the intimacy that is needed to develop a close union with God.

We could also be simply experiencing a trial from God. God sometimes sends us this desolation for the purpose of trying or testing us, to see whether we will be worthy of Him.

We can therefore go from consolation to desolation, or distraction, whatever you might wish to call it. Mostly this will come from the devil, because he wishes to discourage us. He wants us to give up the spiritual life and the prayerful life. When people feel they cannot pray, and are constantly tempted in this way, they sometimes give up and say, "What's the use?" This is where a spiritual director is needed to prod them, and make them realize what is really happening in their souls, and to overcome the devil, so that he cannot succeed. Usually, when this is revealed to the spiritual director, it automatically disappears. Desolation should not long remain in anyone's life. There should generally be a solid, ever-pervading joy and peace in one's heart and soul.

Seek God

We must be very careful that we don't seek the consolation of God, rather than the God of consolation. By that, I mean that we would put excessive trust in visions, hoping to have them or any other gifts that are incidental to spiritual living. This is wrong. If God wishes to give them, so be it. We may be the instrument of bringing much good into the world, through them. We should naturally be open to God at all times, and our prayer life is a time when we might be chosen to receive these gifts, or to be elevated still more in our understanding of God. Many times, in our lives, without our even realizing it, our minds are illuminated about a certain thing. A certain truth becomes very clear and understandable, and we relish the intellectual awareness of these great truths that God has given to us. It's a deep penetration into what God means about certain things. But again, we must discern the Spirit, and see whether this is from God or is from our imagination, or from the devil. The devil is an Angel of Light. He mixes truths with error, and what is true seems so plausible that we fall for everything else that he mixes in.

It is a most terrible thing for people to follow false prophets and uphold them and believe in them, in spite of what the Bishops or people in authority announce about these people.

Obey The Bishop

The best policy is always to obey the Shepherd of the Flock, and do what he points out for us to do. He is the one who is responsible before God. If he tells us that these things are not from Him, from God, then we should abandon them. If they are from God, then we should embrace them, uphold them, and respect them, and put them into practice for whatever God wishes.

Pray Because We Love God

Why are we praying? Are we praying because we love God? Or, are we praying just for selfish reasons? Do we want things just for our *own* honor and glory, so that we will *appear* to be very holy, if these things are granted? Or, are we really humble? Are we truly like the Publican? And, when God gives us what He wants to give us, are we like the ten lepers? The nine went on and never came back to say anything to God, to thank Him. Are we like the one who comes back and thanks God?

We must also be grateful for the gifts that God has given us. We should thank Him repeatedly, over and over and over again, for all the things that He has done for us. I feel that we must really want God in our life, to work with us, to be with us, to be a part of our life. He must become like a second nature to us, just as with the Jews, when they were in the desert. Everything that they saw, everything that happened, they attributed to God.

We Must Want God

I believe we must also do this. We must not blame God for anything, but we must give Him His rightful due. We must want to have Him in our lives. Many say they want to have Him, but they really don't mean it. I think that we must be like a patient in the hospital, with an oxygen tent over him. If they were to remove it, we could not get any air. We want to get that air, and we want the oxygen tent back, so we can breathe freely. *If* we desire God in that same way, *then* I think we truly want God and He *will* be a part of our life.

Be Willing To Change

Many people in the world wish to be without God, because they don't want to give themselves to God. They might have to change. Every time we come closer to God, we have to change. We *must* be willing to change. We must be willing to give up our *selves*. We must be willing to die to ourselves. We must be willing to carry

the Cross. We must be willing to suffer, and we must be very happy
to accept suffering in our lives. That's all a part of being in union
with God. We cannot separate that from our lives. It shows that we
are true followers of God. There *must* be real suffering in our lives.

Follow Christ — Be Christ-like

We have to have a great, generous spirit. It demands great generosity to follow in the footsteps of Christ, to be His true follower.
And, when we are His followers, we are different. We stand out.
We are like something I noticed, when I was a young boy. I once
visited the blacksmith shop. He was heating the horseshoes in the
furnaces, and, when he kept them in the fire, they first looked cold,
black and dreary. After being in the fire awhile, you saw that it
became one with the fire. It became red hot. When it is left still
longer, the horseshoe grows white hot. That is what has to happen
to us!

If we are close to God, we will gradually be transformed and
we will become like that horseshoe. We will become red hot. In
other words, we will become identified with God. Then, if we stay
with God longer and longer, He transforms us and He gives more
of Himself to us, so that we stand out in society. We are then like
the white hot iron. This is giving the witness of God to mankind.
We are no longer, but Christ lives in us and people will witness
Christ in us, they can see Christ in us.

This is what has to happen to us. We must be different, we
must stand out. It is important to accept Christ, because He said,
"You cannot serve two masters. You will either accept one and
reject the other, love the one or hate the other." There can be no in-
between. We cannot be just lukewarm. Christ said He wanted us
either hot or cold.

He said for the lukewarm, "I vomit you from my mouth," and
that is exactly what He meant, when He spoke to the Pharisees. He
said they did all these *things* of religion, all these religious practices, rules and regulations, but they did not have the *spirit* of religion. They did not give themselves wholeheartedly to God, and
they were not willing to be transformed and to do God's Will.

Are We Truly Christian?

So, we may not be like the Pharisees. We should be on the side of God. Many will ask, "What is the difference between good, dedicated people, whether it be to God or to any other cause? The communists are dedicated, too, and so, what is the difference?" The difference is that we are willing to share what we know, what we have, to help others to understand, to preach the message of Christ, to *live* the message of Christ.

We develop this boldness of proclaiming God before mankind by leading a deep prayer life. It is not enough just to pray by ourselves. We must be willing to go out of ourselves and give of ourselves. In this way, "They will know we are Christians by our love." They will be able to see that we are convinced of what we believe, and that we are on the side of God. This is the uppermost thing in our minds, and in our hearts, and in our lives. We *live* the Christian message.

Our Greatest Dignity

The greatest dignity that we have is to be able to stand before God and talk to Him, to address Him in prayer, and call Him our Father. The greatest thing that we do is to show Christ that we love Him and that we accept His love, want to *share* His love with others. People will see only Christ in us then.

Be Transformed

Why is it that, in the early Church, the pagan people in foreign countries, on seeing the Apostles and hearing them preach, were transformed? They had not seen or heard Christ, but they saw the Apostles and the Apostles were witnessing Christ. We must also do this. This is our life. This should be what our prayer brings us to, to be that transformed person, to give ourselves totally to Almighty God, to be used when He wishes, where He wishes, as long as He wishes — for *His* honor and glory.

Power Of Prayer

Perhaps some people relinquish their prayer life because they do not experience the power of prayer. I do feel that we must experience this, and we must realize that the prayer of a good man is powerful and effective. When we are truly near to God, our prayer will be answered, and we will experience the power of prayer. We must give God the chance to work in our lives and hearts. We must surrender our hearts to God, completely, so that we will understand what God wants of us. Some will answer, "God cannot change, therefore our prayer life will not change God in any way." Well, that is true, but Jesus Christ *said* that we should ask, He *told* us to pray. If we do not ask, we will not receive. There are many things that we would not receive, if we did not ask.

He told us to ask, and He said to seek and we will find God. He said to knock and it will be opened to us. This is what we believe. We believe the words of Jesus Christ, *literally*. When we put that belief into our own lives, then we will see that our prayers are answered.

Believe You Will Receive — And Be Grateful

When we pray, we must take it for granted that our prayer is going to be answered and thank Him, before ever it is answered. I remember reading the book *The Cross And The Switchblade* by David Wilkerson, and he had to have a payment for a house. They needed a certain amount of money and they did not have it. They had a couple of weeks to obtain it, so he went to the Chapel and said, "Let's thank God for the gift that we have received." They thought that they had received the check and were all happy and rejoicing. After they had prayed and thanked God, they went out of the Chapel and said, "Where is the check?" And he said, "We do not have it, but God is sending it."

On the last day, they received a check in the amount that they had prayed for. We must also pray and thank God for the gifts that He has given and the gifts that He will give and believe that He is going to give them. If it is for His honor and glory, then He is going to give what we ask.

I know this to be true because of having observed the Sisters of Mary, who are Lutheran Sisters, living in Scottsdale, Arizona, right outside of Phoenix. I visited them at one time. They take the Gospel literally, and they pray to the Father for everything that they need, and they only get what they need. They ask and they believe that they are going to receive. Then they keep on praying, and asking the Father. They thank God for sending what they ask for, even before they get it. They continually thank Him for hearing their prayers. If sometimes they do not have their prayers heard, they say, "Something is wrong, someone must have sinned."

Confessed Sins

Then they go out and they confess their sins to one another. This brings to mind another thing that we must realize. We must pray with an upright heart, with a pure intention, and a *good conscience*. In other words, there should be no sin in our life. We should have asked forgiveness from God, because when we pray, we ask God to forgive us our sins as we forgive. Therefore, if we have anything against anyone, if we have enemies, if we think that someone does not like us, we should ask for forgiveness and forgive them with all our heart and we should pray for them.

This is purifying and it also gives our prayers a very great power, and we will receive what we ask. We will be given what we ask only insofar as we forgive. This is part of the Our Father. In conjunction with this it would be well for us to go to Confession and have our sins forgiven.

Confession Beneficial

Many think that we should not be going to Confession so much any more. I think they are making a drastic mistake. Confession is a very beautiful gift. It is the first gift that Jesus Christ gave to us after His Resurrection. We should use it and we should use it often. I remember my own First Confession. I was a very young boy at the time. I remember the joy of having my sins confessed and forgiven. And I understood. I understood completely what it was all about at that moment, and every time I went to Confession after that, it was not just a routine, but it was a joy and had great meaning to me. We went often to Confession as a family. I think it would be a disastrous thing for young people not to be given the opportunity to go to Confession and have this experience of peace, joy, and happiness with them.

You know, to have sorrow for our sins, does not mean that we must be sad, dejected, depressed, or filled with anxiety. Sorrow for our sins means that we promise God not to commit them again, and then we feel the joy and peace and happiness of going to Confession and receiving reconciliation with God. We know that we are a friend of God, that we are His son or His daughter, and we have a deep closeness to Him.

We know that when we did something wrong as a little person, we felt much better when we were forgiven and told our parents, brothers, sisters, or friends that we were sorry. We were forgiven and we felt much happiness, and oftentimes our friendships were deepened because of this admittance that we were wrong and needed forgiveness and to apologize.

It is the same with God, and the same effect exists in our spiritual life. When our spiritual life is free from sin, then our prayer becomes more powerful. There is nothing so debilitating to one's prayer life as unconfessed sin. We should be willing to go to Confession and be at peace with God, to be reconciled with Him and experience this joy in our spiritual living.

Repent

In the Gospel, we see that St. John the Baptist, Jesus Christ, all the prophets, the Apostles, preached that people should repent and believe the Good News and turn to God. When they repent, they radically turn toward God. They turn away from sin and fulfill the Commandments of God, and love God and serve others in their spiritual lives.

Sin And Its Social Implications

Another point, in regard to sin, is social implication. Everyone in the world is affected by one person's sin. One sin contributes to the suffering of the whole world so that, when we have our sins forgiven, we are really apologizing to other people also. I feel that priests are doing humanity a tremendous good by forgiving sin in Confession. We are working for justice and peace, in this forgiveness. We're bringing Christ's salvation to that soul, and that soul does an act of social justice by confessing its sins.

Sin brings evil, suffering, greed, passions, and turmoil into the world. When we go to Confession and have our sins forgiven, that brings peace to the world, greater benefits to the world. This is something that is very frequently overlooked. We must really try to strive to lead the true Christian life by conquering sin.

Fight Cause Of Evil — Sin

We see many evils in our world. We see abortion, pornography, improper sex education. We must fight the cause, which is sin, greed, and passion. We should go to the very heart of the matter. I feel that, by hearing Confessions, we are doing a very great service to the whole world so that we begin to rid the world of its problems.

The greatest argument for frequent Confession is that it is an effective way to bring God's love into the world, the peace of God into the world. It will not be the peace for which the world is looking, but God's peace, God's love.

The founder of the Methodist Church, John Wesley, made this statement. He said, "Give me one hundred men who desire nothing but God and hate nothing but sin, and I will shake the gates of Hell and plant the Kingdom of God on earth." Well, we have to do the same, and it has to begin with each one of us. We have to stand up and be counted. We have to be on the side of God. If we really love God and hate sin, we will transform the world. This is what the world needs today. It needs witnesses of Christ, true Christians.

Fasting

There is another form of prayer that is very important. We remember in the Gospel how Our Lord sent the Apostles and disciples out to different towns. He gave them the power to cure people, the power to work miracles, and told them to preach the Good News. When they came back, they were overjoyed and one of them said, "Even the evil spirits were subjected to us." He said that they should not rejoice in the fact that they were performing miracles, and that the devil was subject to them, but rather that their names were written in Heaven.

Other disciples came back and said that they could not drive out the evil spirit. They asked why, and Our Lord said, "This type of spirit is driven out only by prayer and fasting." I am convinced that today the devil's power is very strong. He does exist. Hell does exist. I believe this, and I believe that the power of the devil can still only be driven out by prayer and fasting.

Fasting — An Intense Form Of Prayer

Fasting is an intense form of prayer. It is the whole body crying out in prayer, to Almighty God. When we do not eat or drink for a number of hours, or a day, or longer, it becomes a very effective prayer. It makes one strong in the time of temptation. We will be tempted in the same way in which Christ was tempted in the desert.

Forms Of Temptation

We know that the devil came and said that he could change the stones into loaves of bread. He was appealing to the passions of Our Lord. Our Lord was hungry and thirsty, after forty days of fasting, without eating or drinking, and so He was tempted by the devil. But Our Lord did not fall for that temptation. He overcame it, saying, "You should not tempt your Lord." And then the devil took Him up to a pinnacle and said He should hurl Himself down, in other words, do something spectacular. He said, "You will be acclaimed by all people because You will not have hurt Yourself. The Angels will save You."

He tempts us in the same way. He wants us to do things in a glamorous, flashing, glorious way. That is not God's way. God works slowly, methodically, but surely. God's Kingdom is spread in this manner. We must do things the way God wants to do them, not the way man wants to do them. And so, we put ourselves completely in the Hands of God, to do as He wishes. We should not fall for that form of temptation.

If we fast and pray, and we are serious about it, we will *not* fall for that. We will not have the urge to have power, to have a good name, honor and prestige. This is the temptation, mainly, of middle-aged people.

The last temptation was the temptation to possess the whole world. He took Him and showed Him all the kingdoms of the world. He said, "All of these things will be Yours, if You fall down and worship me." He tempts us in the same way. He wants us to have security, to strive for money and power. That is why we have the craze today for material possessions.

The power of the devil is very strong today. We must say with Christ, "Get behind me, Satan, you may not tempt the Lord, your God. You may not tempt God's creatures. Go back to Hell where you belong."

By fasting, we gain power over the devil and over temptation. It becomes much easier to conquer temptation. We should not fear temptation. We should not despise it. It is a necessary part of our spiritual living. It shows what we are made of, and God always gives us sufficient graces and help to overcome every temptation that comes into our lives.

We should put ourselves completely in God's Hands, and ask Him to help us in the time of temptation. Fasting definitely gives us power and strength in time of need, in time of temptation. The main reason we should fast is to give honor and glory to God, and to develop a deeper union with God, so that we are willing to do the Will of God in all things. And I think that, through fasting, this will really develop, because it brings a great interior light to our intellect and helps us to understand better the ways of God. It helps us to discern the Spirit.

When we are fasting, we should not be like the hypocrites, as Christ tells us. We should not go around looking gloomy, sad, and with long faces. He said, "Wash your face, be filled with joy and happiness, so that no one even knows that you are fasting." We can give up a meal now and then. That doesn't mean just giving up a dessert or something that we might like. Perhaps we can even fast completely, without any food, for one, two, or three days. But we should do this only with the consent of our spiritual director, because sometimes the devil will even want us to do this to hurt ourselves, to hurt our health, or our spirit. We might also become proud by doing it, so, if we place ourselves under the obedience of a spiritual director, it will destroy the force of the devil. We will know then that this is really from God.

When we are fasting, if there is any ill effect to our physical well-being, then it is not from God, and we should stop immediately. But, if we do fast for one, two, or three days, abstaining totally from eating, then we should drink liquids or at least water, to give us strength. Fasting is not just a means of practicing asceticism. Asceticism does make one's person hard, but it should lead to a complete surrender of oneself to God.

Fasting should be done with great joy and with the spirit of the Resurrection of Our Lord, Jesus Christ. Happiness and peace should radiate from us, if we are fasting. I also think we can fast more than what we presently do. In the past, when we had the fasting during Lent, many people felt that they could not do this, that they did not have the strength, that they were too sickly, or other such reasons. I think they were tricked by the devil. We have to do fasting. Christ said, "Unless you do penance and fasting, you shall all likewise perish." We should do penance.

We do it to come closer to God, to give ourselves completely to God. It will help us to have a hunger for God that will develop within us. But again, I stress, we must have the permission of a spiritual director to go on an extended or harsh fast.

Many people go on weight-watcher diets which are sometimes much stricter than any fasting that the Church ever asks of people. If people can do this just to lose weight, why can't we do it for God? Why should people have spent hundreds of dollars to lose some pounds so as to have a more shapely figure? Why should they wish to be more pleasing in the eyes of men or women and then do nothing for the honor and glory of God? Their thinking is illogical!

There is another form of fast. It is a forty-day fast, just eating one meal a day, without any water or other liquid, without any food, except for that one meal. Naturally this has to be inspired by

God. We need the permission of a spiritual director. If God has really inspired this and is asking us to do this, we will not be physically harmed by it. We will actually feel a strength in our body. We will feel a greater strength in our souls. This is an intensive form of prayer and we should use it, at times, for the honor and glory of God, and for the good of our souls and for our own selves.

World Needs Contemplative Souls

Prayer and fasting will help us to develop a deeper spiritual life. It is very dangerous to have an undeveloped spirit in a developed mind and body. This is quite revealing. We may not repress our spirituality any longer. I feel that we must learn to rediscover the spirit of contemplation. If we do not, we will see the problems of sex and crime grow still worse.

We know there are people in our world today who are contemplative souls, and that more and more lay people are being called to this state of contemplation, leading a life of contemplative prayer, but we cannot teach you how to pray in a contemplative manner. God is the One Who has to teach that.

When we speak of the contemplative life, we are actually speaking of two phases of contemplation. First we must dispose ourselves by being faithful to the practice of meditation. If we are truly faithful to our meditative prayer life, it should be only a very little while before we are elevated to the state of acquired contemplation. In this stage, we are able to communicate with God on a heart to heart basis, without the need for the expression of words.

The second phase of the contemplative life is infused contemplation. This is, in reality, the mystical state. In the mystical state, it is God Who takes over and prays within us. This mystical state is a deeper understanding of God in our lives, a deeper *union* with God. It seems that there is a light that comes to us after many trials and tribulations. It makes us see clearly that God is in our life, that He is with us and in us always, and that we are with Him and in Him always.

I do not agree with Thomas Merton that only a few are called to the contemplative life. I feel that everyone is called to a contemplative prayer life, that is, to the highest of contemplations, the mystical state. It is most unfortunate that so many in our day do not even know about the mystical state. They read lives of the saints and think it is impossible for them ever to attain such holiness, and so they don't even try. They shrug and say, "Such things are all right for him. After all, he's a saint." Nobody was ever born a saint! Our Blessed Mother was born without sin, yes. Jesus Christ was born without sin. But they both had temptations and resisted them, and did not sin.

We Are Sinners

We are born sinners and we remain sinners. We continually strive to overcome sin in our lives. The more we are successful, the deeper our love and our union with God becomes. We reach a point when we enter a deep, mystical union with God, where intentional sin no longer has a part in our lives. In other words, we would rather die than commit a mortal sin, and we strive never to willfully live in venial sin. If we willfully commit venial sin, we cannot be in the mystical state, and we are not even nearing the contemplative state. We are only struggling still in our spiritual development.

I am speaking here of willful venial sin. There will always be sins in our lives, imperfections, faults, and failings. But, the closer we come to God, the less we will fall into sin. Still, we must always remember that we are what we are because of the Grace of God, no more and no less, because if we forget that, we can become proud and fall easily into sin. We are always capable of sinning, no matter what plane we may reach in the spiritual life. Nor should we strive constantly to figure out where we are in the spiritual life. This is only foolish waste of time and effort.

Give Yourself To God

A soul surrendered completely and totally to God forgets the various divisions in the spiritual life. It's not really important to know where we are on the scale of sanctity. It is of far greater importance to be concerned with the act of constantly giving ourselves to God.

When we reach the mystical state, we realize that there is more to spirituality than just preaching or talking about it. We must truly enter into the saving act of Jesus Christ Himself, that is, we must die to ourselves. We must also be crucified, and that is what we are called to do. It takes power to lay down our lives. It requires a great and generous spirit to be willing to be killed out of love for God, yet this invitation of love is issued to every Christian, to every person in all the world — and each and every one of us should accept it!

When James and John wished for a place of preference, one on His right and one on His left, He said, "Can you drink the cup that I am able to drink, that I am about to drink?" They answered, "We can." He meant the Crucifixion, the sufferings they would have to endure, if they followed Him. We must be also willing to drink of this cup. This should not cause gloom or sadness in our lives, as though we had no reason for joy.

To be crucified is to anticipate the Resurrection. We become participators in the Crucifixion and Resurrection through the events in our own lives. As we accept our own personal trials, we are also accepting the Cross. And, as we experience the joy of this acceptance and encounter Christ more and more deeply in our lives, we experience the Resurrection, because we will know the peace of being able to offer this to God, for His honor and glory.

We enter into the saving mission of Christ, when we become a reconciler with Christ. He achieved this by His death on the Cross, by shedding His Blood. He brought peace to the world and we can also enter into this. We, too, can contribute to the peace of the world and the salvation of the world, if we will only learn how to pray with Him and in Him.

Mahatma Ghandi said that prayer was his energy and his strength. He said, "I can live without food, but I cannot live without prayer. With the kind of life that I am leading, I would go mad without prayer." If we could say the same thing, we would understand the necessity of prayer.

We hear so much today about being "human." Well, no man is human until he has found God, and we only find God when we devote ourselves to a life of prayer and a life of contemplation. It is imperative to develop this contemplative spirit, and to live it. We are often like St. Paul. We have a consuming love for Christ, and to be dissolved and to be with Christ, yet on the other hand, we have a great love for our fellow man. We wish to be among him, to help him, to inspire him, to encourage him — to bring *Christ* to him.

This creates a tension in our lives. There is a constant pull between one form of prayer life and another, our way of acting, because our actions are also a form of prayer, when they are performed for God. This is good and from it will come many blessings to our Apostolate. We will be many times like the Cure of Ars. We will have a desire to do one thing and be in a situation that will require us to do another. He had a strong desire to become a Trappist, yet he had to stay in Ars and be a pastor, a confessor, and a preacher, to give witness. This same thing was true of the Little Flower. She was a contemplative, yet had a very great desire to be a missionary, to go out into the active life. Her desire could not be fulfilled. God gives us such desires to make our Apostolate more fruitful and to keep us close to Him.

Speaking In Silence

As our prayer life develops, the contemplative and, later on, the mystical state, we realize that we must spend time in silence with God, not speaking at all. Many feel that they have to keep on speaking, that their minds must be working, but it is in the time of silence that we can listen to God, and God will speak to us.

He speaks to us in many different ways. Again I point out the importance of seeking to discern the Spirit, so as to see whether the impulse or inspirations that come to us are from God or the devil. The devil is very clever. He can mix truth with his error, and the truth will make it seem palatable and believable. We must sift and judge everything, realizing that not everything comes from God.

False Prophets

This gives me an opportunity to speak about false prophets. We must be most careful of them in our day. There are many false prophets in our world, many who claim to have visions and to work miracles. People are constantly flocking to them. I personally do not believe that they should be doing this. I feel that, if *God* is giving these things to various people, well and good, but we have something far better in our Faith. We have our Mass and the Sacraments. We have the Church and, therefore, we don't really need these things.

I do believe that God gives the power to cure, to prophesy, to speak in tongues, to whomever He will, but it is always for the good of *another.* We have to test any such thing, and once the Spirit is discerned, we will know whether to accept or reject it.

Live The Beatitudes

As our spiritual life advances, we will also realize that it's not enough just to keep the Ten Commandments as people in the world are striving to do. We have realized that Jesus is really calling us to live the Sermon on the Mount. This is new teaching. In the Old Testament, nothing was said about the Sermon on the Mount. It was the Ten Commandments. This was a strange teaching to the people's ears, on the part of Christ. Many people, listening to it, pagans particularly, will say that it is very beautiful, but they don't really live it. Some will try to live it on a natural level, but even believers and especially priests will say it is very difficult to live.

It is not actually difficult to live. Everyone has been called to live in this way, so we should study the passage of Scripture, really delve into the deep meaning and learn just what it is that Christ is asking of us. To be poor in spirit, for example, means that we may not put our trust in wealth. That doesn't mean that we cannot have wealth. It means that we must use it all for the honor and glory of God. I feel that every person should give at least ten percent of his income to charity. It can be any type of charity that he may choose, but it should be given to charity — share with others!

The Needy People Of The World

There are many people who live in poverty and do not have the necessary means for proper nourishment, clothing, or shelter. Two-thirds of the people in the world of today are deprived of the Good News of the message of Christ. They are the ones who are *really* poor, much more so than those who hunger and thirst for this world's food.

It is like the person who saw another person suffering terribly in a hospital with cancer, tubes all connected, under an oxygen tent, and in terrible pain. He said, "I am very sorry for you, that you suffer so much." She answered, "My condition is not as bad as yours. For thirty-five years you have not been with God, have not given God honor and glory. You have been away from Him." That is exactly the way the world is today. So many are away from God. Many do not even know about God. This is a terrible crisis, a terrible suffering. The spiritual suffering in the world is by far greater than the physical.

We should try continually to overcome this spiritual poverty, this spiritual suffering and bankruptcy, this spiritual vacuum that exists in the lives of men. And we can only do this by our prayers, our suffering, our sacrifices, our willingness to follow Christ, our willingness to bring Christ to them.

It is not enough just to feed them. Many say that you have to feed them first and then bring the message of Christ. I don't think so. I think we have to bring them the message of Christ. This is much more important. Many say, "They won't accept the Gospel. They are hungry." I don't believe that. We have many people who are suffering and who hunger, but they are even more hungry for God. When you talk about God to them, they are much more peaceful and happy. We should not deprive them of this tremendous benefit.

CHAPTER 26

PLANNING A MARIAN FAITH PILGRIMAGE

Before bringing this book to a close, I would like to share my experiences while I was on my most recent pilgrimage. Toward the end of 1973, I had the desire to make a Marian Faith Pilgrimage, so I contacted the Herold Tours, in Ontario, Canada, and asked them to make arrangements for this pilgrimage. I had no way of knowing that it would be far harder than I had anticipated. I tried to publicize this pilgrimage in our magazine, but, in the process of publication, the first paragraph was cut out so that people weren't informed in the article as to where the pilgrimage was going.

We therefore had to make most of our contact with people by word of mouth. It looked for quite awhile as though the trip would simply never get off the ground. Even up until the last month, we still had many problems and it looked as if our plans would never materialize. Nevertheless, we were finally able to get sufficient numbers of people to participate, and we were fortunate enough to be able to take part in this pilgrimage.

We Are On Our Way

We left Los Angeles on August 1, 1974, and flew to Chicago, where we met other people who were to travel with us. My Mother was waiting there to see me. I was really surprised because I didn't think she could make such a trip, since she had recently had surgery and been quite ill. Her recuperation had been long and difficult, and I considered it rather imprudent for her to travel from Milwaukee to Chicago under those conditions. But she suffered no ill effects from doing so except for catching a rather serious cold. This did give me some cause for concern.

Blessing A Sick Woman

We left Chicago and continued on to Montreal, where we met more people who were going on the tour. When I arrived, I immediately saw a woman in a wheelchair and I began to think, "This is going to be a real burden to everyone, if she remains in that wheelchair." So I walked up to her, and I blessed her with the relic of the True Cross, and told her to get out of the wheelchair, that she would not need it any more. She did so and, throughout the trip, she never needed the wheelchair again. I don't know that she was cured permanently, but she did receive the Grace to be able to participate in the pilgrimage without serious difficulty.

I did not know, when we boarded the plane in Montreal and took off for Paris, that there had been a question concerning our reservations from Paris to Lisbon. The Herolds were worried about this, and prayed constantly on the way that everything would work out all right. When we got into Paris, the names came through on the computers, and things worked out quite smoothly. The problem over which we had worried didn't occur, and we got on the plane and continued on our way to Lisbon.

Our Words Can Change People

We arrived in Lisbon in the early evening, when the daylight was just beginning to fade away. We went through customs, and then on to the bus that was going to take us to Fatima. When we got on the bus, a young man came forward and greeted me, saying that he was very happy to see me again. This startled and amazed me, as I did not see how anyone there could know me. Later on, I found out how it was that he came to know me.

This young man was our guide on the tour through Fatima. As the bus began to move, he began the tour by telling us a story with which he said he always begins his tours. He said that about ten years ago, he had attended a conference given by myself, in West Covina, California. He was so impressed with this talk that he decided to take his wife and his children and travel to Portugal to live.

The part of the talk that had impressed him so much was my experience in Holland, where the Lord told me that, in order to help the whole world, I must become a saint. He decided that the best place to become a saint would be in the quiet surroundings of Fatima and so he moved, with his whole family to live there. Since that time there are six more children, making a total of nine children in his family. He teaches in a high school. During the summer months, he works as a guide on tours through Fatima, and various other places throughout Portugal. He is quite learned in physics, electronics, chemistry, and, in fact, all aspects of science. He could have his choice among many excellent jobs in the United States or anywhere else in the world, if he chose to do so. But he chooses instead to live and carry out his apostolate and work of trying to sanctify himself and his family by helping the people of Portugal.

Communists Take Over Portugal?

In the course of the trip, he told us that, on April 25, a revolution had taken place in Portugal. According to him, the Communists took over the government at that time. Immediately after the *coup* (a bloodless revolution), Communist literature began to appear in all the stores throughout Portugal, and it is now being infiltrated into the schools. Also, pornography of all types appeared overnight across the country. He was very concerned for the future of Portugal. For himself, he said he did not care, not for his own life, or the lives of his wife and the children. They were all prepared to be martyrs for the Faith if it should become necessary. They would gladly accept such a martyrdom. I greatly admire his courage, dedication, beautiful insight, and deep spirituality.

Apostolate Spreads To Europe

Naturally, they have the message of Fatima, and they have many other programs, but it seems that various priests are push-

ing different ideas in such a way that there is no unity or unifor-
mity of purpose behind one single program. After I had explained
to him about the Apostolate, he said that he felt that this was exactly what they were looking for. He said he would do everything
possible to have my books translated, to have my conferences put
into Portuguese, and to have this work spread throughout Portugal. A hundred men at the meeting he had mentioned had promised to each give $200 monthly, which means $20,000 a month,
to foster a program which would develop the spirituality of Portugal. I am praying that eventually all this will become a reality.
At this time, however, it is impossible for anything really worthwhile to be done with regard to printing books, tapes, etc., because the Communists will no longer allow anything religious to
be printed within the country.

It seems that God was truly with us and indicating His desire
that this will one day be a reality. Three different members of the
Apostolate, from California, had each brought a different one of
my three books. I was therefore able to give him the three books,
so that they would not later have to be smuggled into the country.
Someday, when they are able to be translated and printed, they will
hopefully be able to help Portugal in many ways. They also have
plans for putting these books into French and, later on, into Spanish, so as to get them across the whole world. This is a very wonderful thing for which to pray for the Apostolate. I gave this young
man complete permission to do anything that he wishes with the
Apostolate, the books, and the cassettes. The message of God is
the important issue. We must be willing to share our ideas and our
work with everyone. I hope that much good will be brought to
every place where this work is taken.

Arrival At Fatima

We continued on to our destination in Fatima, arriving close to
midnight. We were very pleased and grateful that the Blue Army
members, with whom we were going to stay, had remained and kept
our supper ready for us. We ate our dinner that night at about twelve
o'clock. Then we went to bed and slept for the rest of the night.

Francesco — A Love Of God

The next day, we had Mass at Francesco's Altar. He was a tremendous little boy, very dedicated. He prayed much, often as many as nine Rosaries a day, because Our Blessed Mother said he had to pray many Rosaries before he could go to Heaven. He died shortly after the apparitions, in 1917. He prayed very hard, and his "many Rosaries" were said in a very short time. His heart was so completely with God that he felt that he did not need to go to school. There was no purpose to it because he would soon die. He was other-world minded, and God took him home very quickly. One cannot help but be impressed with this young man, his dedication to God, and the fulfillment of the message of Fatima in his own life.

Jacinta — A Brave Sufferer

And then there was his little sister, Jacinta. I said Mass at her Altar on the last day. Again we see a little person with a beautiful soul. I am deeply moved at the life that she lived. She lived a life of suffering, making reparation for the sins of men. She predicted the terrible sufferings that would come upon Lisbon and the whole world, that the Holy Father would have to suffer much, and that the immoral fashions would be introduced into the world. She stated that, because of sins of the flesh, many people would go to Hell. She did much penance for the sins of the world. She died alone, as the Blessed Mother had told her she would. This little soul also moves us very deeply, when we read about her life.

The Portuguese people that we met really loved Jacinta. We could see this when we handed out the little holy cards on Jacinta that had been given to us. They kissed her picture, and really showed appreciation. I am sure that she has a great apostolate ahead of her, even if she is dead. She continues to carry out her work from Heaven.

Saying The Rosary And Making The Way Of The Cross

In the afternoon, we had the privilege of making the Stations of the Cross. Between each Station, we had a Mystery of the Rosary, with meditation on both the Mystery and the Station. In that manner, we said the fifteen-decade Rosary. It took us almost two hours to perform this religious service. I think everyone benefited from it. I gave the meditations and, at the twelfth Station, I blessed each person with the relic of the True Cross. Then we continued to the end of the Stations.

The Children's Home

After that we visited Lucy's home, which is quite tumbled down. By modern standards it would be considered unlivable, and yet they had nine children, and the whole family had to live in that tiny little home. We also went to where Jacinta and Francesco lived. I hadn't known this fact before, but the Mother, after the death of her first husband, remarried. When that happened in her day, the people involved were socially ostracized. The town people would have nothing to do with them and the children of that family were also treated as outcasts. People would just not have any part of them. Their lives, therefore, became quite lonely and filled with suffering. The two families, Lucy's and the DeSarto family, were quite close, since they were relatives. They were very good friends, even though the other people of the town were so hostile toward them. The DeSarto home was also quite small. We saw the place where Francesco died, and then later where Jacinta had to be while she was ill, before she went to Lisbon to suffer and to die. It is impressive to see the rustic life that they lived, the privations that they had to endure, the very primitive manner of living. God always seems to choose people in that category to entrust with His messages.

A Surprise Birthday Party

We went back to the Blue Army Headquarters to refresh ourselves, and relax a little bit before going out for dinner that night. I did not know this, but a birthday party had been arranged for me. When we went to a castle, way up in the hills of Ourem, I thought it was simply to have our dinner. It was a very picturesque sight that met us, as we approached this huge castle way up on top of the hill. The bus could not get to the top. It could only go part way, and then a van had to come down and take us the rest of the way.

When we had gone as far as we could go, a white horse and rider came charging down the hill. Trumpets blared from the castle, and still I hadn't realized what this was all about. I thought that this was the way all the guests at the restaurant were greeted. Later on, all the people wanted a picture of me standing by the horse. After all the pictures were taken, we finally got up to the restaurant area in the castle, and were greeted with a small liqueur, by the people who owned the restaurant.

That is when I found out that this was my birthday party! We began to have our meal and, during the course of the meal, we were entertained with a re-enactment of the six phases of the Portuguese claim for independence, and the way in which it was obtained. It was strictly historical, and it was on this very spot where all these things took place.

The restaurant was set up in the form of King Arthur's round table. I was placed as king, and another person as queen. Marian Anheuser sat next to me, and then all the others sat around the table. It was quite an honor to have this birthday party there. The people were wonderful, and there were six or seven courses to the meal. It lasted from eight o'clock until about one, by the time we had singing and the different speeches and stories told to us by several people, about how they joined the Apostolate. It was a very exciting, memorable occasion, one that I will never forget as long as I live. That was the best birthday party I've ever had!

Mass At The Apparition Altar

We went back to Fatima afterwards and I didn't sleep the rest of the night. The next morning we had Mass at the Shrine of the Apparitions. I said Mass, and I noticed that the Bishop had said Mass before me, and then knelt on a *prie-dieu* behind us. I learned that he attends every Mass there on Sunday. After the Masses are over, he spends the rest of his day praying the Rosary for the good of the Portuguese people, and for peace in the world. I could not help but be impressed by this, to see this wonderful prayerful man who realizes the crisis of the world and who is trying to do something about it in his own personal way.

We Go To Coimbra

From there we went to Coimbra, where Sister Lucy lives. We could not see her, but we did hear the nuns singing Office. After it was over, I asked permission to write a message to Sister Lucy. I wrote the message and in it I told her that I wanted to offer the work of the Apostolate as the fulfillment of the message of Fatima, because I truly believe that this is exactly what it is. I learned that Sister Lucy had an apparition from the Sacred Heart in 1925 and He told her that it was His desire that the reign of the Immaculate Heart be brought about, and that, through this reign, peace would be given to the world, and He would then reign as Christ the King. So, I'm hoping that this work is definitely the fulfillment of the message of Fatima. Things would seem to point in that direction.

Heavenly Messages?

When we finished there, the young man whom I mentioned earlier said that he had something to tell me. He told me that he felt that I ought never to build a large Center for the Apostolate. He said that he felt that it is all right to have a center, but it should be one from which I am free to travel in any direction, at any time, to speak to priests, brothers, sisters, or anybody else who wishes to hear me, so that I will always have the freedom to carry on the work of God. He said I must never tie myself down or limit myself to just one place. He said, secondly, that I must not start a new Congregation of priests and brothers, that I am instead to work toward the reformation of my own Congregation. He next told me not to get involved with a certain person who might do serious harm to the Apostolate. This was quite a revelation to me. He could not possibly have known that I had an appointment with this very person for the following week after my return to the United States, nor could he have had any previous knowledge of any of my ideas regarding a Center or my Congregation. I thanked him for his messages, thinking that now it would become a matter of discernment in trying to learn what God wanted with regard to the things this young man had said.

Strangely enough, one of his predictions did come true, some weeks later. On October first, I received a letter from the man with whom I had the appointment after my return to the United States. The first thing this man wished to do was to rewrite my books on the Apostolate. He wanted to change many of the most important ideas concerning the Apostolate, a desire which would most certainly have spelled disaster for the Apostolate. It now remains to be seen whether other things that he said to me will prove to be correct.

The Last Morning At Fatima

At Fatima, the next morning, I said Mass at Jacinta's Altar, and then boarded the plane for Rome. We arrived in Rome quite late in the evening, and there had been a mistake made. We had been flown to the National landing place, rather than the International. We got off the plane, and wanted to board the bus, but some people came up to us and said, "No, you may not do that. You must carry your luggage across the runway and go through the National terminal."

Arrival In Rome

We then had to carry all our luggage clear across the airport area and into the area where the passengers come when they enter the airport. Later the bus came and picked us up, but for a little while, it was a touchy situation. The only thing that really saved the day was the fact that we didn't have to go through customs. People were tired and upset, some were beginning to complain, and then Mark Greer sat down and played and sang some songs. Immediately everybody stopped being unhappy and started singing the song to the Sacred Heart along with Mark. Happiness returned and criticism stopped.

Finally the bus was loaded and we were taken to the place that we wanted to be for the night, at the south side of Rome. It's a funny thing about not having to go through customs. One lady was carrying two thousand Rosaries that she wanted the Pope to bless, and that she wanted to distribute in her own town in Italy. She hadn't wanted to go through customs. She might have had to pay quite a bit of money, so she had prayed that this would happen, that we would not have to go through customs, and her prayer was certainly answered. It's something to think about, the way those Rosaries were looked after.

A Tour Through Rome

The next morning, we went through Rome, and we had a guide who was quite antagonistic toward the Church. Her speech betrayed her, time and time again. We didn't see very many places. She hurried us through the religious places very quickly, and left people dissatisfied. I was terribly disappointed with this, but the morning went quickly and, in the afternoon, we were free to do whatever we wanted. Many of the people did go back and see the different religious things and places that they wanted to see. I did not. I went instead to our Superior General House because I had to deliver some messages. It was wonderful to see the priests there, and be able to talk with them.

Seeing The Holy Father

Later we went back to our rooms and prepared for the next morning. The next morning we had the meeting with our Holy Father, a general audience. It happened that I called beforehand to see whether we would have an audience, and Monsignor told me that we did, and asked, "What can we do for you?" I asked, "What do you mean?" And he said, "I can get special tickets so that you can see the Pope closer." I gratefully accepted his offer, and he got us three tickets. I decided to give one to Father Kroll, who was on the trip with us. He is a very wonderful spiritual person, and he added greatly to the trip. I was quite pleased that he was with us. I gave the second ticket to the woman who carried all those Rosaries and, since I had seen the Pope twice, I decided that it would be nice to have my brother, Dr. James Zimmer, take my place. The third ticket went to him.

It was very nice for me to have my brother, his wife, and my two nieces on the trip with us, and once again to learn more about each person. It's always a wonderful experience to have your own with you. I was very happy that he got to see the Pope.

Our Holy Father came in and gave a beautiful talk that day, and spoke on the importance of Tradition, the Magisterium of the Church, and warned us that we must not abandon the old, but rather *use* it as a basis for the new. After the audience, I had stood outside. You really couldn't see him very close with all the people inside anyway. I had Mark Greer's record with me, and I wanted to give it to the Pope. As the Pope came down, he was very close to me, and I asked the Bishop, who was walking next to him, to take the record and give it to the Pope. He did so, and in this way, I got Mark's record to our Holy Father.

A Gifted Young Man — Mark Greer

Mark is a very gifted young person. He's only twenty-one years old, yet he has a great talent for music and he writes music based on Scripture. His music just comes from him. He can sit down and

Mark Greer

write a song and sing it and hear all the different orchestra parts to it in his head, but he knows only his own part, so we are deprived of the whole ambition of his music. And yet, the music is very, very beautiful. You can't help but admire the talent that God has given to him. I know that Mark will use his talent for God's honor and glory in bringing this message of God to the people. If you listen to the words, you cannot help but be moved. The words are full of meaning, deep meaning, and a great religious message is given. I hope that some day he will become a priest.

Another Prayer Answered

Mark was also hoping to have a second record made. Before we left on the trip, I told him, "I don't know whether we can do that. I don't have that much money to be putting it into a project like that right away. We'll wait and see, and, when we get to Assisi, maybe by that time we will know. Let's just pray for now that we will have an answer to our request by that time."

It so happened that we did go to Assisi one day, while we were in Rome, and we had lunch there before going to the various places we wanted to see. We went there to see the Churches and the places where St. Clare and St. Francis had lived. Over lunch a lady was talking to me about various things. She remarked that she was very impressed by Mark's record, and she asked me how much it would cost to have another record made. I told her that it would cost about $1,800 to make a record and she said, "I will pay for it." And so we are having the second record made, because God seems definitely to have indicated that this is what He wants.

Pope Paul VI

Getting back to our stay in Rome and seeing the Holy Father, he looked very good, very healthy and strong. I hope that he will continue to have a long life and good health, and especially that he will see the success of the Holy Year and the conclusion of the Holy Year.

Brother Gino At San Vittorino

After we saw the Pope, we went to San Vittorino, where Brother Gino lives. Brother Gino has the Stigmata of Christ in his hands and in his feet. He is a very tall person. His demeanor, in its kindliness and friendliness, is deeply moving and impressive. He's very willing to share with others. We said the Rosary there and then we had Mass, and said another Rosary while we waited for about a half hour for Brother Gino to come. When he came in, we were permitted to go up to him and kiss his hand. When we did this, some of us smelled a very strong perfume odor, and some did not. In order to prevent any misinterpretation of this, I explained to the people later that it is a gift that God gives people sometimes, allowing them to smell this "odor of sanctity." It doesn't make one person greater than anyone else. It is simply a gift that is given to strengthen one's faith. We should accept it as just this, and nothing more. Nor should we place any other emphasis on it.

Brother Gino took my Rosary and held it in his hands, and he also took my Crucifix, with the relic of the True Cross, and held it in his hands and kissed it. Then he gave them back to me, and promised to pray for the Apostolate and for the work that we are doing. Then he saw all the other people and gave them a message. It was a very fundamental, down to earth message — to go to Communion frequently, to Confession often, and to help others. This is the Gospel message and this is what he told. The reason he has received the Stigmata is to bring attention to Fatima, and to help to bring about the implementation of that message.

Assisi Again

We left him and went back to the hotel, and the next morning, we were on our way to Assisi. I described Assisi once before. Being there again brought back many memories. It is beautiful to be in Assisi. We didn't have time enough to see everything that we would like to have seen, but at least we were there.

After Assisi, we went back to Rome and, the next day, we flew to Lourdes on the Irish Airline, which was very nice. We got into Lourdes toward evening, and so we just relaxed for awhile, had dinner, and then went to join the Candlelight Procession. I found that quite interesting. It was beautiful and meaningful. This was the first time I had taken part in the Candlelight Procession.

Lourdes

I had said Mass earlier that day, at Lourdes, and, the next morning, I said Mass at the Apparition Altar. We spent all day visiting the shrine, took the bath, and prayed, and also saw the home where Bernadette lived as a young girl, and the mill where her Dad worked. They lost this home and were given one room in which to live, in a prison. Six people had to live in that room. Later, after the apparition, the Bishop gave them a new home. We saw this place as well. It was the first time that I had a chance to really see and appreciate Lourdes.

Revealing A Secret

After we left Lourdes, God chided me because I had been carrying the Blessed Sacrament, and had kept this fact to myself. No matter where you go, in the Marian Shrines, what comes through the most clearly is the message of the Blessed Sacrament and devotion to the Blessed Sacrament. In Fatima and in Lourdes, it's the center of the Marian devotion. Mary always leads you right to the Blessed Sacrament. Our Lord said to me that I had no right to keep it secret from the people on the tour, that I was carrying the Blessed Sacrament. I didn't tell them right away, but, when I did, I quickly realized why God had wanted them to know. From that moment on, they spent an hour every day in silence and adoration, and so we had forty people making adoration every day, for an hour. It was a wonderful thing to behold, and to realize that this was what God really wanted. I was a little sorry that I had not told them from the beginning. I had not intended to tell them at all until I was chided to do so.

Avignon

We left Lourdes by bus and went to Arles. That is only a seashore resort. We stayed there overnight to sleep and then went on to Avignon, where we saw the palaces and the place where the Popes were for seventy years, in France. It was rather a desolate place because all the things there are abandoned. It's just an empty, old ruin. It makes you really stop and think back through the history of the Church about the ways in which people both within and without have tried to destroy the Church and to interfere in Church matters. This is just one more instance of the way people can really mess things up.

Ars — Home Of St. John Vianney

From there we went on to Ars. I was very pleased to be in Ars. I have always wanted to go there. I had not known before that St. John Vianney's body is incorrupt and that only wax was put on his face. The rest of his body is just as it was. I had the privilege of saying Mass there. When I said Mass, I told the people that I did not have only one saint or a few of the saints as favorites, but that I told God about the saints what the Little Flower once said of a basket of toys when she was very young. When they brought a basket of toys to her, she was told to choose what she wanted from among them. She looked at them and said, "I choose them all," and she carried them away.

This is exactly the way I feel in regard to the saints. I take all of them and I accept all. They are all our brothers and sisters in Christ, and are very close to God, and therefore they should be in our lives, and so, "I choose them *all!*"

For St. John Vianney, I have a special love because of his deep devotion for God and the Blessed Sacrament, and his giving of himself to the people of God by hearing Confessions for many, many hours of the day. Fifty thousand people a year came to see him while he was living. Over the course of forty years, that's close to a million people, and he heard many of their Confessions, or I should say, *most* of their Confessions. He was a real man of God. He was considered to be stupid when he was young. He could not pass the tests in the seminary and yet God had designs for this man, and he was given the Wisdom of God, which surpasses the wisdom of men. God made him a model for all priests. If we could but have that wisdom, could have that love, dedication, and zeal that he had, what a tremendous world we would have! He is the patron of all Diocesan priests, but I am sure that we can also take him as our patron and emulate his life and try to follow in his footsteps, because he led a truly Christ-like life.

We saw the house that he lived in. We saw the bed that the devil had set fire to. This brings forcefully to mind the existence of the devil and of Hell, that he hated this man, but he could not destroy him, just as he can never destroy anyone else. We also noticed in the building a large underground Church, standing there under the edifices. For what reason, I really don't know. God must have a reason for this, but it seems strange to my way of thinking to have these things go on.

The next morning, we said Mass again at his Altar. Father Kroll said the Mass this time. This is the Diocesan priest I mentioned earlier. He gave a beautiful talk on the life of St. John Vianney.

Cluny — A Deserted Monastery

From there we went to Cluny. Cluny is nothing but an abandoned monastery. It was destroyed during the French Revolution. Again, seeing the destruction of people who hate God, who try to destroy God, is a thing that saddens me and makes me very thoughtful. How successful they were at that time and in that area! France has not recovered yet from the French Revolution, in regard to religion, religious practices, and faith. It is terribly unfortunate that this is what happened. This is quite forcefully brought to your mind when you view such things as this.

Paray-le-Monial — Receiving A Message

Next we went to Paray-le-Monial. When we got to Paray-le-Monial, we went into the Chapel and I explained about the apparitions, about the body of St. Margaret Mary, which is lying there, and the renovation of the Chapel that is to make it modern, different from what it was in the time of St. Margaret Mary. Yet the atmosphere is still there. It's a great thing to realize that, from the Chapel, came the message of the Sacred Heart, the devotion to the Sacred Heart, that spread so rapidly throughout the world. It's a sharp contrast today to see how very little devotion to the Sacred Heart is being practiced. Let us hope that one day this devotion will be re-enkindled, and brought back to the fore.

As always, at the shrine-convent, I went to see Mother Superior. As soon as I mentioned my name, she said, "Father, I have a message for you." And she went and got an envelope. In this envelope was a typewritten message. It stated that God was very pleased with the work that I was doing, that He was guiding me, and that my Mother was a saint and her prayers and sufferings are helping to spread the Apostolate, that the Blessed Trinity is watching over me, and that this was a message given by the Sacred Heart. I asked the Mother Superior to pray for my work and she said, "We have been, we are, and we will continue to pray for the Apostolate."

From there we went to see Blessed Claude de la Columbiere's body. It was, as before, a shock to me to see the way it is displayed, bone upon bone. The others also went around the town to visit and enjoy themselves.

Seeing St. Bernadette

The next day, we drove to Nevers, where St. Bernadette's body is. Never in all my life have I seen a more beautiful woman. To see her there, in death, with such a lovely smile on her face, is awesome. Her beauty is one of peace and serenity. It's as though she were sleeping and as if she were waiting for the Resurrection, the coming of Christ, at the end of the world.

Lisieux — A Place Of Grace

From there we continued our journey on to Lisieux, where I said Mass. It was here that the majority of the people on the tour, who had not previously done so, all but two, joined the Apostolate of Christian Renewal. What a joy it was for me to have this take place! Only a few years ago, I placed in the Little Flower's hands the charge of seeing to it that this work would be approved by my Superior, and would be successful, and now to receive the Grace of having all these people join the Apostolate in her home, Lisieux, was a source of much Grace, happiness, and gratitude to God.

St. Therese is the most appropriate saint to have been entrusted with the mission of praying for the success of the Apostolate. Her childlike trust in the goodness of God, her deep, sincere love for Him, these are the perfect image for the Apostolate to imitate. To be unnoticed for herself, yet to conquer the whole world with Love — these were her desires. To follow those desires, to renew her zeal in the hearts of all who join in the work of the Apostolate of Christian Renewal, this is the goal for which we should reach.

A Real Retreat

The young people on the tour insisted that I give my talks on Renewal, and I did so. They also insisted that we have the fifteen-decade Rosary every day of the tour and we did this. We had, as I mentioned earlier, an hour of meditation and adoration of the Blessed Sacrament. All of this made this trip, for me, the most intensified fifteen-day retreat that I had ever made in my life. I didn't intend to do these things. It's just that they were requested by the people on the tour. It made the time spent on that pilgrimage twice as beautiful for me.

Going Home

After we finished in Lisieux, we drove back to Paris and waited to come back to the United States. The next morning we boarded the plane. I wanted to come back as far as Chicago, with my brother, and go home and see my Mother for a week. But, in Paris, they would not allow that. They wanted me to go straight to Los Angeles. When we got into Montreal, the Herolds were able to get me off that plane. They waited four hours for me to come and made the arrangements for me so that I was able to visit my Mother and my home, before coming back to California. I am very grateful to the Herolds. They are wonderful people. They are not just tour agents. They are not just doing things for business. It is more like a family. They give of themselves and are really concerned about us and they participated with us in everything. It really made the group feel at home. I would highly recommend them any time for forming a pilgrimage or a tour to go anywhere in the world. Hopefully, next year, we will go again, not to Europe, but to Washington, D.C., and to the National Shrine, where I was ordained as a priest, in 1954, and then up through Canada, to the different shrines there, making a pilgrimage in that way. It would be nice to have many more people going and to have many wonderful and beautiful things to happen along the way.

God Grants Answer To Prayer In His Own Good Time

There is a final event that I must relate before bringing this book to a close. A beautiful thing happened in Milwaukee, Wisconsin, with regard to the Center which had so long been a cause of concern and sorrow to me. When I returned from the pilgrimage, I discovered that a man had rented an office for the work of the Apostolate in that Diocese. He has furnished the office, and is willing to do everything possible to help foster the work of the Apostolate in that area. And so, after a year of no activity, of suffering and worrying and wondering, the work had again begun. I am very grateful to God for this, and I am looking forward to a continued increase in the spread of the Apostolate through the efforts of those working in that Center.

Still another beautiful thing happened which has helped much to further the work of the Apostolate. This is the fact that Archbishop William E. Cousins has now given full written approbation and encouragement to the work of the Apostolate in that area where before he had given only a verbal approval. The following is an article written by him which appeared in the *Herald Citizen*, on December 14, 1975.

Throughout the Catholic world the Holy Year is being anticipated through prayers and words of preparation. We have been called upon to bring into focus in our own lives and relationships the theme concepts of Renewal and Reconciliation. The words themselves have been repeated time beyond number; almost every organization and agency within the Church has referred to these twin ideas in their directives and programs.

All of this, however, can go on around us without making more than a passing impression. We can even grow tired of being reminded that we are expected as individuals to enter into the spirit of the Holy Year with some evidence of personal involvement. We may be tempted to think of this period of spiritual preparation as being practically concluded, leaving us free to think that duty has been discharged and no further demands will be made upon us.

Yet, a moment's serious thought will uncover the error in such reasoning. Reconciliation in the sense of restoring peace, harmony, tolerance, and understanding is certainly not meant to be an intermittent exercise. My relationship with God and everyone about me are part of daily living, so my effort to improve those relations cannot be a hit-or-miss, off-again, on-again matter of concern.

Renewal must also be a lifetime commitment. By passively allowing the Laws of Nature to have their way we grow and are renewed physically, but most of us are sufficiently health conscious to want to help Nature along. Through diet, vitamins, exercise, medicine, we show an evident willingness to do our share in supplementing whatever comes naturally. Spiritual renewal is certainly no less important, if we are to realize our places in the Plan of God and in the mission of the Church.

Renewal, though presently emphasized in our approach to the Holy Year, was fundamental to the deliberations and recommendations of Vatican Council II. In its opening message, we read, "In this assembly, under the guidance of the Holy Spirit, we wish to inquire how we ought to renew ourselves, so that we may be found increasingly faithful to the Gospel of Christ....We as pastors devote all our energies and thoughts to the renewal of ourselves and the flocks committed to us."

Inspired by this basic ingredient of the Council's purpose and by unusual events in his life called to a special ministry, Father Luke Zimmer, SS.CC. (Father of the Sacred Hearts) founded the Apostolate of Christian Renewal with the consent and approval of his Religious Superiors. Pope Paul VI in a private audience on December 17, 1969, told Father Luke, "I bless your work. I bless you and anyone who spreads this Apostolate."

On the West Coast the Christian Renewal Program has met with marked success. Here in Milwaukee, it is being brought to your attention as officially sanctioned and approved. Following a lengthy personal interview and with the recommendation of Timothy Cardinal Manning, Archbishop of Los Angeles, we assigned Father Oswald Krusing, retired, to the Apostolate and approved the naming of Sister Mary Francis, S.S.N.D. as Secretary of the local Center, now located at 6324 West North Avenue, Milwaukee 53213.

We are happy to announce this Program, because we feel that any number of our readers will be interested enough to seek additional information. We are also anxious to promote in every way possible the same ideals as those expressed in II Vatican Council.

The Apostolate of Christian Renewal encourages Consecration to the Immaculate Heart of Mary and Enthronement of the Sacred Heart for families. It promotes in a beautiful way Rosary Devotions, and firmly establishes the Eucharist as the center of Catholic life, with strong emphasis upon the spirit of prayer. In the sanctification of one's self and others greater honor and glory are given to God. Out of a natural growth in love for the Father, Son, and Spirit comes love for neighbor, as expressed through services to the poor, the underprivileged, the sick, the handicapped, and the aged.

We recommend the Apostolate and pray for its success. One does not, however, need to be a "joiner" to make spiritual renewal a force in one's own life. A do-it-yourself kit complete with all the help of Divine Grace is readily available. Simply address a prayer to Mary in care of her Divine Son.

Most Reverend William E. Cousins, D.D.
Bishop of Milwaukee

(From December 14th issue of *Herald Citizen*. Reprinted with permission)

Now that the Milwaukee Center is flourishing once again, I am looking ahead to the time one day when we will have Centers all across the nation. One day, in prayer, I mentioned this to God. The answer I received was from God. It was that I should form a "Thousand People's Club," of one thousand people, each of whom would donate one thousand dollars toward the establishing of Centers all across the country. I will not ask individuals for money for this purpose, only large corporations and charitable organizations. However, if individuals are inspired to donate money, we will gratefully accept it. It would require a million dollars to subsidize the establishing of Centers in this country. It is in God's Hands to see whether or not we will get the money we will need to do this. I am convinced, though, that this is His Will, and that one day we will have these Centers.

One thing is certain. I feel that the idea of renewal and reconciliation is an idea whose time has come and that this is what we should preach to the people. Nothing can resist the power of an idea whose time has come. I feel that the Apostolate of Christian Renewal will transform the world and, in preaching to the poor and the suffering, we should preach the message of Jesus Christ, as St. Paul did.

Preach the Cross, that we must carry the Cross, carry it with Christ, and carry it with joy and happiness. We know that the Apostles walked with Christ and saw Him working and performing miracles, but this is not what brought about our Redemption. It was the Crucifixion, the Resurrection, that brought about our redemption. We are all called to be crucified with Christ, to carry our cross with Christ. I think that this must be explained to all people. I think they must be challenged again to do these things. I am convinced that people are generous and that they wish to respond to this life of love, of sacrifice, of generosity, of giving themselves to God, accepting their suffering, and carrying their cross.

We must realize that, when we carry the cross, it becomes, for us, the power of God. Nothing can stand in its way. Nothing can destroy us. We will be transformed and will become true, contemplative souls in the world, if we do carry the cross with generosity, faithfulness, and persevering love, for His *Honor and Glory.*

PART II

CHAPTER 1

1974

A. Holy Year proclaimed

In 1974, our Holy Father Pope Paul VI proclaimed a Holy Year named, "Renewal and Reconciliation." The purpose of the Holy Year was to bring about a true renewal of Vatican Council II. A true renewal would be one that would lead a person to strive for holiness of life, which would be shared with others. A true renewal would also have to be a theological renewal, which would renew the person's faith, hope and love. In short, a true renewal is the pursuit of holiness.

Throughout the world many people got involved. Many, from all parts of the world, traveled to Rome and actively participated in the Holy Year. They expressed their faith in the Holy Father and in the Church. There were efforts made in various countries to bring about a true renewal. As a result, God's blessings came upon the countries who participated as well as the whole world.

Unfortunately, the preparation period of 1974 did not produce the effects that had been hoped for by Pope Paul VI. Instead, there was much lethargy, lukewarmness and even opposition to the Holy Father's preparation period. In America, we gave, more or less, a token response, which I think left much to be desired. Priests, brothers and sisters should have led the way to prepare the people for a fruitful Holy Year. As a result, there was a lack of true renewal or interior change.

In short, the Holy Year should have been a deepening and renewal of a person's intimate love-relationship with the Lord, but instead there was too much emphasis on the sociological and psychological aspects of renewal. However, renewal must continue. We have to accept things as they are and build upon the blessings which have been received during the Holy Year. We should also be very grateful for what has taken place. Many gifts were given to those who were involved.

1. The Apostolate of Christian Renewal

I was elated that the Holy Father proclaimed 1974 a Holy Year. The reason is because I established the Apostolate of Christian Renewal with the same purpose in mind. First, the Apostolate is intended to be a movement which will bring about a deep renewal of a person's interior spiritual life. This renewal is to be expressed in a person's family life and community life. Through this renewal, a person will develop a deep and intimate love-relationship with the Lord, which will naturally deepen a person's family love-relationship. From this family circle then, each person will go forth into the community to serve others. Second, the Apostolate is to bring about reconciliation, such as between God and man; man and man; man and woman. This reconciliation will bring about peace within the person. Therefore, the Apostolate is intended to be a movement that leads a person from prayer to action.

2. The slow response of the priests and the people

Before 1975, when I was preaching about the intentions and goals of the Apostolate of Christian Renewal, only a few people would respond. Very few priests would even invite me into their parishes. From the time I began the work in December of 1971, I always asked the priests to let me come into their parishes. I begged them to give me a chance to preach and to be with their people. I told the priests that they did not have to give me any money, but just let me come.

Perhaps the slow response of the people was due to the lack of support on the part of the priests. The slow response could have also been the rigidity of my own attitude, my own lack of spontaneity or my own lack of understanding. Maybe I was too impatient or my preaching was too demanding, too narrow or too rigid. There could be any number of reasons for this slow response on the part of the people.

Still, as I continued to preach through the years of 1972, 1973 and 1974, I began to notice an increase in the number of people who were beginning to participate. They seemed to be getting a lot from the Renewal Weeks as well as appreciating what was happening. However, I longed to have many more people come and hear the message because I believed the Apostolate of Christian Renewal is meant for the whole world. However, humanly speaking, I cannot spread the Apostolate by myself. I believe that those who hear the message of the Apostolate need to get involved and also help spread the message.

B. Charismatic meeting with Fr. Bertolucci

In early spring 1974, I attended a charismatic meeting for priests at Loyola University, Los Angeles, California. During the day, I listened to various speakers. One speaker in particular, Father Bertolucci, spoke about his involvement in the Charismatic Movement and what it did for him. In his talk, I became aware that the Charismatic Movement is intended to develop a deep love-relationship with the Lord through the Holy Spirit.

1. Apostolate of Christian Renewal is different from the Charismatic Movement

While preaching the message of the Apostolate of Christian Renewal, I used the same approach as St. Louis DeMontfort, which means going to Jesus through Mary. As a result, the end goal is the same as the Charismatic Renewal. In other words, the Holy Spirit takes over in a person's life and forms us into Jesus Christ, which makes that person a "beloved" son or daughter. Our purpose in life then is to become like Christ and help others become more Christ-like. That is what is means to establish the Kingdom of God on earth.

The Apostolate of Christian Renewal and the Charismatic Renewal are two distinct movements. Both movements, I believe, are from God. However, some people will be more drawn to the Charismatic Movement, while others will be more drawn to the Apostolate of Christian Renewal. I do not see any opposition between the two movements because each movement can enhance the other.

I believe that the Apostolate of Christian Renewal can contribute a lot to the Charismatic Movement because the Apostolate basically teaches people the truths concerning faith and morals. It also upholds and fosters the teachings of the Church, which we all are called to embrace if we want to be true followers of Jesus Christ. As for the Charismatic Movement, it is intended more towards giving a spontaneity in a person's prayer life and joy in Christian living. However, there is less emphasis on the teaching aspect of our religious living.

These two movements need to work side by side, in order to help each other. However, I am not sure how these two movements can accomplish this. I don't even know how I could ever interest those who are in the Charismatic Movement to participate in the Apostolate of Christian Renewal. The only answer to this problem is to pray and ask the Lord, "How can this be accomplished? What can be done?"

Fr. Luke's family - fall of '96 (father and mother of the family are deceased).

CHAPTER 2

1975

A. *Praying for the Holy Spirit*

In June 1975, I attended my annual retreat. I decided to offer up all my prayers, Masses, holy hours, rosaries, conferences and prayers in union with the other priests on retreat for this intention. I offered everything so that these two movements work in harmony with each other. I also made the intention that I would give myself even more fully to the Lord than I had ever done before.

During the retreat, I asked Fr. Patrick Crowley, Fr. Finbarr Devine, Fr. Lane and Br. Ed Campell to pray with me. We began praying and asking the Holy Spirit to come upon us. After praying for awhile, Fr. Crowley laid his hands on the different people who were there. As for me, he laid his hands on me last. At that time, I didn't feel anything and I was a little disappointed because I thought I would receive a greater awareness of the Holy Spirit (Like I did when I consecrated myself to Jesus through Mary on April 28th, 1946). Sometime after Fr. Crowley's blessing, I experienced an awareness of the Holy Spirit working in my life. Still, I was hoping for an even deeper awareness of the Spirit at this time and nothing seemed to happen. I figured the Lord didn't have "anything going" for me at this time. I continued to pray and ask for His help by turning everything over to the Lord. I also asked for His blessings so that He would move people to come and participate in the Renewal Weeks.

1. Jesus blesses me ˙

I was not prepared for what happened the following morning, June 20th, 1975. After breakfast, I went into the Chapel as I always do to make my holy hour. I knelt down and offered myself to the Lord, saying, "Lord here I am. Take me and do with me what you want. You know what I've been praying for. You know my intentions and prayers. I am Yours. Just help me to carry out Your will. Help me to carry out the plan of the Father for me." Immediately, Jesus came from the tabernacle and placed His hands upon my head. I did not see Him, yet I knew it was Jesus. I did not hear anything because He did not say anything. There was just complete silence while Jesus placed His hands on my head. I felt a tremendous power surge through my whole body. This power drew me into a deep union of love and prayer with the Lord. I was not afraid, but I felt acutely my own unworthiness and sinfulness just like any other sinner. As the Lord continued to bless me, His power kept moving through me, from the top of my head to the bottom of my feet. After five minutes of His blessing, He returned to the tabernacle. Throughout that day, I felt a closeness and a deep unity with the Lord. In fact, I continued to feel like this not only during that day, but during many days afterward.

2. Bless people no matter what it costs

I talked this whole phenomenon over with a priest, who told me that God had given me a special grace. He also told me that I should use this blessing so that other people could also receive it. He then mentioned to me that, "You will be ridiculed and misunderstood. You will be persecuted, criticized and misrepresented, but it doesn't make any difference what people will say. You are to use this blessing, no matter what it might cost you." Therefore, from that moment, I began to give this blessing during my Renewals.

B. Blessing people

Since Jesus laid His hands on my head, I decided to lay my hands upon other people. When I blessed them, they began to fall over! The first person this happened to was a religious brother who was sitting at a table. He fell down on the floor and thumped his head on the cement. I was really shook up because I was afraid he was hurt.

Immediately, the reaction on the part of the people was a tremendous thing to witness. People started to come to my renewal talks. At first, the priests who invited me were amazed and a little cautious. However, they didn't interfere or try to stop me from giving the blessing. They didn't even say that I should not give this blessing because it might cause wonderment, curiosity or fanaticism among the people. They simply adopted the position of "wait and see what takes place."

The priests did not give me any encouragement either, and I began to feel as though I was standing alone. Criticism began immediately and I had to explain the blessing to a bishop. He did not say a lot about not giving the blessing, but he carefully cautioned me. He said that I must be very careful that people did not begin to consider me to be a wonder-worker. By that, I believe he meant that I should not build up a cult around myself personally. Naturally, I hope that this never happens because this is not my intention.

1. Results

Ironically, I never expected anything like this to ever happen because I always thought people who fell over were subject to hypnotism, autosuggestion, imagination or hallucinations that caused this phenomenon. I just did not believe in this sort thing and would have been the last person to accept it. So when it began to happen, I didn't know what to think.

a. Not hypnotizing people

In giving the blessing, I was accused of hypnotizing people. I wondered for awhile about that myself. One day a doctor happened to watch me give the blessing. After I blessed about a hundred people, he came to me and said, "Father, some people might wonder when you are giving the blessing whether or not you are hypnotizing them. You most definitely are not! The exact opposite takes place when you give the blessing. People do not go into a trance or lose their power of awareness. Rather, they have complete control over their senses. They are fully aware of what is going on around them. They hear what is said. They are simply under the Power of God's Love and Spirit." I gladly accepted what he had said because it answered many of my questions.

b.   A real blessing—not autosuggestion

The next thing that was brought to my attention was autosuggestion, which is when a person pretends to receive a power when in reality that person has not. But, I often ask myself, "Who are we to judge? We cannot read souls and know what goes on in the heart, mind and soul of any person." Thus, I do not believe this to be a likely answer at all because most people who come for the blessing for the first time are afraid of falling. It is far more natural for people to have a fear of falling than for them to deliberately allow themselves to fall backward. Therefore, I believe that when we are receiving the blessing in a group we should not be looking around at one another to see the different reactions of the people. Rather, we should be praying for them and asking that each person will receive all the blessings, graces and gifts that God wishes to give. We should also be praying for each and every person so that God may touch them, physically, mentally, emotionally and spiritually. I also do not believe that we should ever criticize anyone's actions when they receive the blessing by belittling them or making a great fuss over them. Nor should we think that they are more holy just because one thing or another has happened. This simply should never be done!

c.   The Devil never blesses

People sometimes have accused me of working with the Devil when I give the blessing. Personally, I don't understand their reasoning or how this could even possibly be true. Jesus said, "A house divided cannot stand on its own." I know from personal experience that thousands of people came back to Jesus Christ after receiving the blessing. I know this because they tell me this in the sacrament of Reconciliation. Most of these people have been away from the Church for ten, twenty, thirty or forty years. I also know that the blessing has helped many people to make their peace with God and within their families. How can the Devil bring about this good? He cannot and will not! I always preach that every person must remain obedient to their superiors. I also preach that there must be a complete following of the teaching of the Church. So, how can there be any work of the Devil in this? I strongly reject this accusation and believe that it is totally false. As our Lord said, "When they accused Him of working with the Devil, they will also accuse us of working with the Devil." (Mt. 9). Likewise, even today, I no longer let this accusation bother me anymore.

d.   We are only channels

At first, criticism and ridicule bothered me because I was too sensitive. If a person is too sensitive, then this sensitivity reveals that a person is actually filled with pride. Rather than being proud, a person should be a channel of grace. For example, a person should be as though the Lord was pouring His grace into a funnel. At first, the top of the funnel is very large and the bottom of the funnel is very small. As He pours graces through that funnel, that is, through the person, very little of that person is given to others. In other words, a person does not share with others in nearly so large a proportion as God shares with us. However, as a person continues to be the instrument of God, a person can give more because of the wanting to share everything with others. Each of us must realize then that when a person attacks us, he or she is really attacking God and destroying His work, even though the person might not realize this right away.

2.   Having a healing ministry

Many times, healings are given by God through the blessing, but many people do not let this be known. Usually when I come back to their area in five, seven or ten years, they then tell me about their healings or what took place in their lives because of the blessing. I believe that a person in this type of ministry has to live by faith and give the blessing without wanting to know the results.

However, being human, it is always good to hear what God has done through a person's ministry.

Many people continuously come and demand a healing. I think a person needs to seek, accept and lovingly embrace God's will. If there is no healing, then it is God's will for the person to carry the cross of suffering. The person should accept the illness, problem or whatever it might be and unite it with the suffering of Jesus. If a person does this, then the suffering brings about the gift of conversion, repentance, forgiveness and salvation for others, especially for hardened sinners.

a. Healings

In giving the blessing I hope that people will be healed physically, mentally, emotionally and spiritually. I know that, through the blessing that I have given from 1975 until the present time, there have been many blessings, graces and gifts given. There have also been a few physical healings and some of them instantaneous. Other healings have taken place over a period of time. Still, other people have had an apparent healing, which I believe is given in order to give that person a chance to be more resigned to God's will. An apparent healing is given so the person will be more peaceful and willing to accept the suffering. This healing helps a person to make a better preparation for death. I believe that sometimes God gives a reprieve, just for a moment in this life. He gives strength and courage so that a person can live a better life, which brings a person closer to Him.

b. Healing comes from God

In many cases, no healing whatsoever takes place, no matter how hard a person prays, hopes or believes. This proves that all healing comes from God. In our prayers for healing, we should always pray as Jesus prayed in the Garden of Gethsemane, "Lord, not My will, but Yours be done." He even asked for the chalice of suffering to be removed, yet Jesus said to His Heavenly Father, "May Your will be done." We also have to learn to pray in this manner.

I do not believe that a person should ever say, "If Your will is this, Lord, please cure or heal me" or "I will accept it if it is Your will." The reason why a person should not pray like this is because it allows a certain doubt in a person's mind, an uncertainty, lack of trust or faith. On the other hand, if a person prays the other way, that person is praying with certainty, trust and faith that God's will be done. Then, when He says, "Yes," the person should rejoice, thank and praise Him. Likewise, when He says, "No," the person will be resigned to His Will by thanking and praising Him for the suffering that He has given to deepen a person's love-relationship with Him.

c.   Suffering is a blessing—not a curse

There is a certain redemptive quality in suffering, which can be very beneficial. Some people are called by God to suffer so that they can carry out a special work of giving service to others. Any person who has a special apostolate must have suffering so as to enter into the mission of Christ. With Christ then, a person brings about the work to its fulfillment, completion and fruition. As a result, there is a redemptive quality in suffering from which many blessings flow.

However, I do not believe that suffering is a curse. Even though suffering came into the world through sin, Our Lord conquered sin, death and the Devil through His suffering and dying on the Cross. In fact, Jesus' entire lifetime was filled with suffering both interiorly and exteriorly. His interior suffering was, I am sure, far greater than any of His exterior sufferings, such as the Scourging or the Crucifixion on the Cross.

C. Forbidden to give blessing

After this experience of blessing people, the phenomena of people resting in the Spirit happened quite frequently. I personally never wanted this to happen because so many people referred to this as "Slain in the Spirit." In fact, I always thought people were just over reacting, too emotional or gave into autosuggestion.

Each time I gave the blessing during the Renewal Week, I had to do violence to myself in order to give the blessing. When I gave the blessing, I felt power going through me upon the person. There were many physical, emotional and spiritual healings granted. Many people also came to confession after remaining away for years. Therefore, I knew that this blessing certainly did not come from the Devil.

One day, Timothy Cardinal Manning, other bishops and various pastors said that I should not give the blessing publicly during the Renewal Weeks because a cult could be built around me. People could just come to see me, hear me, be blessed by me and forget the real purpose of life, which is to become a saint. This is very dangerous because a person needs to have a true relationship with God and not for a person who blesses people. Rather, they suggested that I bless people privately. For the next five years, I would only bless people publicly with the permission of the bishop of the diocese and the pastor where I was giving a Renewal. My Provincial said, "God gave you a gift; therefore you should use this gift for His honor and glory and for the benefit of the people."

1. Being obedient to my superiors

I was obedient to the cardinal, bishops and priests and did not give the blessing publicly. I found this hard to understand why I was told not to bless people in public while those who were in the Charismatic Movement or healing ministries were permitted to do so. In fact, people flocked to healing services and to charismatic prayer groups. These ministers were not subject to accusations from the leaders or those giving blessings, praying over people or when gifts of the Holy Spirit were manifested. Rather, everyone was welcome to participate and to talk freely about what took place, such as the blessings, healings and teachings given. I felt like the only person who was not free to use the gifts God has given me. As a result, this whole situation made me look inward and wonder whether this really was from God.

I believe the Devil did his dirty work by suggesting that I was a fake and that what I was doing was useless. I felt that I was an embarrassment to Church officials and that they did not understand me, accept me or support me. I felt that they thought I was a fanatic or just a pious sentimental fool. However, I was still faithful to my prayer life by fasting, praying and doing penance. From my prayer life, I always felt deep down in my spirit a sense of joy and peace. My joy came from always being aware of God within me. I knew and felt His everlasting love for me. That awareness gave me courage to continue through the years without judging, criticizing, being angry or bitter towards anyone. Finally, there were no more objections and I was able to resume giving the blessing in public.

D. All types of people come to Renewal Weeks

Before this blessing was given, very few people came to listen to what I had to say. Now, many people decide to come and participate. Many believe and accept what I say. They also put into practice what I ask or preach. I have seen all different kinds of people, such as those who are conservative, ultra—conservative, liberal and middle-of-the-road. I have seen Charismatics, Cursillistas, Marriage Encounter, and various parish organizations, such as the Legion of Mary, St. Vincent de Paul, Holy Name Society and the Knights of Columbus. You name it, they have come and they all come together. The men, women, boys and girls; the young and the old, the rich and the poor; the professional and the non-professional people; the educated and the uneducated—they are all there as one, as the Family of God.

1. Be child-like

The impact that the Renewals and the blessings made upon the people is varied, according to each person's openness, need and God's grace. Each person is different because I find that the young and child-like souls are the people who believe, accept and live the message. Likewise, the people who are sophisticated, over rationalize and try to figure everything out do not understand the message because it is too simple. People tend to complicate the simple in matters of faith. God intended our faith to be simple and told us to be child-like. When a person is child-like, then that person develops a simple and uncomplicated approach in the matters of faith. Then, when a person hears the simple things, he or she is attracted to these truths because it captivates and motivates the person. Simple truth also helps a person to live a healthy and intensive spiritual life. On the other hand, if a person becomes proud, arrogant and rationalizes the simply truth, then that person destroys the action of the Holy Spirit because the person is not open. Therefore, the person rejects the simple truths and becomes blind and is bound to darkness.

2. Greatest blessing is unity

During my Renewal Weeks, I believe that the preaching and blessings are a source of unity. People who come to the Renewal Weeks learn to accept one another, love one another, encourage one another and inspire one another. The blessing power was given for this purpose.

E. Charismatic gifts to serve others

Any charismatic gift that is given is intended for the service of the Lord and others. The charismatic gifts are not for the holiness of the individual because such a gift does not make the person more holy than anyone else. The person cannot "lord the gift over" anyone else. Rather, the gift should make that person a channel of grace so that the grace can come through that person, as through a funnel. As the gift is given, it must be used. Just remember, one day we are going to have to answer to the Lord for the way we have used our gifts, graces and talents. I would much rather answer to the Lord and say that I have used them than to say that I have not used them. I hope that in using these gifts, I well never misuse them. I believe that they are given not only for the service of others, but to also build up the Kingdom of God on earth.

1. Becoming attached

I think that people can become attached to a person with charismatic gifts. For example, they might stop at the person without going beyond to find God. These people must always remember that the person is only an instrument of God, who should lead the people to a deep love relationship with Him. I also believe that people are searching for God. When they see the goodness in a charismatic person, I think that they are really attracted to God and not the person giving the blessing. If they are sincere, they'll eventually find God and grow in holiness. Then they will see that the person, with charismatic gifts, in the proper perspective. On the other hand, if a person is fickle, curious, fanatical or sentimental, then that person will remain only on the emotional level and his other growth in holiness will be hindered.

2. Receiving a gift

Whenever God gives a person a charisma, such as the gift of healing, then that person should use this gift generously, patiently and lovingly so as to follow the Lord. This gift received must also be used and not abused, misused or never used.

A person must always remember that God gave all the Apostles charismatic gifts. How did they act? Judas betrayed Christ, Peter denied Christ and all the others abandoned Christ. Therefore, it is important to remember the words of Jesus in regard to working miracles in His name. In other words, if a person uses the gift incorrectly or becomes proud, then Jesus will say to them at the hour of death, "Depart form me—I never knew you."

When using these gifts, I believe humility is absolutely necessary. When a person is humble and child-like, the person will always remember that the gift and the result from using that gift comes from God. A person needs to keep his or her eyes, heart and mind on God. If a person doesn't, then that person allows room for Satan to deceive, such as comparing spiritual states of life. As a result, a person can think to be better than others or even envy someone who may be more blessed.

F. Called to fast

Immediately after the Lord came to me and placed His hands on me, I felt the urging of the Lord and His Holy Spirit to begin a strict fast. I felt that He was calling me to a fast without eating any food. I was sort of reluctant to begin this fast because I wasn't really convinced that it was a calling from the Lord. I thought, how could it be prudent to fast in such a manner? Therefore, I hesitated and I didn't do what the Lord was urging me to do. After three months, I still felt that the Lord was urging me to fast so I finally went to my spiritual director and said, "I believe that the Lord is calling me to a strict fast, one without eating and just drinking water." My spiritual director asked me how long I felt that this fast was intended to last. I told him that I didn't know. He said, "O.K., I'll give you permission to fast, but under these conditions: If you get too hungry, too tired, too weak or uncharitable so that no one can live with you, then you will have to stop your fast. But, if none of these things occur, then you may continue with your fast. Check in with me and let me know, from time to time, how things are going."

I began the fast on September 19th. For the first three days I felt a little hungry, but not too much. For the following four days, I felt a little weak and light-headed at times. However, that soon passed and I didn't feel any ill effects in that way again. I began to go through the various days of fasting. I went through seven days, then twelve days. I reported to my spiritual director that all was going well and he told me to continue.

Just before my fast was over, I went to a parish to continue my work. In fact, the volume of work had tripled during the forty day period. I had to answer many letters, see many people and preach Renewal Weeks in various parishes. I just continued to do the work I was doing without slowing down or stopping. I believe the source of my strength came from Holy Communion. I was privileged, during this time, to be able to say two Masses a day. In the morning, I would say Mass and as soon as I received Communion, I would feel strength surge throughout my whole body. In the evening, I offered Mass and was again physically, mentally, emotionally and spiritually refreshed. Therese Neumann, who had the stigmata, also fasted without eating for many years and received great strength from the Eucharist. Personally, a person should not be surprised when he or she receives strength from Holy Communion because Jesus is our strength.

During the last week, when I went to the parish where I was preaching, the cook was somewhat disappointed because she knew that I liked carrot cake, which she made for me. She hoped to give me some of this cake while I was there. I then had to tell her that I was on a strict fast and that she should not tell anyone outside of the rectory about my fasting. The priests could know but I did not want anyone else to know. This was my policy throughout the fast because I did not want anybody to know that I was on a fast. Some people noticed that I was losing weight and perhaps I looked a bit pale, but usually they would ask how I was feeling and I would answer that I was O.K. They would let it go at that so I never had to explain that I was fasting.

On the thirty-fifth day, I opened the Scriptures to see what the Lord had to say about the fast (This is something which I very seldom do, but I didn't have my spiritual director present at the time, so I sought an answer from Scripture). All the passages that I opened indicated that the fast was to continue because they asked for penance and fasting. I decided to go on until the fortieth day.

When I was ready to leave that parish, my fast was nearly over. I had only another day or so left. The cook again made a delicious carrot cake and told me to take it with me. She said I should put it in the freezer so that, when my fast was over, I could eat it. On the fortieth day, I was again away from my spiritual director and I didn't know whether I should continue or stop the fast because I felt hungry. Physically, I felt that this meant that I should stop fasting. Again, I opened the Bible at random, which stated, "Open your mouth and eat what the Lord has prepared for you." So, I decided to end my fast. The first thing I ate was a big piece of carrot cake. However, before beginning to eat again, I asked all the priests who were present at our Center to pray over me. Whenever any person goes on a long fast, the doctor suggests to a person to gradually begin the process of eating. I find this is important because a person's stomach and digestive system aren't able to handle different foods without discomfort or harm to the body. However, when the priests prayed over me, I felt my whole digestive system become reactivated. I was able to begin eating again as though I had never fasted. I was very fortunate because the fast was not too difficult for me.

1. Fasting is good for a person's health

In the book, *The Art of Fasting*, I learned that a person will first lose excess fat. Then the cells that need to be reproduced, or are no longer useful, are washed from the body. From my experience of fasting, I learned that there is a real health process that takes place throughout the fasting period. However, I strongly emphasize that it is very important to have a physical examination before such a fast begins. I had a physical examination shortly after June, when I was home in Milwaukee, Wisconsin. The results showed that my body was sufficiently healthy to undertake a fast. In fact, I was 25 pounds overweight and the doctor suggested that this would be beneficial to my health. This was really an ideal way to loose weight, although I was fasting for another reason.

Anyone who is called by God to a fast must discern the Spirit. The discernment is necessary to see whether this is from God, the Devil or a person's own imagination. A person should also go to a spiritual director and ask permission. If the spiritual director gives permission, then a person may begin to fast. If the spiritual director says no, then a person may not fast. During the fast, a person must use various safe guards, such as checking in with the spiritual director to see how things are going. The spiritual director then discerns whether the fast should continue or not.

I believe that God inspired me to fast. When Jesus was baptized in the Jordan river by John the Baptist, He was moved by the Spirit to go into the desert to fast for forty days and forty nights. For me, it was Jesus Who came and placed His hands on my head and through the Spirit, I was moved to undertake this fast. As I said, I rebelled in the beginning, but it took time to get used to the idea and to accept the call to fast. However, once I accepted and believed that God wanted me to fast, the fast became very easy. God gives His strength and His power to do the things that He wants done. All that a person needs to do is be open to Him.

2. Fasting benefits a person's spiritual life

I discovered that fasting is very beneficial to a person's spiritual life. While fasting, I found that it is easier to think about God. I felt the Presence of God at all times, which made it easier to conquer numerous temptations during the fast. In fact, I became aware that the Devil wants to destroy the good which comes from fasting. However, the power of the Devil can easily be broken or counteracted because fasting makes a person spiritually strong.

CHAPTER 3

1976

A. What approach should be used

At the beginning of 1976, I only had a few Renewal Weeks scheduled. Fr. Regis was visiting us at that time and he said to me, "Luke, you are working too hard. You need a rest. Why don't you go into the desert to pray? You should spend a year just in prayer and not be working yourself to a frazzle, being on the go all the time." When Fr. Regis died in January, I knew that he had been a great friend and brother to me. He inspired me greatly by his prayers and work for the Apostolate.

After he died, I said to him, "Regis, now you know the answers. You are with God. You know whether I am to spend time in prayer, in solitude, in rest and relaxation; or whether I should go to priests, brothers, and sisters to give retreats; or whether I should do parish Renewal Weeks. Whatever God wills, would you please intercede for me and see what can be done so that I have direction in regard to the way that the Apostolate should go at this point of development?"

Within a very short time, I was booked solid for the complete year of 1976, mainly giving Renewal Weeks. I knew that this was what God wanted me to do. I felt that God wanted me to continue, in spite of fatigue, in spite of hardship, in spite of ridicule or whatever might happen. It meant that this was the will of God for me. I was pleasantly surprised at what began to happen. More people started to come to my Renewals and more priests and sisters became interested in what I was doing.

1. Meeting with The International Institute of the Heart of Jesus (IIHJ)

After I finished my preaching assignment, I went to Rome to the Salesianum Seminary in the early part of 1976. I attended a meeting of the International Institute of the Heart of Jesus because I am a member of the advisory board of the IIHJ. This is an organization that has been established to spread the devotion of the Sacred Heart. Since Vatican II, the devotion to the Sacred Heart has diminished. In fact, many people question the mode of spreading devotion of any kind to the Sacred Heart because people have become attached to the idea of having pictures of the Sacred Heart as devotion, rather than the true spirit of the devotion. Some people even suggest that this devotion is no longer appealing to people.

The IIHJ has meetings at different times to see what can be done to overcome any apathy, indifference or opposition to the Sacred Heart devotion. This organization is trying to find an approach which will enkindle a fire of love within the hearts of people. The IIHJ is trying to help people accept the devotion of the Sacred Heart in their spirituality, while trying to inspire the Church to again foster this devotion.

At this meeting, and others like it, I meet many people from various parts of the world. Meeting zealous promoters of the Sacred Heart devotion is an inspirational and educational experience. Many of the people are concerned about spreading devotion to the Sacred Heart. Everyone also tries to find a manner in which the devotion of the Sacred Heart could be presented so that the people of God could be helped in their spiritual life.

The IIHJ has a far way to go before it can make a genuine impact upon the world or upon the Church. In order to revitalize the devotion of the Sacred Heart, a person has to have a deep love and devotion to Mary as well as to the Sacred Heart. In order to develop this love and devotion, I believe that we have to become more Eucharistic in our approach. In this way, the Sacred Heart will not just be fostered or encouraged with just a sacramental or a devotional approach. Rather, a complete theological approach should be used, which means that the love of the Heart of Jesus is the basis of all theological studies, doctrine and spiritual thought. Anything that is sentimental or superstitious must be eliminated. Then we will be able to foster this devotion to help bring about the Kingdom of God on earth—the social reign of Christ the King.

2. While in Rome

Father Superior General came to various sessions. When the sessions were over, I stayed for a couple days at our General house. This gave me an opportunity to speak with Father General and the other priests on the staff. I explained briefly the work of the Apostolate of Christian Renewal to Father General. He was amazed at the success of the Apostolate's work, but as he admitted, he did not fully understand what I was trying to do.

While I was in Rome, I had the opportunity to visit St. Peter's and to attend the Holy Father's Wednesday General Audience. Before the General Audience, I noticed that Pope Paul VI was walking slowly and with great pain. After his talk, he came to the people in the front rows. I was able to shake his hands and briefly speak to him. Although he didn't know it, I secretly blessed him with the relic of the True Cross.

a. Visit with Brother Gino

I also decided to visit Brother Gino, the stigmatist, and spend three days with him at the seminary. I had the privilege of speaking with Brother Gino after I arrived. I asked him whether I should begin a new congregation or whether I should remain in our present Congregation. I also asked if I should try to help reform our own Congregation. Surprisingly, he said that our Congregation has been found wanting and that the Congregation must be reformed or it will disappear from the face of the earth. This news saddens me because I love our Congregation dearly. I believe that our Congregation is relevant for our times and that we have a lot to offer to the world. I would love to see our Congregation have a renewal. However, we must be faithful to the charism of our Founder (Fr. Joseph Coudrin) and live the Gospel message of Jesus Christ. In fact, Vatican II has asked all religious communities to do this. And if we are faithful in living our religious life as proposed by Vatican Council II, then we would never be found wanting.

Brother Gino said that it is a tremendous undertaking to begin a new congregation because a person is supposed to be there to give guidance and direction. The Founder is to express the charism that was received from God to the new community. Brother Gino said that I wasn't going to live long enough to begin a new religious community. I do not know whether he really meant this or whether he was saying this because I had just fasted and lost a lot of weight. I didn't feel too well either while I was at the Salesianum because the food did not agree with me. I may have looked a bit tired, too. Perhaps he made his judgment on exterior appearances. I really don't know whether he was speaking from Divine inspiration or an illumination. I often asked myself if he was giving me a true prophecy or expressing his personal opinion?

b.   Asked to be spiritual director in the seminary

While I was with Brother Gino, I was asked to give the American Seminarians a Day of Recollection. Brother Gino was quite concerned about what was going to happen to these seminarians, how they would develop and live their spiritual lives in the future. He asked me if I would consider coming to live in San Vittorino, to be the spiritual director of the American seminarians. However, even though I would have enjoyed being their spiritual director, I did not feel that was my calling. Rather, I feel that God has given me the work of the Apostolate of Christian Renewal to spread throughout the world. I do not think that the Apostolate can be spread if I went off to a seminary in San Vittorino, Italy, and became the spiritual director. Anyway, I checked this out with my spiritual director and he also agreed with me. He said that he didn't think it was what God wished of me. And so, I decided not to follow this path of being a spiritual director for the American seminarians.

c.   Brother Gino's mission

I believe that Brother Gino is spreading the Message of Fatima, which is the mission God has given to him. Through his stigmata, many people will be drawn to him. He was told to spread the devotion of the Sacred Heart, as well as to the Immaculate Heart of Mary. He said, "How can I do this when I am a 'prisoner,' when I cannot go out among the people to preach?" Our Lord said to him, "I will draw people to come to you and then I will inspire the people to go forth and bring this about."

This is exactly what is happening. People are coming to Brother Gino from all over the world to receive his advice, to be counseled by him, to see him and to talk to him. Some people might object that so many people come just to see Brother Gino. However, I do not think they come just for that particular reason. Many people say that a cult is being built around Brother Gino. Again, I say I do not think this is true because when a person is in Brother Gino's presence, he or she experiences something more. In other words, when a person looks beyond Brother Gino, a person will see Christ and this is the witness that he gives to the world. Brother Gino expresses his faith, gentleness, patience and gives himself to others. Even his love for all people comes through very forcefully. It is not Brother Gino, as Brother Gino, who is important. It is his mission, his teaching, his direction, his guidance and his prayer life. Many blessings for others come through him, since he is a true instrument of God. This way of living is what is really important. He always preaches a very simple message to the people. It is the Gospel message, "To be good, to pray, to have courage, to stay close to the Lord, to have a deep devotion and love for the Blessed Mother, to be faithful and to be loyal to the Holy Father." These are the simple truths that he is teaching.

These are some of my thoughts from the time I spent with Brother Gino. I believe that he is a very humble, beautiful and spiritual person, who is inspired by God. Yet, I do not think all what he says is directly from God. As the Gospel says, we must always see whether the Spirit is coming from God, Devil or self.

3. Spiritualism

I think some people put others on a pedestal, like Brother Gino. They think that someone is holy because God gave that person a special gift. I think sometimes people ask many nonsensical questions. For example, they expect someone to know the future and treat that person as a fortune teller. Some even want to know about the dead, that is, the spiritual condition of a relative, such as being in Heaven, Purgatory or Hell. Only God knows the future and we have no right to ask about it or to know the future. Rather, if God wants someone to know the future, then He needs to take the initiative and reveal it. All of these questions delve into spiritualism and are against the First Commandment.

4.   Using God's gifts properly

The person gifted by God must be careful to use the gifts properly. The person may not become proud and think an answer must be given to every question asked. When a person doesn't know the answer, then the person needs to say, "I don't know, I am not God." This is being honest and telling the truth. If a person acts in this manner, then there will be no fanaticism, misleading of people, or detriment to the Church or the faith.

B. Need to relocate our Center

When I came back to the United States in February, I attended a "Catholics United for the Faith" meeting. I spoke to the people who came and participated in the Forum. While I was waiting for Mass to begin, Cardinal Timothy Manning came over and said, "Did you receive my letter?" I answered that I did not and he said, "Well, we have sold the Center in which you are living so you will have to move. But you have plenty of time and you don't have to worry. We will try to help you move and find another place so that you'll have a place to stay." I then thanked him for all that he had done for us because he allowed us to live at the Center for two years free of charge. The third year we were allowed to remain, but were asked to pay a very minimal rent. We were very grateful to His Eminence for his graciousness and kindness. We also really appreciated his interest and the encouragement that he has given to the work of the Apostolate.

The Cardinal suggested two different places where we could relocate our Center. However, I told Father Provincial and the

Council that I personally did not want to have a separate Center for the Apostolate of Christian Renewal. I felt that this was a burden and a duplication of effort. Financially speaking, we could have combined and had only one community, rather than a double community. The Provincial had been living with me at the Center and we were able to take care of most of the financial matters that came up. Naturally, there were certain expenses that had to be paid by the Congregation. The Provincial paid only Congregation expenses while we managed the expenses of the household. I felt that this was an ideal situation. Perhaps the Provincial may have felt like a prisoner or a burden, but I never looked upon it that way. I never interfered with the Provincial's work or his living in carrying out his ministry or his service to the Congregation. I never told him my ideas or tried to force them upon him. However, I was a sounding board and I listened to what he had to say. I gave him encouragement and advice, but I never tried to run the Congregation just because the Provincial lived in our house.

So, I was hoping that the Provincial would establish a house for the Congregation where I would have a room and an office. I was willing to give financial aid from the Apostolate of Christian Renewal for this type of Center. However, the Council decided that the properties offered by the Cardinal were not suitable to move into or accept as our Provincial house. They were quite inadequate and would not fit the needs for both the Provincial House and a Renewal Center.

Then the Provincial asked many people to pray, through the Charismatic Movement and I asked people to pray, through the Apostolate of Christian Renewal, that we would be able to find a place. We looked around in many areas. We looked in Orange County, California and the prices were out of sight. They were beyond what we could ever pay. These areas wanted prices of $220,000.00, $180,000.00, $175,000.00 and nothing below $150,000.00. One property was offered that might have been reasonably priced, but there was no land and only one building. None of the buildings we looked at were suitable for our purposes. And so, we couldn't find anything.

1. A Mystical Experience

When I was at our Center in Los Angeles, on the Feast of Our Lady of Lourdes (February 11th), Fr. Finbarr Devine, Fr, Kevin Barrett and myself were saying Mass. Fr. Kevin was the principal celebrant and Fr. Devine and myself were concelebrants. As we came to the foot of the altar to begin Mass, I did not expect anything to be different from any other time that I celebrated Mass, but this day was to be different.

Immediately, I don't know whether I was in the Spirit or out of my body. I really don't know how this took place, but Our Lord took me throughout the world. He showed me all humankind in its suffering, its poverty, its degradation and its sinfulness. Then the Lord let me come upon a man who was giant in size and covered with blood from head to foot. Jesus helped me realize that this man represented all the sins of humanity. Jesus then wanted reparation for all the sins of all the world. As I grew in stature to the size of the man, I bent down, picked him up and carried him. I carried him to the throne of the Father. As I was coming toward the throne of the Father, the angels and saints in Heaven, and all the souls in Purgatory were present, praying for all the sins of humankind. As I came before the throne of the Father, I could not even look up because I felt my own sinfulness and my own unworthiness. I laid the man down and I knelt before Him, striking my chest and saying, "Lord, have mercy on me a sinner," just as the Publican did in the Gospels. How could I, a sinner, make reparation for all the sins of humankind? Yet, I knew God was asking me to do this.

Then I thought about the Liturgy, especially at the beginning of the Mass and how the whole Mystical Body of Christ is present with us. At this time, we recognize our sinfulness and the sinfulness of humankind. As we pray as a community, the family of God recognizes and proclaims its sinfulness. We also ask for His mercy and forgiveness. Once we have received His forgiveness, then we can truly sing the Gloria with praise, glory and thanksgiving.

As we began the Gloria, Our Lord came and stood behind me. He placed His hands on my head and I felt once again His power surge through me as I felt on June 20th, 1975. Mary and Joseph also placed their hands on my shoulder. Our Lord let me know that

He was giving Mary and Joseph to me to be the protectors and the guardians of the Apostolate of Christian Renewal. This was done because the purpose of the Apostolate is to help form Christ in others. The Apostolate of Christian Renewal also helps others become a "beloved son" or a "beloved daughter" of God the Father. Since Jesus was the child of Mary and Joseph was as a father to Jesus, they were His protectors. They helped Jesus to live, to grow and to develop into adulthood. Mary and Joseph are also the protectors and the guardians to all of the members of the Apostolate.

After receiving this message, I found myself in Lourdes, where I asked the Blessed Mother's protection, guidance and intercession for the Apostolate. Then I found myself in Fatima. While I was in Fatima, I knelt at the main altar in the Basilica. As a person faces the altar, Francisco is buried on the right and Jacinta on the left. They came forth from their graves, crossed each other's paths and knelt beside me. Francisco knelt on my left and Jacinta on my right. Then they began to pray with me. At that moment, God let me know that He was giving them to me as intercessors and that they would pray for the spreading of the Apostolate. This was done because the Apostolate is to foster the interior message of Fatima, which is the call to live the Gospel message. The real message at Fatima is an invitation to become like Christ and to live His life. When we finished praying, they took me by the arms and raised me up at a forty-five degree angle in the direction of Rome. Next, I found myself in Rome at the Crypt of St. Peter.

At the Crypt of St. Peter, I prayed for the Holy Father. I pledged my loyalty to him and to the teachings of the Church. I did this because we must all be loyal to the Vicar of Christ. We must accept the teachings of Jesus as taught by the Church through the Holy Spirit. I prayed for the Holy Father's strength, health and that his teachings would be accepted by all. I also prayed that all people would be open to the Spirit so that they would be more receptive in accepting the "hard sayings," which the Holy Father teaches if he wants to be faithful to Jesus Christ.

Next, I found myself in San Vittorino, Italy, with Brother Gino praying for the success of the Apostolate. After this, God took me back to the Chapel where the Offertory of the Eucharistic Liturgy was beginning. At the beginning of the Offertory, I saw the whole

Mystical Body of Christ: the angles, the saints in Heaven, the souls in Purgatory and the people on earth. As we were all praying, the offerings of love, adoration, thanksgiving, reparation and intercessory prayer were being offered to the Heavenly Father. This offering was made by the whole Mystical Body of Christ in union with Jesus in the Spirit.

As we began the Canon of the Mass, the scene changed and I saw the Crucifixion scene. I saw Christ carrying the Cross, being nailed and raised onto the Cross. On the Cross, Jesus made His sacrifice of suffering and death. In His offering of Himself, Jesus conquered sin, death and the Devil. He was obedient even until death because He did the will of His Father. During this moment, I again saw our Mother, Mary, the angels and saints in Heaven, the souls in Purgatory and the people on earth, praying in union with Jesus Christ.

At each Eucharistic Liturgy then, we are present at Calvary in a mystical and unbloody manner. This is a supernatural reality that takes place in our presence. We are all part of this sacrificial act, offering everything with Christ the High Priest to our Heavenly Father. This pleases the Father, who accepts the offering of Jesus and that of the whole Mystical Body. Therefore, we are accepted with Jesus and not rejected.

During the Consecration, when the priest says, "This is my Body," I believe that Jesus is truly present because I saw the Body of Jesus present in the Host, which is now no longer bread. Likewise, when the priest says, "This is my Blood," I saw Jesus was truly present in the Blessed Sacrament, in Body, Blood, Soul and Divinity, in His resurrected state—sacramentally present. Jesus is present with us in all the tabernacles throughout the world. In other words, Jesus is with us, He is alive, He is here, He is a part of us and we are a part of Him.

As we continued the Mass, we came to the prayer before the Our Father. In the prayers before the Our Father, we sum everything up by saying, "Through Him, with Him, in Him, in the unity of the Holy Spirit, all glory and honor is Yours, Almighty Father, forever and ever." After this, we begin the banquet of the Mass, which is the meal part. As the Our Father prepares us, we pray with the angels, saints and the whole Mystical Body. We pray that His

Name be hallowed, that His Kingdom come and that His will be done. We also pray for our material needs by praying for our daily bread. We also ask for forgiveness as we forgive those who trespass against us. We also ask for the strength to overcome temptation and to be delivered from all evil. I also believe that the intercessory power is very strong at this moment at each Mass. Therefore, we can expect to receive the blessings of the Father.

As the moment of Holy Communion arrives, we receive Jesus in Holy Communion. I saw that we are within Jesus and Jesus is truly within us. The angels and saints in Heaven and the souls in Purgatory also adore Christ within us. This is such a great blessing and privilege. In fact, when we receive Jesus, He is in us and He transforms us. At this moment of receiving Jesus in the Eucharist, the Holy Spirit takes over and just pours His gifts, graces and blessings upon us. He increases our love for God and enlightens us so that our faith deepens. Our faith, hope and our love become even stronger. Thus, the virtues become more operative in us and the sevenfold gifts become more pronounced. Therefore, the gifts are more fully activated.

When we finally reach the point where the priest gives the blessing in the Name of the Father, Son and Holy Spirit, I saw that it was not only the priest who gives the blessing, but the Father, Jesus and the Holy Spirit Who actually impart the blessing. This happens at every Mass.

God let me understand that we should unite ourselves with each Eucharistic Liturgy that is celebrated throughout the world, each day, day and night. There is never a day or a night, when Mass is not being offered. In other words, Mass is being offered at all times. In this way, we can continually be in union with the Father through Jesus in the Spirit.

In all reality, we are praying twenty-four hours every day when we are praying in union with the Mass. We are able to ask for as many intentions that we wish since the Mass is infinite. Often times, I am asked to pray for many things, such as people who are sick, unemployed and many different spiritual needs. How could I ever, ever pray for any or all of them individually? The only way is to turn it all over to the Hearts of Jesus and Mary and offer all in union with the Eucharistic Liturgy. In this way, our prayer intentions are before the Father twenty-four hours of the day. I believe that all people should make an offering of themselves every day, until the end of time, for our needs as well as for the needs of those who will follow us. The reason why we do this is because we do not know how long the world will exist.

We know that Jesus is the High Priest as well as the Sacrificial Victim. Jesus offers Himself to the Father on our behalf. Through Jesus' suffering and offering of His life on Calvary, all salvation was won for us. Yet, He wants this sacrifice to be offered until the end of time by giving us the privilege to participate in His priesthood.

When the people of God are baptized, they participate in the common priesthood of Jesus Christ. However, they cannot exercise their priesthood unless the ministerial priest offers the Mass. In other words, when people come to Mass, they exercise their common priesthood by praying as a family, with the whole Mystical Body of Christ and as a community.

The ministerial priest, at his ordination, receives a deeper involvement in the priesthood of Jesus Christ. Without the ministerial priest, Jesus could never again exercise His priesthood. But Jesus willed it to be this way. He gave the command, "Do this in commemoration of Me." The ministerial priest then, has the power to change the bread and wine into the Body and Blood of Christ. As a result, Jesus becomes present sacramentally upon our altar and becomes our spiritual food in Holy Communion. He also remains with us in the tabernacle and does not leave us orphans.

I find it strange when people say that they do not get anything from the Mass. I feel this way because they receive tremendous blessings, graces and gifts from each Mass. If we would really understand what the Mass is all about, we would never miss Mass through our own fault. If we are sick, then naturally we are excused. Also, by uniting ourselves in spirit with the Mass, we would participate more fully into this redemptive and glorious mystery.

Finally, if we understood what the Mass is really all about, we would never attend it in a lackadaisical fashion out of routine or duty. Instead, we would have a great joy and anticipation, looking forward to participate in the Mass, to the sharing in the priesthood of Jesus, to praying with others and to building up the Kingdom of God upon earth. We would also do everything in our power to spend some time, even each day, before Jesus in the Blessed Sacrament, where we can pour out our hearts to Him and pray for the needs of the world.

2. We find a Center

Shortly after the vision at Mass, on February 11th, there was an estate in Pomona, California, which was for sale. The estate was a very beautiful Spanish style home. The estate was sufficient, adequate and had two and a half acres of land. Naturally, there were certain things that needed to be done to renovate the house for our use. But, for the most part, I thought the estate was excellent and the price was right. The owners only wanted $95,000.00 in cash. I hoped that the Congregation might buy this Center, but the Council decided against it because they felt that a Center or a Provincial House should be adequate to have rooms where priests could come and relax or where students could come and live so that they could go to various universities.

On the way home from the Council meeting, Father Provincial said to me, "We should not let that beautiful property go without purchasing it. Why doesn't the Apostolate of Christian Renewal buy the property?" And I said to him, "It would be nice, but I don't have the money. I don't have the cash to pay $95,000.00. I would have to borrow money and my philosophy is that, in the work of the Apostolate, I will never go into debt, never do anything unless it can be paid for with cash." He answered me, "That doesn't make any difference. You should go ahead and buy it."

I decided then and there that what we should do was to pray for three days and then have a meeting of our Board of Directors to see what they would say about the purchasing of the property. During the dinner with the Board of Directors, I expressed all the reasons why we should or should not buy the property. I personally did not want to buy any property because I did not want to set up a separate Center by myself, just for the Apostolate of Christian Renewal. I felt this keenly, but I asked for a vote and everyone voted, "yes." I called the people who were unable to attend the meeting to get their opinion. Two said, "yes" and the third said, "yes" with reservations because he knew that I did not want to buy a Center. Anyway, there had been sufficient votes saying, "yes" and my vote really didn't mean anything at that point.

3.   Through prayer, money was received

The Board of Directors decided that we would buy the property. I made the down payment after I had received authority to purchase the property. I also made all the arrangements for obtaining the property. Then we went to the chapel and prayed. As I have said, I had never bought anything without cash and I didn't want to get a loan from the bank because this would have been a real worry to me and might have hindered my ministry. I said to the Lord, "Lord, we have five weeks, until April 28th, to pay $45,000.00 for this property. As You know, we do not ask people for money so we are asking You. You'll have to inspire people to help us, to come to our aid and to raise that amount of money."

Within the next five weeks, the money came from all direction, until we had enough money to pay cash for the property. We also had enough money for the insurance and even to pay for the taxes. (We deliberately paid the taxes because I do not want the neighbors to feel that we are neglecting or taking advantage of Church property in not paying the taxes. I also paid the taxes so that their own taxes would not go up and there would not be any complaints in this regard).

4.   Accused of breaking vow of poverty

I paid for the Center on April 27th, in cash. The property became ours on April 28th, at 12:15 P.M. That evening we were having a meeting at our Center. During this meeting, one of our priests accused me of breaking my vow of poverty, saying that I had no right to spend all that money. He was also concerned about the obligations on the part of the Congregation. This priest thought that the Apostolate of Christian Renewal could not handle the financial responsibilities. He also did not know that I had paid cash for everything and that we did not have any debts or liabilities. Likewise, the Congregation did not have to worry about any financial burden for running the Center of the Apostolate of Christian Renewal.

Because the Apostolate bought the Center, the property is owned by the Apostolate of Christian Renewal. I was being accused of being disobedient, of going ahead and buying property without the consent of the Council. Yet the Provincial had given me permission. I was really concerned about this accusation. I felt that this accusation was made in such a manner that I did not have any time to think or prepare my answer. I believe that I did not fully answer all the questions that were put to me at that time. I thought about it later, though, and I know that I never broke my vow of poverty because I had been told that I could never ask for any money from the Congregation. I also declared to the Congregation that I wouldn't create any financial burdens. I promised, too, that if the Apostolate was able to give money to support the Congregation, then the Apostolate would do so.

C. A gift through Fr. Gerald Fitzgerald

I did not really feel that I had broken the vow of poverty. A short time after this accusation, I went to Albuquerque, New Mexico, to give a retreat. During this whole ordeal, the Devil kept pounding away at me with such thoughts as, "You broke your vow of poverty and you broke your vow of obedience." I suffered terribly over this during the next two to three days and I could not sleep. Yet I knew I had to carry on, giving conferences, giving counseling and running the retreat. As a result, at the end of the retreat, I felt quite exhausted. Fr. Richard Oman, from Anton Chico, New Mexico, came and picked me up at John Koller's home, in Albuquerque, and drove me to Jemez Springs. Jemez Springs is the place where Fr. Gerald Fitzgerald, the Founder of the Paracletes, established his new Congregation. When he established his Congregation, he was still a Holy Cross Father. He envisioned this work and wanted it to be done by his own Congregation. Fr. Fitzgerald then left his Congregation and started a new religious community called, "The Fathers of the Paraclete" in Jemez Springs. He also established a religious community of sisters called, "The Handmaids of the Precious

Blood." These Sisters were to be contemplative so as to pray before the Blessed Sacrament for priests, especially for their problems and for vocations to the priesthood. I think their calling is very beautiful and I hold them in high regard. I also have great respect for the Fathers and the work that they are trying to do.

I went with Fr. Oman to visit the Sisters. As we were driving past the cemetery, Fr. Oman said to me, "Let's go and visit Fr. Fitzgerald's grave." I told him, "I went there last year. I don't see any need to go and visit his grave now." He continued to persuade me and said, "Since we're here, why not go in?" Finally, I agreed. We went through the cemetery and saw various graves of people who had died. Finally, we came to Fr. Fitzgerald's grave.

As I stood before the grave, I felt a tremendous power pulling me toward the grave. I grabbed hold of Fr. Oman and said, "Father, I'm falling! I feel that I am being drawn toward Fr. Fitzgerald's grave." Then I said, "Let's kneel down." As I knelt, this tremendous power continued, which is the same power that goes through my arms and hands when I bless people. I felt this power drawing and pulling me. It was the same power as when Christ came and placed His hands upon my head. I then fell upon the grave of Fr. Fitzgerald and laid there for a long time. While I was prostrate on the grave, all the anxiety, all the fear, all the doubts about whether I had broken my vows of poverty and obedience were taken away from me. In their place, I was given a deep peace, a joy, a strength and a feeling of relaxation. This event felt as if I had slept for many, many hours. When I got up, I felt refreshed and I knew that I did the right thing. Immediately, I knew that it was God's Will for the Apostolate of Christian Renewal to have a Center separate from the Congregation.

1. Which way to go

I do not understand why God wanted this Center to be separate from the Congregation, especially when I desperately wanted the Center to be a part of the Provincial House. Could it be that God intends the Apostolate to be a part of a new community? Could this be the reason? Could it be that the Apostolate is meant to be a movement apart from the Congregation itself? These were some of the questions that remain to be answered. But, more and more, I felt that the Apostolate seems to be moving in a direction totally apart from the Congregation.

This separation is something that I do not wish because I would love to have the Apostolate become a real part of the Congregation. I am hoping, however, that more priests in the Congregation will be more interested in what the Apostolate stands for and does. The Apostolate will have to continue even after I die. However, this is not something that I have to worry about because if this is God's work, then the Apostolate will always continue.

I believe God is going to find a way in which these things are going to be done or brought about. All I need to do is remind myself everyday that the Apostolate is God's work. Then it is in His hands and in His Providence. And so, I must let go and let God. In other words, I may not become too personally involved, lest I begin to think the Apostolate is my work, my efforts and my accomplishments. Therefore, the Apostolate is really God's work that has to be done and God is the One Who is going to bring about whatever has to be done for the future.

a.   Calling to start religious community for women

In regards to starting a new community, I still wonder whether God wants me to do this. I have been thinking about this for more than ten years. This thought is not something new that has recently come into my mine. I definitely think, more and more, that God is calling me to do this. Nevertheless, I will not do this without the necessary guidance, the necessary permission and the necessary discernment of Spirit. I also believe God wants me to begin a new religious community for women. Many young women, as I travel across the country, express a desire to be a part of a new religious community, which would be called the "Handmaids of the Sacred Hearts of Jesus and Mary." The Handmaids would get into catechetical work, census taking in parishes or pastoral ministry while living in a parish situation. They could have people come to the convent for counseling or they could pray with each other. Other Handmaids would work with the elderly, who are home ridden. In other words, the elderly will be urged, if they are well enough and free enough to devote their time and energy to help other shut-ins.

The elderly will also be encouraged to visit, guide, listen and inspire the shut-ins so that they will realize someone really cares. These people must be given the feeling that they are wanted and have a purpose in life. In this way, the sisters can inspire the elderly to be concerned and get involved with others. As a result, the elderly can give a real purpose to their lives, feel wanted and will experience the joy of helping others.

b. The Servants community

In regards to starting a new religious community for priests and brothers, I would call this community "The Servants of the Sacred Hearts of Jesus and Mary." The emphasis in the apostolic life of this new community would be the preaching ministry, the healing ministry and especially counseling or spiritual direction! I would not encourage anyone in the new community to get involved in any other apostolic work. The reason is because the prayer life is the most essential, which has to be strenuous, deep and disciplined. I believe that we must devote a lot of time in prayer. The Servants should prepare themselves to give spiritual guidance more through prayer than through studies. That is why I believe that the Servants should know ascetical and mystical theology. This theology must be stressed rather than the sociological or psychological aspects of spiritual direction. However, the Servants must know when to refer people to psychologists and psychiatrists. In this way, spiritual direction will be based on spiritual values rather than psychological or sociological values. People should, however, be given the guidance and leadership to get involved in social action. We, as priests, can only give guidance, inspiration or dedication. We do this through counseling and spiritual direction.

Social action means to help the poor and the needy in any and every situation. People must be inspired to help each other so that there is a better condition in civil, family and Church life. Each person should be taught to respect the dignity, rights and freedoms of everyone. And finally, each person needs to be taught and guided to peacefully, lovingly and willingly work for the common good, which is true social action.

c.   There is a lot to be done when starting a new religious community

There is a lot to be done in order to establish this community, such as direction and guidance. A way of life must also be formulated and encouragement must be given constantly, in order to bring this about. I believe this is what the Lord is asking of me. Nevertheless, I must wait to see what develops and how things develop. If a new religious community is really from the Lord, then it will be done; however, if a new religious community is not from God, then anything that is done is fruitless.

d.   After Albuquerque

After I finished my work in Albuquerque, New Mexico, I came back to our Center in Los Angeles. Then I went up to the state of Washington for two or three weeks. I preached the message of the Apostolate of Christian Renewal. While I was in the state of Washington, the members of our Center moved to our new place in Pomona, California. They had everything ready when I returned. Shortly after that, I made my annual retreat with the Sacred Hearts Fathers. During an annual retreat, a retreat master comes to give conferences, counseling, hears confessions and participates in other religious exercises. This retreat helped me to deepen my spiritual life. After my retreat, I had the opportunity to give a retreat to a group of priests, which I really loved and wanted to do some more.

D. Others need to foster the work
of the Apostolate of Christian Renewal

In September, I had the opportunity to go to Gilman, Minnesota where Fr. Alfred Kroll was pastor. Fr. Kroll completely understands the Apostolate. In 1974, Fr. Kroll went on a pilgrimage with me to Europe. While on the pilgrimage, Fr. Kroll joined the Apostolate of Christian Renewal at the Carmel convent in Lisieux, France, where St. Therese the Little Flower lived and died. He was very interested in the Apostolate and will do a tremendous amount of good in spreading the Apostolate.

When I came for a Renewal Week in Gilman, I noticed that it was a very small country area, which had a big beautiful Church. I also noticed the sign which stated the population was only 113. I thought to myself, "Certainly we will never be able to fill this Church. I wonder why Father Knoll even bothered to have me come?" As usual, God surprised the dumbest of us. In fact, the morning session was primarily for the elderly, the sickly and those who could not come in the evening. By the end of the week, the people who came during the day approached five hundred people.

In the evening, the week began with about three hundred fifty people in attendance. Before we finished, there were over a thousand people in the evening, who came from all over. Some came from Rochester, St. Paul, Minneapolis and Duluth. I found this to be quite overwhelming to see what was happening. Naturally, we had our critics. A few people were even on a morning radio show and criticized what was going on in Gilman. Some people, who were not even there, said that people fainted when they were blessed. One person said, people had to be carried out on stretchers.

None of these things were true, of course. However, because there was such a spark of interest, many people came to find out what was really happening. God used this event as an occasion to gather people from all over. Then they heard the message I was preaching, which was the charism, spirituality and mission of the Apostolate of Christian Renewal. The blessing then, is only secondary. However, God uses the blessing as an instrument that allows people to get involved.

People who have been blessed know from experience that when the blessing is given, no person ever faints. As I pointed out before, the people are completely in control of their faculties and know what is going on at all times. During this time as well, many people receive blessings, graces, gifts and healings.

My stay in Gilman, Minnesota was really the beginning of the Renewal Weeks. After that, many people began to come in great numbers. I also noticed that more priests became involved in the Renewal because they came and concelebrated with me. This gave me a good feeling, especially when the priests became more receptive and tolerant of me. It was also good to see more sisters come and participate. However, everyone was cautious and waited to see what would happen. They were testing whether this was from God or not. But now it seemed that the priests, brothers and sisters gave, by their actions and their presence, a tacit approval of what was really taking place. This did me much good. It gave me great encouragement to continue the work that God wished to do.

1. The Lord will send other people

In November, I had been told by the Lord that He was going to take away all the people who were working with me in the Apostolate of Christian Renewal. By that, I mean the priests and religious. He said that after this happens, He would send to me the people He wants to work with me. I later told my spiritual director about this in January, 1977. My spiritual director asked me if I was afraid and I replied by saying, "No." However, I would have been afraid if Jesus said he wasn't going to send other people to spread the Apostolate.

Fr. Luke with Don Tesmer

Fr. Luke with niece, Julie Zimmer - Fall of 1996

CHAPTER 4

1977

A. A chaplain to the Holy Lands

When I came back from Gilman, Minnesota, I received a phone call one day. I was asked if I would be the chaplain for a tour to the Holy Land toward the end of February and early March, 1977. The tour was being guided and directed by Pat Boone and George Otis. I knew of Pat Boone, but I never heard of George Otis. Yet, I thought it would be good to be a chaplain on this tour and so I agreed.

I did not know a lot about Pat Boone's life, but I heard that he was a very spiritual and holy person. But, when I was up in Portland, Oregon, giving a mission, a person gave me a book on Pat Boone's life called, *A New Son*. As I read the book, I thought that it would just affirm all my thoughts of what I knew of him. However, in reading the book, I was really surprised. Pat Boone, as a young person, was considered to be quite holy. But after getting married and being in show business, this book says that he started to compromise his principles and began drinking and carousing. As a result of his leaving the Judaic-Christian principles, compromising with the world, and finally accepting the ways of the world, he was at the point of destroying his own marriage.

During this low point in Pat Boone's life, he was asked to play the part of Dave Wilkerson in *The Cross and the Switchblade*. He was going to accept this part, but George Otis told him that he was incapable of playing it. Boone questioned Otis, and Otis replied, "Because you are a bum! You are not saintly and you have to be god-like to play this part. If you want to play the part of Dave Wilkerson, then you must become more god-like. If you portray this part just an actor, then you won't portray an accurate picture of Dave Wilkerson. In other words, if you really want to get into it, then you have to have the same feelings, the same thoughts and the same lifestyle, so that you can portray the truth in your acting. Otherwise, you will be living a lie and will be a hypocrite. You will have two different standards. In one, you will be portraying a person of God, while on the other hand, you will be a person living apart from God."

Pat Boone became quite angry over this painfully true accusation. Later on, after a lot of reflection, Boone realized that Otis was brutally right. Then Pat Boone had an encounter with the Lord and turned himself completely over to Him. There was a complete change in Pat Boone. He again embraced the Judaic-Christian principles and lived a god-like life. He uses his acting as a ministry, which gives witness to others of what it means to be an active Christian in the world today. I believe that Pat is doing a lot of good in his ministry.

As for George Otis, I did not know anything about his life either. I had the opportunity to read his book called, *High Adventure*. This book is the story of his life. As a young boy, George ran away from home and traveled all over the world. He partook in all kinds of worldly pleasures and was very far from God. When I was interviewed by him on TV, he said to me that he was leading a life that would lead him straight to Hell. He was, in reality, leading a very sinful life and was not a very saintly person. One day, George also encountered the Lord and changed his life.

In the course of George's life, he knew how to make a lot of money and became a multi-millionaire. In fact, money came very easily to him because he had the drive, the personality and the knowledge of the world to be very successful. Because of his success, he naturally "wheeled and dealed" in worldly affairs. But, when he encountered the Lord, George knew that he had to make a choice between the Lord's way of living or the world's way of living. Naturally, George wanted the Lord and yet he wanted part of the world. He said that, at the time, he tried to have both. Afterwards, he had to come to grips with himself and see that what he was doing was not from God. He had to make a choice. The choice that he made of course, was to give himself completely to the Lord and accept Jesus as his Savior. After this decision, George began to use his time and his efforts to bring people to the Lord.

As a result of this decision, George established his TV program called, "High Adventure." By this program, he influenced the lives of many people. Through the efforts of George Otis and Pat Boone, many people travel to Israel. These trips to the Holy Land are all about Christianity and giving witness to the Jewish people. Naturally their approach is political as well as religious. But by Pat and George's preaching and witnessing, they show their good will toward the Israelite people. As a result, I believe they make a considerable impact.

During the previous year, they traveled to the Holy Land with 900 people. One of the problems they encountered was that they did not have a Catholic chaplain. That is why I was asked to be the chaplain on this tour. Luckily, I was able to have other priests with me, such as Fr. Alfred Kroll, Fr. Richard Oman, Fr. Kevin Barrett and Fr. Liston.

1. Mt. Carmel

After we arrived in Tel Aviv, we went to Our Lady of Mt. Carmel parish and celebrated Mass. I was hoping that each of the priests could be the principle celebrants throughout the tour. But, most of the people who came were members of the Apostolate and wanted me to preach and be the main celebrant at each Mass.

At Mt. Carmel parish, though, I asked Fr. Oman to be the principle celebrant because he is a member of the Third Order of Mt. Carmel in Albuquerque, New Mexico. In his sermon, Fr. Oman first explained that Elijah lived on Mt. Carmel and the Carmelites claim him to be their founder. He also explained that Elijah was a great prophet, who listened and carried out the directives of the Lord. The Carmelites follow Elijah by living according to his spirit of prayer, sacrifice and penance. Fr. Oman then explained the scapular devotion. He said that the scapular is really the habit of the Carmelite Order. When we wear the scapular, he said, we are truly wearing the habit of the Carmelite Order. The promise that was made to St. Simon Stock is that anyone who would die wearing the habit of the Carmelites would not suffer eternal damnation and would eventually go to Heaven. In order to remain a Carmelite and retain the habit, people have to live in accordance with the ideals and the goals of the Carmelite Order. This means prayer, sacrifice, leading a saintly life, leading a life of the Gospel message and trying to become a "beloved son" or "beloved daughter" of God the Father.

After the people heard about this promise of St. Simon Stock, they wanted to wear the habit and participate in the Carmelite Order. At first, they were permitted to wear the whole habit, but as the habit became cumbersome to wear while working and traveling, they reduced the size of the scapular to that of the scapular worn by the Third Order. As time passed, the size of the scapular was again reduced to the size as we have it today.

a.   Scapular

Many people want to know whether they ought to wear the scapular as is or whether they were permitted to wear the scapular medal. Pope Pius X addressed this issue and said that it is permissible to substitute the scapular medal rather than wear the cloth scapular. Even though most people wear the medal today, I think we should wear the cloth scapular. In fact, women say that the scapular is uncomfortable and too bulky. However, I always say that if the scapular is embarrassing for them because it shifts around and might be seen, then they are not modestly dressed, which reminds me of the complaints of our Blessed Mother to Jacinta, the little girl at Fatima.

In fact, the Blessed Mother appeared in Fatima as Our Lady of Mt. Carmel. I was given the privilege of a vision that allowed me to see the whole scene of October 13th, 1917. In this vision, our Lady appeared first, as she always appeared to the children, as Our Lady of the Rosary. She confirmed that she was the Lady of the Rosary and asked that the Rosary be prayed. Then she appeared as the Sorrowful Mother, in which Jesus and Joseph were also present. Next, Jesus blessed the world. Finally, Mary appeared as Our Lady of Mt. Carmel, who had the Rosary and the scapular in her hands and held them out to the people. I saw this on November 7th, 1952.

In St. Dominic's day, he predicted that in 700 years the world would be saved through the devotions of the scapular and of the Rosary. How can this be brought about, especially when people do not pray the Rosary or even wear the scapular? I believe the answer to this question is Divine intervention so as to help people understand the value of these sacramentals in the Church. I also think it is important that we pray the Rosary and wear the scapular because of the Sabbatine privilege. Many people might laugh at this but the Sabbatine Privilege was given to us by Pope John XXII. He gave the Sabbatine privilege, which means that a person needs to wear a scapular, observe chastity according to a person's state of life and abstain from meat on Wednesday and Saturday. As a result of the Sabbatine privilege, a person who dies and goes to Purgatory will be released on the first Saturday after death. If a person can not abstain from meat, then a priest or confessor can suggest a daily Rosary or some other charitable act. Essentially, a person must live the Gospel message. This means that we must strive to live a holy way of life and become a saint. This is not an exaggerated promise, rather, this promise can easily be fulfilled if we live the Gospel message. We should never be scandalized or think that this is just something superstitious or superficial. This is a promise that has been granted by the Church and we should put our faith in God to honor this promise.

2. Visit to Nazareth

The next day we left Mt. Carmel and went to Nazareth. The trip was a bit hasty, but it was well worth it. As we were driving through the Valley of Sharon and over to Nazareth, we saw a lot of beautiful countryside. The country side was much different from the last time I was in the Holy Land, in 1972. The land was very barren then because it was during the summer months. Now, everything was covered with vegetation and greenery. We also saw the sheep and goats grazing together on the hillside. The guide pointed out to us the difference between the sheep in Israel and the other sheep in the world. The sheep in Israel have a different type of tail, which is shaped like a fan. He told us that in the summertime, there is no grass and the shepherds have to lead their flock to a place where they have food stored. The shepherd calls the leader sheep, which follows the shepherd. The rest of the sheep follow the leader sheep in single file, with each placing its tail over the one following. Only the leader sheep has his head uncovered.

As I reflected on this sight, I thought about the Christian application. At the end of time, Jesus will separate the sheep from the goats. He will put the sheep on the right and the goats on the left. The goats symbolize those who do not do God's will because they are independent, do not share with one another and are not interested in the others' needs. The sheep, however, symbolize those who do God's will because they are dependent, take care of others and are interested in the other's needs (each sheep protecting the next with the shade of his tail over the follower's head). In Christian living, we must also follow the leader, who is the Pope and the bishops under him. We must learn to share with others. Jesus also said that, at the end of time, He would say to the people on the right, "When I was hungry, you fed me. When I was naked, you clothed me. When I was thirsty, you gave me drink. When I was sick, you tended me. When I was in prison, you visited me. Come, blessed of My Father into the Kingdom that has been prepared for you." And then He will say to the people on the left, "When I was hungry, you did not feed me. When I was thirsty, you did not give me to drink and when I was sickly, you did not visit or tend me. When I was in prison, you did not come to me. Depart from me you cursed into everlasting fire."

Christ used the ordinary things that He saw in nature and in life during His preaching ministry. From his preaching, scholars are able to tell what time of the year it is. For instance, when Jesus multiplied the loaves and the fishes, He told the people to sit down on the grass. Scholars can conclude then that the season was late fall, winter or early spring because there is only abundant grass during these periods. Likewise, when Jesus said, "go into the towns and if they do not accept your message, you should shake the dust from your feet." Again, scholars can conclude that Jesus was speaking in the summertime because there is barely any grass and it is very dusty. And so, when a person walks, his or her sandals and feet get very dirty from the dust.

In Nazareth, some people are Catholic, while other are Moslems. As we drove on our way, the guide explained that Archangel

Gabriel could have revealed God's Will either at the well where Mary got water or at her home. These are the two stories that are being examined today. However, the Bible says that the Archangel came to Mary and told her she would be the Mother of the Messiah. Gabriel asked Mary if she would enter into the plan that the Father had for her. Mary, of course, accepted and turned her body, her mind and her soul over to God. The Holy Spirit then came upon Mary and formed Jesus from and within her so that she is truly the Mother of Jesus. We should be very grateful to Mary for entering into the plan of the Father.

Joseph also had to make a commitment to the Lord. He did this when he understood the role that Mary had, by being the Mother of the Messiah. Joseph was told that He who was to be born of her was from the Most High. Joseph accepted the Most High's Will and made his commitment to the Lord by giving his life to the service of Jesus and Mary. Joseph also became the protector, provider and the guardian of the Holy Family. At Mass that night, I preached all of these thoughts.

3. The Sea of Galilee

From Nazareth, we went to the Sea of Galilee. We traveled through the countryside, saw the site of the multiplication of loaves and past the place where Christ gave the Sermon on the Mount. Finally we arrived in Capernaum, which is where Jesus preached in the synagogue and performed many miracles. Capernaum was also the center of travelers, who would come on their way to Egypt to bring their wares and trade. Many people heard Jesus and saw the miracles, but many refused to believe in Jesus. St. Peter also lived in Capernaum, which is also where Jesus cured Peter's mother-in-law. In fact, the city of Capernaum still has the ruins of Peter's house and the synagogue. This synagogue is where Jesus cursed the town and said that it would be destroyed and never be rebuilt. Even to this day, Capernaum has never been rebuilt.

Next, we had the opportunity to cross the Sea of Galilee. The guide told us that the water was as fresh as drinking water. The fresh water comes from the streams which flow from the mountain. The Sea of Galilee also has many fish and is just flourishing with life.

As I was thinking and meditating, all I could think of was that as Christians, we should be like the Sea of Galilee. We should be full of life. We should have the life of God within us. God Himself streams into us, through His blessings, graces and gifts. They flow into us from the sacraments and through our prayer life. So the analogy is quite valid.

4. The Dead Sea

From the Sea of Galilee, we went to Tiberius and along the Jordan river. Our guide explained to us that the Sea of Galilee flows into the Jordan river. We continued our journey until we came to the Dead Sea. The water from the Jordan river flows into the Dead Sea and does not flow anywhere else. The water just stays there and evaporates by the heat because of the hot weather. Even though there is no life in the Dead Sea, there are many rich minerals that are very valuable.

Our guide also explained that if Israel could extract the minerals that are there, especially magnesium, then they could have more money than all the Arab countries from their oil deposits. In order to extract these minerals, Israel would have to run fresh water from the Mediterranean so as to run the turbines, engines or whatever is needed to extract these minerals. Even though Israel is thinking of extracting these minerals, Israel expects that it will take a long time for this to be accomplished.

The leading industry in Israel is tourism. People come from all over the world to visit the Holy Land. They wish to visit and see this little country which is only the size of New Jersey, about 150 miles long and only 40 miles wide.

I believe that the Jewish people are being brought back to the Holy Land because they are fulfilling the plan of God. They were and still are the Chosen People. One day, they are going to be brought into the Church of Christ and will eventually accept Christ as the Messiah. God will fulfill this prophecy and when the time is right, their eyes will be opened and they will embrace the faith.

In the time of 1972, Israel was very materialistic. They were concerned only about the existence of the State of Israel and about material things. But this time there was a great difference, which was that they felt they were fulfilling a mission and that God had chosen them. This was a result of the Yom Kippur war in 1973.

The thoughts that came to my mind, in regards to the Dead Sea and the Sea of Galilee, are the following. I could not help but think about Christians. The Sea of Galilee shares its riches and its life with the world. Likewise, Christians should share their life and experiences that they have from God and others will benefit immensely. The Dead Sea is like Christians we had before Vatican Council II. They are the people who are not open like some people today. As a young seminarian, I was taught in my training that what happens in our spiritual life is between God, my spiritual director and myself. No other person has a right to know about my spiritual riches or my lack of them. I believe that this was a mistake. I believe that God wants us to share our knowledge and the experiences that He has given to us. People must use His gifts and talents to spread His Kingdom on earth. God expects us to use them and if we don't, then we are going to have to answer to God.

In the past, many people were like the Dead Sea and everything has to be dragged out. Many times, great treasures have been hidden or lost by this process. The same is true in regards to the minerals in the Dead Sea, which simply means that they are not being used. Rather, an outside force is needed to extract these rich minerals. Sometimes, in spiritual living, we have to drag the treasures out of people. Many could and should be enriched by these experiences. Rather than being like the Dead Sea, people need to be more and more like the Sea of Galilee and be open. In other words, people need to share their thoughts with others so that many will begin to see the importance of living like Jesus Christ.

5. Jerusalem

As we were going to Jerusalem, it started to snow heavily. This proves that Jesus must have seen snow in His life. He suffered from the cold as well as from the heat. He suffered from the wet weather as well as from the dry. He knew what life was all about. He is a man Who ran into all different situations in life, just like we do. Jesus was truly a man as well as God. As we came into Jerusalem, I thought, "This is the city of the Lord. This is the city where

Jesus wept. And this is the city where He sat on the stone wall and said, 'How often I would have gathered you to myself as a hen gathers her flock, but you would not.'"

Many prophets were killed or stoned to death in Jerusalem. Jerusalem is the Holy City because Jesus preached and died there. We were privileged to go to various places in Jerusalem during the next few days. First, we went to the Upper Room and, as I may have pointed out in Part I, this is the place where Jesus instituted the Blessed Sacrament. In this room, Jesus said the first Mass, that is, the first Eucharistic Liturgy. During the Mass, He conferred the power of the priesthood upon the Apostles and gave them the command to do this in memory of Him. From that time until the end of time, the Apostles and their successors will offer the Eucharistic Liturgy, which is offered 24 hours a day. Finally, there would be a clean oblation offered to our Heavenly Father. The Eucharistic Liturgy is the new oblation, which is Jesus offering Himself as a Victim for all humanity. There could no longer be the offering of sheep, goats, oxen or any other animals because Jesus would be the offering in the New Covenant.

In the Upper Room, Jesus told the Apostles that He would go to the Father and prepare a place for them. During the course of the meal, Jesus prayed the prayer of unity. Even though Jesus gave the Apostles His Body and Blood in Holy Communion, He knew they would abandon Him. For example, Jesus knew Peter would deny Him. Nevertheless, Jesus also knew the Apostle's were of good faith who wanted to give themselves to Him and be His followers. Therefore, Jesus gave Himself to them.

Second, we went to the Garden of Gethsemane. In the Garden of Gethsemane, Jesus prayed and asked the Apostles to remain with Him in prayer, especially James, John and Peter. During this time, Jesus came back to them three times to ask for prayer and to watch only one hour with Him. But they were heavy with sleep as Scripture tells us. They did not pray with him. As Jesus went forward and prayed, He asked the Father to remove this chalice from Him. He said, "Not my will, but Yours be done." The Father said, "No" to Jesus. In saying, "Let your will be done," Jesus made His commitment to the Father. He accepted His Father's Will and made a commitment to us. Jesus was ready and willing to shed His Blood and die for us. Standing in that spot where Jesus made this commitment, a person cannot help but be overawed by the great sacrifice that Jesus made.

In the Garden of Gethsemane, Judas came with the soldiers and arrested Jesus. It was here, in the Garden, where Peter tried to defend Jesus by taking his sword and cutting off the ear of one of the soldiers. Jesus said, "If you take up the sword, you are going to perish by the sword." In other words, Jesus was telling the people that the Kingdom of God is not spread by force. Rather, the Kingdom of God is spread by inviting people to develop a deep conviction and a personal commitment to the Lord. He then told Peter to put his sword away and healed the ear of the soldier. Next, Jesus went with the soldiers and all the Apostles scattered, except for Peter who followed at a distance. Peter wanted to see what would happen to Jesus. Later that night, Jesus' prophecy came true when Peter denied the Lord three times out of fear.

Next, we went to the area where Jesus was condemned. The tour guide explained various happenings during the trial of Jesus. We then walked in the footsteps of Jesus by doing the Stations of the Cross. When we arrived at the Holy Sepulcher Church, we saw the place where allegedly Jesus was stripped of His garments, nailed to the Cross and died on Calvary. A person cannot help but be impressed, over and over again, with what took place in the life of Jesus on this day of suffering. The forces of evil thought they had triumphed, but it was only an apparent triumph. This was a day of victory in which Jesus triumphed over sin, death and Satan.

We also went into the tomb where Jesus was laid. From this tomb, He rose from the dead. We cannot help but think of all the different happenings in the life of the Lord during that day and during the days that followed. In fact, I thought about the beautiful gift that Jesus gave to us. The first gift that Jesus gave to us when He rose from the dead is the gift of reconciliation, the gift of His mercy, the gift of His love and the gift of confession. He appeared to the Apostles and said, "Peace be to you." Breathing upon them, Jesus said, "Receive ye the Holy Spirit. Whose sins you shall forgive, they are forgiven them; whose sins you shall retain, they are retained." This was a gift from His Most Sacred Heart.

We also visited the hill where Jesus ascended into Heaven and where He told the Apostles to wait for Him. When He came toward them, the Apostles all knelt in adoration. Even the Apostles who doubted recognized Who Jesus was. Jesus told them, "Full authority has been given to Me both in Heaven and on earth; go, therefore, and make disciples of all the nations. Baptize them in the name, 'of the Father, and of the Son and of the Holy Spirit.' Teach them to carry out everything I have commanded you. And know that I am with you always, until the end of the world (ct Mt. 28:19-20)!" Therefore, the Church believes that any person who has been baptized in the Name of the Father, and of the Son and of the Holy Spirit, is a member of the Catholic Church. They are members of the Church of Jesus Christ, whether they believe it or not; whether they like it or not. That is why when any person who has been baptized joins our Church, they are not re-baptized. They only have to make a profession of faith and go to confession. This is how they enter more fully into the Church.

When Jesus ascended into Heaven and sat at the right hand of the Father, He was enthroned as the Lord of lords, the King of kings and the Judge of the world. From Heaven, Jesus' first gift from His Sacred Heart was the gift of the Holy Spirit. This gift was given to the Apostles, disciples and the Blessed Mother when they were praying together in the Upper Room. As they were praying for the coming of the Holy Spirit, the Spirit descended upon the Apostles and established the Church of Jesus Christ. The Church of Jesus Christ, then, celebrates its visible birth on Pentecost Sunday. Likewise, Jesus said He would build His Church upon Peter. Therefore, the Holy Spirit established the Church of Jesus Christ upon Peter. This is also when and where Mary gained the title, "Mother of the Church."

The Holy Spirit continually gives His guidance, through the successor of Peter (Today, that means our present Pope). Jesus said that He would send the Spirit to the Apostles in order that the Spirit could bring to their minds all the truths that He had taught them.

We also went to Bethany where Jesus raised Lazarus from the dead. While we were there, we had the opportunity to go into the tomb of Lazarus. The tomb was only big enough to hold twelve people. We crawled through the small opening and entered the little tomb. While there, we joined hands and prayed the Our Father. We also sang the song, "I am the Resurrection and the Life," and went into spontaneous prayers. Then we went from the tomb of the Church and offered Mass. At the Mass, I preached about the bondage of Lazarus. In death, he was bound and had the winding sheet about him. When Jesus asked Lazarus to come forth, he came forth! Jesus told the people to release him by taking off the winding sheets so as to give him his freedom. Perhaps this has to happen to many of us. We have to be called from our mediocre and lukewarm ways of life. Some have to be called back to life after experiencing spiritual death through sin so as to be free from the bondage of sin. People also have to be called to live their faith so as to have the freedom to be the children of God.

6. Receiving the invisible stigmata

When I was in the Garden of Gethsemane, in 1972, I had the privilege to concelebrate Mass with Fr. Patrick Peyton. During the Mass, I do not know whether I had an in the body or an out of the body experience. The Lord took me close to Himself. This experience seemed as if I was standing before the throne of the Father. While I was there, I was told that I would be asked to suffer a lot in my life. God asked me if I would be willing to suffer martyrdom. I thought, at the time, that this meant I would suffer actual martyrdom by shedding my blood. I thought God was asking me to give my life in defense of the faith. Since that time till the present, I have had pains in my hands and in my feet. I believe what has happened is that the Lord has given me the invisible stigmata. At times, these pains feel like a dull toothache, while at other times, these pains feel like a sharp pain that a person gets from an abscessed or infected tooth. These pains come at different times, especially on Friday, which are quite painful. At other times, I experienced a dull pain that lasts for days and sometimes no pain at all. Usually when I bless people who are going to receive great gifts, I encounter the Devil and receive a very sharp and severe pain. These pains have been with me for a long time. At first, I did not think much of it. I thought it was arthritis or something else that was happening. It never really dawned on me that it could be the invisible stigmata. However, today I am convinced that these pains are the invisible stigmata.

a.   My prayer of being an instrument

I find that the invisible stigmata is a profound mystery, espe-cially when God has chosen me for the mission of standing before the world to manifest the sufferings of Jesus Christ, His crucified Son. I am now willing to undergo any pain or any suffering, in order to carry out the Father's Will. I pray that I may be a worthy instru-ment by manifesting His love and compassion to the people of God. I also pray that God will use me to give witness to the Passion of Christ so that all people may be drawn closer to Him. When they see me, I pray that they look beyond me and see Our Lord Jesus Christ, the crucified One. I hope their hearts can be touched so that their minds and souls will be open to the Spirit. I hope that when people see me that they will be filled with a great love and a great longing for the Lord so as to have the desire to receive His love and mercy in the Sacrament of Reconciliation. I also pray that He may use me as His instrument in granting this love and mercy so that people re-ceive peace, love and joy in the forgiveness of their sins. I also hope that through the cross, this gift of suffering, may touch many priests deeply so that they too may be moved by the love and mercy of God. Hopefully, the priests will be more willing to hear confessions and bring God's peace and love to souls. If this is accomplished, then the suffering will never be in vain.

7.   Meeting the Ecumenical group

The involvement that we had with the ecumenical group was limited, but good. We listened to talks by the Mayor of Jerusalem, who was very pleased that Christians were present. He was happy that we contributed to the well-being of Israel. He also expressed a hope that many more Christians would come to Israel, especially the youth. I read in the paper that they wanted Catholic Christians to come to Israel. Perhaps this was due to the fact that the Catho-lics in Lebanon were fighting against the Moslems. Maybe Israel feels that the Catholics are on their side. It could be that they want more Catholics to come to Israel so they could see what is being done in the Holy Land. I think it is very important that as many Catholics as possible should go to the Holy Land. Why? Because we believe that Jesus is the Lord. We believe that Jesus is the Founder of our Church, through the power of the Holy Spirit. We also believe that Jesus is alive and remains with us in our Church and in the Blessed Sacrament. We believe that we are to give witness to Jesus and establish the Kingdom of God on earth. We believe that the Israelite people will one day accept Jesus as the Messiah. Therefore, I believe that we have a mission to fulfill. We are to give witness to the Israelite people and explain who Catholic Christians are. We are to witness to what we believe by being people of good will. We should show everyone that we wish them well. We must demonstrate that we accept people as they are. We prove that we don't force our way or our ideas upon anyone. We only wish to share our ideas, gifts and blessings.

The more we strive to take pilgrims to the Holy Land, the greater the impact will be. Our faith will impress the people of Israel, while our faith will be enriched from the contact with the Israelite people and the various Holy Places in Israel. Visiting the Holy Land also helps us understand the history of Christ, who was born nearly 2,000 years ago in the Holy Land. When visiting the Holy Land, the Gospel comes alive and helps us to appreciate the study of Scripture so as to understand our faith more fully.

8. In Rome

After we finished the trip to the Holy Land, we went to Rome. While in Rome, various arrangements were made to see many of the secular places, rather than many of the religious places. And so, I changed this immediately. I told the guides that we did not want to see the secular areas of Rome. Rather, we wanted to see the churches and the shrines. The guides were very amenable and readily adapted to our requests. They gave us tours to various beautiful places in the Vatican, basilicas and the churches in Rome.

We were also going to see the Holy Father, Pope Paul VI, but we were disappointed because he had the flu. He was too sick for his General Audience. Nevertheless, the Holy Father spoke from his window and said that he was very sorry that he could not be present for his General Audience. He said that he would pray for us and he asked us for prayers.

9. Visiting Brother Gino

As we were waiting to see Brother Gino, we were praying the Rosary. Then he came into the chapel and knelt down next to me throughout the Rosary and the Mass. After the Rosary and the Mass, Brother Gino went to the building where the seminary is located. He greeted all the people for a very short time on an individual basis. Finally, he went into a place where he sees people privately. This visitation was much different from when I was there before. Previously, he saw people in his little area behind the sacristy, where he received the stigmata. In order to see Brother Gino, a person has to wait in line. Each person is given a number because many people want to see him. I chose all five priests who were the leaders, plus three other people who were really in need or had a special reason for being on the tour. When a person visits Brother Gino, there is only a small area in which to stand. In this area, a grille separates Brother Gino from the person who is visiting. He speaks through an opening in the grille and says a prayer. Then he listens to what the person has to say. In some cases, he might give the person advice and then the person is supposed to leave. Then, the next person comes. Usually the other religious brothers try to limit the time of each visit. They usually ring a little bell when the visit is over so that others have an opportunity to visit with Brother Gino.

When I visited Brother Gino, I thought about the suffering that he must go through in order to be obedient to the wishes of his superiors. He does exactly what he is told. The people come to tell their troubles or hardships. Naturally this causes him much pain and suffering. I believe that we should pray for him and make some sacrifice for him. Brother Gino is very humble and willing to give himself to others. Many people say that he should not be doing what he is doing, but he is doing everything under obedience. Brother Gino gives witness to what the suffering of Christ is like. This comes through loud and clear.

When we arrived, there were some Italians waiting to see him. However, Brother Gino wanted us to come ahead of the Italians because he is very fond of American people. The Italian people probably felt a sense of resentment or rejection because they were saying, "Who are these people to go ahead of us?" In fact, I noticed a person who was quite sickly so I took my Crucifix with the relic of the True Cross and asked him if he wished me to bless him. He said he did, and when I blessed him, he felt a tremendous power coming upon him from the blessing. He said, "What is this? What is this feeling that I am getting?" I could not explain to him the blessing because I do not speak Italian, but he asked the others to receive the blessing. And so, all of the Italians received a blessing and some of them fell over. Afterwards, the guide came and also received the blessing. He also felt the power of the blessing, which was explained by Fr. Oman. The guide then explained to the Italian people what had happened. They became excited, peaceful and joyful.

The next day we flew back to the United States. I think that the trip to the Holy Land and to Rome was worthwhile. There are many things that I am sure that I could have said which would make this more interesting, yet what I have pointed out will, I hope, encourage people to visit the Holy Land and Rome so as to see the heritage of our Catholic faith. Catholics have been chosen by God to be the people of God. We have been chosen to be apostolic. Therefore, we should be willing to share our life, our riches, our knowledge and our love with the whole world. We could leave a tremendous impact upon the people, the young and the old, wherever we go. We are ambassadors for Christ and His Church.

B. Two kinds of camp

Upon my return from the Holy Land in the beginning of March, 1977, I continued my work in spreading the Apostolate of Christian Renewal. My preaching ministry took me to various states for one, two, three weeks at a time. When I'm on my Renewals, I have the opportunity to feel the pulse of our nation and see the various impacts of different movements. I become more aware of the sins of the world as well as the struggle that many people encounter when they try to live their faith. I have noticed that there are two different camps in the world and in the United States. On one side, there are the materialists, who want pleasure, possessions, power and prestige. On the other side, there are those who are turning away from materialism, who are sincere, generous and spiritual.

In the 1960's, there was a revolution by many young people that turned against the traditional lifestyle. These young people no longer wanted any part of the rat race. They wanted a more simple, pleasant and peaceful life. Youth turned to what we call the "hippie movement." In this movement, I think there was some good, such as getting away from materialistic living. However, the "hippie movement" also made many mistakes. They took drugs, indulged in sex and drinking. Personally, I believe their lifestyle should be rejected because it is repugnant and leads a person away from God. As a result, many young people have turned away from God and the "institutional Church." These people never really understood the Church and the teachings of Jesus Christ. However, today many of those who left the Church are beginning to come back. Likewise, the young people are more sincere, generous and spiritual. The teenagers are a beginning of a new revolution. They want to take another step forward in spiritual living.

1. Sex education

Many of the young are being corrupted by being exposed to a false sex education program that has been implemented in many of the schools. The problem is that schools are teaching only the biological aspects of sex. Today, they advocate the enjoyment of sex on all levels and explain ways of protection. As a result, some young people have become sexually active at a very early age without knowing any better. Logical problems that follow from advocating the enjoyment of sex at an early age are venereal diseases, unwed parents and abortions. There is an attitude of constant striving for pleasure.

As Catholics and mature adults, we have the duty to teach the youth the truth in regards to sex education. This is primarily the parents' duty. The parents must point out to the youth that this is a God-given gift. The gift of sex is intended to be procreative and unitive, which is to be used only in marriage. In this way, a child can have stability and love so as to become a well developed person. This means the spiritual, intellectual, physical and mental development of the person. Today, only the social, mental and physical development are given attention. Whereas, the spiritual aspect is completely rejected. If we teach our young people the principle of Christian morality, then they will be taught self-control and will respect the dignity of the person. They should also be taught to realize that they are the Temple of the Holy Spirit and the sons and daughters of God the Father. In other words, the youth need to become more like Jesus Christ, Who is the Way, the Truth and the Life. Jesus will show us how to be pure, how to love, how to sacrifice and how to give service to others. If we follow in His footsteps, then we will be true to God, ourselves, our family, our community and our world.

a. Overcoming temptations

All people have temptations, but temptations can be overcome and be very sanctifying. If people learn to ask God for help, then temptations will be a source of grace. People will then lead a life of good Christian morals and will have the power of God to live courageously.

Human nature is weak and when tempted any person can fall into sin. This can happen through weakness, ignorance or in a moment of surprise. A person who misuses God's given gifts needs to ask for forgiveness. We should also be willing to help people with their problems and not ostracize, criticize or destroy them. In this manner, people will be shown mercy, kindness, compassion and love, which will help them to maintain their dignity.

C. Division in the Church

In my ministry, I have found that there is a great division in the Church. There are the conservatives and the ultra-conservatives, the liberals and the ultra-liberals and the middle-of-the-roaders. The greatest danger to the Church are the ultra-conservatives because they think that everything that happened at Vatican II was a tremendous mistake. Ultra-conservatives neither accept Vatican II, nor implement the teachings of Vatican II. In fact, they work against it and try to establish their own Church by keeping the Latin Mass as it was before. They also do not accept the change into the vernacular or the Latin Mass according to the new Ordo.

I believe that helping ultra-conservatives is almost impossible because they don't understand what the Catholic Church is doing. Rather, ultra-conservatives have closed minds and will automatically shut a person off when trying to explain the teachings of the Catholic Church. I believe that a person can only pray and do penance for them.

In regards to ultra-liberals, they want to introduce their own way of thinking and acting. They seem like they want to be the Pope with their own teaching. In other words, ultra-liberals teach modernism, which Pope Pius X condemned. The ideals of modernism are rampant, and are being taught and fostered. Thank God they are only the minority. However, they are vociferous and give the impression that they are the true leaders of the Church.

I believe that the people of God are no longer accepting ultra-liberal teaching. Rather, they are discerning the Spirit and realizing that this is not from God. The impact of ultra-liberal teaching in the Church will be minimal even if they choose to stay in the Church. Ultra-liberals may fight against the teachings of the Church and advocate their own teachings. However, they will not withstand the true teachings of Christ. Their influence might linger on for a short time, but it will eventually be rejected by the people of God. People are uniting and beginning to accept a more well-balanced teaching. The extremes are being avoided. As time goes on, there will be a settling down amongst these groups. Then the true teachings of Jesus will again be taught. I believe that the Church will become stronger through this crisis. More people will accept the challenge of being true apostles, disciples and evangelists. Then there will be a real striving to establish the Kingdom of God upon earth.

D. It is the dawn

On April 13th, I asked some people at our Center to pray with me and over me. While they were praying, I saw the ocean. I was facing the horizon and walking on the beach. I watched the sun, which I thought was setting. The sun was a bright red. I thought to myself that this meant that my waiting for the right time to begin the Servants and Handmaids Communities was over. However, the Lord said to me, "It is the dawn." I understood by His remark that my trials, sufferings and waiting to establish these religious communities was only beginning. I began to cry uncontrollably for over a half hour.

1. The Lord asking me to teach people

The next day, April 14th, while we were praying, I again experienced a bright red sky. I said to the Lord, "What does it mean — that this is the dawn?" The Lord then told me loud and clear that, "It is the dawn of your suffering." Immediately, the words of our Lord, "Take up your cross and follow Me," flashed through my mind. The Lord continued His message by saying, "I love you. I bless you. I consecrate you and I anoint you anew. I will be with you wherever you go and help you in whatever you do. My blessings are upon you and upon your work." I asked our Lord what I should do in order to spread the Apostolate of Christian Renewal. He told me that, for a time, I would continue to preach as I have been doing in various states throughout our country. He then told me that people would come to me from all corners of the earth. I said to Him, "Lord, what is it that You want me to do?" And He answered, "Teach My people." I answered, "What am I to teach them?" His answer was, "Teach them what I have taught you over the years in your spiritual life." I said to Him, "How can the Apostolate have various leaders in different areas if I do not go to them?" He said again, "They will come to you. I will send to you the people that I have chosen and they will spread the Apostolate throughout the country and the world."

E. In Minnesota

In May and June of 1977, I kept busy with the work of the Apostolate. Toward the end of May, I went to Minnesota, where I gave a Renewal Week at St. John's Parish in Foley, Minnesota, and then at Holy Angel's Parish in St. Cloud, Minnesota. I was also privileged to give a Renewal to the Poor Clare Sisters in Sauk Rapids, Minnesota. During the three days, I told the Sisters that they could come and speak with me individually. When they came to speak with me, they opened up and told me about their lives and their spiritual longings to be a saint. I was very impressed with this beautiful community of Sisters.

One Sister came on June 15th, 1977 and told me some things which really made me stand in awe at the workings of the Lord. She told me that God the Father asked her to pray for someone who would have the stigmata and that she should offer her life, her sufferings and her prayers for this person. She was told that she would enter into the apostolate of that person chosen to manifest to the world the Crucified Christ. She prayed for that person and yet, at times, she could hardly believe that it was possible. At times, this calling faded from her mind and was in the background of her thoughts. Nevertheless, she still kept on praying. Then she said to me that at my fist conference, God the Father said, "He is the one." She asked me if I had the stigmata and I explained that I had the invisible stigmata. This is how I met the Poor Clare Sister for whom I have a great respect. Apparently, God confirmed what had been going on in my life since August 17th, 1972. There were many times when I doubted the invisible stigmata. I thought it was just a figment of my imagination. But after Sister told me this, I definitely believed that God has given me the invisible stigmata.

1. A letter I received from a Poor Clare sister

Later, the Poor Clare sister wrote this letter: "Ever since June 15th, 1977, you have been with me in a very special way and my whole life has been bound up with you. But the mystery was so beautiful that I feared it might not be real, so I hesitated to surrender to believing. During February, March and April of 1976, during prayer, the Father constantly spoke to me of His love and how His love was revealed in Jesus, in His last words, and I was so drawn with love to Jesus' wounds. I could think of nothing else except the horrible evil in our beautiful America and in myself. I wept to see such great love and so much ugliness. The Father kept comforting me and making me understand that He was willing to do anything to help the people, because the powers of evil were so great. It went something like this, 'Yes, yes, I am willing. I will give signs and wonders to the United States. I am not through showing mercy. Yes, I will do it. I am willing, even to put a beloved crucified son or daughter in the midst of America, so that, once again, people may see how much I love them and be reminded. Yes, I will give the wounds that Jesus had in His hands, feet and side to someone.' I went through this for three months. The insights were very profound, beautiful and sorrowful. Then this passed into the background only to return forcefully, Father Luke, when I was with you alone on June 15th, 1977. Somehow, we suddenly exchanged very beautiful words and I saw before me the person whom the Father had prepared me to see. The words I spoke to you had not been prepared. After I left you, I walked straight outside and practically fell prostrate in front of the Crucifix. As I said, I do not understand everything. I am lost in a sense of wonder and profound joy. What can I do but love Him in return for the depths of such bounteous mercy?"

2. After leaving Sister and the noticeable change in the people

After leaving Sister, my thoughts were upon her words for many days. During this time, our souls were united in spirit, in prayer, in suffering and in longing for the Will of the Father to be accomplished. I still do not know when, where or how this will take place. Actually, this doesn't matter. The only thing that matters is that we may know and do the Will of God. I pray that I will always have the grace and the strength to do this.

I continued on with the work of the Apostolate, through the months of 1977, without too many other extraordinary things happening in my life. I worked continually to spread the Apostolate. In speaking and dealing with people, I noticed many people showing more respect and love than ever before. I believe God has changed their hearts, minds and souls because when I cross the country, people come in large numbers. They also go to confession, participate in the Mass and listen to my sermons. They also come for the blessing, but not just for curiosity's sake. As a result, I see a tremendous difference on the part of the people. They have always been awestruck, but now there was something deeper and truer. I noticed that I have always been very careful of what I said, because they took me seriously and believed everything that I said. Even when I was joking, they took it very seriously. So I realized, more and more, the importance of really zeroing in on the message of Jesus Christ and staying with that as much as possible, without making jokes or taking anything lightly.

F. Visions

Towards the end of 1977, I was praying in our chapel in Pomona, California, I saw myself in a large open and barren field. As I was walking through this field toward a mountain, I felt the presence of God, the angels and saints in Heaven. Then I fell flat on my face in adoration of God. At that moment, an angel came and raised me up to a standing position. The angel stripped me of all my outer clothing and robed me with new garments. Next, the angel took a horn of oil and poured it over my head, which meant that the angel was anointing me for the Lord's service. Then he gave me a staff and disappeared.

This vision always remained in my mind, and I never forgot it. I believe the significance of this vision was to make me realize more fully that a person receives the gift of becoming a king at Baptism. Kingship means a call to go forth, to give service to others and to be a servant to all.

Another day, while in prayer, I saw the whole world enveloped in complete darkness. I never saw anything so dark or totally black before. Then I saw our Blessed Mother standing and facing the darkness with outstretched arms. From her hands, I saw rays of light which penetrated the darkness. As I was standing next to our Blessed Mother, the angels, the saints in Heaven, the souls in Purgatory and all the people from earth gathered. Next, we all joined in prayer by facing the darkness. As we prayed, we offered everything to Jesus through Mary. Then we offered all our prayers with Jesus in the Holy Spirit as united people to the Father in union with each Mass throughout the world. The rays from Mary became brighter and brighter until they penetrated the darkness. The darkness began to disappear until there was no more darkness anywhere in the world. Everything was clear and beautiful so that every person could see everything.

From this vision, I believe that the Servants and Handmaids of the Sacred Hearts of Jesus and Mary are called to pray with Mary,

St. Joseph, the whole Heavenly court, the souls in Purgatory and all the people on earth to bring about the victory over the darkness of sin, the world and Satan. I believe that an era of peace will be given to humankind. However, prayer, penance, conversion and good works are still needed to be a part of each person's life so that each person can become a saint.

1.   Some women urging me to start a new religious community

I again thought about forming a new religious community of sisters towards the end of 1977. God has been after me for many years to do this. Again, I tried to put this thought off by not doing anything about it. Yet, various people continually asked me about starting a new religious community. They all had the same ideas, the same goals and the same purposes in mind. I continued to put them off and I urged them to enter other religious communities. I told them to pray and prepare themselves so that they could give themselves more fully when they actually entered a community.

Finally, I made a decision that I would put them on a one year probation period. If a sufficient number should persevere, then I would definitely begin the process of founding a new religious community of sisters. I told each one to continue to pray and prepare themselves to work toward that goal. I also asked them to discern if that was God's Will.

During this time, I really stood alone because I didn't have anybody to back me up. God's ways are so mysterious, but I know He was working behind the scenes to accomplish His designs, even though I wasn't sure what He really wanted for the future of the Apostolate. Because I felt alone, I wished I had the support and encouragement of my brothers in my Congregation. Yet, wherever I went, more and more people would come and participate in the Renewal Weeks. More and more would express their desire to be part of the work, yet something was holding them back. I really didn't know where things were heading. I felt so alone and so helpless, so I turned to the Lord in prayer and asked for His guidance and His help.

Fr. Luke just sitting and enjoying a peaceful day - Fall of 1996.

CHAPTER 5

1978

A. Buying a new property

I had an urge to either build or purchase another property to prepare for the future, because underlying all my doubts, fears, loneliness and trials, I felt that God was going to work things out. I believed that He was going to send people to help me as He had promised two years before. I asked a friend of mine to come for breakfast one morning, who happened to be a real estate agent. After breakfast, I told him that I wanted to build another house on our present property. His answer was, "Why destroy this beautiful property? This is an estate and should not be broken up into different packages. If you break the property up, then it will be hard to sell in the future. You will be stuck with a white elephant." So I said, "What should I do?" His answer was, "Buy another property." There was a house down the street at 803 Hillcrest Drive for sale, so I asked him to check it out. He found that the owners wanted $91,500.00 in cash. I asked if I could see the house that evening with Fr. Finbarr Devine, Ray and myself. We saw that the house was in need of repair. The house also needed cleaning, painting and a lot of fixing. Next, we checked with the others to see what they thought about buying this property. I checked with each member of the Provincial Council and each Board Member of the Apostolate. Everyone said we should go ahead and buy the place. We then made an offer of $87,000.00 for the home and the owners accepted.

When I went to make the down payment, I knew I would have to get a loan from the bank in order to buy this property. However,

I always had the policy of buying everything in cash. Therefore, I turned to prayer and asked everyone else to pray that we would be able to obtain the money needed to purchase this property. During this time, I went on another trip to the Holy Land. While we were on the trip, I prayed everyday that we would be able to get money, pay for the property and have everything work out perfectly. When I came back from the Holy Land, I found that we still did not receive any gift of money for the property. Now, we would have to obtain a loan from the Bank of America. The bank said it would take a week longer than the date set for the closing of escrow. With that being the case, purchasing the property would have been impossible because we would not get the loan on time. I told the Lord that this wasn't very good business to get a loan anyway because of the high percentage of interest that we would have to pay. I then said we needed to have a miracle in order to get the money that we needed. Again we turned to prayer. Later in that afternoon, I received a telephone call and the person said, "What can I do for you?" I asked him at that time to just pray. Later on, I wrote to him and told him of our need. He sent the complete amount of money the following Monday so that we could pay cash for the property. This immediately showed me that having this property was God's Will. The purpose of the property was to house the people who might want to come and visit us to learn more about the Apostolate. The house was especially to be used for those who might want to join us in the work of the Apostolate. If it pleased God, then it could be the beginning of the Servants of the Sacred Hearts of Jesus and Mary (priests and brothers). Anyways, if we leave everything in the hands of the Lord, then He will have to work everything out. Therefore, His Will would be done and not ours.

B. Thoughts on pilgrimage

I wish to share my thoughts on my recent pilgrimage to the Holy Land, Rome, Lourdes and Fatima in March. Upon our arrival in Tel Aviv, we quickly went through customs and boarded our various buses. Each person knew which bus to board because every bus was labeled according to a different color (We had a large group, three hundred and forty-six in all, who participated in this pilgrimage). The luggage was identified by having the color of yarn attached to the handles that matched the color on the bus. Name tags were worn by all pilgrims which were also color coded. Therefore, people found it very easy to know which bus to board. Upon our arrival at the hotels, our room assignments did not take long to receive because the roster was all worked out ahead of time. This was a real improvement over the last year's tour to the Holy Land because we had to wait for hours for our rooms assignments. This time the luggage was delivered to our rooms, while last year we had to sort through our luggage and carry it ourselves. Last year, many of us had to also move from one hotel to another every night, thus going through this same "rigmarole" at each hotel. This year, all the "rigmarole" was eliminated in this portion of our trip because everything was done with such precision.

On March 3rd, we left our hotel and went to Cesarea, which was the home of Herod and Pontius Pilate. Since the home was the center of the Roman political occupational force and government, Jesus Christ never came to this city. However, Paul was imprisoned here for two years and gave his famous speech to Governor Felix and appealed to Caesar. From here, Paul embarked to Rome. Today, the amphitheater has been excavated and repaired. During the spring, summer and fall, this amphitheater is used for concerts. The beaches in Cesarea are used extensively in the summer by tourists, who pitch their tents to live or visit for the season. Cesarea is also the place where Christian crusaders built a fortress which was later destroyed.

In regards to the Crusades, they were a total disaster. Could it be because what Jesus said became a reality? In other words, "Those who take up the sword will perish by the sword." The guide explained many interesting things about this spot, mainly the importance of its seaport, its importance to the Roman Empire and its importance to the early Church.

From Cesarea we drove to the Valley of Sharon and to Mt. Carmel. We celebrated Mass at Mt. Carmel, where Elijah lived. This spot is memorable in the history of salvation. At Mt. Carmel, Elijah confronted the prophets of Baal. These prophets worshipped false gods while Elijah worshipped the True God. In Scripture, the writer explains the contest where Elijah convinced the people of the One True God. This resulted in the slaughter of all the prophets of Baal and they were thrown into the river running at the foot of Mt. Carmel. This passage of Scripture makes us wonder and realize the greatness of the Lord. When a person is on God's side, then that person will always be the victor. This was also proven in the life of St. Anthony of Padua when he contested with his enemies in regard to the belief in the Blessed Sacrament. His enemies placed a bail of hay before a donkey, while St. Anthony took the Blessed Sacrament before him and commanded the donkey to adore the Lord. The donkey immediately came and knelt before Our Lord in the Blessed Sacrament, rather than eat the hay that was provided for him.

On March 4th, we visited Nazareth. We celebrated Mass in the Basilica of the Annunciation. This Mass meant a lot to me and I hope that the pilgrims felt the same. Here was the place where Our Blessed Mother said, "yes" to our Heavenly Father (made her total commitment to the Lord) because she gave Him her mind, body and soul over to the action of the Holy Spirit Who formed Christ in her. Mary's whole life was devoted to the service of the Lord. Even after Jesus' death, resurrection and ascension into Heaven, Mary devoted her whole life to Him personally. St. Joseph also made his total commitment to the service of the Lord in Nazareth, that is why he is the protector of Jesus and Mary.

From Nazareth, we made a quick tour to Tiberius, where we boarded a ship to cross the Sea of Galilee. While we were traveling from one place to another, we had an experienced guide on each bus who related to us the religious and political aspects of the areas through which we were traveling. One of the things that impressed me the most during this trip was the close proximity of each area to the other in the Holy Land. This made me realize that Our Lord did not have to travel great distances in His preaching ministry.

After crossing the Sea of Galilee, we arrived in Capernaum. There isn't too much to see since everything is in ruins. The ruins of the Synagogue, the house of Peter, the wine and olive presses and stones strewn all over the area are all that remain. We did not spend too much time there, but we went on to the place where Jesus multiplied the loaves and fishes. Next, we went to the Mount of the Beatitudes where Jesus gave the Sermon on the Mount. To some, this was a very beautiful experience, especially when Jamie Anthony led us in singing the Our Father.

Our next stop was for lunch in Tiberius, where some of us ate "St. Peter's Fish." Actually, we had a choice, we could either have chicken or fish. The chicken, to many, was a more welcome choice because the fish was served whole, head and all. The fish has a big mouth and a lot of bones, which reminds me of the big mouth carp found in the United States. Actually, the food in Israel is plentiful and very well prepared. The only people who might disagree with this are those who are used to eating only one type of food prepared in a certain way. Otherwise, the food was delicious in almost all the places we visited. After eating, we traveled along the Jordan river before spending some more time in Nazareth.

On March 5th, we traveled to Jericho and saw the ruins of the Walls, which date back to the time of Moses and the desert experience of the people of God. Moses was never allowed to enter the Holy Land, but after his death, Joshua brought the people into the area. From Jericho, we went to the Dead Sea area and saw the caves which contained the Dead Sea Scrolls.

In the 1940's, a young shepherd boy lost one of his sheep. In trying to find the sheep, he fell into a cave where he found a jar containing the Book of Isaiah. Immediately, investigations were made into the various caves and now there was a possibility to find all the books of the Old Testament. All the books were found except for the Book of Esther. From this area, we drove to Jerusalem and ate lunch.

In the afternoon, everyone who was on the pilgrimage gathered at the Church of All Nations, which is actually the site of the Garden of Gethsemane. This is my favorite spot in all of Jerusalem and the Holy Land. The Mass was very beautiful; however, we did not have sufficient time to do everything we desired. Wherever we celebrated Mass, we were always limited to one hour because other people wanted to celebrate Mass immediately after we finished. I felt this to be very limiting because these were the only times when we celebrated the Liturgy and we were all able to be together. This could have been an opportunity for me to have spoken to everyone and perhaps touched each person in a deeper way, if only we could have been allowed more time.

From the Garden of Gethsemane, we made our way to the Upper Room where Jesus offered His first Mass, ordained the Apostles, instituted the sacrament of Reconciliation and where the Holy Spirit descended upon the Apostles. The Upper Room today is not the actual one where the Last Supper took place, but is merely a replica. Nevertheless, we all felt the Power of the Holy Spirit. For some, there was an overwhelming experience of His Presence when they received the individual blessing.

On March 6th, we traveled to various places in Jerusalem which proved to be very interesting. The first place we visited was the Dome of the Rock, which is a Moslem Mosque. The Mosque is also on the exact site where Solomon built the Temple. Within this Mosque, there is a huge rock where Abraham allegedly offered his son, Isaac. The Mosque is also the same spot where Mary and Joseph presented Jesus in the Temple as well as where Jesus often preached. Moslems believe that this spot is where Mohammed allegedly ascended into the "Seventh Heaven." Yet, the guide pointed out to us that Mohammed never came to Jerusalem.

Next, we went to the Wailing Wall, which is very precious to the Jewish people. While I was standing at the wall, I saw the Rabbis carrying the Torah, the Old Testament and they unfolded the parchment and began to read from the Old Testament. As they read from the Old Testament, I thought about an incident that happened at Travis Air Force Base. In a vision, a person saw the Scrolls of the Torah on one side and on the other side there were two tablets without any writing. Behind the two tablets, there was a bishop's staff. This vision was seen while I was preaching. The person then drew a picture and attempted to explain the significance. When I was standing at the Wailing Wall, the significance of this vision then hit me very forcefully. The meaning of this vision is that the New Covenant supplanted the Old. After a lot of reflecting, I felt that I should try to bring the Jewish Catholic Christians to the Holy Land so that they could give witness to the New Covenant. In other words, Jewish Catholic Christians can reveal that the Old Covenant is fulfilled in the New and that the Old is abrogated and finished as such. This means Jesus Christ is the Messiah, that He is the Way, the Truth and the Life. If the Jewish Catholic Christians witness to the Jewish people, then they might inspire them to accept Jesus Christ as Lord and Messiah.

That afternoon, we went to Bethlehem where we celebrated the Eucharistic Liturgy. Before the Mass, many of the pilgrims had the opportunity to see the cave where Jesus was born. Others went to this spot after the Liturgy.

On March 7th, we were free to do whatever we wished because the majority of the people did not wish to go to Masada (the tour offered for the day). Masada, to the Jewish people, is a symbol of courage, strength and "death, rather than slavery." Masada is also the symbol for them to carry on, in spite of any hardship, disaster or persecution.

I don't know what others did during those morning hours, but a group of eight people went back to the Garden of Gethsemane and spent three hours in prayer. While we were praying, a group of 25 priests were celebrating Mass. God enlightened my mind to the fact that He wanted priests to come to the Holy Land, make retreats and if at all possible, to provide the means, the money, to pay for the trip and the retreat for the priests. The reason is because priests could have this experience of being in the land of the Lord, so that their priesthood can be embellished and their zeal enkindled. Another reason is that priests can develop a deep prayer life, which would allow them to be more effective in their priesthood, ministry and apostolic works for the people of God.

The last fifteen minutes were spent praying with and over one another. One of the pilgrims saw a wounded lamb and asked me what it meant, which I said I didn't know. Then I asked the other priest if he knew what it meant. He said that when a sheep wanders from the flock, as a maverick, the sheep could be easily hurt. When the shepherd finds such a sheep, the custom is to break the sheep's leg and put the broken leg in a splint so that it could heal. Then the shepherd could carry the sheep on his shoulders until it was well. In the process, the sheep would get to know the shepherd and would begin to love him. When the sheep was completely well, the shepherd placed the sheep into the flock and it would never wander away again. The moral of the story is that the shepherd still loves the sinner and does everything possible to make him whole and thus be able to bring him back home.

I also thought about the present situation of the Israelite people. They wandered from their homeland into the various countries of the world, after the destruction of the Temple, in 70 AD. In our day, the Jews were subject to genocide in the holocaust perpetrated by Hitler. After this horrific period, the Jews began to come home to Israel. Personally, I believe we are seeing the Providence of God being fulfilled before our very eyes. St. Paul, in his epistles, alluded to this, that God would bring the Jewish people back to the homeland where eventually they will accept the Messiah, Jesus Christ.

Also, while we were praying over one another, a priest saw a tree that was knotted and had a deep, hollow, black hole within the trunk. He asked me what I thought this image meant and I said that I did not know. When we got outside, I saw the olive tree in the Garden of Gethsemane. This is actually one of the eight olive trees that some claim still exists from the time of Christ. This tree was knotted and had dark holes in its trunk. One of the people who was praying with us came out and made the remark, "Look at the olive tree." She reminded us that the olive tree never dies. It just "fades away." Over the centuries, the trunk of the tree gets knotty and the trunk becomes hollow. She made an analogy between that and the spiritual life. She said that the tree empties itself so that from the tree will grow new shoots to produce new trees. We actually saw two new shoots coming from this tree, which were beginning to develop into trees. The spiritual meaning I received is that we are to die to ourselves so that the new life may come, and if we are chosen by God to begin a new community of priests, brothers, sisters or a new movement, then the Founder must die to himself so that life will be given to the members. Even if the Founder dies, the life will go on as a tree comes forth from the olive tree. Life continues, even when there is only a shell left from the old tree. The other priest who was with us also made the observation that the man is like a tree, "He grows from within," which is true both physically and spiritually.

Later on, God enlightened my mind and let me see that this tree really represented my life and the work that He has given me. He allowed me to understand that from the Apostolate of Christian Renewal, there would be two branches of religious communities, the Handmaids and Servants of the Sacred Hearts of Jesus and Mary. In dying to ourselves and working to spread the Apostolate, these communities would automatically develop from the various circumstances that would take place. At this point, God let me see that the dying and emptying of myself was sufficiently carried out. Now that God has helped me in dying to self, God will allow other people to benefit from my spiritual life so that new growth can begin.

After lunch, we drove around Jerusalem until it was time to celebrate Mass at Ain Karim, at the Church of the Visitation. When we arrived on top of the hill, we noticed some Arab orphan children who were waiting to attend our Mass. This spot is described very beautifully in Scripture when, "Mary hastened over the hill country to visit her cousin, Elizabeth (about 115 miles)." When Elizabeth recognized that Mary would be the Mother of the Messiah, she was filled with the Spirit. Elizabeth knew that Mary was carrying Jesus within her so she exclaimed, "How is it that the Mother of my Lord should come to me?" At the same moment, John the Baptist encountered Jesus Christ in Mary and was filled with the Holy Spirit by leaping in Elizabeth's womb. This fulfilled the prophecy made by the angel to Zechariah, in regards to his son, John, "He would be filled with the Holy Spirit in the womb of his mother (cf. Lk. 1)."

After the Mass, I blessed the people individually and the Arab orphans received the blessing too. At first, the orphans were afraid, but after being blessed, they crowed around me and asked to be blessed again. As I was leaving, I turned around and saw these beautiful orphans praying over one another.

From the Church of the Visitation, I went to the hospital where I blessed about eighty deformed children, who were all bedridden. Even though they were retarded, they responded to the blessing, which shows that they felt the blessing. I always find my heart to be tender when I see children in this condition, but I also find it heart warming to see the dedication and charity shown in the life of the sisters and lay people who are caring for these children.

On March 8th, we were all supposed to leave the Holy Land for Rome. However, due to mechanical difficulty with our plane, most of us had an extra day in Israel.

Earl Fullerton and I decided to go to Mount Olive, where I offered Mass at the Pater Noster Crypt. This is the place where Jesus taught the Apostles the Our Father. People were milling all over the place and the religious goods store were crowded. I asked a sister who spoke French if I could offer Mass. She was a little flustered, but she got the vestments for the Mass and told me to go to the Crypt. When we arrived in the Crypt, there was a group who was having everything explained to them about this historic site. I vested for Mass and found that we had no hosts, no wine and no water. Earl immediately went and got some hosts, wine and water. When he came back, the people just disappeared and we had no interruptions throughout the whole Mass. Everything was perfectly quiet.

One side note: on October 1st, 1977, Jesus told me that I would find my comfort in the Holy Land, in Jerusalem. Throughout the Holy Land tour, I was waiting to see what this comfort would be. I thought perhaps this comfort was in the Garden of Gethsemane with the experience of the olive tree or possibly what happened at the Wailing Wall. However, the comfort that I received was when I celebrated the Mass. After the Our Father, I began to sing "Through Him, with Him, and in Him." While singing these words, I had an intellectual vision of the Holy Spirit in which I experienced what these words meant. The Holy Spirit anointed me anew in my Apostolate work and allowed me to feel that all of my sins were washed away and that I was standing before the Lord with a clear conscience. I felt that He filled me with His love, peace, joy and I knew that He would guide the Apostolate. The rays from the Holy Spirit came toward the world and passed through it. This signified that the Holy Spirit was going to guide the work of the Apostolate, the work of the religious communities and the work that we would do. I was then filled with a lot of joy and comfort. At the time, Earl was not aware of what was happening. However, he felt the Power of the Holy Spirit and he seemed to be reeling back and forth, trying to remain on his feet. To me, this was indeed the comfort promised.

All that day, I thought about the great privilege Catholic Christians have. The thought that kept coming to my mind was that, "Jesus is alive. Jesus is risen. Jesus is present here in the Holy Land." Many people might think that Jesus only lived there once and never again returned after His Ascension into Heaven. But as Catholics, we know that wherever a Catholic priest offers the Eucharistic Liturgy, Jesus Christ is present, Body, Blood, Soul and Divinity in the Blessed Sacrament. Jesus is Present in the Blessed Sacrament in Bethlehem, Nazareth, Cana, the Mount of the Beatitudes, Mt. Carmel, Jerusalem and in all Catholic Churches throughout the Holy Land. Many will say, "Isn't Jesus Present everywhere?" We agree. Some will say, "Isn't He Present where two or three are gathered in His Name?" Again, we agree. However, in the Eucharist, He is Bodily Present, which has given me food for thought in my meditative prayer since my trip to the Holy Land.

On March 9th, the people who stayed behind in Jerusalem flew to Rome, where we immediately went to St. Peter's Basilica. After our visit to St. Peters, we decided to have lunch, which was more of a dinner. After dinner, we went to the hotel and got settled. All of us stayed in the same hotel, which was very beautiful, but also very noisy. Next, we went to the Catacombs. However, we had to rush back to St. Peter's to celebrate the Eucharistic Liturgy with the cardinal, bishops and various priests.

According to the Italian travel agency, we were supposed to have a general audience with the Holy Father on this day, March 9th. However, three weeks before we went to the Holy Land, I received a telephone call telling me that we would have a private audience with Pope Paul VI. I was a little confused because I didn't ask for a private audience. The reason why I did not feel that it was necessary is because I knew that we would be at the general audience on Wednesday, the 8th. I wondered why anyone would have requested this private audience. Then, three days before we were to leave for the Holy Land, I received another phone call saying that if I wanted the private audience with the Holy Father, our group would have to pay $7,000.00. My immediate reaction and response was, "No way!" I said, "The Holy Father never asks for any money to have an audience. All audiences, general or otherwise are free. Tickets are issued in order to insure the people to be in various sections in the audience hall. I mentioned that paying for an audience with the Holy Father is highly unlikely and that any person who arranges the audiences, would not demand any form of payment. Then, while I was in the Holy Land, I was approached and told that we could still have a private audience if we could come up with $3,500.00. I told the man, "Let me think about it." I actually wanted to have time to consult a well known lawyer about what should be done. He gave me this advice, "Let us go along with this plan of giving the $3,500.00, but with the stipulation that this is to be given as a personal gift to the Holy Father and that I would personally present this gift." The next opportunity I had, I told this person who had contacted me what I had decided to do. He seemed to be shocked and upset, but he didn't say anything. The next day, he said to me, "Well, couldn't you give me the money and I will make out the check from the agency to be presented to the Holy Father?" I said, "Yes, but you will not make out any check. I personally will give the Holy Father the gift." With that, the conversation ended and the possibility of a private audience was shattered because he did not pursue it any further.

When we were in St. Peter's in Rome, the people from the agency who represented us in the United States were arguing with the people responsible for this fiasco about the private audience. A reporter was standing nearby and overheard the entire conversation. After this conversation, the reporter approached our representative and began to ask questions. They told the reporter that if he wanted any information, then he should ask me. I was quite shocked and surprised to find the reporter coming up to me in the middle of St. Peter's Basilica and asking me questions about this whole ordeal. I told him discreetly what had taken place and he reported it through all Catholic newspapers throughout the world. I am sorry that this incident ever took place because the people on our tour were very disappointed.

On March 10th, the next morning, most of us had the privilege of going to the Vatican Museum, Vatican Library and the Sistine Chapel. This guided tour took close to three hours. In the evening, a group of us went to celebrate the birthday of our cook from our Center. Actually, the celebration included all the members of our staff plus the husband of our secretary and the two sons of our housekeeper. We had a wonderful birthday party, which certainly will never be forgotten by our cook.

On March 11th, we went to San Vittorino to visit Brother Gino. All eight buses arrived there at 9:30 AM. We immediately went to the new Basilica of Our Lady of Fatima, where we walked in just before the Liturgy. During the whole Liturgy, I could smell the fragrant odors that came from Brother Gino's hands. During the homily, I explained about Brother Gino's stigmata, how he was chosen, why God chooses certain people and why he is to give witness to the Crucified Christ. I also explained his mission and his work. While I was preaching, an interpreter was translating everything into Italian for Brother Gino. After the Mass, Brother Gino was very gracious because he went to the seminary area where he saw each one of us individually. Then he stood patiently on the hill, where he posed for some pictures with various people until every person satisfied his or her desire for pictures. Finally, he walked back to the small chapel where all of us gathered again to say a few prayers and to receive some departing words. Brother Gino showed great patience, generosity and charity in giving of himself throughout those hours while we visited. Just before we left, Brother Gino spoke to me privately. I am looking forward to bringing others to San Vittorino so that they may witness a man of God. I believe that anyone who comes into his presence will not just see the stigmatist, Brother Gino, but will be led beyond the human and led to think about Christ.

From San Vittorino, we traveled to Tivoli, where we had a most enjoyable lunch in a country restaurant. Someone mentioned the fact that this area was the crucial battle ground before American troops pushed on to Rome in World War II. Having finished our lunch, we went to Rome where we celebrated the Liturgy in St. Maria Maggiore (St. Mary Major's Basilica). As we continued offering the Liturgy, we began to hear shouts from a rally by the communists who gathered outside. We do not know the reason for this gathering, but two days later Mr. Moro was kidnapped by the Red Brigade. We do not know if there was any connection between these incidents. However, these incidents show how forceful and strong the communists are becoming. This made me realize how blessed we still are living in America where we do not witness these gatherings and scenes, inspired by the left wing. In our own country, we witnessed more peaceful demonstrations in the late 60's and early 70's. There is a great difference in the two approaches.

On March 12th, we left Rome and began the arduous part of our journey. In the process of leaving Rome, the rosters of the pilgrims were disrupted, which caused hardships and sacrifices for many. Part of us went to Madrid, while others went to Barcelona,

Spain. Each person then took bus rides from these cities to Lourdes. Personally, I was on the trip from Barcelona to Lourdes, which crossed the entire Pyrenees mountain range. The Pyrenees are very picturesque, and at times, the panoramic view was breathtaking. Sitting in the front of the bus, I could see the hairpin curves, and at some points, the dilapidated roads could easily have endangered the lives of all. Nevertheless, the experienced drivers, who deserve a lot of credit, guided the buses along the roads to safety. On most of the buses, there was sharing, singing and joy, even though the trip was grueling and tiring. Then we arrived at Lourdes late in the evening, which was unfortunate because the Basilica was closed and we were not permitted to celebrate Mass. Instead, we went to the Grotto, where in spite of the protests by the guards, we said the Rosary and departed for a good night's sleep.

On March 13th, we were permitted to offer Mass at the Basilica in the Upper Church before we departed for Madrid. If I had known how many miles and hours this part of the tour would take, I would have canceled that part completely. However, I do know that many did receive gifts from the Lord and even spiritual healing. From that viewpoint, all the sacrifices that we made were worthwhile.

The trip from Lourdes to Madrid consumed many hours. The only thing I can say about this trip is that we saw a part of Spain that we never saw before and never would have seen otherwise. We arrived in Madrid around midnight. Personally, I was happy to be there because my niece was waiting for me. To my surprise, her brother, Dan, was also present because he was visiting her. I hadn't seen Dan for a long time so it was a very pleasant surprise.

On March 15th, we had to get up early so that we could stop in Avila on our way to Fatima. I've always wanted to visit Avila because St. Teresa lived there. This simple, humble woman was chosen by God to reform the Carmelite order. God trained her so beautifully that she was able to speak with great authority on Mystical and Ascetical Theology. She was the first woman to be declared a Doctor of the Church. St. Catherine of Sienna was the second. I was elated to offer the Liturgy in this town because of St. Teresa. The town was interesting to see because it was built on a mountainous area. Then for thirty or forty miles, the land was flat and it had beautiful farmlands. After lunch, we began our long, winding journey through the mountain country of Portugal. We arrived very late in Fatima, but thank God, the roster of the pilgrims was back in order. While we ate our meal, the rooms were assigned, the luggage was delivered and the keys were brought to us at our tables. In the other two hotels that were used by the members of the tour, this may not have been true because the staff of the tour agency from the United States personally delivered the luggage to the various rooms. That day, the weather was dreary and cold because it rained, which also added to the misery for some of the pilgrims. In my own personal life, God showered His blessings and graces upon me in abundance, for which I will ever be thankful.

On March 16th, we had a "sleep in" and a natural awakening. We all were told to be up by noon for lunch. A few of us got up early and went to the place where the Blessed Mother appeared to the children. I asked the Blessed Mother what she wanted me to do in regard to the starting of the religious communities. I was expecting her to give me directions, but she asked me to offer myself as a victim soul for priests. She told me that I would bear the stigmata and witness to the world the Suffering Christ, her Son. I cried like a baby for about an hour and a half. I went to the Basilica immediately and went to Francisco's grave to pray. I laid my hands on his grave and asked for his help. Then I went over to Jacinta's grave and did the same thing. Next, various people joined me in saying the fifteen-decade Rosary. In the Basilica, they have the fifteen decade mysteries shown by picture, placed down one aisle and back down the other. It took us over an hour and a half to pray this Rosary. Then, in the afternoon, we said the Rosary again along with the Stations of the Cross, which was a very moving experience.

Before going back to celebrate the Liturgy at the Basilica, we visited the site where the angel of Portugal appeared to the children to prepare them for the apparitions of the Blessed Mother. The angel instilled in them a great love for Jesus Christ in the Blessed Sacrament. He also gave each child Holy Communion. Lucia received the Host, while Francisco and Jacinta drank the Precious Blood from the Chalice. The angel also taught them a beautiful Trinitarian prayer. When we read about the apparitions of Fatima, most literature explain that the children received an instruction in their faith.

A person cannot help but be struck by the simplicity of Fatima. Everything seems to bare nothing of importance. Yet, everything is there because the whole area speaks the message of Fatima as revealed by Our Lady to the children. This makes us realize that the Miracle of the Sun was not the great happening. Rather, the miracle was the change and transformation in the lives of the children.

Francisco was lackadaisical, lukewarm and a care-free individual. He did not see the Blessed Mother until he started to pray the Rosary. Nevertheless, Francisco never heard the Blessed Mother speak. He always had to be told what she said. The sight of Hell which the Blessed Mother showed to the children moved him deeply, and from that time on, he continually prayed so as to, "console the Lord Jesus." He felt that Jesus suffered so much because souls deliberately chose to go to Hell for all eternity. Francisco spent this time in prayer. He often prayed the Rosary, since the Blessed Mother said that he would go to Heaven, but that first he would have to pray many rosaries. He spent most of his day in prayer before the Blessed Sacrament in his parish Church. The reason he was free to do this was due to the fact that the whole area was destroyed by the numerous people who came to visit. The grazing ground, the gardens and everything else was trampled and destroyed. Therefore, the sheep had to be sold. The reason Francisco never went to school was because the Blessed Mother said that he would die soon, so he didn't see any sense in studying. Well-meaning people asked him, "Do you want to be a doctor? Do you want to be this or that?" His answer was, "No." When they asked him, "What do you want?" He said, "I want to go to Heaven."

Jacinta was a rambunctious, spoiled and arrogant child. She always had to have her own way, and when she did not, she would pout until she did. This young girl, at a very young age, wanted to be with Lucia watching the sheep. She wanted this mainly because she wanted to play, as we read about in her life story. Jacinta devised different games to play so that she would win. Even though transformation in Jacinta took longer than Francisco, she became a penitential and saintly young girl. The vision of Hell left such an impression upon her that she prayed and did penance to a heroic degree for the conversion of sinners. This vision bothered Jacinta tremendously because the souls in Hell would be there for all eternity. She constantly asked Lucia about this. Finally, Jacinta came to the conclusion that the only thing that could be done was to try to save people from going there. That is why she led such a penitential life from then on until her death. Jacinta died alone in a hospital, in Lisbon, just as she predicted would happen.

Even though Lucia did not know how to read or write, she knew enough about her religion to instruct Jacinta and Francisco. She was asked to learn how to read and write so she could remain on earth and spread the message of Fatima. The Blessed Mother promised her that she too would go to Heaven. We might be over-awed at the fact that she was promised sanctity and we would think that she was the only one living in the world who was promised that gift. But as I was reading in an article, the writer pointed out that we, too, are promised Heaven, if we receive our Lord Jesus Christ in the Blessed Sacrament. The reason is because Jesus said, "He who eats my flesh and drinks my blood will have life everlasting." Lucia is now ninety years old and is living in Coimbra, Portugal, as a Discalced Carmelite Sister. Lucia did not want to enter the convent, but she entered at the request of the bishop. She also went because the bishop said she must be out of the limelight and avoid curiosity seekers. I believe that her privacy and her mission to fulfill the requests of our Blessed Mother made it necessary for her to live a life of solitude and prayer. In 1967, Sister Lucia came to Fatima for the 50th anniversary of the apparitions. During this anniversary, Pope Paul VI urged the people of the world to heed the message of Fatima and do what our Blessed Mother asked so that we could have peace in the world.

Actually, the apparitions of Fatima withstood the meticulous scrutiny and investigations of the clergy and the bishops. The Church declared that these apparitions were from Heaven and worthy of belief. Pope Pius XII also said that Fatima proclaims "The Gospel Message." Why did he say this? Pope Pius XII knew our Blessed Mother asked us to pray the Rosary daily, to do penance, to consecrate ourselves to her Immaculate Heart and to make the First Five Saturdays. These are the external practices that allow our souls to be open to the Holy Spirit so that He can help us to be transformed like unto Jesus Christ. If we imitate Jesus, then we are living the Gospel message. I believe that the majority of people who heard about Fatima missed the interior message, which is to live the Gospel message. I believe in the words of Pope John XXIII when he said, "Fatima is the hope of the world." I believe that the true message of Fatima is manifested in the documents of Vatican Council II. Therefore, the Apostolate of Christian Renewal has the privilege of spreading this message.

I believe that the message of Fatima was not fully accepted because the Devil played a part in trying to discredit this apparition and its true meaning. Therefore, I believe that the Devil is responsible for many alleged apparitions of the Blessed Mother in various parts of the world to distract people from the truth. In the time of Lourdes, there were one hundred various apparitions, but only one withstood the test of authenticity and that is Lourdes. Today, we have to be very careful in regard to any other alleged apparitions. I believe we should always follow this maxim:

If the Church approves an apparition, then we may believe and foster the message. However, if the Church does not give its approval, then we must obey the Church and not become involved in spreading any message claimed to be coming from God, even if we think that person is holy. We must always test the spirit. But how can we know the true from the false? The answer to this question is found in Scripture, "By their fruits you will know them" A person with a true message from God will always be obedient to the Magisterium of the Church, which is the Pope and the bishops.

On March 17th, I went back to the spot of the apparition early in the morning. I asked the Blessed Mother, "Is it, yes or no, that I should begin new religious communities?" She answered, "Leave it to me." Then we gathered for the last time in the Basilica for the Liturgy. This Liturgy was very inspiring for me and I hope it was for all who were on the tour. Immediately after the Mass, those who flew to France left for Lisbon, while the others who were going to Madrid left a little later. We flew from Lisbon to Madrid so as to rest before the long flight home on the 18th.

On March 18th, we arrived in Los Angeles around 9:00 PM I finally ended the tour with a Mass in our own chapel, on the feast of St. Joseph. Interestingly enough, we began the tour on a feast of St. Joseph and ended on his great feast day, the solemnity of St. Joseph which was moved this year from the 19th to the 18th. After

a short talk before the Offertory, I offered myself as a victim soul
for priests, as our Lady requested while I was in Fatima.

I personally did not feel any of the hardships on the trip because I was always looking for the spiritual growth that could come
from any incident that occurred. Therefore, for me, the trip was a
joy, in spite of any problems or difficulties that arose. Some of the
others, I know, suffered deeply. One young boy made a funny remark, and someone said to him, "Why don't you offer it up for the
souls in Purgatory?" The young boy's reply was, "I emptied Purgatory a week ago." Even though some people might think that
this is a scandalous remark, I thought it was a witty and very funny
response. I was deeply moved by many on the trip, especially those
who were in their 80's, who seemed to be strong under the trials
and difficulties. I was disappointed by a few, who complained about
everyting. Even God would not have been able to satisfy them.

1. After my trip

I noticed immediately after the trip to Fatima that various priests
expressed a desire to work with us and take part in the work of the
Apostolate. Fr. Ed Wojniak, who had accompanied me on various
Renewal Weeks, came from Pennsylvania. Fr. Wojniak then went
back to Erie, Pennsylvania, where he is spreading the Apostolate
by giving Renewal Weeks in that area. Monsignor Robert Nash,
the former President of Gannon College, who was very moved by
reading my book, *Chosen* and the *Mystical Mass Prayer*, also
spreads the work of the Apostolate. I believe things are beginning
to move a little faster which reveal more interest on the part of the
priests, brothers and sisters, especially wherever I go in the work
of the Apostolate.

C. Annual retreat

In June 1978, I made my annual retreat, which was given by
our Vicar General, Fr. Finton Sheeran. He was very good in his
presentation of the material for the retreat. The presentation was
really a summation of what I believe is the work of the Apostolate
and our spiritual life, as members of the Congregation of the Sa-

cred Hearts of Jesus and Mary. I was hopeful that the Provincial Chapter, which followed our retreat, would be very productive. The Fathers were very congenial, serious and concerned about the religious life, yet I felt that our Congregation does not live the charism of our Founder and the life that the Congregation represented when I joined the community.

Despite my Congregation's good will and seriousness in following the Lord, I feel that the purpose and the goal of our Congregation, as it is practiced today, really do not have any meaning to me anymore. I still long for us, as a community, to be Eucharistic centered; to make reparation for the sins of humankind through the adoration of the Blessed Sacrament; to have a deep love and devotion for our Mother Mary; to spread the devotion to her Immaculate Heart, so that we would have a deeper devotion to the Sacred Heart. Likewise, I longed for the work of the Enthronement to spread in such a way that there would be a manifestation of the Covenant between the family and God. I wish that as a community, we would pray more and live a life of prayer in community. But what I envisioned as a community and what my Congregation envisioned as a community were two different visions.

During this retreat, I again felt that God is urging me to begin a new community. Fr. Finbarr Devine, a member of the Congregation, was rather provoked and discouraged also. He felt that our community was not living the charism of our Founder either and that we were not living the Gospel message. Fr. Devine also said that he would be willing to join the new community if I began the Servants of the Sacred Hearts of Jesus and Mary and that he would help in spreading the work of the Apostolate. Fr. Devine also said he would withdraw from being involved full time in the Charismatic Renewal, but remain in an advisory capacity. He said that he would help where there was a need in the Charismatic Movement, but that he would like to enter into the preaching ministry of the Apostolate. I said that we would pray about this and try to work this out.

D. Giving retreats to sisters

I gave retreats to two groups of sisters, one group in Nevada, Missouri and the other, a group of Felician sisters in Chicago, Illinois. Both groups were small in size and were elderly. The latter group had some young and middle-aged sisters. I found out that the community life was lacking and left much to be desired. Personally, I think it's a tragedy when a person visits various communities and sees the division between the conservatives, the liberals and the in-betweens. In these communities, a person recognizes the lack of following the charism of the Founder and the lack of living the Gospel message. As a result, most of these communities are falling apart and dying a painful death.

In many religious communities, there isn't sufficient charity being practiced. A person has to challenge each community to be faithful to the Lord, to have Christ as the center of their lives and to have devotion to our Mother Mary. If religious communities live a life of charity, then they will build up community rather than destroy community.

1.　Renewal Weeks

After I finished giving retreats to the sisters, I again began Renewal Weeks. When I was at Sacred Heart Parish, in Harrisburg, Pennsylvania, a sister attended whom I had never met before. She later wrote to me and told me that she saw my hands bleeding during the Mass. She asked me if I had the invisible stigmata. I wrote to the sister telling her about the invisible stigmata, but that she should not mention this to others. I find that wherever I go more and more people are beginning to see the invisible stigmata. They either see blood running, dark spots on my wrists or rays of light coming from my hands, while others even see me wearing white gloves. I often wonder why the Lord is letting people know these things, but I always tell them to be quiet. However, as in the Gospels, when Jesus told people to be quiet, they spoke of it all the more. Therefore, this news is spreading throughout our country, without my desire or intentions. This sister also said that the stigmata would become visible when I had totally prostrated myself before the Lord. I take this to mean that I will have to die to myself, humble myself and become more like a child.

2.   Women who want to be Handmaids

When I returned to the Center, six of the women who wished to join the Handmaids of the Sacred Hearts of Jesus and Mary came together. We spent four days talking about the lifestyle and the apostolate that they would be following. The decision was made that they should begin on September 18th, 1978. In the meantime, these women were to work on a document to comprise the various points we discussed. Because I had to be on the road preaching Renewals, I wasn't able to spend a lot of time with them. However, before I left, I wrote to Cardinal Timothy Manning and Bishop Ward of my intentions.

3.   The sudden death of Paul VI

In early August, I began a Renewal in Tulsa, Oklahoma, at the Cathedral. While I was there, I heard about the sudden death of Pope Paul VI. I always admired Pope Paul VI because he suffered so intensely, both internally and externally. I felt that he died from a broken heart and was a real martyr of love. Paul VI loved the Church, the people and God. He was a faithful Pope and I hope that, when he died, on the Feast of the Transfiguration, August 6th, he could say, "Lord, it's good to be here!" I have prayed for him everyday since he became Pope. Now I feel that it is his turn to enter into intercessory prayer for the Apostolate. All during the mourning period and the election of the new Pope, I felt very close to all the Cardinals, but especially Cardinal Timothy Manning.

4.   Beginning the Handmaids

After the Tulsa, Oklahoma, Renewal, I returned to the Center for a few days. When I was home, I wrote to Fr. Patrick Crowley, my Provincial, that I had decided to begin the Handmaids of the Sacred Hearts of Jesus and Mary and that I was definitely thinking about establishing a new religious community for priests and brothers called, "The Servants of the Sacred Hearts of Jesus and Mary." I knew that for the latter, I would have to work through my Superiors, in order to be released from the Congregation. However, for the sisters, I did not think this was required because it was completely separate from the Congregation. Even though I was acting more as a spiritual director, I would be considered to be the Handmaids' Founder, since my preaching inspired them to give their lives to God. I also thought that my Superiors should know my intentions so that I could communicate the proper information to his Eminence Cardinal Timothy Manning and Bishop John Ward.

5. Renewals in Minnesota

I then flew to Minnesota where I had another Renewal Week at St. Stanislaus Parish, in Bowlus. While in Bowlus, I heard the news about the election of Pope John Paul I. There was a great joy on the part of all over his election. John Paul I seemed to begin a new era in the history of the Church. This joy was also evident when I gave another renewal at St. Mary's Cathedral, in St. Cloud, Minnesota. The Renewal Week at the Cathedral was very successful and I am looking forward to going back there again next year. Before leaving Minnesota, I again had the privilege of visiting the Poor Clare Sisters, in Sauk Rapids, Minnesota. Somehow the news of my stigmata was known by other's in the community. Therefore, I asked the whole community to pray for me so that I would be a worthy instrument of God witnessing the Crucified Christ to the world.

6. Starting the Handmaids

I returned home from Minnesota on September 16th because on the 18th, the Handmaids wanted to begin with the intent to strive to become a religious community. We had a discussion on the night of the 16th about a habit to be worn. I then called Bishop John Ward's office and I talked to the secretary. She said that they should be wearing habits. I asked her to speak to Bishop Ward, and if they were not to wear habits, that he should call me immediately. I do not know what happened, but we did not receive any call. I also checked with another Canon lawyer and he told me that it was essential to begin wearing the habit immediately. The habit that was worn was not the official, final habit, but a habit that the postulants would wear. Therefore, I thought I was acting correctly in this matter, only to find out later that I was wrong.

The women who joined the Handmaids of the Sacred Hearts of Jesus and Mary continued to formulate a document that would explain their lifestyle. This was rather difficult for them because they did not have any experience in religious life. Nevertheless, Madelyn Lane, the woman chosen to be their leader, put everything together in an outline form which they used as a basis for their document. They began to live a community life of prayer and work. They also lived at our new community house on a temporary basis because they were to either rent or buy a place for themselves.

I was told that whenever a new religious community is to be started, there must be three essential steps before any approbation can be given. First, there must be a number of people who are interested in becoming religious. Second, they most follow a spiritual and scheduled life. Third, they must be financially sound. Many times, a new religious community takes years to be accepted by Ecclesiastical authority. The Handmaids were only in the early stages of formation and they knew that they were not religious. I often told the members that they should explain to the people that they were working toward establishing a religious community. The Handmaids also attended a Scripture class, listened to tapes on religious life and received a conference once a week by Fr. Finbarr Devine. They lived a deep spiritual prayer life which gradually formed them into a real community.

7. In Washington

Next, I went to the state of Washington for Renewal Weeks. While at St. Charles Borromeo Parish, in Tacoma, we received the shocking news that Pope John Paul I had died on September 28th, 1978. I found it hard to believe that the new Pope was dead after such a short time since his election. Now, the people would have to pray and wait for the election of another new Pope.

The Renewal Week was a great success. The Church was overflowing. God's blessings were poured upon the people in abundance because many came back and were reconciled to Him through confession.

The following week, I went to St. James Cathedral, in Seattle, Washington. While I was there, I had the privilege of meeting Archbishop Hunthausen. We had a lengthy talk about the Apostolate and the blessing that I give at Renewals.

8. In New Mexico

Then I flew immediately to Albuquerque, New Mexico, on October 9th, where I began a Renewal Week in Our Lady of Fatima Parish. The people again responded very vigorously and I was pleased that more than sixty percent of the people who attended were Spanish-speaking Americans.

The following week, I was at St. Mary's Cathedral in Santa Fe, New Mexico. However, before going to the Cathedral, I had a meeting with Archbishop Sanchez. During this time, I was very concerned because my whole body was racked with pain and I wondered if I could continue preaching. While visiting with Archbishop Sanchez, he asked me if I would bless him. And so, we went to the chapel and I prayed over him and gave him the blessing. Then he prayed over me and all the pain disappeared.

While at the Cathedral, I learned about the election of the new Pope, John Paul II on October 16th, 1978. He was a Cardinal from Poland, who is very intelligent and seems to have a deep and solid spirituality. John Paul II also upholds and believes staunchly in the teachings of the Church. I believe the whole Church should begin to pray that he will be a source of unity and a beacon of hope so as to bring about human rights.

The Renewals in New Mexico were extremely successful. In fact, I was told that Our Lady of Fatima Parish has not been filled in the last eight years, while the Cathedral had not been filled in fifteen years. In both Renewals, the Churches overflowed with the people of God. Before returning to California, I also visited Immaculate Conception Parish, Las Vegas, New Mexico, for a one-night Renewal; St. Joseph's Parish, in Anton Chico, New Mexico; and Jemez Springs, New Mexico, to visit the Servants of the Paraclete and the Handmaids of the Precious Blood. After the Renewals in New Mexico, I flew back to California for a few days.

9. In Oregon

Then I flew to Oregon to give Renewal talks. While in Oregon, I went from one parish to another almost every night, rather than staying at a parish for a full week. The turnouts were numerous, but I realized that a Renewal should be given for a full week and not just for a day. Nevertheless, God showered His blessings and graces upon the people, because many came back to Him through the Sacrament of Reconciliation.

10. National Catholic Women's dinner

On November 9th, 1978, I was invited to attend the National Catholic Women's Dinner along with the Handmaids of the Sacred Hearts of Jesus and Mary. At this dinner, I permitted the Handmaids to wear their habits. The comments on the part of the people were very favorable. The people at the dinner were deeply impressed by the habits. Unfortunately, some of the Handmaids told the people that they were Fr. Luke's Order, rather than instructing the people that they were not a religious order and were only working toward approbation. This was a big mistake. I found out afterwards that permission was never given for the Handmaids to wear habits. This was an unfortunate misunderstanding on my part, especial when Timothy Cardinal Manning was present and saw the Handmaids.

a.   Receiving a letter from Father Provincial

When I returned to the Center in California, I received a letter in the mail from Father Provincial. The letter stated that I was to meet with the Council at the Alemany Faculty Residence at 1:30 PM, on November 22nd. There was no explanation why, just the statement that my presence was required.

b.   Our Lady of Guadalupe

Before this meeting, I was scheduled for another pilgrimage. On November 14th, we went to Our Lady of Guadalupe, in Mexico.

Unfortunately, our guides scheduled many secular sites and commercialized everything by stopping at the gift shops for long periods of time. And even when it came to spiritual things, we were told to hurry because our time was limited. However, on November 19th, Fr. Devine and fifty others, including myself, went to the shrine of Our Lady of Guadalupe where we prayed all day. I think the shrine is a magnificent place and I was deeply impressed by the number of people who came to Mass. One Mass was followed immediately after the other, from early in the morning until late at night. There was a constant stream of people receiving Holy Communion most of the day. On the following day, we prayed two more hours at the shrine. In late afternoon, we flew back to Los Angeles on November 20th. I thought it was a well worthwhile trip, but I don't think I'll ever go on a similar pilgrimage. If I ever go again, then the tour will be with a very few select people so that each person can really benefit spiritually.

c.   Meeting with the Council

After returning to California, I kept my appointment with Father Provincial and the Council at Alemany High School Faculty Residence on November 22nd. I was asked to explain the activities and happenings at Christ the King Center. I explained to them that many women have been interested in joining a new religious community, which was to be called "The Handmaids of the Sacred Hearts of Jesus and Mary." I told the Council that various people, over the past three years donated money for this purpose. These benefactors simply gave money without my asking or saying anything about starting a religious community of sisters. I told the Council that I have been thinking about this for many years and that the women themselves have been coming to me, encouraging me and even urging me to begin this community. I also told the Council that I wrote to His Eminence Cardinal Timothy Manning in July and September. I told them that the Cardinal had not answered my letters. I thought the reason why the Cardinal had not responded was because he hadn't had sufficient time, perhaps even to read them, because of the elections of the two new Popes. Then I told the Council that I wrote to Bishop Ward in July, September,

October and November about the lifestyle of the Handmaids. Next, I explained to the Council about Bishop Ward's replies.

Unfortunately, I forgot to tell the Council about the letter I sent to Father Provincial on August 14th. Because in that letter, I informed Father Provincial about my proposed activities and that I had asked him to share this with the Council. I then realized on October 26th that Fr. Provincial did not share my letter with the Council. Perhaps he may have forgotten. I realized this because I began to speak to a member of the Council whom I thought knew all about the Handmaids and my plans to eventually begin the Servants of the Sacred Hearts of Jesus and Mary for priests. The Council member told me that nothing in my letter was discussed among them. However, on the next day, he planned to talk about this letter at the next Council meeting.

When I finished speaking, Father Provincial said that he went to Cardinal Timothy Manning and asked him if he had given approbation for me to begin the Handmaids of the Sacred Hearts of Jesus and Mary. In my response to the Provincial, I said that I did not ask Cardinal Manning for approbation because I knew this was premature. I did, however, ask for the Cardinal's blessing upon what I was undertaking. Then Father Provincial told me that Cardinal Manning said that I had to disband the sisters. I was shocked, first of all, that Father Provincial did not come to me and ask me what I was doing or even give me the opportunity to explain everything to him, especially since I had written to him on August 14th. Immediately, this whole ordeal seemed that the decision to disband the sisters had already been made, even before asking me to give an explanation at the Provincial Council meeting. At that point, all I could do was ask them to consider giving me permission to continue this beautiful work for the Lord. I wish that Father Provincial had used the Scriptural form of fraternal correction, that is, to come to me first in private. Then, if I was adamant, the next step would have been to go to the Council and, finally, as a last resort, to go to the Cardinal.

This ordeal reminded me of St. Paul and St. Peter. In other words, when Saul was persecuting Christians through ignorance, he encountered our Lord. Through this encounter, Saul was converted and became St. Paul. When Peter denied our Lord, our Lord went to him and said three times, "Do you love me?" thus forgiving and reinstating him to his former position. In regards to these two men, I find myself acting like Saul. In other words, I acted out of good will, but in ignorance.

11. Documents from Bishop Ward

On November 24th, I received some formal documents from Bishop Ward, with various corrections and encouragements. He did point out that the Handmaids should not wear their habits, which was again a shock to me, since I thought that I acted correctly. As spiritual director of the Handmaids, I asked them to remove their habits, in obedience to the directions of Bishop Ward. Within twenty minutes, the Handmaids removed their habits and returned to secular clothes.

12. Documents from Father Provincial

I was at St. Boniface Parish, in Anaheim, giving a Renewal Week, when I received the reply from Father Provincial and the Council to disband the religious community of sisters. Since the Handmaids already removed their habits, I thought there was nothing further that needed to be done. I told them the news in late November. They decided that they wished to go forward and continue to try to form the Handmaids of the Sacred Hearts of Jesus and Mary. They understood that I was not to be considered their Founder, but that they had to make a go of it on their own. Since they did not join a community to follow Father Luke Zimmer, but to serve God, they felt they had an obligation in conscience to go forward. I told them they could remain as lay guests at out Center until they had moved into their newly purchased property.

a. The Handmaids move

On December 1st, the Handmaids moved to 1329 Indian Hill, Pomona, California. I decided to give them a loan through the Apostolate of Christian Renewal. The agreement was made that they would pay the Apostolate of Christian Renewal as soon as they had sufficient funds. The reason why this agreement was made was so that the Congregation cannot accuse the Apostolate of Christian Renewal or me, of fostering this new lay religious community through financial aid. Personally, I feel that these women are very sincere and I have the highest regard for them. I do not consider these women to be fly-by-nights or fanatics, rather they have their feet on the ground and will be a great asset to the Church. These women are willing to work in order to pay the money that is owed for their property. If everyone pools their resources, they will be able to succeed financially because most of these women are professionals. They will also continue to live a prayer life and hopefully work closely with a canon lawyer and Bishop Ward so as to establish a community in accordance with canon law. The money for the loan will come from the savings of the members in the community.

I hope that my involvement with the Handmaids will not be a detriment for their final approbation because that would be a tragedy. Just because God chooses an ignorant instrument to bring something about doesn't mean that the mission or work is not from God. I admit that I acted like St. Peter, in an impulsive manner, but never out of ill will or deliberately trying to do things behind any person's back. In fact, in my 1978 yearly report to every member in the Province, I told them about the plans to establish the Handmaids community. I also told them that I was thinking about starting a new religious community for priests and brothers. Perhaps no one took me seriously!

b. My thoughts on the disbanding

I think I need to explain my own feelings on what has happened. After getting over the initial shock, I was obedient to all concerned. I constantly preach that every person is to be obedient and if I didn't live it, then I would be a hypocrite or a Pharisee. Even though I do not have any ill feelings towards anyone, I feel sorry for Father Provincial and the Council in the way that this matter was handled. During this time, I definitely prayed for them as well as for all who were involved.

I do not want anyone to speak ill of them either, especially if they find out the full story. In living a life as a religious, sometimes there are reasons why certain things are done, even if the person doesn't understand. Likewise, obedience is essential in order to maintain community life. As a result, when a mistake is made, the person who makes the mistake is responsible and not the person who is obedient. As I reflected on this matter, I was reminded of what our Blessed Mother said at Fatima, "Leave it to me." Everything is in her Heart and she is the one who is the Foundress. She does not want anyone else to stand in the way and that is why I believe she removed the obstacle, which is myself. However, I will always pray for these women and keep them in my heart. Our Blessed Mother has been instrumental in bringing these women together. There are twenty others who have expressed the desire to join the community. There is no other explanation than that God is visiting His people and stirring them up.

c. The counsel of my spiritual director

My ordinary spiritual director told me that I have a duty to explain my side of the story to the Cardinal and that he has a right to hear it. I do not intend to plead with the Cardinal to reinstate me as the Founder of the Handmaids. I just want to explain the facts, as I see them, and give him the opportunity to ask questions, give advice and/or correction. I have always tried to be obedient and with the grace of God, I will continue to do so. In conscience, I still believe that God wants me to start a religious community for priests and brothers, which will be called the Servants of the Sacred Hearts of Jesus and Mary.

Fr. Luke kept his joy of talking on the phone until the last days of his life.

CHAPTER 6

1979

A. Results of a letter from Fr. Provincial

Before going on my annual retreat with our Congregation in June, 1979, I wrote a letter to Fr. Provincial and his Council asking permission to seek a bishop in order to begin the Servants and Handmaids of the Sacred Hearts of Jesus and Mary as religious communities. I had no idea that about the same time Father Provincial and his Council had decided to inform me that I would not be able to do this. The letter from the Provincial and the Council told me to do the following:

1) To sell the properties at 890 and 830 Hillcrest Drive
2) To disband all who were living there
3) To forget the idea of founding a new religious community

I found this letter to be quite vague because there were no reasons given as to why I should do this. In fact, I was not even given an opportunity to speak to the Council over this matter. I was just told—you do this! Since our letters crossed, I was not obliged to do anything immediately. I later contacted Timothy Cardinal Manning, but he remained neutral in this affair because he had to deal with the Congregation and myself. I then wrote to Fr. Superior General in Rome.

Fr. Luke and Ann Holcomb.

CHAPTER 7

1980

A. A letter from Father Superior General

In early February of 1980, the Superior General sent two representatives to look into the matter. The result of this meeting and a meeting with Father Provincial and his Council was:

1) We were to disband the community living at 890 and 830 Hillcrest Drive
2) We were to sell both properties
3) I could have an office where my secretary could continue working, which was one room in her home.
4) Nothing was mentioned about the financial situation, therefore we continued as we were already doing.
5) Nothing was mentioned about not beginning the religious communities. Therefore, I decided to continue to try to establish these communities, even though I didn't realize how hard that would be or how long it would take.

We then put the properties up for sale, which did not take too long before they were sold. The people in our community had to leave and go elsewhere. I felt very badly for them, but I could not do anything because obedience comes first.

1) Fr. Finbarr Devine moved to Holy Name of Mary Parish, San Dimas, California.

2) Fr. Kevin Barrett, W.F. returned to his community in Los Angeles, California.

3) Fr. Ed Wojniak, S.V.D. lived with his community in Riverside, California. He continued to preach Renewal Weeks until the last few months of his life. He died from cancer.

4) Fr. Richard Oman lived at St. Louis of France Parish, La Puente, California. He, too, continued to preach Renewal Weeks throughout the country.

5) My secretary continued to work for us in her home.

6) My mother, who lived with us seven months of the year returned to Wisconsin, where she lived with my brother Larry in Waukesha. While she was with us in California, she went to various Renewal Weeks. In regards to my mother, many people loved her dearly. She was our best publicity person because she loved life, people and God. Many people came to her and listened to her words of wisdom.

7) The other lay people who were working for us returned to live in the world.

8) Ann Holcomb, who was my housekeeper decided to go to travel school. She passed with top honors which was a tremendous achievement. She established "Angeles International" travel agency for the purpose of making pilgrimages to various countries and shrines. This was done under the umbrella of the Apostolate of Christian Renewal, yet remained a separate corporation. She had many hardships, heartaches and problems to deal with over the years, especially in doing this work for the Lord. She has weathered the storm and does her very best. She would never do this work except for the honor and glory of God.

9) I moved to Damien Faculty Residence at 2150 Damien Ave., La Verne, California. I began to live there in December, 1980. My office was 18 miles away: Christ the King Center, PO Box 467, La Puente, California. 91747. I also continued to publish our little newspaper, "Christian Renewal News," answered all personal letters addressed to me, was a chaplain for pilgrimages to other countries and shrines and preached Renewals, days of recollection, retreats and workshops throughout the country.

CHAPTER 8

1981

A. *Being cut off from the Handmaids*

In 1981, I received a letter from Father Provincial stating that I was to cut off all contact with the lay Handmaid's community. There was no explanation given why I should do this. I called him and said, "Am I to ring a bell every time I see a Handmaid and say, 'unclean'?" He said that he did not mean that. Rather, he said that I should be nice to them when I met them. Likewise, I was left in the air as to what I could do or could not do. I then spoke to my spiritual director who said, "If any of the Handmaids approach you for spiritual direction or confession, then accommodate them." Therefore, I followed this approach.

B. *A prophecy by Fr. Carl Hammer*

Later, when I was in New Mexico, I went to visit Fr. Carl Hammer, who was assigned to help priests by visiting them, encouraging them to pray, and being with them. He established a house of prayer for this purpose in Albuquerque, New Mexico.

I asked Fr. Hammer to pray for me and with me. I asked him to pray whether God really wanted me to begin the Communities of the Servants and Handmaids because I always felt in my heart and mind that I was to be the founder of both communities. As he prayed over me, he said, "The Handmaids community will almost disappear. Most will leave, but from the embers will rise a large and vibrant community." In regard to the Servants, Fr. Hammer said,

"The Servants will receive a lot of opposition from Church authorities, from my own Congregation and others." He said, "After a time passes, your Congregation will give you permission to begin. They will not oppose the founding of these communities, but they will only tolerate what you feel God is calling you to do. Finally, they will help you begin these communities." Likewise, Fr. Hammer said, "You are called to be the Founder of these Communities. Remember, you must put new wine into new wineskins."

During this period, I was going through tremendous opposition from everyone. Even my spiritual director did not believe in me and withdrew his direction, which meant that I needed a new spiritual director. I felt that people were ashamed to be associated with me. Even though I felt alone, I became more determined than ever to continue to do God's Will. The reason I became more adamant to do God's Will was because young men continued to contact me over the years. I had them attend colleges, seminaries and universities throughout the country. I even helped with the tuition of some of these students.

Fr. Luke's mother, receiving Communion from him in his early years.

CHAPTER 9

1982

A. *Receiving permission to seek a benevolent bishop*

In 1982, I kept explaining to Father Provincial that I still felt, more than ever, that God wished me to establish the Servants and Handmaids of the Sacred Hearts of Jesus and Mary. As a result, Fr. Provincial and the Council wanted me to update my theology by taking some courses at Berkeley. I spoke with my spiritual director and he said, "That would be a waste of time and you should not and may not pursue that course of action." I told Father Provincial and his Council what my spiritual director said. Father Provincial expressed his dissatisfaction and had each Council member express his views. They asked me what I really wanted to do. I stated I wanted to be given permission to seek a bishop who would allow me to establish the Servants and Handmaids. From the comments made by Father Provincial and the Council members, I thought the permission would not be given. I left the meeting with a very heavy heart. The rest of the day I spent in prayer and totally surrendered everything to God. Later, one of the Council members told me that they decided to grant my request.

I officially received a letter from Father Provincial telling me that I could seek a benevolent bishop to begin these communities. The decision was made on the Feast of the Sacred Heart and Father Provincial wrote the letter on the next day, which was the Feast of the Immaculate Heart.

I really did not want to go back to school because I studied a lot on my own ever since my ordination. In fact, I studied all the

Vatican Council II documents and renewals that were taking place in the Church. I read the L'Osservatore Romano faithfully each week, the encyclicals and the documents from the Vatican and the Bishops' Conferences. I read many books as well as listened to many people who were ultra-conservative, conservative, ultra-liberal and liberal. I firmly believe that I have a very good idea of what was being presented in the Church in the modern world. The reason why I personally continued educating myself is because I made up my mind that I should believe, accept, live and preach according to the authentic teachings of the Holy Father and the Magisterium of the Church.

In regards to the beginning of the religious communities, I still had opposition from Church authorities. I felt that Timothy Cardinal Manning was unwilling to give permission because he would be resigning soon and that he wanted the new Archbishop to decide. In a private conversation with Cardinal Manning, he said others tried to establish communities, but failed to do so. He used one person as an example. He then told me, "Once you put your hand to the plow you should never look back." As I reflected on this meeting, I felt that this example could be taken in two ways, either give up the idea of beginning the Servants and Handmaids or once being committed to do so never look back. I felt that the Cardinal meant the former, giving up the idea of beginning the Servants and Handmaids. Nevertheless, the Cardinal was always gracious to me whenever we spoke. I truly admired this man and I was always deeply disturbed whenever anyone spoke ill of him.

As for the Vicar of Religious, Bishop John Ward, D.D., J.C.L., I always thought that he was opposed to the Servants and Handmaids. He said that I should remain in the Congregation of the Sacred Hearts of Jesus and Mary and that I should try to renew this community. Unlike Cardinal Manning, Bishop Ward was not so gracious because he spoke to me several times very forcefully, which seemed to be in anger. Beyond this, I always respected Bishop Ward and I pray for him everyday.

B. Meeting Eduardo Cardinal Pironio

In the fall of 1982, I made another pilgrimage to the Holy Land, where I met Eduardo Cardinal Pironio, who was the Prefect of the

Congregation of Religious. I told him that I felt God was calling me to be the founder of a new religious community. When I mentioned the name I wished to call it, Cardinal Pironio said, "I heard about you," and asked me to send him the constitutions, etc. I believe he must have heard about us from (then) Archbishop Eduardo Gagnon, who was the President of the Commission of the Family.

C. Archbishop Gagnon

While I was in Rome, I met Archbishop Gagnon, who was on the advisory board of the IIHJ with me. During this time, we developed a good friendship. One day, I stated to Archbishop Gagnon that I would like to start a new religious community because I had a tremendous devotion to the Sacred Heart, Immaculate Heart of Mary and St. Joseph. Then Archbishop Gagnon suggested that I call this new religious community the Servants and Handmaids of the Sacred Heart of Jesus, Mary and Joseph because it symbolizes the one heart, love and unity of the Holy Family. Naturally, I was very inspired because the name of this new community expresses what I felt God was calling me to do.

Before Archbishop Gagnon gave me the name of the new religious community, I always called it the Servants and Handmaids of the Sacred Hearts of Jesus and Mary. But now, the name Heart, rather than Hearts, express the love and unity of the Holy Family as reflected in the Blessed Trinity.

Later, when Archbishop Gagnon was made a Cardinal, I asked him if he would present the Constitutions and the Statues.

A Journey Through Life: Chosen

CHAPTER 10

1983

A. Selling of the property

In 1983, the buyer of our former property at 890 Hillcrest Dr. sold this home to another buyer. The person who bought the property from us made investments in other properties and then would sell them for exorbitant prices. Finally, the person was caught embezzling funds from his employer and put in jail where he later died. The person who bought the property from him refused to make payments so the Apostolate was forced to foreclose. When the Apostolate reclaimed the property, I asked Mr. and Mrs. Roman Oman to be caretakers while we tried to resell. When we finally sold the property 14 months later, the Apostolate demanded cash to avoid any future problems

When the buyer of 830 Hillcrest Dr. began to have marital problems and separated, they stopped payments too. After many months, the Apostolate began the process of reclaiming the property once again. However, after this couple reconciled, they refinanced their loan and immediately paid us the full amount they owed us.

1. The Handmaids on the move

In 1983, the Handmaids sold their property at 1329 Indian Hill, Pomona, California. They then moved to Saint Anthony's Mission in the Monterey Diocese. In order for the Handmaids to pay off their property debt, I obtained donations so that most of the mortgage money was paid. Therefore, the Handmaids had sufficient money to live until they could become active in their ministry. I felt that living at St. Anthony's Mission for six months was an insightful experience for them since they had to really be on their own. Then the Handmaids moved to Ventura, CA, where they settled and pursued various courses to train themselves in religious education and spiritual living. They developed a prayerful community and began to work in various ministries, especially in San Buenaventura Mission. Alice Chinn was the Superior of the community and leader in the work at the Mission. Others worked at Our Lady of Assumption for a year in youth ministry.

B. Seeking permission

In 1983, I finally began to seek admission into other dioceses, such as Sacramento and Monterey. Bishop Francis Quinn of Sacramento said the diocese was not interested in any new religious communities, whereas Bishop Thaddeus Shubsda showed great interest in the Servants and Handmaids of the Sacred Heart of Jesus, Mary and Joseph.

Fr. Luke giving a daily homily in Dr. Jim's home. - Fall of 1996.

CHAPTER 11

1984

A. Ignatian retreat with Fr. John McAnulty, S.J.

During the month of May, 1984, I made a thirty day Ignatian Retreat at the House of Prayer in Los Angeles, California, with Fr. John McAnulty, S.J. During this retreat, I realized that St. John's Gospel expressed our charism better than any other Scripture writer. The passage of the Last Supper struck me very deeply, especially the prayer for unity (Jn 17: 20-23). As I focused on this passage, God spoke to me about many things, especially while I was walking. Fr. McAnulty recognized that God would manifest Himself and His teachings to me while walking. He also told me to walk everyday as long as I had good health, but especially for the next two years. I believe that this retreat was a great blessing. I felt that this Ignatian Retreat was one of the greatest highlights of my priesthood and life. I would highly recommend anyone to make such a retreat.

B. Meeting Archbishop Augustine Meyer

In the summer, I went on pilgrimage to Germany, Austria, Switzerland and Italy. When I was in Germany, I visited Theresa Neuman's grave in Bavaria, Germany. While I was there, I asked her to intercede for the Apostolate since I had not heard anything from Rome about our Constitutions. The next day, we went to St. Conrad's shrine in Attoling, Germany. I met a priest who was tall and thin. I said to him, "Father, I want to offer Mass." He then introduced himself as

Archbishop Augustine Meyer, who was the Secretary for the Congregation of Religious in Rome. I told him about what was transpiring and how I was waiting to hear from the Congregation of Religious in regard to the Constitutions I sent to them. Before he departed, he said, "I am going back to Rome and you will hear from us." He was later transferred to be Prefect of the Congregation of Sacraments and Worship and was also elevated to Cardinal.

Two weeks latter, I received a letter from the Congregation of Religious by Archbishop Vincenza Fagiola. The letter explained the procedure of establishing religious communities, that is, the various steps of development. He said the Congregation of Religious would be willing to help us in any way and at any time.

C. Revising the Constitutions

I wrote to Bishop Thaddeus Shubsda, in Monterey, giving him this information. He wrote back and said I should submit the Constitutions to a canon lawyer. He made arrangements for this with Father Richard Hill, S.J., to go over the Constitutions. After Father Hill studied this document, he had a meeting with me and commented that they were too detailed and needed to be simplified. He said a new document should be drawn up to meet the requirements for establishing a Diocesan lay association. He actually wrote this document after further consultations with me. I personally felt this document was too weak and did not really express what I believed the Lord wanted for us to live and foster. However, I had to be satisfied with at least that much for our beginnings.

This document was submitted to Bishop Shubsda, but he kept putting the process off. I thought that he might have done this to test our perseverance or maybe he wasn't really interested. Anyway, he maintained that he was interested, but that this process was something entirely new to him. He also stated that he wanted everything to be done correctly. Bishop Shubsda then had the Handmaids submit various documents on each member. He also wanted me to send information regarding the Servants. Bishop Shubsda then contacted the Apostolic Delegate's office and followed the advice given by them. However, the process just kept dragging on and on.

D. Visiting Medjugorje

On September 29th-30th, Ann Holcomb, Julie and I made our first trip to Medjugorje. One of the reason's why we went to Medjugorje was to see whether the trip was feasible or not. When we arrived in Dubrovnik, a taxi driver named Tony took us to Mostar for lunch and then we proceeded on to Medjugorje. We arrived in Medjugorje about 3 PM. Then we went to the apparition room, where there were a number of priests praying the Rosary in Italian. Then Ivan, Maria and Jakov came into the room and began to pray the Our Father. Halfway through the prayer they fell to their knees. Allegedly, our Blessed Mother was present. Each of the children was speaking with our Blessed Mother. Even though their lips were moving, we did not hear anything. After the apparition, we returned to the main body of the Church and prayed the remaining part of the Rosary and celebrated Mass. When Mass was finished, the pastor said that I should come back the next day to offer Mass at 10 AM.

The next morning, September 29th, was the feast day of Archangels Michael, Gabriel and Raphael. While I was vesting for Mass, four Italian priests came. They wanted to concelebrate with me, but one of the priest wanted to have Mass in the apparition room. He then asked where I was offering Mass, but I didn't know because the pastor never said anything. After this priest talked with the pastor, we were allowed to celebrate Mass in the apparition room. However, I had to wait until the Mass being offered was over. When I entered the apparition room for Mass, the room was full of Italians. As I was to begin the Mass, a priest came and told all the Italians to leave. Therefore Ann Holcomb, Julie and myself were all alone in the room. No one disturbed us throughout the Mass.

When I began the Mass, I felt the Blessed Mother's presence throughout the Mass. I also felt St. Joseph, the angels and the saints were also present. Our Blessed Mother said, "Ask whatever you want to have and it will be given to you." This message meant that each person who was present could ask for anything. I felt that the only thing I wanted was to know and do God's Will. Whereas Ann asked for the grace of conversion for her husband so that he could overcome a problem. As for Julie, I'm not really sure what she asked. This great gift seemed to answer every question I had during the Mass. After the Mass, we remained in the apparition room for a long period of time in thanksgiving.

After we left the apparition room, the driver insisted that we visit the village where the children lived as well as the hill of the apparitions. However, because of the rain, we were not able to climb the hill. The driver then asked an elderly woman where the visionaries lived, she said that Maria lived in the next house. The driver then knocked on Maria's door and asked if we could visit.

As we entered her home, she was praying with two of her friends. One of Maria's friends could speak English, so we were able to communicate with Maria. We asked Maria many questions, which she gladly answered. She said that it is necessary to pray from the heart so as to have peace of heart, mind and spirit. She also said that if we pray this way, then we would have peace in our families, communities, countries and the world.

Next, I prayed over each person and blessed them with the relic of the True Cross. Then Maria prayed over me and blessed me with the relic. Finally, she traced a cross on my forehead. After that we had some coffee and cookies, took pictures and talked some more.

Finally, we left Maria's house. The driver drove us to a very nice place for lunch, which actually turned out to be a big meal. When we were eating, a few communist officials came into the restaurant for dinner. Our driver, being a communist himself, went over and spoke with them. Then they sent a bottle of wine to our table. Before the communist officials left, they came to our table and shook our hands. They seemed to be very friendly, but the leader seemed suspicious because he would never look at us and stared at the floor.

While we continued driving back to Dubrovnik, the driver asked Ann if she would send him some of the pictures she took at Maria's home. He also said he would like to have the address of her home as well as the names and addresses of the other two women. Ann agreed.

The next morning, September 30th, when I woke up, I looked into the mirror. When I looked into the mirror, I saw a large black cross on my forehead. The cross resembles the cross of the early Christians. When a person goes to the Holy Land, he or she can see this cross engraved on rocks, walls and in various Christian places. This cross is also on the Pope's Pallium.

I was amazed and wondered what I should do. First, I tried to wash it off, but was unable to do so. Then, I decided to see if Ann and Julie were up, so I went to their room and rapped on the door. When they answered the door, they did not seem surprised so I realized they were unable to see the cross. And then I said, "Thank God." However, I went back to my room and I could still see the cross.

Even though I haven't seen this cross since, it still remains on my forehead because many people say they see it, such as during Mass, Renewal Weeks and pilgrimages. I find that these people are deeply moved and it seems to have a very beneficial effect because they resolve to live a life of virtue.

1. Don't send those pictures

After our flight home to California on September 30th, I was driving to the office from La Verne, California, to La Puente, California. During this ride, I heard our Blessed Mother say, "Call Ann and tell her not to send the pictures and addresses to Tony in Yugoslavia." I said, "Why not? He seems to be such a nice person and even prayed with us at Maria's home." Then our Blessed Mother said, "So, was Judas a nice person?" Then I understood that he could use these pictures as evidence of Maria and her two friends breaking the law. In other words, at that time in Yugoslavia, the law only permitted people to pray in the Church, which means people were prohibited from gathering anywhere else for prayer, even in a person's own home. I called Ann and gave her the message. Needless to say, she did not send him any pictures.

A Journey Through Life: Chosen

CHAPTER 12

1985 & 1986

A. *Mystical Mass Prayer enlightened*

I also noticed after my trip to Medjugorje that I started to pray the Mystical Mass Prayer differently. Every morning, while I was walking, the Lord gave me new insights and showed me the magnitude of this prayer. The prayer has changed drastically from the time I first wrote it. The first prayer, which appears in my other books, was written after twenty-five years of meditating on the Eucharistic Liturgy. The new prayer was more meaningful to me, which was really fulfilling and effective in having prayer requests answered for others.

All during 1985, I kept this new version. Then I explained it to the Handmaids. Debbie Hensler said, "Father, you have to give us a copy and make it available for the people." Finally, I wrote the Mystical Mass Prayer and sent it to Father Provincial and asked him if I could send it to Archbishop Roger Mahony to obtain the Imprimatur. Fr. Provincial said that he liked the prayer and everyone he showed it to also liked the prayer. Therefore, I sent the Mystical Mass Prayer to Archbishop Mahony and asked for the Imprimatur.

On January 3rd, 1986, I went on my daily walk early in the morning. While I was walking, I was praying the Mystical Mass Prayer and was moved to pray to Pope Pius XII and Pope John XXIII. I said to Pope Pius XII, "You prepared everything for Vatican Council II," and to Pope John XXIII, "You convoked the Council, so pray for me." Then I said to the both of them, "You know the reasons why God moved the Church to have Vatican Council II in our time. I believe the Mystical Mass Prayer reflects the spirituality God wants for our day. If this prayer is really from God and reflects Vatican Council II spirituality, then move Archbishop Mahony to give the Imprimatur."

The next evening, January 4th, I celebrated a home Mass for a group of people. At the end of the Mass, a good friend of mine, Jerrie Castro said, "Father, I have something to tell you. I don't know what it means, but I must tell you." Then she said, "The prayer you prayed to Pope Pius XII and Pope John XXIII has been granted." Naturally, I was very surprised because I did not say anything to anyone about asking for the Imprimatur.

Four days passed before I received a gracious letter from Archbishop Roger Mahony granting the Imprimatur for the Mystical Mass Prayer. The letter was dated January 7th, 1986.

B. The Mystical Mass Prayer

Eternal Father, we offer to You, through the Immaculate and Sorrowful Heart of Mary and the Just Heart of Joseph, in the Holy Spirit, the Body, Blood, Soul and Divinity of our Lord Jesus Christ, in union with each Mass celebrated today and every day until the end of time.

With Mother Mary, St. Joseph, each angel and saint in Heaven, each person in Purgatory, each person in the Body of Christ and the family of God, we offer each act of love, adoration, praise and worship. We offer each act of thanksgiving for blessings, graces and gifts received. We offer each act of reparation for sins that have been, are being and will be committed until the end of time. And we offer each act of intercessory prayer. We offer all of these prayers in union with Jesus in each Mass celebrated throughout the world, throughout all time.

We prostrate ourselves before You, Triune God, like the Prodigal Son with our weaknesses, limitations and sinfulness, asking for Your mercy, forgiveness and acceptance. Like the Publican-tax collector, we ask for mercy and forgiveness. Like the Paralytic, we ask for healing and strength. Like the Good Thief, we ask for salvation. And like Mary Magdalene, give us the gift of

Your Unconditional Love of the Blessed Trinity as reflected in the Holy Family.

We consecrate ourselves and all of creation to You, O Triune God: Father, Son and Holy Spirit.

Eternal Father, we ask You in the Name of Jesus, through the power of His Most Precious Blood, through His death on the Cross, through His Resurrection from the dead and Ascension into Heaven, to send forth the Holy Spirit upon all people.

Holy Spirit, give an outpouring of Your blessings, graces and gifts; upon those who do not believe, that they may believe; upon those who are doubtful or confused, that they may understand; upon those who are constantly living in a state of sin, that they may be converted; upon those who are weak, that they may be strengthened; upon those who are lukewarm or indifferent, that they may be transformed; upon those who are holy, that they may persevere.

We ask You to bless our Holy Father. Give him strength and health in body, mind, soul and spirit. Bless his ministry and make it fruitful. Protect him from his enemies and in his travels. Supply for all of his needs.

Bless each cardinal, bishop, priest, deacon, brother, sister and all those aspiring to the religious life, especially..., and grant many the gift of a vocation to the priesthood and religious life. Bless all married and single people. Bless each member of our families, relatives, friends, enemies and persecutors, especially..., Bless the poor, the sick, the underprivileged, the dying and all of those in need, especially..., Bless those who have died and are in the state of purification, that they may be taken to Heaven.

We offer and consecrate ourselves and all of creation to you, Sacred Heart of Jesus, Mary and Joseph. We ask you Joseph and Mary to take us with all of our hopes and desires. Please offer them with Jesus in the Holy Sprit to our Heavenly Father, in union with each Mass offered throughout all time.

We consecrate ourselves to Archangels Michael, Gabriel and Raphael and each angel, especially our own Guardian angel. We ask in the Name of Jesus, through our Mother Mary, Queen of all Angels, that You, O Heavenly Father, send forth legions of angels to minister to us: Archangel Michael with his legions to ward off the attacks of the world, the flesh and the Devil; Archangel Gabriel with his legions to teach us that we may know and do your will and that they may help us to catechize and evangelize; Archangel Raphael with his legions to heal our woundedness, supply for our limitations, strengthen us in our weakness, to break all demonic depression and bondage, to give us joy in the spirit, to protect us in our travels and to supply for all of our needs.

Finally, we ask for the gift of Unconditional Love, that we can live the Family Life of the Blessed Trinity as reflected in the Holy Family at Nazareth, thus bringing to fruition Jesus' prayer for unity, and peace in justice throughout the world. Amen. (Revised 1996).

C. Being in Pontevedra, Spain

During the summer of 1986, I was the chaplain on a pilgrimage to Fatima, Lourdes and Spain. While traveling through Spain, we stopped at the convent in Pontevedra, where Sr. Lucia had various visions. One day, while taking care of garbage, she met a young boy who spoke to her. She asked him if he knew the Hail Mary. The little boy responded that he did. She then told him to go to the chapel and pray. Two weeks later, while doing the same chore, she met the little boy again. This time he said to her, "Why don't you do what my Mother asked you to do?" At that moment, she realized that the boy was Jesus. However, when she explained to her Superior what happened, they said that they did not believe her so the request could not be carried out.

When I was offering the Eucharistic Liturgy in this chapel, the Holy Spirit moved me to pray for Steve Lawrence. Steve was a young man who had a very bad heart. His heart was so damaged that it was impossible to have an operation. He became a Catholic and had a new lease on life. Steve was joyful and had a real zest for life. Everyone who knew Steve knew that he did not have long to live. As I was offering Mass, the Holy Spirit prayed through me for his eternal welfare. I told the Lord that he knew every aspect of Steve's life and that He knew his heart. I begged God to forgive all his sins and to bring him safely to Heaven. I offered the Mass and each Mass throughout all time in reparation for any and all his sins, in thanksgiving for every grace received and that he be taken to Heaven without going to Purgatory. After this prayer, I felt a tremendous peace come over me as I left him in the mercy and love of God.

After the pilgrimage, I was told that Steve Lawrence died on a Sunday while he was with his family at a picnic. Before he died, he reconciled with his family. His death occurred on the same day I prayed for him in Pontevedra.

D. Still having problems getting religious communities started

The remainder of 1986 and 1987 was filled with Renewal Weeks, retreats, and waiting for the Lord's direction in regards to the Servants and Handmaids. People began to express doubts about whether these communities would ever receive approval from a bishop.

However, I was told by a priest and members of my own Congregation that I should become more aggressive in dealing with bishops, especially Bishop Shubsda. I was really convinced of bishop Shubsdas' sincerity when he said he wants to proceed in a manner which would assure everything to be done correctly. I was willing to give him time, but I also knew he was very busy running his Diocese, preparing for the Papal visit and working on Junipero Serra's cause. He was also having financial problems in his Diocese so I felt that being too aggressive was not very prudent.

Some of the seminarians who had expressed the desire to become Servants began to pursue other interests in life. Some decided to get married, while others joined other religious communities or diocesan seminaries. A few people just returned to the world and waited to find out what they were to do. However, each person is free to decide what to do with his or her life, so all that could be done was to let go and let God. I still pray for each of these people and hope that the decision they made was the right one. Likewise, I always will be supportive of any decision a person makes in regard to a vocation in life.

In the Handmaids' community, I felt a restlessness. They, too, were becoming tired of waiting. Some left and returned to previous lifestyles, while others remained. However, for those who remained, some people did not have their hearts in what is necessary to live our charism, spirituality and mission.

With all that was happening, I never doubted God's will in establishing the Servants and Handmaids. I knew I had to patiently withstand the bombardment from others and continually remind them that I had not changed my beliefs in what I felt God wished me to do.

I received encouragement from a few loyal and faithful friends, who always urged me forward. I also remembered that Helena Maxfield, Steve Martinez and Mary Buytaert had offered their lives for the founding of these communities.

1. Helena Maxfield

Helena Maxfield was a very intelligent and self-willed person. She became a convert to the faith and then began to live a humble and saintly life. She was a person who, once she made up her mind, would do anything no matter what the cost. When she became ill with terminal cancer, I gave her the book, *Cissie* to read. This changed Helena's attitude in regard to her illness.

Cissie was a young girl who had bone cancer and suffered greatly. She decided not to take pain-killers so that she could offer her sufferings in reparation for abortion. She did this even before the Supreme Court decision of 1973. Cissie died when she was thirteen years old.

Since Cissie did not take pain-killers to ease her pain, Helena decided to do the same thing. She offered her sufferings for the founding of the Servants and Handmaids communities. Before she died, I asked her to become the first Handmaid, which she did. I also asked her to offer her life for the Servants and Handmaids, which she did in my presence. The last days of her sufferings were horrendous, but she persevered. She would say "Jesus" over and over again. She died on April 7th, 1973.

2. Steve Martinez

Steve Martinez was a teenager in Bakersfield, California, who had a cancerous brain tumor. His parents were hoping that he would receive a miraculous healing. Therefore, they went on a pilgrimage with us to Fatima, Spain and Lourdes. We kept praying for his healing, but God had other ideas. I asked Steve if he would offer his sufferings for the founding of the Servants and Handmaids communities and he agreed. Even though Steve was not healed, other people were, such as Bob Wilson, Ph.D., a psychologist. Bob was given only a few months to live because he had bone marrow cancer. However, Bob was healed and is healthy and strong even today, six years after being diagnosed.

Steve returned home and continued going to high school until his sufferings became unbearable. I visited with him several times during the last few months of his life. I heard his confession, gave him the Sacrament of the Sick and Holy Communion. Steve publicly professed he would offer his sufferings for the Servants and Handmaids. I also allowed him to become the first member of the Servants.

During the fifteen months of suffering, Steve was a living example of God's love, compassion and courage. He insisted that no person should feel sorry for him because he felt there was always someone less fortunate than he was. Steve showed unconditional love toward all, which uplifted his friends and his family during his last days.

Steve died on May 23rd, 1983. His life was not in vain because his suffering and death touched everyone at Garces High School, especially his close friends. His friends and family were able to become better people from what he shared with them. In making his suffering redemptive, he affected lives of people he never knew or met.

When Steve was young, his grandmother said, "He does not belong in this world because he looks like a little saint and he belongs in Heaven." In fact, when he was young, he would pretend he was a priest and would offer Mass. He would ask other children to join with him and to pray. He always thought of others rather than himself. This is probably why he wanted to become a priest.

After learning about the Servants, Steve began to pray the fifteen-decade Rosary everyday until he was unable to do so. Steve's parents, schoolmates, teachers, friends and the clergy all agreed that his humor and acceptance in the face of his growing disability and death were nothing short of extraordinary. They all agreed that the acceptance of his suffering and death was only possible through his faith in God. This faith helped him console his parents when they cried and kept him from any bitterness about his illness. After Steve's death, his parents received letters from people they didn't even know, who wanted them to know how Steve touched their lives.

Before Steve died, he wanted everyone to know he received a gift from God which was better than a cure. This gift was the desire of meeting His Heavenly Father and Mother. This gift also helped him never to go through any stages of depression and denial in facing death.

At the graduation of his class in June, each student presented a red rose in his memory. Then they sang the song, "I Will Never Forget You."

3. Mary Buytaert

Mary Buytaert, who joined the Handmaids community for a time, also offered her sufferings and life for the founding of the Servants and Handmaids. Unlike Helena and Steve, she was left by God to remain on earth to suffer many trials and difficulties. Her suffering was not so much physical as it was spiritual. The spiritual struggle she battled was dryness, darkness and being bombarded that God has or will abandon her. This suffering is equivalent to death. In other words, Mary suffered a real spiritual martyrdom.

CHAPTER 13

1987

A. A prophecy?

There was a sister from France who was known as Sr. Joseph. She too wanted to begin a new religious community. She predicted that the community would be founded when there would be a great crisis in the Church and the world. She said that, when the Name and Life of Jesus would be blasphemed in movies, and when His Name would appear on the marquee of the movie houses, then the Holy Spirit would give an outpouring of His graces and gifts in a renewal of the faith. She said that there would be a spiritual revolution which would bring, from America, great blessings upon the Church and the whole world. I have been told by people who knew and spoke to her that the Servants and Handmaids are those communities. She said these things in 1968. Today, we have seen movies blaspheme the Name and Life of Jesus.

B. Annual retreat

At the end of my annual retreat in June, I told Fr. Provincial that I would pray for the particular intention of whether God wanted the Servants and Handmaids to begin or not. I said, if they are not going to be considered, then I would just remain in my Congregation and forget about going further. Yet, deep in my heart, I still felt I was called to found these communities.

C. Analogy with the sun

In July, I was giving a Renewal Week in St. Cloud, Minnesota, at St. Mary's Cathedral. One morning, I went for a walk. The street lights were still on and the sun was just beginning to break. As I was walking, I noticed two shadows: one was long, which came from the sun; while the other was short, which came from the street lights. This reminded me of the saying that there is a little bit of good in the worst of people and a little bit of bad in the best of people. As I reflected on this experience, the longer shadow can represent all the good qualities in the good person, while the shorter shadow represents all the bad qualities, such as the sinfulness, faults, failings and weaknesses. Likewise, the shorter shadow hinders the person and wounds a person's relationship with God.

On the other hand, the larger shadow can represent all the evil in the person who is constantly living in the state of sin. Thus, there is more sinfulness than there is good. Still, there is always a little bit of good in a person. If they have a change of heart and a change of life, then they can overcome the sinfulness, faults, failings and weaknesses.

However, when a person walks towards God, that person never loses sight of God. Likewise, the closer a person moves towards God, the closer a person becomes totally filled with God. This happens to any person who becomes humble and gladly cooperates with God in living his or her life. Then, doing God's Holy Will becomes all-important and worldly things become less and less significant. Spiritual things also become more important because a person begins to divest self of worldly things, cares and interests. As a result, a person begins to see and understand things from God's viewpoint and not from a human's viewpoint. For example, a person begins to see and understand God's plan for life, for the world, for the Church and just for everything. In surrendering and abandoning all to God, a person becomes completely free and experiences the joy, peace and happiness of finding a loving and personal God. This personal love-relationship is fulfilling and leads a person to be concerned about others, which leads to a greater joy and happiness. The person becomes God-centered, other centered and all selfishness disappears.

Later, I thought about this analogy some more. I then realized that when the sun is directly over a person, the person does not see any shadow. Similarly, when a person is totally united with God, he or she always knows and does God's will and any suffering, trial or problem is seen in the proper perspective. The peace, then, within a person is never disturbed. Therefore, a person's relationship with God ultimately brings a person to do God's Will.

D. A new Handmaid leader

In December, Alice Chinn told me that her position as leader of the Handmaids community and Religious Education Director at the San Buenaventura Mission was too much for her. She needed to be released from the pressure of running the community so she could be more effective in her apostolic work. Since she was the leader for many years, I decided that a change was needed. Looking at the Handmaids' community, I felt that there were two different ideas of living our charism, spirituality and mission. Therefore, I felt that there was only one person who, with the help of God, could lead the community, Marcella Mei.

Marcella often spoke with Bishop Patrick Ziemann, who always encouraged her to work towards establishing the Handmaids as a religious community. Now that she was appointed by me to be the leader, she began to proceed in this manner. Marcella tried to help each member discern their vocation so that they could make a commitment wholeheartedly as a Handmaid and live the charism, spirituality and mission. This meant that each member would have to make a choice, either remain or leave, which caused a lot of pain.

A Journey Through Life: Chosen

CHAPTER 14

1988

A. *The unfolding of the Mystical Rosary*

During the whole month of January, I was praying the Mystical Mass Prayer with the intention of the founding of the Servants and Handmaids communities. On January 1st, while praying the Rosary, the Lord let me know that I should add a portion of the Mystical Mass Prayer as intentions before each mystery. At first, I thought this would not work because the intentions would not fit the Rosary. However, over the next few months, God revealed to me insights and that the intentions do fit the mysteries. Then I began to see how everything beautifully unfolded and the magnitude and power of praying in this manner.

Mystical Rosary

Introductory Prayer: Eternal Father, we offer to You the mysteries of our salvation in this Rosary, in union with Your dearly Beloved Son, our Lord Jesus Christ in each Eucharistic Liturgy, celebrated throughout the world, throughout all time; and with Him in each tabernacle throughout the world. We invite you Jesus, Mary, Joseph, each angel and saint in Heaven, and each person in Purgatory to pray with us and for us.

The Joyful Mysteries

The First Mystery: **The Annunciation and Incarnation** (Lk 1:26-28)
May it be done to me according to your word. (Lk 1:38)

Eternal Father, we offer to You, through the Immaculate and Sorrowful Heart of Mary and the Just Heart of Joseph, in the Holy Spirit, the Body, Blood, Soul and Divinity of our Lord Jesus Christ; from the moment of His conception and embracing the totality of His entire existence; in union with each Eucharistic Liturgy celebrated throughout the world, throughout all time; in atonement for our sins and the sins of the world, to bring peace in justice to the whole world.

The Second Mystery: **The Visitation** (Lk 1:39-56)
My soul proclaims the greatness of the Lord;
my spirit rejoices in God my Savior. (Lk 1:46-47)

Come, O Mother Mary, into our lives, so that we may intimately encounter Christ through you and be filled with the Holy Spirit. We ask for the grace to go forth to live and share the Good News.

With You, Jesus, Mary, Joseph, each angel and saint in Heaven, each person in Purgatory, each person in the Body of Christ and the family of God, we offer to You, Eternal Father: each act of love, adoration, praise and worship; each act of thanksgiving for blessings, graces, and gifts received; each act of reparation for sins that have been, are being and will be committed until the end of time; and each act of intercessory prayer. We offer all these payers in union with Jesus, in each Eucharistic Liturgy celebrated throughout the world, throughout all time.

The Third Mystery: **The Birth of our Lord Jesus** (Lk 2:1-20)

We offer our lives to You, Infant Jesus, the God-man, promising You to live the spirit or vows of charity, chastity, poverty and obedience to Your Church, according to our state of life.

We prostrate ourselves before You, Jesus, like the Prodigal Son with our weaknesses, limitations, and sinfulness asking for Your mercy, forgiveness and acceptance. Like the Publican-tax collector, we ask for mercy and forgiveness. Like the Paralytic, we ask for healing and strength. Like the Good Thief, we ask for salvation. And like Mary Magdalene, give us the gift of Your Unconditional Love of the Blessed Trinity as reflected in the Holy Family.

The Fourth Mystery: **Presenting Jesus
in the Temple** (Lk 2:22-40)

We entrust and consecrate ourselves, everyone and all creation to You, O Triune God, Father, Son and Holy Spirit, at the Offertory in each Eucharistic Liturgy so that our united common life becomes meritorious, redemptive and infinite in value. We express our sorrow and wish to make reparation for each of our sins. We wish to thank You for every blessing, grace and gift You have given us. We ask You for the grace of continual conversion, so that we may be open to the Holy Spirit, in order to be transformed to be a saint by becoming Jesus for and to others. We ask for the gift to be confirmed in grace and final perseverance.

The Fifth Mystery: **Finding Jesus
in His Father's House** (Lk 2:41-52)

Jesus, we ask You to bestow Your mercy upon us sinners, that we may not leave our Father's house. We ask for a special grace for those who have left our Father's house. Help them return home, to find and keep You in their hearts and lives.

Eternal Father, we ask in the Name of Jesus, through the power of His Most Precious Blood, through His death on the Cross, through His Resurrection from the dead and Ascension into Heaven, to send forth the Holy Spirit upon all people.

Send forth Your Holy Spirit and we shall be created and You shall renew the face of the earth. Come, Holy Spirit, fill the hearts of Your faithful and enkindle in us the fire of Your Divine Love.

The Sorrowful Mysteries

The First Mystery: **The Agony of Jesus in the Garden** (Lk 22:39-46)

United with You, Jesus, in the Holy Spirit,
may each of us, like You, pray to our Father:
not my will but yours be done. (Lk 22:42)

Holy Spirit, give an outpouring of Your blessings, graces and gifts upon those who do not believe, that they may believe; upon those who are doubtful or confused, that they may understand; upon those who are constantly living in the state of sin, that they may be converted; upon those who are weak, that they may be strengthened; upon those who are lukewarm or indifferent, that they may be transformed; and upon those who are holy, that they may persevere.

The Second Mystery: **The Scourging of Jesus at the Pillar** (Mk 15:15)

In a spirit of silence, we accept all bodily, mental, emotional and spiritual sufferings. We offer the sufferings of each person with You, Jesus, in the Holy Spirit, to our Father, in union with each Eucharistic Liturgy celebrated throughout all time, that they may be meritorious, redemptive and infinite in value.

Holy Spirit, give an outpouring of Your blessings, graces and gifts upon the sick who suffer in body, mind, soul or spirit, the underprivileged and all those in need. Bless each person who is dying, that each may receive special graces and gifts to choose Eternal Life (Jn. 17:3) and not eternal damnation. Bless each person in Purgatory, to be quickly taken to Heaven.

The Third Mystery: **The Crowing of Jesus with Thorns** (Mk 15:16-20)

Behold Jesus, the God-man! Accept Him as our King, our Lord, our Savior, our Brother, our Friend and Bridegroom of the Church. Behold the Vicar of Christ and accept him as the Visible Head of the Church.

Holy Spirit, bless and give an outpouring of Your gifts upon our Holy Father. Give him strength and health in body, mind, soul and spirit. Bless his ministry and make it fruitful. Protect him from his enemies and in his travels. Supply for all of his needs.

The Fourth Mystery: **The Way of the Cross** (Lk 23:26-31)

Jesus, help us to carry our cross and follow You in love, joy and peace. Holy Spirit, bless each cardinal, bishop, priest, deacon, brother, sister and all those aspiring to the religious life. Grant many the gift of a vocation to the priesthood and religious life. Bless all married and single people.

Holy Spirit, bless our families, relatives, friends, enemies and persecutors. We ask for a growing awareness and love of our role in Jesus' mission, given to us at our Baptism and Confirmation. Help us to develop Your gifts and virtues, so that we may go forth to catechize and evangelize everyone to be Jesus for and to others.

The Fifth Mystery: **The Crucifixion
and Death of Jesus** (Each Gospel)

Let us rejoice and be glad! Jesus, our Savior and Redeemer, won salvation and redemption for us. May we accept this act of love by responding in love.

We entrust and consecrate all we have prayed for to the Heart of Jesus, Mary and Joseph. We ask You, Joseph and Mary, together with Jesus, in the Holy Spirit to offer all to our Father at the Consecration in each Eucharistic Liturgy celebrated throughout all time, to bring peace in justice to the whole world.

The Glorious Mysteries

The First Mystery: **The Resurrection
of Jesus from the Dead** (Jn 20:1-18)
*Then the angel said..., He is not here,
for He has been raised just as he said.* (Mt 28:5-6)

We entrust and consecrate ourselves and everyone, to all the angels, especially Archangels Michael, Gabriel, and Raphael and our own Guardian angel.

The Second Mystery: **The Ascension of Jesus into Heaven** (Acts 1:3-14)

I am going to my Father and your Father, to my God and your God (Jn. 20: 17)

Lord, seated at the right hand of the Father, You will come to judge the living and the dead, intercede on our behalf. We offer ourselves to Your Justice, while thinking of our own judgment and eternal life.

We ask in the Name of Jesus, through our Mother Mary, Queen of all angels, that You, O Heavenly Father, send forth legions of angels to minister to us. Archangel Michael, with his legions, to ward off the attacks of the world, the flesh, and the Devil. Archangel Gabriel, with his legions to teach us that we may know and do Your will; that they may help us to catechize and evangelize. Archangel Raphael, with his legions to heal our woundedness, supply for our limitations, strengthen us in our weakness, to break all demonic depression and bondage, to give us joy of the Spirit, to protect us from our enemies and in our travels and to supply for all our needs.

The Third Mystery: **The Descent of the Holy Spirit** (Acts 2: 1-12; 40-41)

Come Holy Spirit, into our hearts! Give Yourself more fully to us, that we may live the Family Life of the Blessed Trinity, as reflected in the Holy Family. Give us a growing desire to bring to fruition Jesus' prayer for unity, at the Last Supper:

> *I pray not only for them, but also for those who will believe in me through their word, so that they may all be one, as you, Father, are in me and I in you, that they also may be in us, that the world may believe that you sent me. And I have given them the glory you gave me, so that they may be one, as we are one, I in them and you in me, that they may be brought to perfection as one, that the world may know that you sent me, and that you loved them even as you loved me.* (Jn. 17: 20-23).

Holy Spirit, give us an increasing desire to long for Jesus. Help us to make frequent spiritual communions: uniting with Him at

Holy Communion in each Eucharistic Liturgy celebrated through-out all time.

The Fourth Mystery: **The Assumption**
of Mary into Heaven (Sacred Tradition)
Hail, favored one! The Lord is with you. (Lk. 1: 28)

We ask you - Jesus, Mary, Joseph, each angel and saint in Heaven, each person in Purgatory, to pray with us for the Triumph of the Immaculate Heart of Mary, for the conversion of Russia, the reunion of all Christians, peace in justice throughout the world, and for all those in the process of canonization, especially for Jacinta, Francisco and Alexandrina.

The Fifth Mystery: **The Crowning of Mary**
as Queen of the Universe (Sacred Tradition and Rev 12:1-6)

Mary, conceived without sin, pray for us who have recourse to you. We believe, you are our mother, sister, friend and queen!

We invite you, Jesus, Mary, Joseph, each angel and saint in Heaven, each person in Purgatory, to pray for all religious insti-tutes and all lay, private and public associations of the faithful.

O Triune God, give an outpouring of blessings, graces and gifts upon all benefactors and provide for them generously, ac-cording to Your Will. Inspire the hearts and minds of many people to help all religious communities to do the work of God in build-ing up His Kingdom, by spreading the Good News of Jesus Christ. (Revised 1996).

B. A flight in spirit

On January 25th, I was praying the Rosary when God took me in spirit to the Archbishop's meeting with my Provincial. I was standing behind Archbishop Mahony's chair. Then the Holy Spirit prayed a prayer through me as I laid my hands on the Archbishop's head. The prayer was for the founding of the Servants and Handmaids of the Sacred Heart of Jesus, Mary, and Joseph as reli-gious communities. Shortly after this experience, Marcella Mei called and said that Bishop Patrick Ziemann spoke to Bishop Shubsda about the Handmaids being accepted in the Monterey Diocese. However, Bishop Shubsda did not give a satisfactory reply. Rather, Bishop Ziemann told Archbishop Mahony to have Sr. Mary Glennon, the Vicar of Religious, to check into this matter.

On February 3rd, I wrote Marcella Mei the following letter: "On January 25th, while praying the Rosary before the Blessed Sacrament, I was taken in Spirit to the Bishop's Provincial meeting. I stood behind Archbishop Roger Mahony and laid my hands on him while the Holy Spirit poured forth a prayer unto him so that he would be enlightened to be open and accept the Servants and Handmaids into the Archdiocese of Los Angeles. I was deeply moved by this experience and really did not know what to expect.

When you told me what Bishop Ziemann did and what Archbishop Mahony said, I was not surprised. However, I wanted the Servants also to be included because of the prayer of the Holy Spirit through me. I had written and also orally expressed the desire that Bishop Ziemann be made the protector of the Handmaids and Servants with the approval of Archbishop Roger Mahony."

1. The visitation with the Vicar of Religious

On February 7th-9th, I scheduled a few days of retreat with the Handmaids. Later, Sister Mary Glennon also scheduled a meeting with the Handmaids during this time. On February 7th, I arrived at the Handmaids home, where some of the Servants were visiting the Handmaids'. Shortly after, Sister Mary Glennon also arrived.

When we finished with that meeting, we went downstairs. Sister Mary Glennon spoke to the Handmaids in a group. She asked each Handmaid various questions, such as who they were and why they wanted to be a Handmaid. She let each person speak freely about their thoughts on religious life, the spirituality, expectations and hopes for the future. In the course of these discussions, I noticed that some of the Handmaids were experiencing a vocational crisis and were thinking of pursuing vocations elsewhere.

Sister Mary Glennon stayed overnight and was at prayers and Mass the next morning. She spoke to Marcella for over an hour after breakfast. Then all the Handmaids gathered in community and she said that the charism and calling to begin the new religious community was from God. She said a study would begin on how to establish the Handmaids as religious so they could begin the novitiate.

Sister told us that she was new in the position of being Vicar of Religious and that she did not know what the procedure should be, but that she would find out. She also urged me to gather the Servants into a community, but I was hesitant because the Servants were scattered throughout the country.

Sometime later, I spoke with Sister Mary Glennon in regard to the Servants. She again encouraged me to gather the Servants into a community. She said that I needed to write Bishop Ziemann of any development. A few days later, I received a letter from her that stated that after the study concerning the Handmaids was completed, the same study and process would be done for the Servants. Then I decided that I would gather some of the Servants into a community.

C. Satan's method of attack

In April 1988, God allowed me to understand that any person who is serious about becoming a saint would experience Satan's hatred and attacks. Satan tries to tempt a person at his or her weakest point. When he tempts the person to fall into sin, he begins with small sins, then mortal death bearing sins, so that the person belongs to him and his power. Likewise, Satan doesn't have to bother a person who is living in sin because that person belongs to him already. Satan also easily controls the person who is lukewarm because that person is satisfied with the way he or she is. These people are willing to go through life without a conversion of heart and even without wanting to change. I think these people need to be pitied and each of us needs to pray and do penance for them so that they may awaken and be converted. However, if the person continually succeeds to overcome temptation after temptation, then Satan begins a new method of attack.

First, Satan tries to distract a person and retard the spiritual growth by having a person compare self to others. If a person meets a very saintly person, Satan urges that person to be envious by wanting to become like that person. In response to Satan, I think that a person must never try or want to become like any other living person. The reason is because Christ is the Model and a person should learn to be Christ-like.

Likewise, if a person meets another who isn't very holy, then the Devil inspires the person to think that he or she is better than the other person. This is bad theology because a person never knows the state-of-soul of another unless the other person reveals this or if God gives the gift of reading souls. Because a person does not really know the other person, we may never judge another person - ever! Each person should always be careful never to make a rash judgment, which is really jumping to conclusions. A good rule of thumb to remember is this: If a person wants to compare him or herself to another, then let it be Jesus Christ because the person's body, mind, soul and spirit will be Christ centered.

Second, if Satan does not succeed in having a person make comparisons with others, then he inspires others to turn against that person. In other words, Satan will invoke misunderstandings, ridicule, rash judgment, slander and/or persecution so that people begin to abandon the upright person. This could lead to discouragement, lack of self-esteem and self-introspection, which could become detrimental. However, if a person remains faithful to prayer, penance, love for everyone and has a spirit of forgiveness, then God gives the gift of fortitude to withstand any opposition and perseverance to carry the Cross lovingly, generously and joyfully.

In sum, Satan will always attack the person who becomes Christ-like. He will try to destroy the person's ministry, way of life, reputation and even urge others to kill the upright person. However, Satan can never do anything beyond what God permits. God's special protection is always there, especially in martyrdom, where God's grace is always sufficient to defeat the Devil.

1. Jesus in me

On May 2nd, I was praying the Rosary before the Blessed Sacrament at Damien High School, Laverne, California. I felt myself drawn to Jesus' presence in the tabernacle. I also felt my heart expanding and enveloping the tabernacle. Then I felt myself embrace Jesus in each tabernacle in the whole world. That evening, when offering Mass, I felt my chest mystically open. I felt the Presence of Jesus within me as in a monstrance. Rays of light then came from Jesus upon the people who were present. During the "Our Father," great graces were given to each person who was open to the Holy Spirit.

I was allowed to understand that Jesus is truly present within me and that wherever I go, I bring Jesus to others, just as Mary brought Jesus to Elizabeth and John the Baptist. Any person who is open to the Holy Spirit will recognize Jesus within me and not me per se. That person will also be filled more fully with the blessings of the Holy Spirit, just as John the Baptist was while in his mother's womb. There will be great joy in the person's heart, even though that person really does not know the source of this gift. However, for the person who is not living a god-like life, he or she will be convicted and feel called to respond to God by asking for mercy and forgiveness. If the person is open to the Spirit, then they will be moved to go to confession. However, if the person hardens his or her heart, then the person will walk away without realizing or accepting the visitation of the Lord.

2. All that I have is yours

On May 3rd, while praying the Rosary before the Blessed Sacrament, I felt drawn again more forcefully to Jesus in the tabernacle. Jesus drew me into Himself and mystically led me to the throne of the Father. The Father embraced me as a son and I felt that God the Father was truly my Father. He said to me, "All that I have is yours. Ask Me anything and I will give it to you." The reason why He said this is because Jesus is truly present within me. Naturally, what I ask for must be according to God's will and His plan for me and others.

I was given a gift to love God the Father with a filial love and to love Jesus more as my brother. Then God the Father gave me a deeper love for the Holy Spirit because I was brought to the Holy Spirit Who anointed me with His power. Joy and peace flooded my whole being and I felt like shouting from the mountain tops for all in the world to hear that God loves me and that I belong to God.

I felt the presence of the Blessed Trinity within me for many days. I knew the Triune God was within by the gift of faith and knowledge. To find God, a person only needs to visit Him within a person's heart. This is the secret and heart of what St. Paul preached. God is within a person. Christ is within a person. He is present. No person ever needs an appointment to visit Him because He is always there. This is a very generous and gracious gift, which is also a message of hope and peace.

3.   That all may be one

On May 23rd, the Lord let me understand that the charism of the Servants and Handmaids is the prayer prayed by Jesus at the Last Supper, "That all may be one as He and the Father are one." This is brought about through accepting, living, and sharing the gift of unconditional love and mercy. When each person lives this way of life, this charism brings peace in justice to the whole world.

The Lord also let me understand that living unconditional love brings justice, peace and unity because it prepares the Church and the world for the Second Coming of the Lord. Our prayer should be, "Come, Lord Jesus." In other words, a person should be like St. John the Baptist, who prepared the way for the Lord. All people, then, are called to repentance by accepting and living the Gospel message in a radical way.

When unity between all in Heaven and people of good will on earth has been effectively brought about, Jesus will come and present all to His Father in Heaven. I believe that this will be the final completion of the mission given to Him by His Father.

4.   The blessing

On May 24th, the Lord told me that in the Cross of Christ, we are to conquer. He said I should hold the relic of the True Cross in my hand and bless people with holy oil by tracing a cross on the person's forehead. I should pray, "Through the Sign of the Cross, may God deliver and protect you from all evil. May God the Father, Son and Holy Spirit bless you." The Lord let me understand that when I bless a person in this way, the person may feel conviction if he or she is living in the state of sin or are lukewarm. As a result of the blessing, the person will be strengthened if he or she is living a deep spiritual life. I believe everyone should use this blessing, such as parents blessing their children and families blessing each other because many blessings, graces and gifts will be granted to everyone. The Lord also let me understand that evil meant physical sickness, emotional and mental illness and spiritual evil, which is the result of sin, Satan, temptation or any attitude that is not of God.

5. Life from God

On May 27th, God let me understand that He alone gives life which begins for each person at the moment of conception because only God exists from all eternity. In creation, God willed life to be shared because He gave and gives life to each animate being. This life is handed down from generation to generation whenever the laws for procreation are fulfilled, such as life in plants, animals and humans in which the life of God is shared. This makes a person realize that only God is the giver of life and that only God has the right over life and death.

D. Why do you rob my people?

One day while I was preaching, the Lord told me that I was robbing the people. I said, "How can that be? I don't rob people." Then He said, "Yes, you are robbing them of the blessings, gifts and graces that they would receive if they were charitable by giving money to help the work that I have called you to do." At that moment, I realized the importance of people being charitable in supporting the work of God, no matter what type of charity it may be. I also realized that the money given must be used according to the intentions of the person who gives the money.

As for the Apostolate, I know that we would use this money for God's honor and glory. In fact, I've never enjoyed asking people for money. Rather, I would sell books, tapes, pictures and rosaries so as to make an income for God's work. Even on Renewal Weeks, I would only ask once for money during a free-will offering.

I think that a person must always remember that God gives money to people and ultimately that money is not our money. In other words, the money God gives us should be used for His honor and glory as well as for the building of His Kingdom.

Throughout my ministry, I believe the American Catholic people only give about 5% of their income to charity, when they should be giving 10%, unless they are unemployed or under employed. I believe that to obtain the blessings of the Lord, a person must pray and do penance, which can mean fasting or almsgiving. When praying, a person must keep in mind four elements of prayer

1) Praise, worship, adoration and love
2) Thanksgiving for blessings, graces and gifts received
3) Reparation for sins, such as personal and others
4) Petition.

Prayer disposes a person to be open to God and obtain graces, whereas penance is necessary to overcome Satan, the flesh and the world. Likewise, almsgiving is necessary so as to obtain God's blessings, graces and gifts to overcome temptations.

1. Almsgiving

Even though most people think that almsgiving refers to money, this is not the whole truth. Rather, almsgiving also means giving of self, such as a person's talents, gifts and graces. Almsgiving can also mean spreading the work of the Servants and Handmaids throughout the world. In other words, a person can give alms by carrying out the work of the Lord. Therefore, I urge people to obtain the literature, cassettes and other material the Apostolate of Christian Renewal has to offer so that they can spread this work throughout the world.

E. Marcella Mei officially appointed

Bishop Patrick Ziemann came to celebrate Mass for the Handmaids on the Feast of the Sacred Heart. During the Mass, Bishop Ziemann officially appointed Marcella Mei to be the leader of the Handmaids' community. In the course of the day, five of the Handmaids decided to take a leave of absence or just left for good. This left only Marcella Mei and Alice Chinn as members. Afterwards, Sr. Mary Glennon was still willing to proceed with the study and preparation for the novitiate. This event with the Handmaids made me remember the words of Fr. Carl Hammer: "The Handmaids community will almost disappear. Most will leave, but from the embers will rise a large and vibrant community."

F. Contacting other bishops

Since I had been bombarded by so many people about beginning the Servants and Handmaids, I decided to contact other bishops and not wait for Bishop Shubsda to make up his mind. I wrote to Bishop Francis Quinn, of Sacramento; Bishop Joseph Madera, of Fresno; Bishop Philip Starling, of San Bernadino; and Bishop John Steinbock, of Santa Rosa. Bishop Francis Quinn referred my letter to the Vicar of Religious who informed me that they were not interested in establishing a new religious community in the Diocese. Bishop Joseph Madera was sympathetic, but said that his advisors were against having the Servants coming into the Diocese. Bishop Madera said they were afraid that the Servants would take vocations away from the Diocese. However, he said he was willing to have any of our seminarians who were ready to be ordained and work in his Diocese for a three-year period. Then they could join the Servants' community if it was established by then. Bishop John Steinbock said he was only a new bishop and did not know the needs of his Diocese. He said I should contact him again in January of 1989, which would give him enough time to know more about the Diocese. Bishop Philip Starling asked me to come and speak with him. During the meeting, he said that he wanted to know more about the Servants. Therefore, I should supply him with information, such as books, tapes and other documents.

1. Buying property for the Servants

In May, Marcella Mei and Alice Chinn looked at some property which was located at 411 First Street, Fillmore, California. They thought this would be an ideal place for the Servants to begin and reside.

As for me, I was praying during this time for a place where there would be two houses. In the main house, I wanted it to be used by the Servant candidates and myself. While the other build-ing, I wanted it to be used for priests who would begin to join us as well as for those who could come for a visit. On May 17th, I visited 411 First Street, Fillmore, California. I found that my prayers were answered. However, the main house was old and needed a lot of repairs and cleaning, while the duplex was only a few years old. I signed the papers and the escrow was to close on July 28th, 1988, the anniversary of St. Louis de Montfort's canonization. The price paid for the property was $430,000.00. We moved into the house on July 30th, while the Servant candidates moved in by September 1st.

Next, I wrote to Sr. Mary Glennon and Bishop Patrick Ziemann of what was transpiring. I then wrote to Fr. Provincial and his Council asking if I could live with the community in Fillmore, but that I wanted to retain my office in La Puente, California, because I still wished to be affiliated with my Congregation at Damien High School, in La Verne, California. They gave me per-mission to do this.

2. In Fillmore

During 1988 and the beginning of 1989, I had various young men join me in Fillmore, so as to begin to live the life of the Ser-vants of the Sacred Heart of Jesus, Mary and Joseph. They came with the idea of learning the charism, spirituality and mission of the Servants. They also learned how to pray and work together so as to form community life. These young men also became involved in the parish community by teaching catechism and evangeliza-tion. They learned to develop their spiritual lives and undertake their studies in a proper manner with the right attitude to prepare for the priesthood. And so, I felt that they were receiving a fairly well-balanced training in preparation for the seminary. This was the purpose of gathering these young men.

G. Another trip to Medjugorje, Rome and Fatima

While in Medjugorje, I took an excursion to the Immaculate Conception Church, which was about twenty-five miles away. I listened to a sermon by Fr. Josef who was the pastor in Medjugorje when the apparitions began. He explained that at first he did not believe in the apparitions. But, when the children were in danger, Fr. Josef heard a voice that said, "Protect the children," which he did. He wanted to believe and know what he should do so he asked Jakov, one of the alleged apparitionists, to help him. Jakov said, "I cannot help you, Father, because you do not believe." When Fr. Josef heard this, he realized he had to pray for faith. Finally, Fr. Josef had an experience which convinced him that the apparitions were authentic.

1. Receiving a piece of wood

When Fr. Josef finished speaking, I went to the bus. A woman came who had something in her clenched fist. She said that she wanted to give me what she was holding, so I took the object. When I looked at it, I saw that the object was a round piece of wood with a cross on it, which was the same that had been impressed on my forehead.

She then told me that she was from Ohio. She explained that she use to live in Guatemala, where there are trees that grow on the highest mountains. These trees are considered to be sacred and may not be cut down. When the branches fall from these trees, the people gather them and cut them into small pieces, like the piece I received from her. Each piece has this cross because it is ingrained in the wood. She also said that the sap, which comes from these trees, is used to cure various illnesses.

Because this woman gave me this wooden cross, I believe even more in what God is doing in my life. I always have doubts concerning the Cross on my forehead, but when these doubts come something usually happens to make me believe.

Personally, I rejoice and thank God that He usually keeps these manifestations hidden. I prefer that they will always remain hidden, unless it is for the honor and glory of God and the salvation of souls. If God so chooses to make these manifestations visible, then I would say, "Yes" to His Will.

2. The insight I received in Assisi

When I was in Assisi, I celebrated Mass in the upper Church. This Church is where St. Francis is buried. During the Mass, the Lord let me see how every person is united in the Eucharistic Liturgy from the time of the Last Supper, down through the centuries and until the end of time. I wanted to lay prostrate in spirit before the Triune God, but was not allowed to do so. I saw myself united with the angels, saints, souls in Purgatory, members of the whole Mystical Body of Christ and the family of God. I saw how each person's prayers are offered with Jesus in the Spirit to the Father. I saw how the Father grants blessings, graces and gifts won by Jesus through His suffering and death. These are offered by the Holy Spirit to all who are open, willing and desirous of receiving them. I saw how God wishes to share His love, mercy, life, blessings and gifts with everyone. I also saw how God was not able to give anything to those who refused to accept or who were closed to Him. From this insight, I understood the difference between a humble person and a proud person, between a child-like person and a self-centered person.

I also understood more fully the importance of the Mystical Mass Prayer, living the Mass with awareness and the unity of prayer. Therefore, I became aware of the importance of the vocation of the Servants and Handmaids of the Sacred Heart of Jesus, Mary and Joseph. The Servants and Handmaids are to help bring unity, peace and love to all through the Church so as to help bring victory to the Church over all her enemies.

3. St. Joseph

On Father's Day, I had the privilege of being present in the House of Loreto. While praying there, I understood that St. Joseph was assigned by God to be a father, protector and intercessor for the Servants and Handmaids. Because of this assignment, the Servants and Handmaids are to go to St. Joseph for help so as to spread the charism and spirituality throughout the world so as to increase our members to help us evangelize and spread the Good News.

Likewise, every person should listen to St. Joseph's direction and follow where he wishes to lead, so that he can be a real father to us. Each person is also called to be close to St. Joseph and to actually be a part of the Holy Family as family. Therefore, a person needs to understand the theology of St. Joseph and his role in salvation history, spiritual living and in our battle against the forces of evil.

4. Padre Pio

When praying at Padre Pio's grave, I asked him to be a spiritual father to the Servants and Handmaids of the Sacred Heart of Jesus, Mary and Joseph. Padre Pio then brought my dad and the members of my family tree, as well as other relatives and said, "There is your father. Ask him to pray for you since his prayers are very powerful." Then he said, "I will be a spiritual father for the Servants and Handmaids."

5. Unconditional Love

When I was flying home from the pilgrimage on June 26th, God revealed to me that unconditional love is a Person. This Person is the Holy Spirit. Then I saw how at Baptism the Blessed Trinity lives in each person. Since the Holy Spirit is the love spirated from the Father and the Son, every person who possess the Trinity within has the love of God always present. In other words, Jesus commanded us to love one another as He loves us. It is only by the love of the Holy Spirit within us that we are able to love others with God's love.

From this revelation, I understood the importance of always living in God's love and the terribleness of sin. God, the angels, the saints and the souls in Purgatory see us at all times. They desire to help every person grow in God's love and likeness. However, each and all are constrained because of our free will. They rejoice when anyone perseveres in living a god-like life, while they can only pray and hope that a sinner will be converted and repent. When a sinner comes back to God, there is great joy by all. God also let me see this scene in all its ramifications.

Later, when I spoke to Anita Morse, she explained how God is merciful by not allowing us to always have a Mt. Tabor experience. She said that the greatness of God's presence and divinity would fill a person with awe and fear. The light of His Being would also blind any person and he or she would be overpowered with awe. Thus, God allows a spiritual darkness to envelop the soul to the point that a person feels abandoned by Him. A person then is unable to pray as before. The desert experience is necessary, she said, but the suffering and pain are very intense. The darkness, however, does not blind a person because God's gentle light and guidance, even if not perceived, are directing the person on the path of purification and holiness of life.

6. Dream of the Sacred Heart in Medjugorje

On June 29th, I had a dream that I was back in Medjugorje, Yugoslavia, on Cross Mountain. While I was there, a bright light from the sky lit up the Cross. Even though the light came from behind me, the light fully enveloped me and people started to come up from behind me.

I was praying with my arms stretched out in the form of a Cross. I was also praying for the conversion of the world. I looked to my left and saw a statue of the Sacred Heart and behind Him a statue of the Immaculate Heart of Mary. As I walked towards the statue of the Sacred Heart, the head of the statue began to move from side to side, as if He was searching for someone or looking into the hearts of the people. Then I saw tears flow from the eyes of Jesus that ran down His cheeks. This dream left a very deep impression upon me.

H. In Fatima, August

In August, I went on another pilgrimage to Fatima. While I was there, the Blessed Mother revealed to me why some statues weep tears or blood, such as the International Pilgrim statue of Our Lady of Fatima. She said that some people, who are open and have a regard for motherhood, are deeply moved whenever a person's mother cries, such as St. Monica (St. Augustine's mother). The tears of our Blessed Mother are meant to touch the hearts of those who appear to be devoted to her, so they will make reparation for the sins of humankind. The tears of Mary are meant to touch the hearts of sinners, especially those who are constantly living in the state of sin so that they have a conversion of heart. Any person who witnesses Mary's crying should be deeply moved to live a virtuous and holy life. Likewise, a person knows that Mary cannot suffer in Heaven and that she cannot cry. This phenomena is permitted by God to move people to repentance or to make a more total giving of self in doing God's will.

I was also given the understanding that our Blessed Mother cries through the statue because people who come do not change their lives. The people keep on being like the Pharisees, who judge everyone, complain about problems and sin in the world, but don't do anything about it.

Also in Fatima, I felt the Presence of the Triune God, which was enveloping me with His power, grace and light. I felt as if God's blessings were being given to each Servant and Handmaid as well as the work of the Apostolate. Then I felt that Mary, St. Joseph, each angel and saint in Heaven, and each person in Purgatory were interceding for us. They again took us under their special care and protection. The presence of the whole Heavenly Court stayed with me all day. The effects of this experience were with me for many days.

In Fatima, Fr. William Wagner gave a talk on the work of the angels. He pointed out that, when St. John and St. James asked for the favor of being on His right and the other on the left, when He comes into His Kingdom that they could and were willing to be martyrs, even if they were unaware of what they were agreeing to.

Fr. Wagner then stated that the cup a person drinks from is the Precious Blood of Christ. He said that in the early Church, the Christians received the Eucharist under both species. They understood that they were willing to suffer martyrdom for their faith. Father pointed out that in the Easter Rite Churches, they always received Communion under both species, which revealed the importance of persecution.

Fr. Wagner also pointed out that the angel gave the Host to Sr. Lucia and the Precious Blood to Jacinta and Francisco in 1916. This is the manner in which Holy Communion is received in Russia. When Jacinta and Francisco received the Precious Blood, they were drinking the cup of spiritual martyrdom. I am sure that they were willing to suffer much during their lives. Both of the children willingly accepted suffering and death. While Fr. Wagner was speaking, I understood that Jacinta, Francisco and Lucia were true martyrs because they were willing to accept death rather than reveal the secret to the Mayor of Ourem. They were threatened to be thrown into a vat of boiling oil yet they kept the secret. When they were taken separately from the room, they believed that they would be killed.

When Father Wagner said that the angel set the stage for modern times to receive Holy Communion under both species, I thought this meant that all the countries receiving both species are called to martyrdom. But he stated that the United States is one of the few countries that allows people to receive Holy Communion under both species.

The Bishops of the United States are urging people to receive Holy Communion in this way. I understood that the people of the United States are called to spiritual martyrdom just like Jacinta and Francisco. Later, I realized that our Blessed Mother, St. John and Mary Magdalene also suffered a spiritual martyrdom while standing at the foot of the Cross. Each person, then, should be willing to suffer misunderstanding, ridicule and persecution from people of ill will or those who do not understand the Catholic faith.

People who fight to overcome alcoholism, drug abuse, sexual problems, emotional illnesses, or any other mistreatment need to offer their sufferings patiently. In this way, they will suffer spiritual martyrdom. People who suffer from poverty, lack of clothing, food, shelter also suffer spiritual martyrdom. People whose families are broken through abandonment, divorce, crime, violence, hatred and war also suffer spiritual martyrdom.

If every person would offer their sufferings and struggles with the offering of Jesus on the Cross, with each Eucharistic Liturgy, then many graces and blessings would be given to the person, family, community, nation and the world because through the seeds of martyrdom comes faith.

1. Offer myself to His Divine Justice

On September 8th, while praying the Mystical Mass Prayer, God let me understand that I should offer myself to His Divine

Justice. I did so and pictured in my mind the moment of my death. I asked forgiveness for every thought, word and action of sin in my whole life. I thanked God for every gift, grace and blessing He has given me throughout my life. Since I am still living, I asked God to bless me, to give me the gift and grace of final perseverance. I felt my whole being flooded with God's Love and Presence.

2. Peace in Justice

On September 14th, God let me understand that our Lord wants to give all people peace through Mary, our Mother. In order to obtain this peace, each person needs to abandon and surrender completely to God through an act of consecration. In order to surrender completely, a person needs a conversion, that is, to put on the mind of God so as to think the way God thinks and not the way the world thinks.

To have a true conversion then, a person needs to forgive everyone, especially his or her enemies. To forgive, a person needs to pray much, personally and with others. When that person prays for others, a love develops for them and for everyone. Love of God and of others is absolutely necessary to begin this process which will bring true peace in justice to the world. Peace must begin within the person, which is a gift from God. Then the person brings peace into the family circle, the community and to the world. Likewise, in order to bring peace in justice and true love into the world, a person needs to become a saint; i.e., a true mature person.

3. Our charism is the spirituality of Vatican II

On September 16th, when I was at St. Peter's in Rome, a lady pointed out a statue of St. Louis de Montfort. I wanted to explain to her that the Servants and Handmaids spirituality is an updating of his devotion to Mary.

The Lord then said to me, "No, the spirituality of the Servants and Handmaids of the Sacred Heart of Jesus, Mary and Joseph is not that of St. Louis de Montfort." He showed me that our charism and spirituality are something completely new for and in the Church. The charism is the spirituality of Vatican II for the renewal and unity in the Church as well as for the victory of the Church over all her enemies.

There are elements of various spirituality in what the Servants and Handmaids are to live and foster. Every spirituality must be based on the truths of our faith as given to us in Scripture, Tradition and the teachings of the Magisterium of the Church.

The Servants and Handmaids are called to explain the developments of this spirituality as God inspired us to know and live over the years. The charism is centered on the love-offering of the Lord in the Eucharistic Liturgy, the Eucharistic devotion and is the center of all spirituality as the source of unity.

Unity is when Heaven and earth are united as one. This happens whenever the Eucharistic Liturgy is offered. In other words, the angels, saints, souls in Purgatory, and people on earth are united in, with, and through Jesus Christ in His sacrificial offering to His Father in the Holy Spirit.

In praying and living the Mystical Mass Prayer, each person actually becomes a part of this unity through unconditional love and mercy for peace in justice. The Mystical Mass Prayer also prepares the way of the Lord for the final offering of everything to His Father at the end of the world.

When I was speaking about the martyrdom for those who receive the Precious Blood of our Lord, He gave me a deeper insight into the bloody martyrdom of Jesus, the Apostles, the early Christians and people down through the centuries. He also let me understand the spiritual martyrdom of our Mother Mary, St. John and numerous other Christians and people down through the centuries to our present day.

God let me understand that more people today, especially in the United States, would be more like our Mother Mary and St. John in suffering spiritual martyrdom.

To be true to God today and wanting to help others accept Christ, a person's heart will be pierced by a sword of sorrow. This will be true because a person of good will likes the best for all people, yet will be rejected, misunderstood, ridiculed and persecuted.

The Lord also let me understand why people should be more willing to receive the Precious Blood of our Lord. When a person receive the Precious Blood, the blood goes directly into our bloodstream and flows throughout the body. From His Precious Blood, a person should receive strength in body, soul and spirit. His strength is our strength so as to truly carry out the work of the Lord; to have the strength to resist temptation; to have perseverance in doing good; in striving for sanctity, to carry the Cross, and to do His Will.

4. Entrustment to the Triune God

The Lord again let me know the importance of making a consecration or entrustment to the Triune God, the Holy Family and the angels. God gave each person a free will and no person in Heaven will ever violate that gift. In freely making a consecration, a person gives God, Mary, St. Joseph and the angels the right to work in his or her life, which also gives the person the right to be used as an instrument to accomplish God's Will.

To develop a true friendship based on love, a person needs to be able to communicate with the other. In communicating, it is necessary to listen, to understand completely what the other person is saying and means. Sometimes a clarification needs to be given in explaining the meaning of a word, phrase or sentence. Perhaps the whole subject spoken about needs to be explained better.

In speaking, a person might disagree, argue and at times, meet a crisis point where communication is broken off. If there is a true love and friendship, then disagreement, arguing and fighting over a point or issue does not break the friendship. Actually, the friendship should deepen the love for one another and help the person to want to understand the other better, to see and ask forgiveness if pain and suffering were inflicted.

5. A meditation from Vicka

On September 16th, the group spoke to Vicka today. She pointed out that we should do the following for three days and then repeat it again and again. First day: Pray the Our Father slowly and meditate on the greatness of the Father in all His attributes. Meditate on Him as a loving Father who wishes to give us His mercy, truth, love, peace and salvation. Second day: Pray the Hail

Mary slowly and mediate on the greatness of our Mother Mary. Think of all happenings in her life, the gifts she received, her role in Heaven, earth and in the Church, but especially in a person's own life. Third Day: Pray the Glory Be, while slowly meditating on the Blessed Trinity.

I. Pilgrimage to Russia

In the early part of 1988, I was asked by Dan Lyons, who lives in New Jersey and runs a travel agency, if I would go to Russia with a group of people during October 7th-16th. Dan wanted me to be a chaplain on this pilgrimage with three other priests. Dan also wanted me to encourage other people to go on this pilgrimage so that we could all pray, as silent agents of God, for peace in the world and for the triumph of the Immaculate Heart of Mary. As for me, I thought this was a great opportunity to go to Russia, to pray for what was always in my heart, to see Communism in a country and how it limited people. And so, I consented to go on this pilgrimage.

When we went to Russia, we first stopped in Copenhagen, Denmark, where we boarded a Russian plane. This plane was an army aircraft that was used in World War II. Even though we arrived in Russia safely, there were a few times that I wondered if this was my last pilgrimage anywhere.

When we arrived in Moscow, I immediately noticed the poverty, suffering and joylessness of the people. I also noticed that the Russian people did not smile and looked very unhappy. In fact, the young, the middle-aged and the old all seemed to be going through life as if other people didn't exist. The Russian people seemed to be very worn, which means the hardness of life was wearing them down. For example, many of the young people were disabled, many of the middle-aged had strokes and many of the old were suffering disabilities because of World War II.

Even the Russian peoples' clothing was worn and dreary with very little light or bright colors. The apartments were also worn, dilapidated and very dangerous to live in from a sanitary and humanitarian viewpoint. Likewise, the people still made sacrifices to live in these run-down apartments because of the poor economy.

When we arrived at our hotel, I noticed that we were treated a lot differently. Many of us were given the royal treatment and put in the finest buildings. At the hotel, we were assigned to a certain floor, which required papers. When we arrived at our floor, there was a man who sat at a desk and gave us our keys for our rooms. However, when we left our rooms, we would have to give our keys back to the man who took them. In other words, even though we were free to go and leave as we wished, we still felt like we were in prison because we were always being watched. In fact, there was nothing to prevent the person who was on the floor from going into our rooms and searching our property and luggage. And so, we didn't know if they went into our rooms or not.

In my room as well as in the rooms of the other priests, we had our Mass kits so that we could offer Mass. For most of the Masses, we celebrated them in my hotel room so that we could all be together. On one occasion, we had an open room where people could come publicly. In fact, some people who were workers in the hotel came to Mass because they were Catholic. Naturally, celebrating Mass in the open was dangerous because the KGB could arrest any person they wanted. However, we celebrated Mass without any interference. This was a great experience to celebrate Mass in a Communistic country.

Next, the guides took us to various places in Moscow. The first place they took us was Red Square, which seems like a very large place on TV, especially when they had parades. For instance, on May Day, Red Square seems huge because they had their missiles and all their military equipment in the parade, which seemed to go on and on. The impression I received is that Red Square is a large place where leaders of the Communist Party would stand up on a wall and observe everything. However, after seeing Red Square, I found the area to be quite small.

While I was in Red Square, I took my Crucifix out of my pocket and held it in my hand and prayed, "Eternal Father, I offer You the Body, Blood, Soul and Divinity of Our Lord Jesus Christ in union with each Mass celebrated this day and each day throughout all time, for the conversion of Russia, for the Triumph of the Immaculate Heart of Mary and for peace in the world." I said this prayer the whole time I was in Red Square. Likewise, I said this prayer in all four directions so that this prayer would be for everyone in Russia, the world, the defeat of Communism, the Triumph of Mary and peace throughout the world.

After we walked through Red Square, we entered the Kremlin, which is about 120 acres. Inside the Kremlin, we saw the Parliament Building and all the other buildings. Then we saw four former Basilica's, which were turned into museums. We then went into one of the Basilica's called St. Basil's, which was a very beautiful place to see. There still were many articles of faith in St. Basil's, such as ornaments and worship vessels etc... However, being in St. Basil's, I realized that Russia indeed separated the Church from the State.

Our guides then took us on Russia's subway system, which was the most modern subway in the whole world. I think our guides just wanted to use the subway as an example that reveals how great and modern Russia seemed to be. However, the only thing I observed was that Russia was very much enmeshed in the world. The reason I say this is because everything they spoke about was about worldly ways of living. I think this is quite a tragedy because there was no sense of purpose for life. In other words, even though Russia had many modern things, they still did not have any joy or peace.

Next we went to Lenin's tomb, where we lined up two by two. While we were waiting to see Lenin's body, the guides told us that we had to observe silence in respect for Lenin. Because I never read anything about Lenin's tomb, how he was buried and preserved, I really didn't know what to expect. And so, I was quite surprised when I found out what really took place.

When we got near the entrance of Lenin's tomb, there were two soldiers who stood guard. As we walked past them and went down the steps, there were two more guards. Then when we got to the bottom of the steps, we had to turn and go up more steps. When we arrived, we could see Lenin's body on our left. There, Lenin was preserved in a glass coffin wearing a blue suit. One of his hands was raised and clenched, while the other hand was at his side and clenched as well. When I looked at Lenin, I noticed that he had red hair and a red beard, which was neatly trimmed. Next, we walked up to the top of the steps and turned, where we were supposed to stop and look at Lenin for a moment.

While I looked at Lenin, I felt inspired and courageous to say to Lenin, "I'll defeat you and all of Hell." I meant every word of this because I felt God's presence and I felt that God was praying through me. Then I said the prayer, "Eternal Father, I offer to you the Body, Blood, Soul and Divinity of our Lord Jesus Christ from all the altars throughout the world celebrated throughout all time for the defeat of Communism, for the destruction of this insidious and diabolical regime. In the Name of the Father, the Son and the Holy Spirit." Then, I walked on and kept saying that prayer over and over.

As we came out of this area, we walked past the wall where the other leaders were buried. At each place I stopped, I said that prayer for the defeat of Communism, overcoming of the enemy, Satan and evil. Then God allowed me to understand that Russia was not being run by Mikhail Gorbachev, but by Satan and his agents. They were the ones who were bringing about corruption and imprisonment in the world. I believe that every person under Communism seemed to be in a prison world even if they were working, traveling or whatever. Their lives are regulated and are not their own. In other words, the Russian people could not move without the leaders, police and others knowing what they were doing, which means imprisonment and no freedom.

I believe that freedom is a gift given to all humankind. All people have a longing for freedom, just as a man or woman has a longing for love. In faith, I believe freedom will prevail, truth will prevail and love will prevail. Even though it will take some time, God will give all humankind this gift because no person can ever suppress freedom, truth and love.

From Moscow, we went to another little town that the Communists always used as a showcase so as to convince people that Russia was a great country and that their way of life was truly the way to follow. Even though this was a beautiful little town, I noticed that the hamlets, places where people lived and worked, were very impoverished. I then said to myself, "Why should anyone ever fear Russia? They do not even have sufficient money to wage a war, even though they have many nuclear armaments and technological equipment that could wreak great havoc." In fact, Russia was still suffering the effects of World War II when they were reduced to poverty. A person only has to look at the buildings that were damaged because they show that Russia didn't have enough money to rebuild them.

Then we went to Leningrad, formally known as St. Petersburg. Leningrad was more or less Russia's pride and joy because it's the city where the Communists Revolution took place. Again, we saw the same things that we saw in Moscow, such as poverty, the humdrum way of life and the terrible suffering that people were going through under the Communistic regime.

In Leningrad, we were able to visit a Catholic Church. The tour guides said that we could have religious services in the Church. Because we were in a Communistic country, the gates to the Church were locked before and after we entered. After we were in the Church, I decided that it would be better if one of the other priests would be the main celebrant of the Mass while the other priests, including myself, would concelebrate. The Mass was very beautiful and moving, especially because we were in a Leningrad Catholic Church.

That afternoon, while I was in Leningrad, Mark Sielewicki, a former Servant seminarian, and I went for a walk along the beach of the Baltic Sea. As we were walking, we prayed the fifteen-decade Rosary, which was very beautiful because we prayed for the same goal, the defeat of Satan and Communism.

As I reflected on this trip, I realized the many freedoms that we take for granted. For example, in America, we can worship whenever we want, wherever we want and how we want without any repercussions. Even if we are ridiculed, misunderstood or accused of various things because of our faith, we still have the gift of freedom to worship.

The trip to Russia was truly a very spiritual experience for me. Even though I dressed as a Catholic priest in my clerical garb, I never had any fear of my room being bugged or being harassed by the Communists, KGB or police. The people from the State Department of the United States were a little paranoid. They thought that we would never get out of Russia and that the Russians would take away our passports and put us in jail. Other than that, I just went about my business praying continuously those prayers, praying the

Rosary and uniting myself with God throughout the trip. Finally, we got on the plane and flew out of Russia to Copenhagen, where we switched to another plane and came back to the United States.

1. Spiritual battle

On October 16th, I arrived back home in California. I explained to my secretary all that happened in Russia. Then I wrote all the articles for my newspaper, *The Christian Renewal News*. Because my trip to Russia was still fresh in my mind, I decided to devote one of the articles to my trip. In this article, I explained what I said to Lenin at his tomb, "I will defeat you and all Hell." Because I said this statement, I expected spiritual warfare. And so, I decided that I would increase my prayer life so as to counteract anything that could happen, especially from Satan and his forces of evil.

I believe that if a person is living a God-like life, then spiritual warfare should be expected because Satan hates God and all that is good. However, if a person is living a life of sin, then Satan does not have to do anything because the person is not living a god-like life. In other words, as soon as a person decides to live a life of God by trying to be holy and trying to bring about the Reign of God, then Satan will do everything in his power to destroy that person's faith, spirituality and holiness.

Today, many people do not believe in Satan and the existence of Hell, but any person who lives a god-like life knows that Satan and Hell do exist. As a result, we are in a spiritual battle. And, with God's grace, we will win against Satan by doing penance, reparation and praying. If we do this with God's grace, we will be transformed into the image and likeness of Jesus Christ. Then we will be able to live lives of holiness and journey through life with peace, joy and victory.

2. Mystical Marriage

After my trip in Russia, I experienced the Mystical Marriage as St. Teresa of Avila describes in her Interior Castle. The Mystical Marriage is a deep union between the person and God. There is nothing a person can do to obtain this gift, rather it is a gift given by God to those whom He wishes. This experience was rather startling because I never expected this great gift to be given to me. At first, I thought I was deluded. But then, I knew that God gives many gifts even though we are not worthy of them. During this experience, I was brought to the throne of the Trinity where I was unvested of my garments and given new garments. Then, a ring was placed on my finger. At that moment, I knew I received the Mystical Marriage with God.

I believe every person is called to the Mystical life and Mystical Marriage. As for me, I was brought into the mystical life at a very young age, yet it took me many years before God gave me the Mystical Marriage. I believe that I was filled with the things of this world and other things that prevented a deeper relationship with God. But once I began to surrender everything to God, I was more open and willing to cooperate with His gifts.

CHAPTER 15

1989

A. God always forewarns me

In my life's experiences, I have found that whenever any great difficulty is about to come into my life that God forewarns me. Even though I won't have an idea as to what will happen or how bad the difficulty may be, God will assign me different people in Heaven to help me through the difficulty. For example, God assigned Jacinta, Francisco, Padre Pio and Archangel Raphael to help me with what was about to occur with my secretary and all the events that were to follow from this incident. God also told me that he would assign all the angels and saints in Heaven and souls in Purgatory to be with me and to help me through all the other events that were going to come into my life.

At that time, I realized that I needed to renew my commitment of doing God's Will in my life again. In the past, I often prayed, "If it is in Your Will, O God, please grant this or grant that." But now, I became aware that I should pray in accordance with God's Will by saying, "Let Your Will be done." In other words, I became aware that if I said, "If it is Your Will," then I would be limiting God because of my doubt, uncertainty and hesitation. As a result, I wasn't fully responding to God's Will. Even though a person may never be completely aware of God's Will, the person will know God's Will when He brings about events in a person's life that manifest His Will. So, a person should pray according to God's Will so that a person can accept what God's Will is.

In the Divine Office, it states, "I promise to grant to you anything you ask the Father in my Name." The reason why I state this is because I believe in all of Jesus' promises. And so, I believe that whatever a person prays for will happen as long as it is in accord with the Will of God. Therefore, when Jesus prayed at the Last Supper for unity, he prayed that all would be one. As for the Servants and Handmaids of the Sacred Heart of Jesus, Mary and Joseph, we believe that this will happen because Jesus prayed for this unity. Even after I was told that the Servants would not be accepted in the Archdiocese of Los Angeles, I still felt that the Servants should be started. I also strove to be obedient in carrying out the directives of the Archbishop and my Provincial. I think that God honored that obedience.

1. My secretary

During Holy Week of 1989, I went to my office on Holy Thursday to dictate some letters that I wanted to send. During the day, I noticed that there was a change of attitude on the part of my secretary. I also noticed this attitude in one of my secretary's daughter as well as in my secretary's husband. Her husband came to me and thanked me for everything I had ever done for his family and how proud he was to have me and my office at his home. Then he said that he enjoyed working with me and that he was glad he knew me. Therefore, I was quite confused as to why there was this sudden change in attitude by my secretary, her daughter and husband.

The secretary then left to work in the parish the way she did on various occasions. When I was driving home to Fillmore, the Lord told me that my relationship and work with my secretary would end. The Lord told me about the suffering that was about to occur in my life. He then assigned Padre Pio, Jacinta, Francisco and Archangel Raphael to be with me so that I could ask for their help in overcoming the situation that was developing. And so, I was forewarned about the development of this separation, but I did not think it would happen the way it did.

On the very next day, Good Friday, I received a letter from my secretary that was dated the day before, which was Holy Thursday. Her letter stated that she resigned her position as my secretary and that I could no longer have my office at her home. The letter also stated that I should collect my things as soon as possible and that she never wanted to see me again. Then, she listed a few reasons why she was resigning, even though the reasons were unclear to me.

Naturally, I couldn't understand why she made this decision because I always treated her with highest regards. In fact, I thought of my secretary as being a confidant and friend. However, in this abrupt way of acting, I was deeply hurt and really didn't know what to think. Even though I wanted to clarify and reconcile this situation, I was unable to do so because of her request. In other words, my secretary didn't want me to call, visit or even talk to her about this situation. My hands were tied and the only thing I could do was to forgive my secretary.

At that point, I made arrangements for all my office materials to be moved to Fillmore. Then I decided that I would do most of the secretarial work on my own. However, I asked a very close friend of mine, Don Tesmer, if he would be willing to help me with the book work. Graciously, Don agreed and offered his help, which was very beneficial, especially during this time of inconvenience.

2. Don Tesmer

Don Tesmer was born in Milwaukee, Wisconsin. He moved to Fresno, California when he was young. In 1983, Don came to a Renewal Week I was giving in Porterville, California. Like many people, Don came to the Renewal for the blessing. After I blessed him, he thought I was pushing him so he didn't want anything to do with me or the blessing. However, Don was inspired by my message and arranged a Renewal Week at St. Anthony's Parish in Fresno. Don also invited me to stay with him at his house because there wasn't any room in the Parish Rectory. During this time, Don and I got to know each other and by the time the Renewal Week was over, we became very good friends. After the Renewal Week, Don would arrange more Renewal Weeks in the future. I would also stay with him whenever I would pass through Fresno. Don even allowed me to sleep in his bed during these times, while he slept in another room.

During one of my visits, we were talking about the priesthood and brotherhood. When he finally decided that he would like to become a brother, I said to Don, "Why did it take you so long?" Naturally, I knew that Don would be very helpful in getting everything set up in Fillmore because he is a very hard worker and faithful servant to God's work. Don then became my right-hand man who helped me with the book work concerning finances, entered the names and addresses of people into the computer for the Christian Renewal News, went with me on days of recollection and Renewal Weeks, took care of the Book ministry and was a Eucharistic Minister and Lector. Don also studied the charism, spirituality and purpose of the Servants of the Sacred Heart of Jesus, Mary and Joseph.

3. Not having the proper spiritual direction

Many people have accused me of not having proper spiritual direction. As for me, I have always had a spiritual director ever since I was in the seminary. I know that no person can be a good judge in his or her own case. As St. Bernard said, "If you do not have a spiritual director, then you will have a jackass directing you." This, of course means oneself. My first spiritual director was a member of my Congregation. Fortunately, we always seemed to be assigned to the same place. I found that this priest helped me a lot during my days at the seminary and afterward.

When I was moved to a place where I no longer could visit my spiritual director, I went to others to be guided. For the first 24 years of my priesthood, I had members of my Congregation as spiritual directors. Then, I chose an elderly diocesan priest for my spiritual director. This priest was very intelligent, down to earth and gave excellent spiritual direction. Later, I chose another spiritual director who was younger. He was also very intelligent and knew theology very well. However, this priest also understood mystical theology and mystical experiences, which helped me tremendously.

Even though I kept both of these priests as spiritual directors, I always found that whenever I asked my spiritual directors the same question, they both would give the same advice. I knew then that I was on the right track. As regards to starting the Servants community, they both believed that God was calling me to start this religious order.

4. Retreat with Fr. DeGrandis

Shortly after Holy Week, I had the opportunity to go on a three day priests' retreat with Fr. Robert DeGrandis. During the retreat, I prayed with some people who were helping him. I shared with these people all that happened in regards to my secretary. Then I asked these people to pray with me, for me and for my former secretary. As they were praying over me, I felt a tremendous and uplifting peace within me.

After this little prayer meeting, I thought about my secretary. Even though this situation still bothered me, I knew I needed to let go and let God. When a person rejects another person, the experience is very painful. At that moment of rejection, I was really able to relate with Jesus when, in His painful experience, Judas and Peter denied Him and all the other Apostles ran away. And like Jesus, I too felt alone.

5. Calling Fr. Provincial

A short time after my secretary wrote me that letter, I called Fr. Provincial and told him that I needed to move my office from La Puente to Fillmore. During the conversation, I told Fr. Provincial about the letter and all that happened. Then Fr. Provincial told me that he just received a letter from Archbishop Roger Mahony. The letter from Archbishop Mahony said that my former secretary wrote many things to him in opposition to my being qualified to start the Servants of the Sacred Heart of Jesus, Mary and Joseph. She also stated that I claimed to have the invisible stigmata and that I complained about the pain. Finally, she stated that I prayed that the invisible stigmata would become visible and that I predicted that this would happen.

6. Fr. Provincial meets with Archbishop Roger Mahony

Archbishop Roger Mahony then had a meeting with Fr. Provincial in regards to the letter. During the meeting, the Archbishop and Fr. Provincial reviewed this letter. However, Fr. Provincial was quite adamant that I should speak with the Archbishop before any decision about the Servants and the Apostolate of Christian Renewal were made. And so, Fr. Provincial and I went to Archbishop Mahony's office for this meeting.

7. Meeting with Archbishop Mahony

When we arrived at the Chancery office, I could tell that the Archbishop had already made up his mind. I also knew what he was going to do and that no matter what I said or did, he would not change his mind. The Archbishop then asked me a few questions and asked me if I was willing to speak with Fr. Luke Dysinger, who is a Benedictine monk from St. Andrew's Abbey in Valyermo, California. Fr. Dysinger is also a psychologist who sometimes consults Archbishop Mahony on various occasions, such as my situation. And so, I told the Archbishop that I would be willing to meet with Fr. Dysinger.

Fr. Luke celebrating Mass.

CHAPTER 16

1990

A. Meeting with Fr. Luke Dysinger

As I was waiting for Fr. Luke Dysinger to contact me, I found out that he met with a former housekeeper of mine, Ann Holcomb. I guess the reason why Fr. Luke Dysinger met with Ann Holcomb was because she knew both my secretary and myself.

About two months past before Fr. Luke Dysinger met with me. He spent about twenty minutes asking various questions, such as about the Charismatic Movement and the Apostolate of Christian Renewal. When I responded with my thoughts on the Charismatic Movement, I said that this movement is mainly geared to foster the charism of the Holy Spirit. However, I told Fr. Dysinger that I thought the teachings of faith and morals were lacking in the Charismatic Movement. I then said that if faith is taught more diligently, then the gifts of the Holy Spirit will bring to fruition what was already taught. Then I went on to explain that the Charismatics should have a deeper devotion to Our Mother Mary because she is the Spouse of the Holy Spirit. Finally, I told Fr. Dysinger that the Apostolate of Christian Renewal has a lot to learn from the Charismatic Movement, especially concerning the gifts of the Holy Spirit.

Next, Fr. Dysinger asked about the invisible stigmata. I told him that I didn't say a lot about it because I didn't want to draw attention to myself. However, I told him that one of the priests who was helping the Apostolate spoke about the invisible stigmata many times, even though I instructed him not to do so. Fr. Dysinger also asked me about the accusation of taking and misusing money given to me. In regards to this accusation, I told Fr. Dysinger that people gave me money freely so that I could use it for the work of the Apostolate.

1. Receiving a letter from the Archbishop

Within a few weeks after my meeting with Fr. Dysinger, I received a copy of the last three pages of Fr. Dysinger's report from Archbishop Roger Mahony through his Chancellor. The report stated that I claimed the Apostolate of Christian Renewal was better than the Charismatic Renewal. Personally, I think Fr. Dysinger simply misunderstood my thoughts because there are fundamental difference between these two movements. I believe if a person understands both movements, then a person will be able to easily understand how they compliment each other.

Fr. Dysinger also stated that there was no such thing as the invisible stigmata in the history of the Church. He stated that neither I nor anyone else should ever talk about this condition. He also said that if I were asked about the invisible stigmata in private that I should not even give the impression that I have the stigmata. Finally, he concluded that my condition was more pathological than anything else and that I should submit to a psychological evaluation.

I did some research and found, to the contrary, many people down through the centuries have had the invisible stigmata. Some of those people are great saints in the Catholic Church. For example, St. Jean-Marie Vianney, St. Catherine of Sienna and St. Gemma Galgani all had the invisible stigmata. As for St. Teresa of Avila, she also had the invisible stigmata where her heart was transpierced. Perhaps she suffered the stigmata in her hands and feet as well. During the twentieth century, Padre Pio had the invisible stigmata for eight years before it became visible, then he had the visible stigmata for 50 years. However, Padre Pio always prayed that God would take away the visible stigmata, but God did not listen to him until the lasts days of his life. Then finally, God removed the visible stigmata. In our times, Brother Gino, now Fr. Gino, has had the invisible stigmata for 10 years before it became visible. Therefore, I sincerely believe it is possible for people to have the invisible stigmata.

I also believe that those who have the stigmata should keep quiet and hidden so that cults will not be built around them. Then, those who have the stigmata can carry out God's plan without any unnecessary persecution. As a result, he suggested that there could be something pathologically wrong with me. Fr. Dysinger then recommend psychological evaluation.

In regards to a psychological evaluation, I just had completed an extensive psychological evaluation. The evaluation was very favorable and I passed with flying colors. However, Archbishop Mahony objected to this psychological evaluation because the psychologist who administered the psychological test was not a clinically licensed practitioner, rather, he was merely an educational psychologist. I thought that this was an unfounded objection because the educational psychologist was a professor who teaches and conducts counseling services at a regular university. He does this for students who are preparing to become counselors and psychologists. Therefore, I felt that he was very qualified to administer, interpret and evaluate the test that I took from him. I also did not see any further need for psychological evaluation neither did the Archbishop nor my Congregation.

Fr. Dysinger also stated in the report that if any of the present Servants wanted to apply to enter the seminary, then they should be evaluated more carefully than other's who applied.

a.   In regards to my stigmata

I really do not know whether the pains in my hands, feet and side come from a pathological cause or not. Regardless, all I know is that on August 17th, 1972, while I was praying in the Garden of Gethsemane, I had a religious experience where my spirit was taken outside of my body. During this experience, Jesus said, "Are you willing to suffer?" And I responded, "Yes." Then he asked me, "Are you willing to become a martyr?" Again, I responded, "Yes." Even though I was willing to suffer, I never thought that the Lord would allow me to suffer the pains of the stigmata, whether visible or invisible. Because I never asked for the stigmata, I personally think that any person, who wants to have the stigmata along with their other suffering that comes from life, is in need of psychological evaluation.

b. People who see the stigmata

Sometimes when I celebrate the Eucharistic Liturgy during my Renewal Weeks, some people see my hands bleed, even though they know nothing about the invisible stigmata. Later, these people would come and tell me about what they saw and ask me, "Do you have the stigmata?" Because I was in an awkward situation, I would not say anything. Normally, I would tell them, "Please do not speak about what you have seen to others." However, just like the Lord telling people to be quite in the Gospels, most people speak about it anyway.

c. Not special

Just because I have the invisible stigmata, I don't consider myself special or holier than anyone else. Likewise, the charismatic gifts do not make anyone holier than another. We must remember that the Apostles had charismatic gifts and Judas betrayed Jesus, Peter denied Jesus, Thomas doubted Jesus and all the Apostles ran away from Jesus, except for John. From the Gospels themselves, we can see that charismatic gifts do not make people holy. Rather, the charismatic gifts are given to be of service to others.

d. Dr. Jim and my pain

I asked my bother, Dr. James Zimmer, who is a physician, if he would examine the pain I was having in my hands, feet and side. However, I never told him about my experience in the Garden of Gethsemane. After he examined me, he said that I did not have any arthritis. Then he asked me if I knew what I had. I responded by saying that, "I'm not really sure." Dr. Jim then said, "I believe you have the invisible stigmata."

Later on, I had numerous x-rays of my hands, feet, side and other parts of my body. The x-ray examinations were conducted by a friend of mine, Dr. Anthony Sneed. These x-rays showed that I had a separation of the bones in my wrists and feet, which normal people do not have. He also confirmed Dr. Jim's analysis that I did not have arthritis in my hands or feet. However, the x-rays did show signs of some arthritis in my back and neck. Even though the technician who took the x-rays was not my physician, he told me that I should be in constant pain because of the arthritis in my back and neck. However, I seldom felt any pain in these areas.

e.   Rapid heart

I also consulted a doctor because I felt my heart beat very rapidly. When the doctors administered a sonogram, they found that my heart was rather small for the size of my chest. The sonogram also showed that one side of my heart was prolonged, as if a spear had been plunged into my heart. Because the doctor wasn't so sure what he was seeing, he wanted another test. Again, the test showed that my heart was prolonged in one area. Then the doctor called in another physician and asked if he saw the same thing. While they were discussing the results of the sonogram, I asked if they could explain it to me. They told me that my heart was prolonged and that this condition was very unusual. In fact, he said, "I have never seen anything like this in a person's heart."

f.   Suffering

During my life, I have always suffered a lot. Usually, the suffering that I experience has been because of persecution, misunderstanding, rejection and ridicule. Even though I don't enjoy suffering, I do know the value of suffering. This is why that whenever I suffer, I never say to God, "Why me?"

Suffering can come from many sources. I believe that suffering is an element in the human condition caused by original sin. Because of the sin of Adam and Eve, every person is effected from this fall and will suffer the consequences of sin.

Many people suffer because of their own fault. In other words, many people live a life of sinfulness by doing things that are not of God. As a result, they suffer the consequences of sin. Next, there are accidents that just happen to people, such as drowning, being burned, being injured in an accident or finding themselves diseased because of various causes. There are also sufferings that come from man's inhumanity to man. Personally, I think that this type of suffering is the most prevalent and widespread. Finally, there are those people who have been asked by God to suffer for His honor and glory for the conversion of sinners. I believe that this is the type of suffering that God has asked of me. And so, I accept and offer all my sufferings with Jesus in each Eucharistic Liturgy until the end of time for all bishops and priests.

I find that suffering is a blessing because it helps a person realize his or her own sinfulness and helps to overcome sinful habits. Suffering also helps a person remain free from vanity and reveals the emptiness of the world. However, in having received this gift of suffering, there are times when I am writing letters that I have to stop writing because the pain in my wrists are so pronounced. Like I said earlier, the pain is usually like a dull toothache, which is constant. At other times, the pain is like a badly infected tooth, which is sudden, sharp and intense. Most of the time, this type of pain catches me off guard and I moan. As for my secretary, she thought my moaning was an act of complaining. Even though I wasn't complaining, this is what my secretary seems to have understood it to be.

B. Meeting with Archbishop Mahony

After reviewing the results of the report from Fr. Dysinger, the letter sent to me by the Chancellor of the Archdiocese stated that I needed to schedule a meeting with the Archbishop. This meeting was scheduled for July 14th. Personally, I thought this meeting would be a great opportunity for me to dialogue with the Archbishop about all that had happened. I was even hoping that everything would finally be straightened out before he would make a decision about starting the Servants of the Sacred Heart of Jesus, Mary and Joseph. However, when I walked into the Archbishop's office, he handed me a letter that was dated July 12th. I then realized that Archbishop Mahony already made up his mind.

As I read this letter in the Archbishop's office, he stated that I could continue to reside in Fillmore and continue my work for the Apostolate of Christian Renewal. Second, he said that I could not start the Servants of the Sacred Heart of Jesus, Mary and Joseph. Therefore, all the men who were living in Fillmore were to be disbanded and could no longer have the intent of starting a new religious community. Third, he suggested that these young men who were preparing for the community should be urged to become priests for the Archdiocese of Los Angeles. He said that they could attend St. John's Seminary in Camarillo, California. Finally, he suggested that I should start a confraternity for priests, which would express the charism and spirituality of the Sacred Heart of Jesus, Mary and Joseph.

After reading this letter, I was quite shocked! Again, there was nothing I could do, except be obedient. The only thing I could do was go back to Fillmore and try to explain to the young men the decision of the Archbishop.

1. The response of my Congregation

In light of this letter, the Congregation's response was that I should not try to establish the Servants of the Sacred Heart of Jesus, Mary and Joseph. They also said that they would not give me permission to start the confraternity for priests. According to their words, they said that the Archbishop was only making a token offering to appease me so that I wouldn't feel too bad that he did not give permission for the founding of the Servants.

Even though I assented to my Congregation's directives, I still believed that Archbishop Mahony wanted the confraternity to begin. Nonetheless, I was obedient to my superiors and I did not pursue the starting of the confraternity. Interestingly, a bishop talked to me and said that my body language and my attitude expressed that my main interest in carrying out the work that God has called me to do, was to establish these communities. I believe that this bishop spoke the truth because starting the Servants is always on my mind. I firmly believe that it is God's Will that this community should be established.

2. Telling the Servants the results of the Archbishop's decision

When I met with the Servants, I reviewed with them the letter from Archbishop Roger Mahony. I said that they should discern God's Will and that if they wanted to enter St. John's Seminary, then they should do so. Since they were no longer Servants preparing for a new religious community, I felt that there was nothing wrong in having them continue to reside in Fillmore when they went to the seminary. I told them that they still could come and go anytime they pleased during the year, such as Christmas, Easter, holidays or weekends home from the seminary.

After the meeting with the men, all of them discerned God's Will and decided to apply to St. John's Seminary. However, because Fr. Dysinger suggested that these men be subjected to careful psychological evaluations, I felt that they were discriminated against because of all the extra tests. Naturally, I felt a lot of hurt when I heard how they were treated in their evaluations. But because these men were well-balanced and strong in their faith, they passed with flying colors.

a. A vocational abuse

I felt that disbanding these young men was an abuse to their vocations. I believe that no person ever has a right to do this. I believe each person is called to a specific vocation, either to a vocation of becoming a diocesan or religious. Likewise, a person cannot force another person who is called to a specific religious community to join another religious community. The reason, of course, is because they will not find their happiness, their joy and they will not persevere.

If this happens, I believe the person will go through a lot of needless trials, tribulations and suffering. I believe this needless suffering that people are put through when they are coerced into doing something that God is not calling them to do is a great sin. I always use the example that a person cannot take a round peg and put it into a square hole. I felt that this is what happened with these young men. In other words, they were forced to become diocesan priests when they felt called to be a part of a specific religious community.

b. The men going to the seminary

When these men entered St. John's Seminary, they were accustomed to a deep prayer life and a community lifestyle. As a result, they found that praying together was very, very difficult because of the diocesan seminary training. In other words, because these men had a community type of attitude, they found that the seminary training allowed little room to foster this attitude. For example, many of the men often prayed the fifteen-decade Rosary together, but this form of prayer and praying together was viewed by many as being pious and/or too traditional. In fact, many times these men were ridiculed for what and how they prayed. As a result, these men decided to carry out their prayer lives as they wanted in the privacy of their own rooms.

c.   No doubt about Servants being founded

After the young men in Fillmore entered St. John's Seminary, I never urged them to be Servants, although this was the desire of my heart. Likewise, I know that one day the Servants will exist. And so, the only thing I could do is surrender everything to the Lord.

3.   Spiritual centers

This is why I would like to have a spiritual Center so that the Servants can assists people in discerning their vocation. Even though starting these centers may take a long time to develop, I believe that people should have this opportunity to discern, especially today when we live in a society where young people are afraid of commitment or not mature enough to live the commitment they make. Therefore, many young people need guidance and help to make a lifelong commitment.

a.   Discerning a vocation

I believe each person needs to discern what God's Will is when it comes to a person's vocation. I also believe that God always makes a person's vocation known because there is a great difference between a religious way of life and a diocesan way of life. If God calls a person to a religious way of life, then I believe that God calls a person to a particular religious community. Next, I believe that the person can discern a particular religious community by looking into the depths of his heart. If he is motivated to a certain charism or spirituality, then that is where he belongs.

If God calls a person to a diocesan way of life, then I believe that is where he belongs. I wholeheartedly believe that nobody has the right to interfere with this discernment. Rather, we have the duty to help each person to discern their vocation in life in a prayerful manner. If there is no vocation to be a religious or a diocesan priest, but the person is called either to the single or married life, then that person should also be guided accordingly.

b. Helping to discern

We have to be open to these young people by being there for them, listening to them and helping them. Likewise, we should never force a person to accept a vocation they are not meant to have. Just because we may want them to be priests, brothers, sisters or deacons, we cannot urge them to join just for the sake of numbers. Rather, we should urge the young people to be the best they can so as to help them discern their true vocation from God. We can do this by helping them become aware of their vocation and by encouraging them to follow their call. I believe this is the way we can help young people discern their vocation. I think this has been sadly neglected in the past as well as the present. So, there has to be a change in the approach of how to help people to know and do God's Will.

c. Parents

Naturally, parents have a great obligation in this regard. I find it amazing to believe that parents do not encourage their children to consider the priesthood, brotherhood or sisterhood. I also find it amazing when children express their desire to me to be a priest, brother or sister and that these children find a lot of opposition. Parents have an awesome responsibility to their children, especially to help them fulfill God's Will. Once they know God's Will, parents should accept it, encourage it and be supportive of this child's vocation in life.

d. Prayer Life

People need the encouragement and strength that comes from prayer. A true prayer life is so very important, no matter what walk of life people are called to live, whether they are single, married, religious or diocesan. If a person does not have a prayer life, then the support that is so needed to persevere, to do their work diligently and to develop and maintain their love relationship with God is almost impossible.

I think the first things that need to be taught are what prayer is and how to pray. Some people say that their work and ministry is their prayer. However, their work is only a part of their prayer life and is not the fullness of their prayer life. That's why I believe there is such a great struggle in the lives of people to be faithful to their calling, to their vocation and to their commitment.

4. In Rome

In December 1990, I had the opportunity to go to the canonization of St. Marguerite d'Youville, who lived in Montreal, Canada (1701-1771). She founded a religious community called the Sisters of Charity. St. Marguerite d'Youville is also related to Blessed Brother Andre, C.S.C. (1845-1937) and Blessed Marie Rose Durocher (1811-1849). All three of these people are related to Don Tesmer, who lives with us in Fillmore.

While in Rome, I had the opportunity to speak with Father General. He told me about Fr. Lombardi, S.J., the leader of the Better World Movement. Fr. Lombardi was recently exonerated and his work was being emulated by the Jesuit Order and Rome, where he was previously looked down upon, ridiculed and persecuted. Then Father General said to me, "What you need to do is follow your conscience and go forward to live your life and spread the work of the Apostolate of Christian Renewal." He also said, "You should discern whether you are called to live the spirituality of the Sacred Hearts community or if God is calling you to do something else."

Personally, I think Father General was hoping that I would understand the charism, spirituality and mission of the Congregation of the Sacred Hearts of Jesus and Mary more clearly. However, I felt that I needed to make another Ignatian retreat so as to discern if I was really called to be the Founder of the Servants of the Sacred Heart of Jesus, Mary and Joseph.

a.   Private Mass with Pope John Paul II

Before I went to Rome, I wrote to Cardinal Gagnon asking for an audience with the Holy Father. He responded by stating that I should contact the Pope's secretary asking for permission. When I received a letter from the Pope's secretary, he said that I could concelebrate with the Holy Father in his private chapel.

On December 12th, I concelebrate with nine other priests and two bishops. There was one deacon and twenty-five other people, including Don Tesmer and Andy Pittelkau. Don came with me because of the Canonization of his relative St. Marguerite d'Youville and Andy came with me because I felt that this was a great spiritual experience for him. Andy and I always spoke about spiritual things. Many of his insights would give me much food for thought. Often times, I meditated and pondered many of his insights that helped me to see the value of the development of the spiritual life. This is why I think it is important to talk about spiritual things, especially with the young. Many times, they have tremendous innocence into the spiritual life. And so, I think each of us should be willing to learn from anyone because God always speaks through others, no matter if they are young, old, intelligent, not so intelligent, disabled etc...

We celebrated the Mass of St. Jean Francis de Chantel. I was deeply moved during the Mass because the Holy Father was so absorbed in prayer and in God. Even after Mass, the Holy Father spent about ten minutes in silent thanksgiving. After Mass, we were ushered into a large room where the Holy Father visited each of us briefly. He also gave each of us a Rosary.

CHAPTER 17

1991

A. Eight-Day Ignatian retreat

In February, 1991, I made an eight-day retreat with Fr. John McAnulty, S.J. In my discernment process, I studied and prayed about the various aspects of why I belonged to the Servants community rather than the SS.CC. community.

In the SS.CC. community, our Founder was involved in many different types of work because he responded to the needs of the Church. And so, he was willing to send his men as well as himself to fulfill these needs. As a result, our ministry is to be available to the Church and respond to Her needs.

According to our Founder, we were founded with the charism of making reparation for sins through Perpetual Adoration of the Blessed Sacrament, while our spirituality was spreading the devotion to the Sacred Heart of Jesus and Mary. Our community was to urge lay people to make reparation for sins through Eucharistic Devotion. We are also called to do missionary work, parish work and to teach in schools just like our Founder. I believe that our vocation is a very sublime and worthwhile vocation.

On the other hand, the Servants and Handmaids of the Sacred Heart of Jesus, Mary and Joseph have the charism to bring to fruition the prayer that Jesus prayed for at the Last Supper, "That all may be one" (Jn. 17:21). The Servants and Handmaids are to work for the unity between humanity and God; one person to another. As a result, the Servants and Handmaids are to give witness by their lives to this charism. The spirituality is to express their prayer life and their work in the charism of unity through the Mystical Mass Prayer, Mystical Rosary and our work. In other words, every little aspect of a person's life is a prayer. Therefore, to bring about unity, a person must live a deep spiritual life. The Apostolate is to share this charism and spirituality with others, so that they will also be a living witness to the unity that Jesus prayed at the Last Supper.

1. Charism

a.   Unity is an intimate relationship with the Triune God

When Jesus prayed for unity, His desire was that we share in the intimate life of God. In other words, Jesus' desire for unity is that we may have an intimate relationship with God the Father, God the Son and God the Holy Spirit. If we live an intimate relationship with God, then we will truly be in union with God, the angels and saints in Heaven, the souls in Purgatory and all the people on earth. This is unity that we need to live and bring about for a solid foundation for true Ecumenism.

b.   The mystical union given at Baptism

In the Sacrament of Baptism, a person becomes a "partaker of the Divine nature of God," (2 Cor. 5:17, 2 Pet. 1:4, Gal 4:5-7) and lives the life of the Blessed Trinity. This means that because of Baptism, God has given us the grace to share in His Divine Nature. Because we share in His Divine Nature, all baptized people belong to the Mystical Body of Christ. Mystical union then, exists between each person thus becoming one. Therefore, through Baptism, we are one body with Christ and this is how our intimate relationship with God begins.

2. Spirituality

a.   The Life of the Blessed Trinity

The Life of the Blessed Trinity is the manifestation of God's tremendous love that the Three Person's have for One Another. This Love unites them as one, yet they are Three Persons in One

Divine Nature. God is a Family and a community. And God is call-ing us to live the life of the Blessed Trinity. Therefore, the Servants and Handmaids of the Sacred Heart of Jesus, Mary and Joseph are really dedicated to live the Life of the Blessed Trinity as reflected in the Holy Family.

Over the years, I thought a lot about this charism, which has been developed gradually, sometimes painfully while at other times joyfully. The pain that I experienced in my life came from the trials and tribulations from others, but this pain always brought me closer to the Blessed Trinity. And so, this book and charism is really a sharing of my own personal experience in living my life.

b.   Blessed Trinity and Holy Family are the perfect model

Because each person is different, they should not try to be-come like Fr. Luke or any other person. Rather, a person should zero in on the Blessed Trinity and look to the Holy Family so that they live their lives totally for God. We are all called to be instru-ments of unity so as to bring this spirituality and way of life to others.

3.   Purpose

a.   Mystical Union includes Ecumenism

Naturally, mystical union includes the Ecumenical Movement, where we strive by our prayers, by our witness, by our sharing, by our dialogue with other Christians to help them understand that there is only one true Church of Jesus Christ. This Church is the Catholic Church because it is the one Jesus, Himself, established. True ecumenism, then, is to bring all people to the fullness of the Catholic Church. However, this must be brought about through the work of the Holy Spirit.

b.   The Servants and Handmaids pray for an outpouring of the Holy Spirit

The Servants and Handmaids of the Sacred Heart of Jesus, Mary and Joseph are to pray for an outpouring of the Holy Spirit.

They should also accept any charismatic gifts that the Holy Spirit might give. The Servants and Handmaids should use these gifts for the honor and glory of God. These gifts should be also used by spreading the Kingdom of God and bringing about the unity that Jesus prayed for at the Last Supper. However, in order to do this, each person must be willing to love, accept and appreciate each person as he or she is. Therefore, we cannot force anyone to do anything against his or her conscience. We can, however, help another to respond to God's Will

c. Sharing our gifts with others who are not in the Church

When God gives us gifts, they should be used for others. These gifts need to be used because it is God's Will that we do so. By sharing our gifts and explaining these gifts, we can teach other people how they should use their gifts in their lives. In that way, people have the opportunity to see how God is working in their own life. People need to have the insight to evaluate, discern and respond to any gift or grace that God gives to them. As a result, the person will be able to respond freely, lovingly and willingly to the Church of Jesus Christ. By doing this, we are not proselytizing, but we are just stating the facts that we have a mission to carry out. This is the mission that we have been given by God.

4. Who is called

a. Everyone is called to live the charism and spirituality of the Servants and Handmaids

Every person is able to live the charism and spirituality of the Servants and Handmaids: the Holy Father, cardinals, bishops, priests, deacons, brothers, sisters and all lay people, man, woman or child. Everyone person is called to live this charism in his or her personal life, family life and community life. That's what we are striving to bring about so that there will be a change in the way society lives and a change in the culture.

b.   The Servants and Handmaids are a movement

I believe that the men and women who are ready to become Servants and Handmaids should realize that it is a movement. I do not think that the Servants and Handmaids should ever become an organization with a president, vice-president, treasurer, secretary etc. . . . The reason is because these organizations seem to stifle the work of the Holy Spirit.

Rather, the Servants and Handmaids should be like the early Christians, who had tremendous zeal and were very dedicated, even to the point of martyrdom. In other words, the Servants and Handmaids should have the same zeal and dedication. They need to inform and help people to understand the charism, spirituality and mission of the lay Servants and Handmaids. In this way, other people will know what to do and how to live this charism and spirituality.

Likewise, we need to be sensitive to others because each person is different and will express themselves differently. We have to be open so that we don't stifle the Spirit. For instance, if a person prays the Rosary by him or herself, in a small or large group, each person will have different thoughts, different inspirations, different gifts and graces from praying the Rosary. Our growth in the spiritual life and growth in holiness, will be in accordance with our capacity in our state of spiritual development.

If they are more like children, they will develop their spiritual life very quickly. For instance, if children are raised in the proper manner by their parents, they will have a great love in their hearts for God. I see this love in many little children, such as their qualities of innocence, talents, gifts and graces. If we become like these children, then we will not put the obstacles in the way of the grace of God. And so, we are to become like little children in developing the spiritual life. Jesus said, "Unless you become like a little child, you shall not enter into the Kingdom of God." We can also learn a lot from the elderly people too, who have experienced life, trials, tribulations and have become child-like.

In short, we have a lot to learn from the little children and the elderly. For example, when the Lord met Nathaniel, He said, "Behold a true Israelite, one without any guile." People who are without guile are single-minded and single-hearted. These people have only one purpose in life, which is allowing God to be the center of their lives and never to deviate from God. In other words, people without guile are always open to God, ready to do God's Will and are willing to surrender themselves to God. These child-like qualities are needed in everyone's life, especially the Servants and Handmaids.

c.   Culture

The culture people live in is what really guides and motivates people in living their lives for others. We should have a great impact on culture and society. Likewise, we should be people of respect by upholding a positive attitude in a culture for life, rather than a negative attitude in a culture of death. If we are upholding a positive attitude, then we must be optimistic and never criticize others, look down upon others or reject others. We must learn to love each person as he or she is. Through our love, we will manifest God to others and He will change people's hearts.

d.   Having a healthy heart in the Church

As the Church continues to grow, we need a true and healthy heart in our Church. In other words, in order for the Church to have a good heart, we have to have a good heart because we are the Church. Even though we may become discouraged in the Church, we must never lose heart. Rather, we must be faithful to the heart of the Church, which is really the Heart of Christ. Then Mary, who is the Mother of the Church, our mother and the Mother of Jesus will also help us to be the Heart of the Church. Then St. Joseph, who is the protector and provider, will help us to have a great love for the Church.

5.   Thoughts I learned

These thoughts that I just expressed are what I learned in the discerning process in the retreat with Fr. John McAnulty, S.J. I mention these thoughts because many have made accusations or said things that would give the impression that I am not to continue to try to bring this way of life to others. However, because I have no doubt in my mind, I will always believe that the Servants and Handmaids are God's Will. Therefore, no matter what obstacle, trial or tribulation comes my way, God's grace will give me the strength to carry on His Will. As I always say, "God's grace is sufficient."

B. Other thoughts

1. Fillmore

Some people say to me that I am too permissive and not strict enough in correcting the faults of others. The reason why they say this is because of some events involving people who came to live at our Center. One of the problems living a community lifestyle is that I was usually the last person to find out if there was something wrong.

Because of my schedule of giving Renewal Weeks, I was gone most of the time. While I was away, sometimes people did things that they should not have done. However, when I would return to the Center, nobody ever mentioned anything about the problems that arouse or the personality clashes that occurred. Again, I was not aware of any of these things taking place because nobody ever told me. Naturally, I thought the best of every person living at the Center, such as being good-hearted, loving, charitable, accepting and forgiving. And so, I believe that those people who have accused me of not being strict enough are wrong.

There is a saying that if you spare the rod, then you spoil the child. I believe this is true in all walks of life. I believe that we all need a healthy sense of discipline and that if we are doing wrong, then healthy fraternal correction is a source of great grace. People need to be shown the right way, what is expected, how to live in harmony and peace.

Some people even say that others took advantage of me, walked over me and manipulated me. These people usually say this is a weakness in my character. However, I have found that these accusations often came from people who are disciplinarians, self-righteous, perfectionists and letter-of-the-law people. These people want everything to be 100 percent perfect. Well, I believe this is unfortunate because there is never anything 100 percent perfect. Rather, each person should strive to do their best and we should encourage people rather than criticize them.

Often times, we can crush people by the way we treat them. For instance, if we constantly tell people that they are not doing the right thing or that they are no good or that they are stupid, then we are abusing these people to the highest degree. In fact, there are many different types of abuse, such as physical, mental, emotional, verbal and non-verbal abuse. I believe that none of these types of abuse, nor others like them are permissible. The reason is because abuse stifles the spirit and breaks a person's self-esteem. As a result, people lose heart and become emotionally sick. In fact, emotional illness is a detriment to everyone involved, to the person, the family and the community. Rather, we should encourage people to be their best by allowing them to use their talents, graces and gifts. Therefore, if a person continually beats on some theme with a person, then the results are meaningless because the person just doesn't mature when people are being negative toward them.

a.   Being a good parent or leader

In order to be a good parent or a good leader, a person learns not to break the reed, but bend it so that the spirit of the person will not be crushed. If a parent or a leader learns this method of correction, then the spirit of the person will be uplifted and inflame within the person a deeper love and appreciation toward everyone in the community, especially the parent or leader. In fact, there should never be any family or religious community that is run in a dictatorial or military fashion. This I believe wholeheartedly!

When I was being trained in the seminary, I thought that there were many things done incorrectly. Even though I cannot blame anyone, I believe there should be a different approach to train people in the seminary. For example, I believe we should teach people to see Jesus Christ in each person. In this way, people will be helpful and loving so as to live in true unity, "That all may be one as the Father and I are One." If the seminary training is focused on this approach, then I believe we will be able to bring the best out of these people and many problems would dissipate.

Another point that we have to realize is that we can destroy everything by speaking too forcefully or by being too aggressive and ambiguous. Rather, we should be willing to be long-suffering at times, just as God is with us. In other words, if God waits for us, our return, our conversion and does not interfere, then we should to the same with God.

b.   Might not see the founding

Although I believe that I am called to start the Servants of the Sacred Heart of Jesus, Mary and Joseph, I also realize that the founding might not occur until I die. In other words, "The grain of wheat must die before it can grow." In St. Louis de Montfort's day, he had only one person willing to study for the priesthood and only two women who wanted to be sisters when he was ready to start his community. However, St. Louis de Montfort died prematurely at the age of 43. Yet, only after he died, did his religious communities begin. This is also true with Sr. Faustina, who was told by God that she was to start a new religious community. In fact, Sr. Faustina asked her superiors many times to permit her to leave so that she could begin these communities, yet they always refused. Then, finally, she got tuberculosis and died. Today, these communities exist and are flourishing. As for myself, I think something similar will happen to me.

c.   God's time is not our time

God's time is not our time and God's way is not our way. Each person should wait on the Lord, just as Sr. Lucia has for so many years. Even though Sr. Lucia had so many obstacles in her way and tried so diligently to do what God has asked of her, many events are still not brought to fruition. Therefore, each person should be open to surrendering everything to God. If each person puts his or her faith, hope and love in the Providence of God, then the person will receive everything that the Lord wants to give.

d.   Total abandonment

I was given the book, *Total Abandonment*, I noticed that it said that each person is to surrender to the Will of God. After reading this book, I again made a total commitment of surrendering to the Will of God no matter what that may be, especially in regards to the founding of the Servants community.

2.   Easter Sunday

On Easter Sunday, April 19th, 1991, I decided that I would surrender everything to the Lord on a daily basis. Even to this day, I have kept my decision. I believe that surrendering everything to God is essential because as it says in Scripture, "Surrender to God everything, and He will do all things for you." Although a person should never surrender just so that God will do everything for the person, rather a person should want to surrender everything to God so that God can work within the person's life. As a result, God can fulfill His plan for that particular person.

God is also long-suffering and waits upon a person to be motivated, to do things, to get rid of obstacles and return to a life of grace. And this takes time. For example, when the Blessed Mother appeared to Lucia in Fatima, she told Lucia that she would have to stay in the world for a time. Also, the Blessed Mother wanted Sr. Lucia to spread the messages of Fatima so as to make them known to the world. The Blessed Mother then could bring about the Triumph of her Immaculate Heart and the conversion of Russia. The Blessed Mother told Sr. Lucia that she would see all of this happen. Like the early Apostles, many people had the impression that this event would take place right away. Yet, today Sr. Lucia is 90 years old and all those things have not been fully developed. Even though Russia has changed drastically, the Triumph and Reign of the Immaculate Heart of Mary still needs to be brought about in its entirety.

3.   Surrender Song

During a prayer meeting in Fillmore, Joe Arledge, a seminarian, started to sing the "Surrender Song." This song really touched me. Then, I started to sing the "Surrender Song," and gradually as I sang it, the song began to change. So, I asked Joe to change the words and put this song into music. In order to sing the "Surrender Song," each verse is said twice:

Come Lord Jesus, Come.
Come Heavenly Father, Come.
Come Holy Spirit, Come.
Come Blessed Trinity.
Make Your home within me (us).

I (we) surrender all to You Heavenly Father;
I (we) surrender all to You my (our) God;
I (we) surrender all to You my (our) Dad.

I (we) surrender all to You Lord Jesus;
I (we) surrender all to You my (our) God;
I (we) surrender all to You my (our) Brother.

I (we) surrender all to You Holy Spirit;
I (we) surrender all to You my (our) God;
I (we) surrender all to You my (our) Spouse.

I (we) surrender all to You Blessed Trinity;
I (we) surrender all to You my (our) God;
I (we) surrender all to You my (our) God.

Heart of Jesus, I (we) adore You;
Heart of Mary, I (we) implore You;
Heart of Joseph, ever Just;
In this Heart, I (we) place my trust.

C. The separation of the Apostolate of Christian Renewal from the Congregation

Many people say to me that I will never be able to start the Servants because of my age. In other words, because of my age, they felt that my health could fail or that I could become incapacitated or even die. This is why my Congregation told me that I should make provisions to separate the Apostolate of Christian Renewal from the Congregation of the Sacred Hearts of Jesus and Mary.

Even though I was quite surprised that my Congregation wanted this separation, I knew that I must obey the directives of my superiors. I felt a lot of hurt in regards to this separation because I always wanted the Apostolate of Christian Renewal to be apart of the Congregation. However, I realized that opposition always prevented this union.

When I began to carry out the directive of my Congregation, I had to work with the State of California for legal purposes of separation. I also had to make sure that everything done was according to canon law so that there would not be any repercussions, such as bringing harm to the Church or the Apostolate. Finally, after the legal separation of the Apostolate of Christian Renewal from the Congregation on May 30th, 1991, I was able to work for the Apostolate while residing in Fillmore.

1. Apostolate of Christian Renewal & Servants are the same

The Apostolate of Christian Renewal does nothing different from what the Servants and Handmaids of the Sacred Heart of Jesus, Mary and Joseph will do. In other words, they are synonymous. After the Servants are founded, the Apostolate of Christian Renewal will be phased out so that the Servants are able to carry on the work. Legally, the Servants will have to change the name of the Apostolate of Christian Renewal to the Servants of the Sacred Heart of Jesus, Mary and Joseph.

a.   In regards to the Servants

In regards to the Servants, we should not be too aggressive or ambitious for a bishop to found the Servants of the Sacred Heart of Jesus, Mary and Joseph. Neither should we be too aggressive by forcing our way of life on other people. Rather, we should be patient and allow the charism to mature and develop.

As for me, the charism came to me over a period of time in my life and it did not come easily. Only during a 40-day Ignatian Retreat in 1984 did I begin to see how the charism developed. Even after this retreat, the charism took until 1987 before I began to understand it more fully. Then I was able to articulate the charism and formulate it into words so that others are able to understand. We have to be patient and willing to be long-suffering so that the charism matures slowly and truly in the mind and lives of others. Then our foundation will be as solid as a rock and the edifices built upon it will never fall.

2. Reflecting on this experience

In reflecting on this experience, I believe that this separation was providential. The reason is because the separation allowed the Apostolate to go forward and do what we needed to do. Naturally, all the members of the Congregation of the Sacred Heart of Jesus and Mary resigned from the Board of Directors. As a result, the Apostolate needed to establish new membership for the Board of Directors. I remained the President; Sr. Mary Rose Chinn, a Handmaid, became Vice President; Ron Butler became Chairman of the Board; Don Tesmer became Treasurer, Mary Shearer became Secretary, Sr. Mary Joseph Mei, Allen Shearer and Carol Butler became Board Members. Therefore, the Apostolate of Christian Renewal, guided by the Board of Directors, will carry out the charism, spirituality and purpose until the Servants of the Sacred Heart of Jesus, Mary and Joseph are founded.

When I die, and if the Servants are not founded, then the Board of Directors will continue the work. I hope and desire that the lay people, who are Servants and Handmaids, will live this way of life, spread this way of life and financially assist this way of life so that the work of the Apostolate will continue.

In the past, all sources of income received were because I was on the road giving Renewal Weeks urging people to become lay Servants and Handmaids. As a result, many people were able to spread the work of the Apostolate and contribute money so that the work could continue. However, the amount of money received was just enough to keep the Apostolate out of the red. Because of this situation, the Apostolate was limited in what it could do. We wanted to begin building Spiritual Educational Renewal Centers, but because of the lack of money, we were unable to carry out what we really would like to have done. Perhaps we were not aggressive enough or did not make our needs known sufficiently or perhaps did not urge the people to come forward to make a sacrifice to help us establish these spiritual centers that God is calling us to develop. Likewise, we were unable to urge people to help with the Servants communities because we were not permitted to do so at this point in time.

I hope that after I die, the work will continue to flourish. I sincerely believe that I am only an instrument, which means that the Apostolate does not depend on me. Rather, I believe that the Apostolate depends upon everyone, especially the lay Servants and Handmaids. I also invite and challenge you, who are reading my autobiography to consider helping establish the lay Servants and Handmaids with the gifts, graces and blessings that God has given to you.

D. Way of life

1. Called to be a saint

Each person is called to be a saint, which means we are to be holy. In other words, Jesus says, "Be holy as the Heavenly Father is Holy." And so, each person should ask for the grace to have the desire to become a saint. Even though we cannot become a saint on our own, we can become a saint with God's grace. Therefore, if we are united with God who gives us His holiness, then we can be holy as our Heavenly Father is holy.

Some people might think this is very idealistic, but in all reality nothing is further from the truth. This way of life is a commandment because Jesus said this in the Gospel. Jesus expects us to be holy and it's only possible with the blessings, graces and gifts He has given us. If we respond to Jesus, then we will implement Jesus' command in our lives so that we will have this deep relationship with God.

a.   Everyone is called to be holy

I believe every person has the call to live a true spiritual life, whether the person is holy or whether the person is sinful. And with God's grace, a sinner can always change and be converted so as to live a life of holiness. In fact, the Church has many great sinners who are now saints, such as St. Augustine, St. Francis Xavier and St. Mary Magdalene. Therefore, every person needs to always ask for God's love and mercy so that they may be what God has called them to be: saints.

b.   Just ask

I sincerely believe that each person needs to just ask for God's mercy and compassion and He will give these virtues to that person. We need to accept these gifts from the Holy Spirit and live a life of holiness, while constantly begging for the mercy of God and making reparation for the sins that we have committed. Every person has sinned, some more and some less. That is why we need to make reparation for the sins of others so that God can give His mercy to others by touching their hearts.

In order to begin to live a life a holiness, God will move the heart of the sinner. If the sinner responds, then God will transform the sinner's heart so that the sinner begins to imitate and follow the life of Jesus Christ. In fact, many people's lives have been changed because God has touched their hearts. These people give witness talks at prayer meetings or even write a book about their life stories.

I believe that no sin should ever prevent a person from striving for holiness and living the life of the Lord. Even if this sin is extremely mortal, I still believe that if God touches the heart of a person and when the person responds, then they will commit themselves to a new way of life. However, often times before a person changes their life, he or she has to hit rock bottom before a true conversion takes place. But when the person is converted, he or she is receptive of God's love, mercy and forgiveness.

2.   Our prayers are not magical

I have also been accused of praying prayers that are magical or pious. For example, many people who pray the Rosary, as I do, are often looked down upon because of praying this prayer. Detractors say to me that the Rosary is just a repetitious prayer and that we should not be praying these types of prayers. The reason is because they say there is too much danger in having routine in prayer because a person will no longer be aware of what he or she is doing when praying.

However, if a person puts his or her mind to it, then the person can pray with a greater awareness of God at all times, especially when praying the Rosary. Even if a person repeats the same words over and over again, the prayer still is sanctifying. For example, when a person begins to pray a formal prayer like the Rosary, often times it starts out as repetitious prayer. But, gradually, as the person prays the Rosary and perseveres in this prayer, he or she begins to mediate on the various mysteries of the Rosary. As a result, they no longer think about the words per se. Rather, the words are like a symphony in the background that allows a person to think more attentively about the various mysteries. These awesome mysteries attract the person, who becomes more insightful as a person grows in God's mysteries. The person then begins to know God on a very personal level and gradually becomes more and more aware of His presence.

The person's spiritual life also begins to change because as his or her relationship with God develops, they want to keep sin out of their lives for fear that they will turn away from God. Then, the person slowly overcomes temptations and begins to eliminate sinful habits. He or she will also recognize God's grace from within. By praying the Rosary, the person will go through a process of purification, which is necessary to know God more purely.

Gradually, the Rosary meditation will bring the person into the Dark Night of the Senses, which prepares the person to enter into the contemplative prayer life. Every person is called to experience this type of prayer so that he or she may know and love God more intimately. In other words, each person is called to be a mystic.

a.   The Rosary

When a person prays the Mystical Rosary, as God has revealed to me, I believe that it will lead a person to an intimate and personal relationship with the Lord. As a result, the person will have a greater love for God, others and self. And so, I invite people to pray the Mystical Rosary and to persevere by being faithful to this prayer. Even though some people may criticize a person for praying the Mystical Rosary as being too Marian or pious, I believe that the Mystical Rosary is Christological, Trinitarian and encompasses the mystery of our faith. Therefore, if a person prays the Rosary faithfully, by meditating on the mysteries and being open to the Holy Spirit, then through the gift of understanding and knowledge, the person will know God intimately and personally.

Likewise, we never have to apologize to anybody for the way in which we pray the Rosary. When I asked a theologian to investigate the Mystical Rosary, he said that there was nothing against faith or morals. In fact, he said that praying the Rosary is an excellent way of expressing love for God and others. The theologian also encouraged the spread of this way of life throughout the world.

3. Called to be a mystic

I believe each person is called to be a mystic. A mystic is a person who is in union with God. A mystic is a person who is aware of God's presence and strives to live a life of holiness. This life of holiness makes the mystic more like Jesus Christ and more like God the Father.

a. Contemplative life

Each person should dispose themselves as best they can so that they may be ready for God to bring them into the contemplative life. Even though a person can do nothing to reach this way of life on his or her own, God will give this gift of contemplative prayer to any person if the person is generous and persevering in prayer.

4. Contemplation is a gift

A person can attend many seminars and retreats where speakers explain various aspects about the contemplative life. Some of these seminars and retreats will even try to direct the person into that mode or way of prayer. However, even though most of these discursive methods are very beneficial, I think many of these speakers forget that contemplative prayer is a gift. As I mentioned before, a person needs to be open to the Holy Spirit so that when the gift is offered, a person can respond affirmatively and truly begin to develop the person's spiritual life through contemplative prayer.

In the beginning of contemplation, a person will experience various aspects of prayer. A person might go back to discursive prayer, then to meditative prayer etc . . . This process lasts as long as God wills, especially until the person is more rounded in a contemplative way of life where God gives this gift to the person as a state of life and a way of living. This is what St. Teresa of Avila speaks about in her book, *The Interior Castle.* It is in her Seventh Mansion where a person reaches the Mystical Marriage and receives contemplative prayer as a permanent way of life.

5. The Dark Night of the Soul

The Dark Night of the Soul is a purification that strips the person of attachments, even spiritual attachments. If a person goes through the Dark Night of the Soul, then the person will be open to God, who floods the generous soul with blessings, graces and gifts. At this point, God will begin to transform the person more and more so that he or she becomes Jesus for and to others. God will also enlighten a person's mind in regards to the spiritual life as well as the personal relationship the person has with God.

During this time, God uses the gift of understanding to illuminate a person's mind about any teachings of the Church, such as the teachings of Jesus concerning the mysteries or dogmas of our faith. God also uses the gift of knowledge when He allows a person to see his or her own unworthiness. As a result, a person sees himself in relation to God and finds that the things of the world are meaningless and are valueless without God. The person then discovers that material things are empty, which invites the person to be willing to give up those attachments that keeps the person away from God. In other words, when a person has an encounter with God and feels His presence within, the person becomes aware of his or her sinfulness and unworthiness. However, the person feels grateful because this personal encounter with the Living God also brings peace and joy.

a. Waking up the sleeping giant

I believe that we need to wake up the sleeping giant, who are those people that live a life of being lukewarm. These people think they can just go through life because they feel that they are good enough and do not need to change. They also think that they do not have to enter into the mission of Jesus. In fact, lukewarm people have no fervor and function more out of duty than out of love or conviction. As a result, they are lethargic and just vegetate in their spiritual life.

6. My work has been reviewed by proper authorities

All of my books have been reviewed by proper authorities. In fact, I have never printed a book without the consensus of the proper authorities. The reason is because I wanted to make sure that there was nothing that I have written that was against faith or morals. And so, I do not have to change or apologize for anything that I have ever written. In all my writings, there is nothing that would lead people astray. Rather, my writings can be beneficial for those who are open to the development of their faith, morals and development of the spiritual life.

7. Schedule

a. Being a workaholic

Some people have accused me of being a workaholic. They say this because of my demanding schedule of giving Renewal Weeks, letter writing, writing articles for *The Christian Renewal News* and counseling people. Even though this appears to be many attributes of a workaholic, I believe that I am just doing God's Will.

Personally, I think a workaholic is a person who does their work for his or her honor, glory and success. As a result, they can say, "Well, this and that is what I did and I hope that you appreciate what I am doing for you." However, a person who does God's Will never becomes a workaholic because he or she is always totally dedicated to live the life of the Lord by spreading His Kingdom for His honor and glory.

I know that I have worked hard over these past twenty-five years so as to establish the Servants and Handmaids of the Scared Heart of Jesus, Mary and Joseph. However, the only reason why I worked with such love, dedication and commitment is because God willed it that way.

b. I'm not a workaholic

I do not think I am a workaholic, obsessed with driving to do things, holding power, obtaining possessions or controlling. The reason why I am not a workaholic is because there is a certain joy in working for the Lord. I think that this joy is the reward that God gives to those who do His Will. Likewise, I work not for the reward, but I work for God.

In working for the Lord, a person is given the gift of perseverance. In fact, the person who works for the Lord's honor and glory is filled with a tremendous peace and joy. As a result, the person works day in and day out, week in and week out, month in and month out, and year in and year out until death comes. Then, I believe, the person is ready for the Lord.

c. My schedule

I know that my schedule can be very strenuous, but God gives me the grace to endure it. For example, I would get up at 4:15 AM every morning and be in the chapel by five o'clock where I would pray the fifteen-decade Rosary. Then I would walk for an hour. During this time, I was able to meditate and pray another fifteen-decade Rosary. Often times, I became more aware of the things of God by being open to the Holy Spirit. This is when God would enlighten my mind about the various mysteries of the Rosary, our way of life and the direction in which He willed. Also during this time of walking, God revealed to me certain aspects of my spiritual life, which was a tremendous source of grace. After my walk, I would go back to the chapel and pray the Liturgy of the Hours with whoever was there. Then, we would pray the 15-decade Rosary and celebrate the Eucharistic Liturgy. After Mass, I ate breakfast and began to work. So, from the time I got up to about 9:15 AM, my prayer was continuous.

8.   Letter writing

While I was at home, I would write letters from breakfast until noontime. Then I would take a little time to eat and finish writing letters until about 4:00 PM. After this, I would spend some more time in adoration, praying the Liturgy of the Hours and the Divine Mercy Chaplet.

I think that every priest, brother and sister should pray the Liturgy of the Hours because of the richness in the writings, especially in the first and second reading in the Ordinary. These writings usually contain the writings of the early Church Fathers. These readings are still relevant today and provide a source of great thought and interest. They also teach a person a lot about the spiritual life. Finally, the Liturgy of the Hours is a great treasure and is a "pearl of great price."

Even though the monastic way of life is centered around the Liturgy of the Hours, all people are called to pray this prayer of the Church. This may take some sacrifice, but if a person sacrifices a little sleep and uses breaks throughout the day efficiently, then I believe that the person can pray most of the Liturgy of the Hours.

9.   St. Teresa of Avila

St. Teresa of Avila said that each person should pray at least two hours a day if he or she is serious about the spiritual life. As for me, I believe that those who are priests, brothers and sisters are to pray more than those who are not ordained or professed. The reason is because they have more time to pray than those who are married or single. Even though some of these people say that they are busy doing the Lord's work, I believe that the development of their prayer life is essential. In this way, they not only grow in God's love and awareness, but they also touch other peoples lives because of their holiness. Personally, I think praying for many hours is very beneficial because this helps a person change his or her life.

As I pointed out earlier, when a person is aware of God's presence, everything they do is prayer, such as praying before the Blessed Sacrament, praying the Rosary, eating, working, sleeping, recreating, traveling and preaching is all for God's honor and glory. And so, a person truly becomes a living prayer and does pray always. This is what we have to keep in mind so we will not be workaholics.

10. Strength comes from the Eucharist

I believe that a person receives tremendous grace and strength to carry out the work of God, especially from the Eucharist. When a person receives the Eucharist, he or she receives the strength of the Lord. This is why a person has to adopt a right attitude regarding Jesus in the Blessed Sacrament. In other words, a person needs to prepare for Jesus coming into his or her heart and being within his or her life. Likewise, a person should never forget this and should never allow the receiving of the Eucharist to become just a routine.

11. Surrender

I think that every morning a person can begin the day with total surrender to God. In doing this, the person sets a tone for the day. Hopefully, this will allow the person to be more focused so he or she may be in the presence of God. This is the attitude all of us should strive for everyday.

12. Too much involvement

I know that for those people who are involved with various programs within their parish that most of the meetings take place in the evening. As a result, most people go to bed very late. However, if a person becomes too busy to pray, then I think something is out of balance. A person should realize that prayer is first and the activity should spring from prayer. Therefore, if there is too much activity or involvement, then I think a person should eliminate some of this activity so as to allow for more time for prayer.

E. Renewal Weeks

1. In the preaching ministry

In my preaching ministry, I have realized that every person needs to do what Jesus did. In other words, we need to teach and explain why and what we are teaching. We need to urge people to accept this teaching. Also, I believe that every person needs to teach from the heart so that others can see that what is taught is done with conviction. There is nothing so powerful than teaching with conviction.

a. Preaching

When a person is giving a mission, Renewal Week, retreat or working in a parish, the person should always be prepared to preach. I think a person can do this by his or her prayer life, reading various material and thinking about God during the day so that a person can preach or give witness from the heart. I have found that when a person preaches from conviction, the people are more apt to respond to God.

2. My sermons

I think that God has given me a great gift of preaching, especially when it involves preparing my sermons. The reason is because I really don't have to work too hard to prepare my sermons. In fact, people tell me that when I preach from my heart that it touches their hearts as well. They say, "You speak from the heart and you speak with authority." I believe this to be true and I think that every person should speak this way too. Somehow, the Lord is able to speak clearer through the heart than by fancy little gimmicks in sermons. I think that preaching flows from our lives, the way we are living and what we are doing. I also find this to be true when I write letters because the Holy Spirit guides me very quickly to know what to say to people about various questions and the spiritual life.

a. Reading encyclicals

I have read every encyclical and every writing by the popes since Pope Pius XII. Consequently, I believe I know the teaching of the Church and Jesus Christ. This is why I desired to present these teachings to the people of God during my Renewal Weeks. My main desire was not to give the blessing or healings, but to teach the truth. Although, when I gave the blessings, there were many physical, emotional and spiritual healings.

3. Reading

I have taken three speed reading courses in my life and I am able to read very rapidly. As a result, I am able to cover a lot of material in a very short time. God has also blessed me with an acute memory so that I can remember things for a very long time. For example, when I read a book or a magazine, I am able to remember a particular page and refer to it quite easily. Also, when I speak to people or refer them to various readings, I am able to mention where they can find the material they need. I am very grateful for this gift.

I believe that people should read extensively, especially the encyclicals of the Holy Father, documents from the *Catechism of the Catholic Church* and the *L'Osservatore Romano*, which is the official Vatican Newspaper. The *L'Osservatore Romano* prints the true teachings of the Holy Father. This newspaper prints all the encyclicals, meetings and other documents of the Holy Father. These articles are very extensive and reveal what is being taught regarding various matters in the Church. Even though the *L'Osservatore Romano* is very expensive, the paper itself is invaluable. If a person spent just a few hours a week reading this paper, they would know exactly what the Church teaches. I know that many lay people cannot always do this, but certainly, priest should be more aware of this paper so that they are more informed of Catholic Church writings.

Personally, I think priests should be more involved in learning Church doctrine so that they can teach the true teachings of the Lord. I know that reading can be a discipline, but I also know that the *L'Osservatore Romano* can be very beneficial. In fact, I find a great joy in reading this paper because the Pope speaks about many mystical themes (The Pope, himself, is a mystic). The many articles speak to a person's heart and nourishes a person's faith. The articles also feed a person's spiritual life.

I hope that all the Servants and Handmaids will always avail themselves to these articles in the *L'Osservatore Romano* so that they can learn them and share this valuable information with others. I believe this will keep a person's faith alive.

4. Charismatic gifts

I believe that God has given me many charismatic gifts, which I need to use in a proper manner so as to bring about the Kingdom of God. Even though these gifts are a tremendous blessing, they have become a heavy cross to bear. In other words, ever since the gift to bless people as I experienced in June 20, 1975, I have been accused of many things and have received a lot of opposition on the part of others. In fact, many people judge me by these charismatic gifts.

As I said earlier, people from all walks of life came to my Renewal Weeks. Unfortunately, the ultra-conservative, who do not like any change at all in the Church, accused me of many different things in regard to the blessing. They reported me to the bishops, and as a result, I was not able to give the blessing for five years. As I pointed out, I was the only priest in the United States who was not able to give the blessing publicly. Rather, I could only give the blessing privately.

a. Being misunderstood

When a person receives various charismatic gifts, that person will often be misunderstood by many because others do not understand these gifts. In order to understand these charismatic gifts, a person has to be open and willing to receive them so that they can be used for God's honor and glory.

b. Being judged

Throughout most of my priestly life, I have been judged by mainly those whom I've never met. These people have judged me purely on hearsay. This has caused me a lot of hurt. I believe that many of these people don't even know what I am trying to do. For instance, the people who judge me without ever hearing me speak, reading my books or listening to my tapes are often my most critical judges. These people reject, ridicule and just don't understand who I am when they say these things.

I believe that a person needs to listen to what other people have to say. Even though they may say things that we may not agree with, we still need to give them respect by listening to them. However, this does not mean that we have to agree with them. If they say something that is not true or doing something that is not of God, then we have the duty to explain to them the truth. Sometimes, people will say, "You are judging us." However, we are not judging them per se, rather we are judging an action that is not of God. If we truly love another person, then we will explain and be witnesses to the truth. Then they will know the truth and be inspired to change their lives so as to find the Lord.

c.   Why I taught with firm conviction

I feel people judged me without knowing me and without knowing what I was teaching. Some thought I was teaching too firmly and being too strict in adhering to the teachings of the Catholic Church. Even though I was always outspoken and taught what was in my heart and from a firm conviction about the teachings of the Church, I always taught what was in Scripture, Tradition and the Magisterium. In fact, I have always been faithful to the teachings of the Holy Father, his encyclicals and the documents of Vatican II. Whenever a new document was released, I always read it thoroughly so that I was able to teach and implement what the document said.

In today's society, I have diligently taught the teachings of the Church, especially those of Pope John Paul II. As a result, I have taught against many of the false teachings of our present society. In other words, the many "isms" of our day, which have their roots in Modernism. Yet, the reason why I taught so forcefully was because I was trying to zero in on the true teachings of the Church that are now explained very beautifully in the new *Catechism of the Catholic Church*. I believe that if all the faithful would begin reading the deeply rich material that the Church has to offer, then many of the false teachings of our present society would dissipate. I believe we need the guidance of the Holy Spirit so that we are able to discern what is true and what is false.

I believe that when the Holy Father says that something is not of God, then we should follow his guidance. I think people need to listen to him so that we can respect and accept what he teaches. We also need to practice what he teaches so that we can share his teaching with others. The Pope is the universal teacher, who is guided by the Holy Spirit and is infallible whenever he teaches about faith or morals.

The Holy Father can exercise his infallibility whenever he expresses his teaching in a definitive way. In other words, the Holy Father, who is guided by the Holy Spirit, can make a definitive statement on his own. Indeed, the Holy Father does not need the College of Bishops to reinforce what he is saying so long as he is stating a definitive teaching, makes it known, binding and tells people that if they want to be Catholic, then they need to accept this teaching. However, most dogmas that are proclaimed from an Ecumenical Council come with the input and the agreement of the College of Bishops.

Sometimes people think that he is being dictatorial and is usurping his rights, but he is not. Rather, the Pope is acting within his teaching role that Jesus Christ has given him so that he can explain, proclaim and defend the truth. This is why I have taught the writings of the Holy Father on my Renewal Weeks so that people would be open to the teachings of Jesus Christ. In fact, the people who are open and child-like always accepted the Holy Father's teachings. As a result, I found that these people always believed and were filled with great joy and peace.

5. Gift of Confession

One of the greatest blessings during Renewal Weeks was that many people would flock to Confession. I believe that this Sacrament is a great gift that allows sin to be forgiven and obstacles that we place before God to be resolved. The Sacrament of Confession is the first gift that Jesus gave us after He rose from the dead. I believe that every priest should be willing and ready to make this gift available by hearing Confessions. The priest should also be like Jesus during the Sacrament of Confession.

At times, we have to follow the principals of Jesus and say that we cannot give absolution. We may not deviate or do things that we might think are compassionate, charitable and considerate just to be kind. Rather, we must remain firm in the truth and give the proper guidance prudently. For instance, if a person gets a divorce and marries outside the Church and comes to Confession, then the priest must explain that absolution cannot be given until they stop living with this other person. Likewise, the priest needs to see if there is a possibility of the first marriage to be annulled so that the new marriage can be blessed in the Church. If the marriage cannot be annulled, then the priest needs to encourage the person and the other to live as brother and sister. The priest also needs to explain that absolution is impossible while they are still living together. The priest also needs to instruct them that they are unable to receive Holy Communion while they are in sin.

Another invaluable lesson I learned over the years is the importance of being charitable, which means explaining and living the truth. The reason why this is such an invaluable lesson is because the truth will set a person free. This allows people to live their lives as God wants them to live. Even though truth can be painful at times, I believe that the truth is better than allowing people to live in the state of sin. I believe that a priest also needs to express compassion and sorrow when people are in these painful situations. As a result, the priest should let the penitent know that he will pray for them and try to help them in any way possible so that the situation can be rectified. These have been the concerns that are uppermost in my heart and mind.

a. Hardened sinners

A hardened sinner needs saturating prayer and penance for conversion. This breaks the power of Satan and helps create a desire for mercy, forgiveness and acceptance by God. Many times, people are so wrapped up in self that they are unable to see the value of suffering. They think God is punishing them.

I find it hard to help people, especially when they refuse to hear or accept what another has to say. Most of the time, I can only be silent, listen, pray, do penance and give it all over to God. Later, when the person is not under stress, he or she may be more open and receptive to listen, to change and accept the help needed.

I find it essential to meet people where they are at in their lives. However, a person should never be satisfied to have anyone remain where he or she is at in life. We should help people grow, develop, mature and become the person that God wishes them to be. This help should be given with true Christian charity.

b.   Giving a penance

One day, the Lord told me that I should give the following as a penance: "They should offer the next Mass that they go to in reparation for each of their sins and in thanksgiving for every blessing, grace and gift that God has given them throughout their lives." Ever since that day, I have been faithful to Jesus' request, except for little children who might not understand. Then, I will give them another penance that will make more sense to them. However, when I offer Mass, I will offer the child's prayer of reparation and thanksgiving so that the penance is done the way the Lord requested. Personally, I think this penance is tremendous because proper reparation and thanksgiving is given through the Eucharistic Liturgy.

6.   What I have learned

a.   People have a lot to learn

Even though we live in an age of great technical advances, we still have a lot to learn about the human person. For instance, if we say we are as great as we are, then why is there so much pain, suffering and injustice in the world. I believe that in order to contend with the various happenings in life, such as being judged, ridiculed and misunderstood, a person needs to be God-centered. If a person is God-centered, then all these various persecutions can be a source of great grace. Although these various persecutions may hinder or be an obstacle for God's Will, they will eventually work themselves out. Therefore, I believe that a person who finds himself in this type of situation should be forgiving and pray for these people so that the work of God may continue.

b.   Dealing with others

Many people say that I am gullible and naive because they think I believe everything people say. Personally, I try to believe that people are honest and mean what they say, that what they say is true and what they say comes from their hearts. The reason why I treat people like this is because I always try to be open, sincere, truthful and say it as it really is. However, many times I find that what some people say is not true, and therefore it leaves me open to be hurt and misunderstood. As I have said, I have always given people the benefit of the doubt.

I think that a person should just accept people as they are. Even if a person is dishonest, I think that judging them does no good. Rather, I think a person should pray and forgive the person. I also think that many people do not even realize that they are dishonest. Therefore, the problem is a weakness of his or her own human nature. I believe that if we pray for this person, then they may receive the grace to realize what they are doing so as to change their way of life.

I also feel that we must discern what others say. But, when people are totally off-base, teach errors and say things that are not true, then we should know their errors because they make their beliefs quite evident.

Usually when a person meets someone, that person expects them to be straight-forward. On the other hand, many people "wear a mask." These people may have a number of reasons for being dishonest, but I think this is a sin against human respect. Even though they may not realize this, they are still being dishonest and showing disrespect. Certainly, the person needs to overcome this sin and each of us should try to help him or her remove the mask.

I also believe that we have the duty to teach people what is right and what is wrong so that we do not enter into their sinfulness. In fact, we should be very sad and concerned about people who are not living correctly. If they are living sinful lives, then I believe that we need to make reparation for them so that they will have a change of heart. We can do this in many ways, such as being a witness to the truth, explaining the truth and defending the truth. However, if people are doing good, then we also need to learn from them by being grateful. We can also be inspired by others to live the life of the Lord.

c. When giving advice

I hope that I can always be open to the people of God and be willing to listen to them. Sometimes, I notice that I don't always listen sufficiently or even patiently to the questions or things people ask me. I find this to be one of my greatest weaknesses because many people seemingly preach to me or just ramble on and on. This is quite difficult, especially when a priest has so many things to do and so many people to see. However, I know that I need to be patient so as to accept each person as if they were the only person in the world, thus being more considerate. Still, a person must learn the importance of interrupting or even stopping a meaningless conversation. In other words, I am not obliged to give my time to those who waste it. Otherwise, a person is caught up in something that is nothing more than a gossip session. In such a case, the conversation must cease. I think that I have to learn, though, to be a little more careful about the manner in which I bring such a conversation to an end. I have to learn to be a little more kind and careful in my dealings with people, more considerate of their feelings and try a little harder to be more open in listening to them.

Many times people don't even want a solution. They just want a person to listen to them about their problems and difficulties, even though the things they say may seem trivial to me. This is definitely not the case with the person experiencing problems or difficulties. When encountering other people, we all have to be open and willing to listen. If need be, we can give advice or correct wrong thinking. In helping other people, a person must be firm and loving. At times, we must say things to people that might hurt them, but is good for their soul. This compares to a person who goes to a physician and finds it necessary to have surgery. In other words, we must perform some sort of "spiritual surgery," which seems to hurt the person, but brings about a healing within the soul of the person. We also have to be kind when giving advice so that we can really help people.

When helping others, we are not being charitable by simply being silent or by agreeing with them when something definitely is not from the Lord. When something is not good for their spiritual well-being or their eternal salvation, then we must speak out. If we remain silent, then we become a partner in their evil ways or thoughts. As a result, we will also be held accountable by the sin of omission. We must always proclaim the truth prudently, even if people reject us, because it is our duty. We should pray for such people so that they will see what we have tried to do for them and that we have their good will at heart. We want them to have peace, joy and happiness rather than sufferings, problems or difficulties. We want them to understand that we really do love them. Sometimes by our fraternal correction, we can wake them up and make them look at themselves. Maybe then they will see themselves as they really are. In this way, we might be able to help them to truly come to know the Lord.

d.   Breaking people's confidence

Some people have accused me of breaking their confidence about certain things that they told me in spiritual direction or in a counseling session. I totally reject this accusation because I have never broken anyone's confidence. When people go to spiritual direction, I believe this matter should be treated like the Sacrament of Reconciliation. This seal is very strict and the priest cannot say anything to anyone. This allows a person to tell the priest anything with the confidence of secrecy. The spiritual director is not free to say anything unless he has the permission of the penitent to do so. However, there are times when unusual cases occur, in which a priest might need to consult others so as to give the proper advice in whatever is being asked or confessed. I believe that there has never been a priest who has broken the seal of Confession.

The same is true for counseling. A priest would be very foolish to violate the confidence of a session of counseling. If anything is ever said by a priest from what he knows, then his knowledge must come from other sources and not from counseling, spiritual direction or Confession. However, a priest should be prudent and careful so as to never talk about anything that is ever confided in him.

e. In summary

In summary, there were certain people who only came for the blessing, just like in the time of the Lord. The Lord healed and blessed many people, but some of them never benefited from His teachings. Yet, the Lord longed that people would understand His real message, "Love one another as I have loved you." If people would have understood His message, then they would change their ways and live a life of holiness. However, because many people did not understand Him, He cried when He sat on the walls of Jerusalem and said, "How I would have loved to gather you people to Me as a hen does her chicks under her wings." In fact, even the Apostles did not understand, because Jesus said to them, "I have been with you all this time, and still you do not understand?" Therefore, the Lord had to continually explain to people His teachings, especially by the use of parables.

F. Apparitions

In the last ten to fifteen years, there have been many apparitions in various parts of the world. Many of these apparitionists claim that they are from God. Yet, I believe that many of these alleged apparitions are false. In order to discern these apparitions, the Church deliberately investigates with a very slow and cautious attitude so that a true discernment takes place. The reason why the Church has this attitude is because there are eternal consequences whether something comes from God, the Devil or the person's own imagination. The official who discerns these alleged apparitions, ecstasies or locutions is the local bishop who also makes the final pronouncement about the authenticity of such events.

1. Today's apparitions

In our time, God is intervening in the world more than ever. He does this by Himself, Mother Mary or through one of the saints.

I think this Divine intervention is because of the crisis that the world is in today. The crisis of today is coined by Pope John Paul II, when he says in *Evangelium Vitae*, that the world is following a "culture of death rather than a culture of life." This crisis stems from practical atheism, where people act as if God does not exist and is not needed. Therefore, God intervenes in the world so as to counteract this mentality and attitude.

Because of this lack of belief in God, there are many false prophets that are leading people astray, especially those prophets who teach against the very teachings of Christ Himself. Likewise, Christ fosters and nourishes a culture of life and not a culture of death. Therefore, we need to be careful today because many people have itchy ears and they want to hear what they want to hear. Consequently, they accept all of the things that seem to be not of God and accept these errors hook, line and sinker. Often times, when the people are told that various apparitions are not of God, they rebel and are disobedient by not accepting the guidance of the Church. Likewise, many of the apparitions that are of God seem to be rejected or opposed by many. As a result, they remain hidden for a time until they will be accepted.

a.   God is not a fortune teller

Some people who seek messages use God as a fortune teller. Even though they may not realize this, they are in fact breaking the First Commandment because they are using God to know events about the future. For example, some people try to find out where a dead person is and what is going on with him or her. I believe that a person should never use God in this manner because of the gravity of this sin. When we are trying to live our lives for God, we should never rely on apparitions or visions unless God takes the initiative.

Likewise, if there is an apparition, locution or an enlightenment from God, He will always take the initiative. In other words, when God speaks to a person the mind is illuminated and a person sees, yet does not see; a person hears but does not hear; and a person knows the message and the One who is giving the message. The message is clear, simple and to the point. If a person has an authentic message from God, then the person will remember this message forever.

b. The angel of darkness dressed as an angel of light

The Devil can often disguise himself in many ways, such as appearing as an angel of light, a saint or a particular person. A person needs to be very careful when they receive any vision so that they are able to make the proper discernment of spirits to see if it comes from God, the Devil or the person's own imagination. But, we need to be open to anyone who has God working in his or her life. Each person should be careful not to judge without knowing or seeing the facts so that a true discernment and evaluation may be done. However, as I said earlier, the Church will either officially affirm or reject whether something is of the Lord. For example, during the time of apparition in Lourdes, there were about one hundred other alleged apparitions, yet Lourdes is the only one that stood the test of time and was affirmed by the Church.

c. Being accused of being gullible

In regards to myself, I have been accused of believing in everything and being naive and gullible in accepting these happenings and apparitions. One of the reasons people say this is because I have been on pilgrimages throughout the world, even to places that have not been officially approved by the Church. My philosophy is, "wait and see." The reason is because no person really knows about the authenticity of an apparition and so the only thing to do is, "wait and see." Even though I've been to places that have not been officially approved by the Church, I believe that if there is good virtue in the message, such as fasting, penance and prayer, then these virtues can be practiced. Likewise, these messages that invite a person to fast, do penance and pray are nothing more than the Gospel message. And so, there has been much good coming from various areas in the world where there are alleged claims that the Blessed Mother is appearing or that someone has been receiving messages.

d. Victory 2000

Personally, I do not believe in the gloom and doom prophets, whose messages say that we have to accept, follow and believe what they are saying. Rather, I believe Pope John Paul II, who is more optimistic and positive in his attitude. He says that the year 2000 will be a great time of victory for the Church and a time of the Triumph of the Immaculate Heart of Mary.

The Pope does not speak about the Three Days of Darkness, the Rapture and the end of the world. Rather, he speaks about hope, such as in his book, *Crossing the Threshold of Hope*. John Paul II wants all people to work faithfully and diligently for the future so that the true teachings of Christ can be taught, evangelized and lived. Again, this is what we have been trying to accomplish in the work of the Servants and Handmaids of the Sacred Heart of Jesus, Mary and Joseph.

Fr. Luke getting ready for daily Mass.

CHAPTER 18

1992

A. Being gracious receivers

On June 14th, I saw that each person, who is of God, tends to be a giver. However, each person also needs to learn to be a gracious receiver and be willing to accept the blessings, graces and gifts that God has for each of us or that other people wish to give us. When we recognize all that God has given us, we need to express our joy and gratitude. The reason, of course, is that God loves the cheerful receiver, just like He loves the cheerful giver. For instance, when the Lord healed the ten lepers, only one leper came back and expressed his gratitude. Then Jesus said to him, "Where are the other nine? Were they not healed as well?" The lesson to be learned is a foreigner, who was not even a Jew, came back to express his gratitude. Each person needs to express gratitude for everything God has given in the spiritual life.

1. Realizing who God is

Each person needs to think about who he or she is as well as who God is. When we do that, we will realize the importance of continual acts of surrender as well as how we are totally dependent upon God. We will also feel a more intimate union with God, each angel and saint in Heaven, each soul in Purgatory, each person on earth and the rest of creation.

During our prayers, we should realize who God the Father is because Jesus gave us the awesome prayer of the "Our Father."

The "Our Father" reveals all the various aspects that a prayer should have. This is very important because Jesus, Himself, gave this to us. We should also remember that the prayer says, "*Our* Father" and not "*My* Father." In other words, we are praying not only for ourselves, but for others as well.

2. God's will

God invites each of us to fulfill His plan many times throughout our lives. Even though we are weak through our faults and failings, God always reminds us of His will so that we can live our lives the way He wills. In order to do this, we need to listen to God because He speaks to us in the silence of our hearts. We need to pray so that God can teach us how to pray. As I have said many times, I believe that the Rosary can teach us how to pray because it teaches us to be silent by meditating on the mysteries of our faith. Then, in the silence of our hearts, God will teach us and enlighten our minds to know His Will.

3. The need to die to self

During another time of meditation, I saw the need to die to self in order to really live in God because we are His glory. The fact is we participate in God's Life. And so, we should take up the Cross and follow the Lord. We need to be willing to accept any cross and be thankful because carrying our Cross willingly will sanctify us. Likewise, without God's help, we are totally helpless. We should also realize the need to surrender to God so that we can be sanctified through the Cross. Lastly, we are to glory in the Cross.

4. Dying to self

In dying to self, a person should realize that the joy of dying without sorrow is worth the pain of living without pleasures. In other words, a person should die to self and overcome any sin that keeps a person away from God. Even though this is painful, especially trying to conquer habitual sins, the joy a person receives when living with God is worth all the pain and dying. As a result, a person will have more time to think about God and all the blessings, graces and gifts that He has given. Therefore, dying to self and sinful pleasures allows a person to develop his or her spiritual life and love relationship with the Lord.

5. Jesus' death

When Jesus came into this world, He was naked and Mary wrapped Him in swaddling clothes and laid Him in the manger. When Jesus died and left this world, Mary wrapped Him in the shroud and He was placed in a tomb. As a result of His death, Jesus gave birth to the Church, which is symbolized by the opening of His side with water and blood flowing forth. The water symbolizes Baptism, while the blood symbolizes the Eucharist. Therefore, Jesus' death was the birthpangs of the Church. Just like Eve was taken from the side of Adam, so too the Church came forth from the side of the New Adam, Jesus Christ, when He died on the Cross.

B. Death of Mom

Before my mother died, I had the gracious opportunity to visit with her two weeks prior to her death. Mom was always afraid of death because her biggest fear was going to Purgatory for a long time. During my visit, Mom told me that she knew that she was dying and that she no longer had any fear of dying or going to Purgatory. Rather, Mom knew the people in Heaven were calling her Home and she felt a lot of peace and joy.

Two weeks later, on July 6th, at 11:45 PM, Mom passed away. However, she was officially pronounced dead on July 7th. On the morning of July 7th, I checked my phone messages from the previous night. One of the messages was from my brother Larry who told me that Mom had passed away. When I heard this, I exclaimed, "Thank God, Mom is Home." As I said this, I startled one of the seminarians, Kyle Finken. I think he was a little surprised over my reaction about the death of my mother. But Kyle also knew that I prayed that Mom would die in peace and with members of her family and not in a nursing home. Mom died in Larry and

Ann's house. They took care of Mom for fourteen years and they took care of her in a very wonderful way.

I flew back to Wisconsin for the funeral. On the morning of the funeral, July 10th, I was praying the Rosary with Larry, Ann, Sr. Mary Rose, Andy Pittelkau and Aunt Lolie. During the Rosary, I saw Mom dressed all in white. She was walking from the right, while I saw my Dad dressed in a black tuxedo walking from the left. Then, they met in the center and turned and began to walk towards Heaven. Next, they walked into a cloud that enveloped them and I no longer could see them.

From this experience, I knew that both Mom and Dad are in Heaven. At that moment, I realized that God intended them to be together and that there marriage was blessed in Heaven. Mom and Dad were married fifty-five years and had nine children. Now they are enjoying eternal life with God.

1.　Mom's wisdom

I knew Mom was a very holy person. In fact, many people were very attracted to Mom and asked her for words of wisdom, counseling and prayers. Mom was a very balanced person, she had common sense and was very spiritual. She always spoke about the things of God. I believe that God used Mom as an instrument of His Own love.

2.　One hundred fifty Masses said

After mom's death, I was asked by various people to offer a Mass for her. In the end, I offered over one-hundred fifty Masses for Mom's soul. On December 18th, 1992, I was thinking if these Masses were beneficial for Mom because I knew she was in Heaven. But, the Lord revealed to me that her accidental glory in Heaven increased because of these Masses. This means that her love and knowledge for God increases for all eternity. Next, God let me understand that Mom received more glory for those one hundred fifty Masses than she did from almost all ninty-five years of her life.

C. Resting in the bosom of the Father

On August 23rd, God allowed me to understand that I was resting in the bosom of the Father. At first, I did not understand what this meant. Then I asked myself, "What does it mean to rest in the bosom of the Father?" After some reflection, I believe that "resting in the bosom of the Father" is what each person should strive for in this life so as to be in God and have God in us. In reality, this is what Heaven is and that's why Jesus said, "The Kingdom of God is within you." In other words, Heaven is already within a person. People who are in union with God are in union with all the angels and saints in Heaven, souls in Purgatory and each person on earth because each of us is in God and God is in us. Therefore, every person who is in God is in us. This is a great mystery, but nonetheless, it is true.

Jesus said that at the end of time, when the world will come to an end, He will call each person from the grave. Then He will gather the sheep on the right and the goats on the left. In other words, those who do God's Will and follow Him are the people who are blessed (sheep) and will be taken to Heaven so that they may rest in the bosom of the Father. While those who do not do God's will are the people who are banished from God (goats). These people will never rest in the bosom of the Father and will never have rest for all eternity. These are the people who did their own will and became selfish. They will be in Hell for all eternity.

One day while I was offering Mass, I again pondered the question, "What does being in the bosom of the Father really mean?" Suddenly, I saw a small light, like a meteorite, but it was not coming down to earth, rather, the light came from my heart and went towards the Throne of God. Then I saw the bright light pierce the Heart of God the Father. The light disappeared into Him. Again, I believe this affirmed what I thought before, that is, when any person is in the bosom of the Father he or she is in the Father.

Naturally, when a person is in the Father, he or she is also in Jesus Christ (the Son of God, the God-man) as well as the Holy Spirit because there is only one God in Three Persons. This is the great Mystery of the Trinity, but this is also the beauty of the Trinity. To be in the bosom of the Father is a great blessing. If a person is in God, then the person is in each Divine Person of the Blessed Trinity.

1. Being in union with each person

While meditating on the prayer of Jesus at the Last Supper, "That all may be one," I was given the grace to be in union with each person throughout the whole world. Even though this seems to be impossible, this is what actually happened. This allowed me to realize and understand the unity that Jesus experienced while He was in the Garden of Gethsemane praying for each person from Adam and Eve until the end of time. When Jesus was in the Garden of Gethsemane, each person was present in His mind simultaneously. During this time, Jesus saw the state of each person, those who believed, those who did not believe, those who were doubtful or confused, those who were lukewarm or indifferent, and those who were weak and living in sin. Jesus also saw those who were striving for holiness, doing their best to be faithful and those who were in grace. As a result, Jesus saw each person as he or she is and offered His life, prayers and suffering for each one individually. That is why He shed His blood in the Garden of Gethsemane. He was in agony because of His tremendous love which flowed from the Love of His Heart.

2. God's love for us

Each person needs to realize that God loved us so much that He was willing to suffer and die for each of us. All of the events which happened to Jesus when praying in the Garden of Gethsemane are contained in the prayer for unity. In fact, Jesus wants this unity more than we do. Anytime we are in the state of grace, we are in union with God and are carrying out the prayer of unity, "That all may be one." In order to do this, we need an outpouring of the Holy Spirit.

3. Spousal relationship with the Holy Spirit

I believe that each person is called to have an intimate spousal relationship with the Holy Spirit. This is an awesome hidden truth that many people do not realize. However, when a person realizes that the Holy Spirit is our spouse, that He gives us the gifts that Jesus won for us on the Cross and that He gives these gifts because it is the Will of the Heavenly Father, this tremendously beautiful truth will inspire and encourage each of us to live a life of holiness. As a result, each person will be filled with a deep joy and peace.

a.   Holy Spirit is the source of unity

The Holy Sprit is the source of unity because He is the love between the Father and the Son. In the Trinity, then, Love brings forth unity. Like the Trinity, each person should love so as to bring about unity. When we are in God, that unity is everlasting. The only thing that could ever break this unity is when a person no longer loves and lives a life of sin and not a life of holiness. However, if a person keeps the Commandments, lives the Beatitudes, dies to self and strives for holiness, then the person will never lose that unity with God, the Heavenly Court, the souls in Purgatory and the people on earth.

D. Blessing people with the Cross

As I have already explained, the Relic of the True Cross has pieces of the True Cross, the veil of the Blessed Mother, the bed of St. Joseph, the habit of St. Anthony of Padua and the habit of the Little Flower. Later, I put some hair of Padre Pio inside the Cross as well as some oil that exuded from a Eucharistic miracle. On September 20th, the Lord told me that He wanted me to use a different prayer. So, God dictated the prayer that He wanted me to pray:

"I seal you with the Sign of the Cross and the Precious Blood, in the Name of the Father, and of the Son, and of the Holy Spirit. May God protect you through the Sign of the Cross and the Precious Blood from all dangers and evils. May the blessing of God the Father, Son, and Holy Spirit come upon you and remain with you forever. Amen."

E. Giving a retreat to the Discalced Carmelites

On October 11th, I gave a retreat to the Discalced Carmelite nuns in Ada Carmel, Michigan. When I entered their chapel, I noticed a statue of the Little Flower. The statue showed St. Therese holding a cross covered with a bouquet of roses. However, this statue, unlike the others, was a little different because there was an angel holding a basket of picked roses while the other angels were looking up at her with expressions of joy.

When I saw this statue, I again was inspired to read St. Therese's autobiography, *The Story of a Soul*. St. Therese suffered tremendously throughout her life, but she carried the cross with surrender, love and joy. Through her cross, she received many graces that helped her sanctify her life. When she died, she said, "I will shower roses upon all." Since her death, she has showered roses on many people, especially for the conversion of sinners. St. Therese truly is a model for Christian living and anyone can do what she did as long as they can surrender everything with love.

In the Little Flower's book, she speaks about her "little way," which is loving God with her whole heart, mind and soul. Again, her "little way" is just doing the ordinary things with love and in doing so, she received great strength. Even though she did not seem to have a lot of experiences during her life, her "little way" is nothing other than extraordinary.

1. *The Story of a Soul* **inspired the development of the charism and spirituality**

As I was reading *The Story of a Soul*, I began to understand that St. Therese played a great part in the development of the charism and spirituality of the Servants and Handmaids of the Sacred Heart of Jesus, Mary and Joseph. Her "little way" is love, which brings about unity. However, I believe that we have taken this "little way" a step beyond, through our expression to live a life of holiness.

At Baptism, a person is brought into an intimate unitive relationship with the Blessed Trinity. Our union is a spousal union in and through the Mystical Body of Christ. By the grace of God, each person posseses God and partakes of His Divine nature. Jesus Christ is true God and true man. He also is a Divine Person. Therefore, our spousal relationship extends to the Father and the Holy Spirit. The Holy Spirit, who is our Sanctifier, transforms us like Jesus and thus like unto the Father and Himself.

The Little Flower's "little way" was offering everything in love to the Father with Jesus. However, the difference between her "little way" and "our way" is that we unite everything with Jesus, in each Eucharistic Liturgy celebrated through all time until the end of the world. Even though I have never read that St. Therese expressed this in words, perhaps she expressed this way in her heart and prayers.

2. Interdependence

While I was offering Mass, the expression, "our union in God with one and all in the Communion of Saints" made me realize that each person is interdependent upon another. Our prayers also interpenetrate each other. We offer everything to the Father, through Jesus, in the Holy Spirit and in union with each Eucharistic Liturgy, as a continuous offering to the Father until the end of time.

In praying this way, a person will mature in confidence and trust, which makes the person's faith and love in God increase profoundly. Then a person will realize that he or she is able to ask the Father anything in the Name of Jesus and it will be granted.

F. Divine Friendship vs. human friendship (i.e. Friendship in God)

On October 25th, God allowed me to understand that there is a great difference between a human friendship without God and a human friendship that is of and in God. A mere human friendship is usually conditional, limited, shallow, fickle, empty and temporary. A human friendship based in God is uplifting, brings peace, joy, happiness and is everlasting. God will always be there for us because He loves us and is a true Friend. He helps anyone who lives a god-like life. Therefore, I believe that a person should not get too bogged down in earthly and worldly friendships because these friendships have the potential of leading us away from God. In fact, often times human friendships lead us away from God and into a life of sin, especially if a person does not have a deep love relationship with the Lord.

G. Evils of sin

On November 1st, God allowed me to see the evils of sin. When St. Bernadette was living, she said that a sinner is a person who loves evil. God let me understand more fully that a sinner is a person who does not love God, neighbor and self. That is why St. Augustine could say, "Love and do what you wish." Likewise, when a person sins, he or she usually thinks they are doing what is good for self at that moment. A person also does not think about God or the consequences when he or she sins. I think this is why Jesus said on the Cross, "Father, forgive them, for they know not what they do."

The effects of sin are tremendous. Adam and Eve's sin affected every person in the world, even until the end of time. Each person is born with Original Sin. In Scripture, we read that, "The sins of the parents are visited upon their children to the third and fourth generation." Even though children are not responsible for their parents' sins, the consequences of the sins of the parents are brought into the lives of their children, which affects each child and person in the whole world. On the other hand, the good a person does affects the whole world and is always greater than evil. The problem is that we always hear about the evil in the world, but we don't always hear about the good in the world.

1. Temptations from the body, world and Satan

In regards to temptations, the Lord let me understand that temptations come from the body, the world and Satan. As a result, Satan will have an effect upon a person to the degree of a person's union with God. If a person is weak, then the person is more susceptible to fall into sin more easily and quickly. However, if a person has a deep union with God, then the person will not sin. Likewise, God will help the person overcome his or her temptations. Also, when a person lives the life of God, temptations become very repugnant and the person is always ready and able, by the grace of God, to overcome these temptations no matter what they may be.

Temptations are not sinful. Rather, temptations can be a time when a person can show his or her love for God. Temptations are also a time to grow in holiness by overcoming temptation. When a person overcomes temptations, the person becomes stronger in living his or her spiritual life and overcoming the evil works of Satan. God gives each person the power to overcome Satan, which allows us to live holier lives. Essentially, each person is able to become a co-redeemer with Christ when he or she leads a life of holiness.

2. Death of Jesus

The death of Jesus on the Cross won Salvation for each person. Jesus won all the graces and blessings when He died on the Cross for the sanctification of all humankind. In other words, if we cooperate with Jesus and do the things that God wills, then we will become like Jesus and will live a holy way of life. *Each person is called to be Jesus for and to others.* Each person is also called to be a saint. A saint is a tremendous gift for the world and impacts the whole world until the end of time. Yet, by ourselves, we cannot become saints. Rather, we have to surrender to God in order to let Him help us to become saints.

3. Solidarity of good

The solidarity of good is greater than evil. John Paul II said, in speaking about our times, "the solidarity of evil seems to be greater than the solidarity for good." Yet, if a person realizes that Heaven and earth are united as one, as we pray in the way of the Mystical Mass Prayer and the Mystical Rosary, then the solidarity of good is greater than evil. In reality, it will be greater than any evil and all evil put together. For example, when a person repents from a life of sin, the penitent's action reveals that God draws good from evil. God blesses those in abundance when they do good and avoid evil. So, our intent should be one of striving to overcome sin in our life by doing good.

H. Mary's heart being pierced

On November 8th, God let me understand that our Heavenly Mother's heart was pierced with a sword of sorrow as she stood beneath the Cross so that we could pass through her heart into the heart of Jesus. The heart of Jesus, after He died on the Cross, was opened by a lance by a centurion's sword so that each person could enter His heart. We are also able to drink from this fountain of His love.

On November 15th, I saw Jesus on the Cross and He raised me up to drink the Love from His open side. This may seem strange, but later I read that some of the saints experienced the same thing. So, this experience is not something too unusual.

I. Mark Miravalle

On November 22nd, I spoke to Mark Miravalle, STD., professor at the Franciscan University of Steubenville, about the work of the Apostolate of Christian Renewal as well as the Servants and Handmaids. He said that the charism and spirituality are an expression of the Doctrine of the Mystical Body of Christ and the Communion of Saints. Dr. Miravalle believes that we are combining these two Doctrines and that the unity we express is the charism that Jesus prayed for at the Last Supper. In other words, Dr. Miravalle believes that there is nothing theologically incorrect when it comes to our approach in carrying out the charism, spirituality and purpose.

Dr. Miravalle believes that the Heavenly Father is able to assign the Blessed Mother, St. Joseph, each angel and saint in Heaven and soul in Purgatory to be agents in the work that we are doing. He also said that because God assigned them to me, they are able to work with, in and through me. In addition, I believe that they are also able to work with, in and through the Servants and Handmaids. For example, as a father in the world is able to assign certain tasks for his children, so too the Heavenly Father can do the same from Heaven. I think that every person should be grateful that God has allowed us to develop this charism and spirituality. However, we are only instruments, and as instruments, God is able to work through us. This is an important point that must never be forgotten.

That's why the booklet, *A Way of Life: Be a Saint* is so very important. The booklet teaches more than a way of life. In this booklet, we call people to become lay Servants and Handmaids of the Sacred Heart of Jesus, Mary and Joseph. In living this charism and spirituality, they will be called to live lives of holiness so as to really and truly become saints.

J. Entering the mission of Christ

St. Paul tells us that we are able to make up in our bodies what is lacking in the sufferings of Jesus Christ. By this he means that each person is called to enter into the mission of Christ, which is to overcome sin and establish truth in the world. In other words, preach Jesus to all nations because Jesus is the Way, the Truth and the Life.

In entering this mission, a person realizes that he or she walks with God as an individual. However, a person also walks with God and others. We belong to the human race, we are social beings and we need others to become holy and saints. Upon entering into the mission of Christ, we become co-redeemers with Christ in helping others to come to Him, to know Him and become like Him.

K. Power of the sign of the Cross

On December 27th, God gave me the grace to understand the power of the blessing when we give the blessing of the Sign of the Cross. When we make the sign of the Cross, we express our belief in the Blessed Trinity. At the time of the blessing, many great blessings, graces and gifts are given to us. The blessing also gives us God's Power, God's Love and God's Mercy. If people understood the Sign of the Cross, they would make the Sign of the Cross more often. They would also wait to the end of Mass to receive the blessing that is given through the Sign of the Cross from the Blessed Trinity. For those who do not remain, they do not receive the blessing of God, which is essential to live our lives today.

Fr. Luke working on his letters. He prided himself on answering each one.

CHAPTER 19

1993

A. *Incarnation*

On January 17th, God allowed me to understand that everything that is created is created through the Second Person of the Blessed Trinity. This means that the Second Person of the Blessed Trinity also created His own mother and His own human nature. The Second Person of the Blessed Trinity assumed a human nature from Mary as she remained a virgin and became a mother. This happens according to the Will of the Father and by the power of the Holy Spirit.

In the Mystery of the Incarnation, the Divine and human nature are united in His person and His person is Divine. Because Jesus is a Divine person, all this is offered with Him to the Father in the Spirit and becomes infinite in value, redemptive and meritorious.

A person must always realize that Jesus has a Divine nature and is a Divine Person. So, as God, Jesus cannot change, cannot be added to and he cannot be subtracted from. Jesus always remains God, who is always equal to the Father and the Holy Spirit because They are One.

However, as man, Jesus' human nature is in union with God and there is a potential of changing and growing in God's likeness. Therefore, Jesus' human nature, being in constant contact with the Divine Person, is always becoming more holy (Divine).

In our lives, we too can become holy in our nature and in our personhood insofar as we have contact with the Divine. Just as Jesus did in his human nature, we too grow more like God. Because we are human, our growth is much more limited. In other words, we can never become as holy as Jesus.

The only obstacle that can limit or prevent God's Will from being done is a person's free will. And so, any time we refuse a blessing, grace or gift by living a life of sin, a person's relationship with God is either broken or wounded. As a result, sin will hinder the growth of holiness and sanctity.

B. Throne of the Father

On January 31st, I had an intellectual vision, where I was taken to the Throne of the Father. As I knelt before Him, the Father placed a scepter on my head and then He placed it on my right shoulder. After that, He embraced me and drew me to Himself. He finally touched my lips with His fingers as though He was anointing them. I believe that this means what I teach will come from Him, through the Holy Spirit so that it will touch the minds and hearts of people.

I asked the Father for the gift that whenever I come into the presence of people, they will see Jesus in me. Next, I asked Him to move the people to look into their spiritual lives so that they may see where they are in their relationship to God, where they need to change and how they need to grow in holiness. I also asked Him that when I give the blessing with the relic of the True Cross that people would have an experience of looking into their hearts and receive many blessings, graces and gifts so as to help them transform their lives and grow more fully into being like Jesus.

C. Unconditional Love is the Holy Spirit

On February 7, I was praying for the unconditional love of the Blessed Trinity as it is reflected in the Holy Family. God allowed me to understand that unconditional love is the Holy Spirit. He is the love that exists between the Father and the Son. This love brings unity in the community and the family life of the Blessed Trinity. When the Holy Spirit possesses us, we truly love with the love of God. The Holy Spirit is in us and we are in Him. He works in us, through us and brings others to know and love God. This love is the work of the Holy Spirit, which is continual even though we might not be aware of it. The Holy Spirit brings about unity within a person, family and community.

D. Bi-Location

At various times, people say that they had an experience of me either giving them a blessing and/or spiritual direction. Sometimes, this experience happens to them in a dream, in prayer or just going about their business throughout the day. When this happens, sometimes I am aware and sometimes I am unaware of my going to them or their experiencing these different things. Sometimes, I even receive letters telling me of healings that have taken place in the same way, either through their dreams when I bless them or while they are aware of what is transpiring. In any case, I am always amazed when people tell me, write to me or call about these experiences. I am amazed because I have only prayed for them.

E. Dignity of women

On March 7th, God let me understand the true role of women. He showed me that those who act like Eve, have an evil influence on men, while those who act like Our Blessed Mother, have a good influence on men, the Church, the world and the families. So, women have a tremendous role and vocation to carry out God's plan to help men, to be a companion to men and to be helpful in inspiring people to become even more holy. Likewise, Mary never enticed anyone to sin. She is the perfect model for women because she is humble, pure, generous, charitable, unconditionally loving and a leader. Mary also encourages everyone to fulfill his or her role in life.

F. Hiddenness

On April 4th, I realized that God acts through His hiddenness and silence. He does this through the use of His attributes by manifesting Himself clearly so that His divinity shines through those who remain hidden. For example, all of creation reveals His splendor, even when a person sins and repents, God reveals His splendor by being merciful. We also see God's splendor in redemption as He gives each person blessings, graces and gifts so as to live a life of holiness. In this holiness, God reveals His hiddenness to those whom He wishes. In fact, if a person lives a life of God, then he or she will see God's power, existence and awesomeness.

When a person truly lives by faith, the person will know that Jesus Christ is Lord, Savior, brother and friend. The person will also realize that Jesus is present in the Eucharist. A person can meditate on the hidden life of our Lord as He lived in this world, as well as on Mary, who seldom spoke and on St. Joseph, who never spoke (in the recordings of Scripture). However, through their hidden life, each of these people are the perfect model because God acts through their hiddenness and silence. So, hiddenness and silence are great mysteries to be lived. I believe that when a person is silent, he or she can learn many things, especially wisdom. Then, when that person speaks, he or she will speak with wisdom and will bring forth much fruit. An important point to remember, although each person has the tendency to explain who he or she is, as well as what he or she has experienced in life, is that God acts through a person's hiddenness.

1.   God's gift of humility and wisdom

Each person should use God's gifts with humility, which means living truthfully. Likewise humility does not mean that a person cannot speak out; rather humility demands that a person should speak the truth so that God can manifest His Will. Thus, the person will not be susceptible to doing his or her own will. If the person does God's Will, then the person will reveal God's honor and glory.

In order to really learn humility, a person needs to learn prudence. In other words, a person needs to learn when to speak and when to be silent, when to act and when not to act, and when to suffer and when not to suffer.

G. Pilgrimage

In April, I went on a pilgrimage to Italy. While we were in Loreto, Italy on April 13th, I celebrated Mass at "the Holy House," which is the home of the Holy Family in Nazareth. After Mass, some people explained to me that they saw my hands bleeding while I was offering Mass.

The next day, April 14th, we visited Padre Pio's home in San Giovanni Rotondo, Italy. While we were there, I celebrated Mass in Padre Pio's chapel. During this Mass, I felt the presence of Our Lady and two angels standing behind me. After Mass, I spent some time praying in the chapel, while the others explored the monastery. These were some great moments for me because God gave me many great graces as well as His blessing.

On our way to Rome the next day, while driving through Sorrento, we saw the sun spinning and changing colors. There was a red heart that appeared in the sky. The red heart came within one hundred feet of the bus. The heart then stopped and stayed with us for awhile. Even though I don't know what this really means, I believe that it might signify the Sacred Heart of Jesus, Mary and Joseph. Those on the bus who witnessed this event undoubtedly experienced an increase of faith. I never expected anything like this to happen. It was just one of those miraculous occasions. Why God does these things, only He knows.

Later, one of the buses broke down. While we were waiting for the replacement bus, one of the ladies came to me and told me that she saw the Blessed Trinity within me in a very profound way. She also said that the Blessed Mother is watching over me and that the Holy Spirit comes through me and touches people's hearts. Interestingly, she said that when I look at people, my eyes penetrate into their very souls. As a result, these people become more aware of their lives, examine their consciences and are moved to go to Confession. Even though I am very careful about what people say to me in regards to things like this, I think this insight affirms the gift that God has given me so that when people see me they see Jesus in me.

Again, we need to be open to anything God wishes to do with us and we should accept these gifts and be grateful for them. Although I am often overwhelmed by God gifts, I try not to make a big deal out of them when miraculous events occur. Rather, I just try to go on with my daily life and live my life for the Lord.

1. Way of the Cross

On May 12th, while in Fatima, I was praying the Stations of the Cross. I came to the tenth station where Jesus is nailed to the Cross. The thoughts came to me that Jesus' left hand was nailed to the Cross first, then His right arm had to be pulled to the place where the soldiers were able to nail His hand to the cross because the cross beam was too long. More than likely, the soldiers pulled His shoulder out of His joint. Next, the left foot was placed over the right and nailed.

When Jesus was dying, He had to pull Himself up to get air, then He had to let himself down. As a result, He would get cramps. Next, He would have to pull himself up again. Jesus did this for a continuous three hours. In moving this way, His left arm and hand were used more than His right arm and hand because He was compensating for His right shoulder being dislocated. His right foot was used more than the left because He had to put more pressure on that foot so that the pain in His shoulder would not increase too much. This is the reason why any person who has the stigmata has more pain in the right foot than the left and more pain in the left hand then the right.

H. Ascension Thursday

On Ascension Thursday, I had a vision of Our Blessed Mother while I was praying the Rosary. (Whenever I say "appeared to me, I'm talking about an intellectual vision. I see, but I do not see. I hear, but I do not hear. An intellectual vision is an enlightenment of the intellect. I know who is there and I know the message the person wants to give.) Mary was wearing blue and she gave me the Servant's blue habit. I said to her, "The Servants are not even founded yet." Mary just similed at me. I also knew that it is up to Jesus, Mary and Joseph to bring the Servants into existence. I knew then that I had to turn everything over to Jesus, Mary and Joseph and place it all in Their Heart.

During this vision, Mary came holding the Rosary and the scapular and said, "We should propagate these two devotions." Then I remembered what St. Dominic said, "Someday, the world will be saved through the Rosary and the scapular."

I. Apparition in Santa Maria, California

On May 30th, I attended an alleged apparition of Our Blessed Mother in Santa Maria, California. As we were praying the Rosary, I received the following message: *"Anyone who has problems or temptations against purity should invoke Our Blessed Mother Mary as the Immaculate Conception in honor of her Virgin Motherhood, and the person will overcome the problems or temptations."* Then, God told me that I should preach this on my Renewal Weeks, which I did on many occasions. Often times, people would thank me after I preached this invocation because they told me the message helped them tremendously in keeping pure and conquering temptations.

J. Visionary in Fillmore

On June 26th, this visionary from Santa Maria came to visit us in Fillmore. During her apparition, she invited a little boy named Jesse White to kneel beside her. When he was kneeling, the visionary, guided by the Blessed Mother, did various things. While Jesse was kneeling beside her, he too was able to see the Blessed Mother.

Jesse then described the Blessed Mother in detail. After the visionary came out of ecstasy, the visionary told us that the Blessed Mother was wearing a white veil, a white dress with a blue sash, had bare feet, was standing on a cloud, had gray-blue eyes, chestnut-brown hair, rosy cheeks, and was very happy and joyful. Miraculously, Jesse explained the same description as the visionary. There is one little twist to this miraculous event, Jesse White is blind.

The reason why I give this testimony is because most people do not see anything while this visionary is in ecstasy. Everything has to be accepted in faith. Yet, the various events that do happen, such as conversions that take place or blessings that are given, are so pronounced, a person cannot but believe these things are truly occurring.

K. The Mansions vs. the Beatitudes

I realized from all my studies that the spiritual life is developed insofar as a person practices the Beatitudes. Each stage of the Beatitudes parallels the Seven Mansions explained by St. Teresa of Avila.

One of the Beatitudes will be more or less pronounced in a person's life as he or she develops a spiritual walk or journey with the Lord. For example, in the Seventh Beatitude, "Blessed are the Peacemakers," a person who lives this will experience the Mystical Marriage. In this Beatitude, a person realizes that peace comes from God and not from self. The Peace of God is given as a gift, which is totally mystical and within the contemplative state. This gift of peace is not the peace as the world thinks of peace, not love as the world thinks of love, and not holiness as the world thinks of holiness. Rather, this gift of peace is God Himself. Even though every person is called to receive this gift, few receive it because of the lack of generosity.

The people who do not reach the mystical state have only themselves to blame. Even though they may have a number of excuses, such as fear of suffering, trials and tribulations or even perhaps they have become indifferent or lukewarm and have become enmeshed in the world rather than in spiritual living, they still only have themselves to blame. As I always say, God is never outdone in generosity.

L. Feast of St. John Vianney

On the Feast of St. John Vianney, August 4, the Lord took me to Himself in a state of absorption prayer while I was praying the Rosary. During the first mystery, Jesus came and stood before me. He placed His hands on my head and prayed a blessing prayer. After that, Jesus blessed my lips for a long time. Taking a flask of oil, He then poured it over my head. Next, Jesus gave me new garments that He put over my other clothes. Then, He gave me a ring and stood beside me and placed His arm around me while God the Father confirmed all that was done. Next, God the Father blessed me. After that, Jesus stood behind me with His arms folded over my chest and said, "I give you a golden heart so your love will be as gold. I give you a gift that when you preach, your words will be as gold."

Even though I heard, "I give you a golden heart," I have no idea what this means because I have never heard of such a thing. However, on various occasions after that I saw "the golden heart" in various places. First, I saw "the golden heart" in Beauraing, Belgium, where people were to consecrate themselves to the Immaculate Heart of Mary. Second, I saw "the golden heart" in France, in the Montmartre district of Paris, where the golden heart of Jesus is in a beautiful fresco above the altar in the Sacred Coeur Basilica.

Since this experience, some people said that when a person has a golden heart, he or she has a pure heart. This means that the person is filled with the love of God, single-minded and without guile. One person even bought me a little gold heart and a little gold rose which I have placed on my Rosary so as to remind me of the occasion when I was given a golden heart.

I still do not understand completely what receiving a golden heart signifies, such as my vision, but I am always open and ready to learn more. Maybe someone else knows more about the significance of a golden heart and will be inspired to enlighten the Apostolate regarding its true meaning.

1. Golden heart card

I received a card from Sr. Loretta Jacobs called "The Golden Heart of Our Mother of Perpetual Help." In this card, the Redemptorists community states, "The Golden Heart symbolizes the heart of Our Mother of Perpetual Help, the Mother of God. The heart of Mary represents the profound love of a Mother for her Child, Christ. It also denotes the deep abiding love for all her spiritual children given to her beneath the Cross, when Christ said, 'Woman, Behold Thy Son.' Within this heart, all children of Mary become as one, and mankind is immersed in the saving graces of Christ. Each person enrolled in the Golden Heart is joined through Mary with Christ, the source of eternal life."

M. Feast of St. Clare

On the feast of St. Clare, August 11th, God allowed me to understand that when a person is purified and sanctified, he or she becomes a new creation. He revealed to me that the Holy Spirit transforms the person to become like Jesus Christ and restores the person's innocence as it was before the fall of Adam and Eve. This innocence includes holiness, single-mindedness, purity and love.

The Lord also revealed that if a person has lost the virtue of virginity, then spiritually the person's virginity can be restored when he or she is purified and sanctified. Even though I really do not understand how or why God does this, but in faith I believe this to be true. This also helped me realize more fully that without God, a person can do absolutely nothing.

The Holy Spirit must bring about a change within a person. God has to work within the person's limitations, weaknesses and sinfulness. The Holy Spirit patiently waits for a person to open up to Him, to let Him bring the person to holiness and to be transformed to be like Jesus. We too must realize that we have to be patient with ourselves and others. Therefore, we need to pray, do penance and ask God to transform and sanctify us. Also, we need to accept ourselves and others so as to cooperate with the Holy Spirit in bringing about this transformation.

1. A week after this experience

For a whole week after this experience, I reflected upon the state of my life and soul. On September 5th, I realized that there were many times that I did not cooperate with the blessings, graces and gifts that God has given me so as to bring about the full effects of His will. However, I asked God to grant me the gift to completely make up for the lack of responding correctly so that all would be rectified as if I had cooperated to accomplish His Will through me. I also asked God to let me walk in the light and not darkness so as to be a true light to the whole world.

I think that each of us can do this, especially to receive the place in Heaven that God wishes us to have when we die. I think that doing God's Will is the most important aspect in our lives, even though we may have not done what He wills all the time.

N. Angels

On October 10th, I realized that the angels in Heaven neither sinned nor suffered. Rather, the angels in Heaven are pure, holy and powerful in carrying out the Will of God. Each angel lives and does everything for God's honor and glory. As messengers, angels help us in our battle against the world, the flesh and the Devil. Each angel is ready to help us reach eternal life, especially our Guardian Angel, who has uniquely helped us from the time of our conception.

From the results of this meditation, I became more aware of being in true union with each angel and saint in Heaven, each person in Purgatory and each person throughout the world. The prayers that I offer to God are for each person. These prayers are offered with each person who is in union with Christ, for those who do not pray and for those who are in need of reconciliation. In other words, no person is ever left out, no matter where they are in the sight of God.

On October 17th, I realized that to be united with every person in Christ is an awesome realization of the great mystery of the Communion of Saints. Each person should realize that every person lives within us and is praying with us and for our intentions. Naturally, this should help us to realize that we are all brothers and sisters in Christ.

On October 31st, I also realized that each person is a great mystery. Even though we do not know the thoughts or hidden life of others, God knows and He will judge each person accordingly. And so, we should never judge anyone. Like Jesus said, "Let the person without sin cast the first stone."

O. A young man living in Fillmore

In the late fall of 1993, a young man came to live in Fillmore so that he could learn more fully the charism, spirituality and purpose of the Servants of the Sacred Heart of Jesus, Mary and Joseph. One of the reasons why he wanted to live in Fillmore was that he felt that God was calling him to found the Servants. Even though I allowed him to do what he felt was God's calling, I believed in my heart that he was not the man to begin the founding process. However, because God works in mysterious ways, I surrendered to God's Will. And so, if this young man was the person to begin the community, then so be it. Likewise, if there is someone else to begin the Servants, then that should be honored as well.

As for me, I believe that one day the Servants and Handmaids will exist working together, side by side. I think that in order for this to happen, there need to be priests who can lead, give guidance and administer spiritual direction so that the charism, spirituality and purpose can be spread far and wide.

P. Masses for Mom and Dad

On November 7th, I was asked by my brother Larry to offer fifty Masses for my Mom and Dad. Larry also asked me to include the whole Zimmer family and relatives. While I was offering these Masses, God enlightened me to include my extended family and their families. Later, God let me understand that we can include every person in the Family of God because Jesus was crucified for everyone. He offered His sacrifice for each person in the Family of God individually. Therefore, each Mass is offered for every person until the end of time.

This enlightenment is a great grace and blessing so as to be aware that each person is being blessed at each Mass that is offered. This is a great insight and should be in kept in mind when we celebrate the Eucharistic Liturgy.

Q. Commit our lives to becoming like Jesus

On November 21st, I was meditating on Jesus Christ. I realized that each person should commit his or her life to becoming like Jesus. Through the offering of Jesus, each person is called to share in the life of the Blessed Trinity. When a person is in the state of grace, the person also participates in each attribute of God. This process begins at Baptism. Through Baptism, we are brought into a relationship with each Person of the Blessed Trinity and we become members of the Mystical Body of Christ. We as individuals, then, are the Church, which is sacramental and hierarchical. As the person lives his or her life in union with God, the person grows in His likeness more and more.

As Church, each individual needs to be guided and taught by the Magisterium because no one is able to interpret Scripture and

Tradition by oneself. The Holy Father is the visible source of unity in the Church. Being in union with him, we are in union with Jesus Christ, the Invisible Head of the Church. Thus we, in Jesus Christ, are in union with God, each angel and saint in Heaven, each soul in Purgatory and each person on earth.

Even though we are individuals, we are still interdependent so that all is done in union with God, which becomes meritorious, redemptive and infinite in value. This is true because we offer all with Jesus in each Eucharistic liturgy until the end of time. As a result, we will all be one for all eternity. Because of God's grace, I am personally aware of representing each person in my prayer life, which is an awesome experience.

R. A person with a prophecy

There is a person I know who receives authentic locutions. Her spiritual director told her to come to me and give me a message. So, she came to tell me this message on November 27th. She told me that Cardinal Mahony would come to believe in us after a miracle would happen. She said she saw me hold a Church in the palm of my hand and that the Church was gold. She saw many future priests dressed in blue habits. She also saw two officials of the Church who came from Rome to confirm all that we are. They stated that the Servants and Handmaids of the Sacred Heart of Jesus, Mary and Joseph are definitely from God. However, she did not know who these people are or when they would come. In the meantime, all is to be placed in the protection of Our Blessed Mother who will bring everything about as God wills. She pointed out that these priests dressed in blue are to be "preachers of the truth" to all peoples.

She also pointed out that in the future, Our Blessed Mother will come to those who are more mature in the faith. Whereas before, she came to those who did not know the faith or who were weak in the faith. She then said that the people need prophets who speak the truth in a prudent and forceful manner so as to call all people to live a life of holiness.

S. Consecration to the Immaculate Heart of Mary

On December 25th, I was praying for people to make a consecration to the Immaculate Heart of Mary for the conversion of Russia and peace throughout the world. This consecration is the request of Our Lady of Fatima. And so, I was hoping that millions of people would respond, but the Lord said that the quantity of people who make the consecration is irrelevant. Rather, the quality of people who make the consecration is relevant and is most important. In other words, if millions or billions of people make this consecration and live it in a minimal way, then the effects would also be minimal. However, if only a few people would make this commitment and live it to the full, then many blessings, graces and gifts would be given. I thought about the passage in Scripture where Gideon was asked to send away soldiers who were not fully committed. He sent many of them home until he was left with only three hundred soldiers to fight in the battle. The Lord allowed this to happen so as to show Gideon and us that it does not take too many people to win over evil, Satan and the world. This story reveals that God is the One who creates, redeems and sanctifies and not the people, who create, redeem or sanctify. So, if we give ourselves totally and completely to God, then He will give us what we need so as to be His honor and glory.

CHAPTER 20

1994

A. Gift of knowledge

On January 9th, 1994, God allowed me to understand that the gift of knowledge operates and helps bring a person through the Dark Night of the Senses, while the gift of understanding operates and brings a person through the Dark Night of the Soul. However, all the gifts of the Holy Spirit are operating when a person sincerely seeks a life of holiness. Likewise, a person must always proceed with prudent and ardent zeal so that a flame of love and desire spurs a person to be open to the working of the Holy Spirit. This will transform us and make us more like God.

B. Offering all of creation

On January 30th, a very close friend of mine, Andrew Pittelkau, and I were talking. He told me that he was praying for the safe birth of his soon to be god-child, who was expected to be born sometime in September, 1994. As I was thinking about this, I realized that we can offer all of God's creation with each angel and saint in Heaven, each person is Purgatory and all the people on earth, from the moment of their conception and embracing the totality of their entire existence. We can offer all this to the Father, with Jesus and in the Holy Spirit, in union with each Mass until the end of time. I believe this is an awesome spiritual reality. This also gave me a closer spiritual bond with each person who exists and will exist until the end of time.

I also realized that while I was praying the Rosary, the Communion of Saints in Heaven and the souls in Purgatory are praying with me in all the mysteries that are offered to the Triune God. When we realize this, the Rosary becomes more meaningful than ever.

C. Incident between a young man and the Cardinal

One day in February, 1994, Cardinal Roger Mahony came to St. Francis of Assisi Parish in Fillmore. A young man who was discerning to start the Servants decided to attend the service. After the service, the Cardinal asked the young man what he was doing. The young man explained to the Cardinal that he was living with me in Fillmore. Evidently, there was nothing else said.

1. Telephone call from Father Provincial

On March 13th, I received a telephone call from Father Provincial. He told me that Cardinal Mahony had written him a letter asking him to remove me from the diocese. The reason the Cardinal wanted me removed was because he said that I had too much influence on the seminarians and other young men who already had become priests. The Cardinal thought that I was disobedient in trying to establish the Servants community. Therefore, he wanted me out of the Archdiocese of Los Angeles so that I would no longer have this influence on the seminarians and young priests. The Cardinal wanted me to live with my Congregation and be assigned to other work within the Congregation, which meant that I would no longer be able to carry out the work of the Apostolate of Christian Renewal.

Father Provincial also explained to the Cardinal that I was having prostate problems, which might mean that I would not be able to work for the Apostolate of Christian Renewal. On March 30th, I had biopsies done so as to see if I had prostrate cancer. Fortunately, the biopsies were negative. I also had a cystoscopy that showed that I didn't have any tumors, stones or infections in my bladder or kidneys. The doctor said that my bladder and kidneys were normal and healthy. However, through some medication, the problem with my prostate could be corrected.

Because of my age and with the problem of the prostate gland, Father Provincial told Cardinal Mahony that he did not want to remove me from the Archdiocese. In answer to that, the Cardinal said I could continue the work of the Apostolate in the Archdiocese, but that I may not have any contact with the seminarians.

After I agreed to the Cardinal's wishes, Father Provincial then wrote me a letter stating that the former Servants could not visit, call or contact me. By this action, it was very evident that Cardinal Mahony and my Congregation did not want me to ever begin the Servants community whether it was in the Archdiocese of Los Angeles or any other diocese.

Again, I really did not get the full story from the Cardinal himself because he never saw me and there was no dialogue. And so, I just had to be obedient and carry on my work as I was doing in the past. I believe that this was an injustice done to me. I also feel that this injustice was definitely an abuse against the seminarians as well as the young men who were already ordained priests and who wanted to be Servants.

This whole incident was a severe and heavy cross to carry because I was very close to many of these young men. In fact, I knew many of these men as well as their families for many years. Naturally, I am sure that these young men also found this extreme action to be very difficult because they were used to visiting, coming to Confession and sometimes talking about their spiritual life. Then, all of sudden, they were completely cut off, without any explanation, recourse or dialogue on my part. This was disheartening and painful to say the least.

However, everyone decided to remain obedient to the Cardinal's directives. As a result, some of the seminarians lost hope that the Servants would ever be founded. And so, they began to explore their options.

One of the young men decided to go back to his home archdiocese and make his affiliation there. After he spoke to the Archbishop, made all the arrangements and was accepted, he then informed the Cardinal about his decision and told of the permission given to him by the other bishop. After that, he asked the Cardinal that since he was no longer affiliated with the Archdiocese of Los Angeles if he could come and visit me in Fillmore. Since this young man was no longer under the jurisdiction of the Archdiocese of Los Angeles, the Cardinal said that he could visit me in Fillmore. The Cardinal also expressed to the young man that he should finish his seminary training at St. John's Seminary until he was ready to be ordained.

2. Broke the camel's back

Once this young man was able to come back and visit, the others asked themselves the question, "Why can't we do the same?" Personally, I really think that this was the straw that broke the camel's back. After that, many of these young men opted to go to other dioceses. Some of them first decided to continue and finish college and then drop their affiliation with the Archdiocese. Because the Servants had not been established, these young men seemed to be in "nomad's land." Perhaps, this was God's way of testing them so as to help them discern their vocation even more.

Because of this whole ordeal, I learned once again to let go and let God. I also honored each of these young men's decisions as they prayed, discerned and received guidance from their spiritual director. When I saw these young men suffer, I also suffered because I never intended these young men to go through what they did. If I had know this would be the outcome, I would never have allowed them to come in the first place to prepare to be Servants or to go to the seminary. However, I believe that each of these young men received many blessings, graces and gifts. Other than the degrees they received, I believe that their education will be very beneficial to them in their spiritual life, their ministry or vocation, no matter what that may be. Personally, I never thought I did anything wrong, but if I have done something wrong, I sincerely ask them for their forgiveness.

3. A lesson to be learned: communication

I believe that this incident caused needless trials and tribulations for everyone involved. One of the main problems during this incident was the lack of true discernment. In other words, if there was true discernment, then there would be a lot more communication or dialogue. However, this did not happen. Rather, there was a decision made without any dialogue. During this time, there was no inquiry about where these young men were coming from, no attempt to understand what these young men wanted to do, no asking what these young men desired in their hearts and no questions as to why they all left their families so as to seek the life of being a Servant. None of these different inquiries were ever asked or examined. This is why I believe that many of these needless trials and tribulations could have been avoided.

These are some of my personal feelings. However, what is done is done and everyone needs to move on in life. Therefore, I hold no hatred, criticism or animosity towards anyone. Rather, I pray that I can learn from this experience so that in the future, I can avoid other needless trials and tribulations.

D. Place in Heaven I was created for

On March 27th, 1994, I had a great desire to ask God to grant me my place in Heaven as if I had cooperated with all the blessings, graces and gifts that He has given me. First, I asked Mary, Joseph, the angels and saints in Heaven and the souls in Purgatory to bring this about through their intercessory prayer. Second, the thought came to me that I should remain on earth until I reach the place God wanted me to be in Heaven as if I had cooperated with these graces. But then, I thought that I would be here on earth until the end of time. And so, I thought the first way was much better because the prayers of the angels and saints in Heaven and souls in Purgatory are extremely powerful.

E. Person from Australia

In 1990, I met a stranger from Australia. This woman explained to me that God wished to have great work and spirituality spread throughout the world. She said that I was the person to do this work. At the time, I really did not pay any attention to what she said because my philosophy is to "wait and see." Sometime later, this woman wrote to me on March 30th, 1992. In the letter she stated that I was definitely called by God to start new religious communities. She also said that I would encounter even greater opposition, but that through obedience to my bishop and superiors, God's plan would finally be fulfilled. She also said that all opposition would eventually cease. As for me, I believe that I have remained obedient to my bishop and superiors.

F. George Timmerman

On Good Friday, George Timmerman, a Presbyterian from England, came to visit our Center in Fillmore. He also had a great love for the Lord and was spreading the Divine Mercy devotion of Sr. Faustina. Because of his great love for this devotion, I showed George a life-size picture of the Divine Mercy in our chapel. The Divine Mercy picture was given to me many years ago by a woman named Zelda Weber. She told me that this picture needs to be displayed so that people would be moved, have a conversion of heart and a longing for holiness.

When we were looking at the picture, Jesus came alive. He was radiant, smiling and His eyes showed tender love. Both of us were very moved by this experience. Later, George went back to England. After eight months, he wrote to me. He stated that the reason he waited so long was to wait for the emotional effects to wear off so that he could think more rationally. He said that he would like a life-size picture of the Divine Mercy just like the one we have in Fillmore. However, this was impossible because it would have cost a lot of money. Rather, I decided to have a professional photographer take a picture of our Divine Mercy as well as the statue of the Scourged Christ and Jesus in the Garden of Gethsemane so that I could send him a copy of each.

1. Scourged Christ

The statue of the Scourged Christ came from Little Rose Ferran, who was born in Canada. She was the tenth of fifteen children. Her mother dedicated her to the tenth mystery of the Rosary. She also dedicated each of her other children to other mysteries of the Rosary. When Little Rose Ferran was born, her mother was moved to go to the barn and give birth in a stable. Later, they moved to Woonsocket, Rhode Island, where Little Rose received the visible stigmata. Because Little Rose received many supernatural gifts, her mother kept her hidden because she thought Little Rose was emotionally disturbed. But over the years, the mother realized that God blessed Little Rose by using her as an instrument for the conversion of sinners.

Anyways, one day Little Rose had a vision of the Scourged Christ, which showed a gory and painful scourging. The vision also showed how much Jesus really loves us by all the suffering He went through for our salvation. She then had three statues made. One statue was given to Blessed Brother Andre, which is at St. Joseph's Oratory in Montreal, the second statue was given to my Congregation and the third statue was kept in her home. After many years, nobody in my Congregation wanted this statue so I decided that I would take it and put the statue in our house in Fillmore so that everyone could see it.

2. Jesus in the Garden of Gethsemane

In 1960, someone gave me a painting of Jesus in the Garden of Gethsemane. I always relished this painting because it always moved me emotionally. When I was a little boy, I suffered from a club foot that needed to be broken. Because this caused so much pain, my grandmother would rock me for hours and explain to me two pictures on the wall in my home. One picture was Jesus in the Garden and the other was the Immaculate Conception of Mary.

When I moved to Hawaii, I asked someone to take care of this painting. When I returned, I found this painting in the dumpster. I then cleaned the painting up and hid it so that this would not happen again. When I moved to Fillmore, I decided to have the painting framed and hung in our gathering area. Since then, I have had many compliments on this painting and many people have been deeply touched.

G. Pilgrimage to Belgium, France and Portugal

In May, I went on a beautiful pilgrimage to Belgium and France. The reason for this pilgrimage was that Fr. Damien, the Leper Priest, was going to be Beatified. However, the Beatification was canceled because Pope John Paul II fell and hurt himself. Although, after the Holy Father recovered, he conducted the Beatification the following year. Nevertheless, we went to Fr. Damien's shrine in Louvain, Belgium and celebrated a very beautiful Eucharistic Liturgy. While in Louvain, I had the opportunity and privilege to visit Robert Mondoy, whom I taught in the seminary, while I was in Hawaii. He was also the director of music for the celebration Mass in honor of Fr. Damien.

While visiting Belgium, we stopped at the shrine in Banneaux, which is an approved apparition. The message from the Blessed Mother was to pray much and to surrender yourself to God's Will. In Banneaux, Mary appeared with a golden heart. The priest in charge said that we are to make our prayers pure as gold, help families to have golden hearts and to help people become people of prayer. He also pointed out that we should become a living prayer.

After that, we went to France. While we were in France, we visited Joan of Arc's shrine. She was a very strong and spiritual leader against Satan and his army when the English tried to capture France.

Then we went to Lisieux where St. Therese the Little Flower lived. I think St. Therese is a perfect model for us today because she teaches us her "little way" of mercy and love. In October 1996, we will celebrate the 100th anniversary of her death. Hopefully, people will turn to her and learn more about how to love, be merciful and help change the attitudes of the world.

Next, we went to Paris to visit Rue de Bac, where the Blessed Mother gave St. Catherine Laboure the Miraculous Medal. When people wear the Miraculous Medal, it brings many great blessings and gifts. Hopefully, people will wear this medal and spread these blessings and gifts around the world.

While we were in France, we visited Our Lady of Victory Church in Paris. In this Church, there is a very beautiful shrine in honor of St. Therese and a shrine in honor of St. Augustine, who is holding a golden heart. This is where the father of St. Therese of Lisieux had requested that Masses be offered for the cure of his little daughter, Therese, when she was very young. The result of that offering and request brought about the incident where the Blessed Mother smiled at St. Therese. She also came to this Church before she made her pilgrimage to Rome to ask the Pope for his permission to let her enter Carmel at the age of fifteen.

The Augustinian Fathers are in charge of the Church and when King Charles was living, they asked him to build a Church in honor of his military victories. This is why the Church is called Our Lady of Victory. King Charles consented to this and now the Church is there. But since the Church is located in very remote area, very few people go to visit this Church. At one time, the pastor even thought of closing the Church, but then he decided to consecrate the parish to the Immaculate Heart of Mary and have various devotions in honor of our Mother Mary. Immediately, the people started to come to Mass and participate in these devotions. Today, the Church services go on all day long. This was a real eye-opener when I realized that other parishes across the world could do the same thing. That is, to consecrate their parishes to the Immaculate Heart of Mary and have some devotions to Mary in her honor. I am confident that many blessings would be given to the world if parishes would consecrate their parish in this way.

From Paris, we went to Fatima. While we were in Fatima, we were again reminded that this is where the Blessed Mother gave us the peace plan for the world. We know that very few of the faithful put her messages into practice. While in Fatima, people recite the Rosary in procession each day as they always do from May until October. Because I was not feeling very well, I decided that I would retire early. Even though I have participated in the procession many times, I felt a tremendous sadness because I could not participate.

Next, we went to Nazare, Portugal, and saw where the Blessed Mother had also appeared. We also saw the cross they erected in that area. This cross is very beautiful and I was moved to go up to the cross. As I went to the cross, I felt a great blessing given to me such as I experienced when I was on Cross Mountain in Medjugorje, Yugoslavia in 1990.

On the way back from Nazare to Fatima, we prayed the fifteen-decade Rosary. During this time, I was thinking about the fact that I had missed the Rosary procession during the pilgrimage. Then the Lord said, "the Mystical Rosary (with the thirty people on the bus) is more efficacious than all the prayers from the Rosary processions at Fatima down through these years." I was rather surprised at this, but once I though about it, the Lord is right. When we pray the Mystical Rosary, this prayer is not just something fanatical or pious. Rather, the Mystical Rosary is a tremendous prayer, especially when we unite ourselves with the angles and saints in Heaven and the souls in Purgatory united with each Mass celebrated throughout the world.

H. 101 Foundation trip

In October, I had the opportunity to go on a world pilgrimage with the 101 Foundation. We first flew from Kennedy Airport to Lisbon, where we visited the shrine in Fatima. Unfortunately, we were not able to stay in my favorite apparition shrine very long. From Fatima, we flew to Rome because this is the center of Catholicism and the center of Christianity. However, like Fatima, we only stayed a short time. From Rome, we flew to the Philippines, where we attended the Congress for the Family.

Being in the Philippines was a tremendous experience because the faith is alive and vibrant. I believe the Philippines is the country that God has chosen to influence the whole Asian world. Perhaps, the Filipinos will even contribute to the well-being of the whole world, by sending some of their numerous vocations as missionaries.

While we were in the Philippines, we attended the Congress for the Family. At the congress, there was a great concern about the meeting that had been held in Cairo, Egypt in September. In that meeting, they tried to redefine the definition of marriage and the family. They only wanted to speak about the rights of the individual and did not want to face the fact that a marriage and a family need a man and a woman as a couple and as husband and wife. This is necessary to have a true family. In the Cairo meeting, there was tremendous opposition to family values and fortunately they did not win in regard to their agenda.

The Filipino's thought that there was a tremendous danger in the future where marital and family life would be attacked. The family is the most important core of society. In fact, the family is the cell of society. As much as the family is healthy and strong, so too will the nation and the world be healthy and strong. If family values are not fostered according to the natural law and Judaic-Christian principles, the values of our society will disintegrate into a dangerous situation as we are witnessing now in our country and in the world today.

The Filipinos are dedicating themselves to work for the good of the family and against artificial birth control. We know that today contraception is being spread all over the world by the use of condoms and other artificial means to prevent birth. Obviously, this is a dangerous attack against an individual because this practice leads to taking the life of an unborn child. These means are being carried out as birth control methods, limiting the family and destroying the rights of the unborn.

Today, people are so worried about the explosion of population that they cannot see the forest from the trees. The problem is that they cannot see and understand the value of a person. They also do not see that in order to have a sound economy, the country needs population growth. I believe that we all need to learn to work together and cooperate in this global endeavor so that we can uphold the dignity of a person. The resources for everyone in the whole world are available. Likewise, every person needs to learn how to use these resources so that everyone in every country can live in harmony and be taken care of properly in all aspects of life.

I thought that being in the Philippines was a great experience because it was uplifting and our spirits were inspired. The Philippines is truly a god-like country. Although, all countries have some factions that militate against the faith, against goodness and against the values of family life. So, I hope that the Philippines will be a true shining light to the whole world, especially in the Asian world.

From the Philippines, we flew to China via Japan. When we arrived in China, we found out that the plane had developed a bad engine. While we were there, the plane flew to Hong Kong to either have the engine repaired or a new engine installed. During our visitation in China, we went to various places. First, we went to Beijing, which is a very pleasant city. The people were more free and open with us than in other places in China. Yet, we were warned, by the Vatican, not to participate in any government sponsored National Church activities.

Nonetheless, we visited a seminary that was run by the National Church, which was not in full union with the Catholic Church because they don't have anything to do with the Holy Father. The clergy in the National Church are extremely loyal to the Chinese government. Maybe they feel that this is the only way they can function as priests or carry on Christianity. Personally, I think they have deluded themselves.

In China, there still is an underground Church. The reason the Vatican was so concerned about our welfare was that two priests in the underground Church were caught offering the Eucharistic Liturgy and were shot. So, the Vatican warned us that we should not publicly offer Mass and not display our faith openly. In other words, they warned us not to proselytize and not give out any religious articles.

So, we had to offer our Masses in our rooms at the hotel. We would gather the different people we wished to have with us while we offered Mass. Since the Vatican called and told us to be very careful, and I was the leader of the group as a chaplain, it was my duty to warn the other priests not to offer public Mass against the wishes of the Vatican.

I had to tell the people that they were not able to do anything in regard to spreading the faith. However, some disobeyed the wishes of the Vatican. This could have jeopardized our whole group because we could have been put in jail.

The mechanic in Hong Kong found that the plane was not able to function without a new engine. So, we had to wait for the installation and spend an extra day in China. Each of us also had to pay an extra $35 so as to extend our visa for another day. We spent our extra time in Beijing. Many of us noticed that the attitude had changed because there were more police officers that were watching us as well as greater surveillance. Likewise, there were always agents with us no matter where we went, whether in the hotel, walking or visiting various places, such as the Chinese Square.

When I was in China, I prayed the same prayers that I did when I visited Russia. I constantly prayed the Mystical Rosary and the Mystical Mass Prayer. Even though I said the Mystical Mass Prayer in a shortened form, I offered everything to the Father with Jesus in the Spirit in union with the Eucharistic Liturgy for the Conversion of China and for peace in the world. However, I did not pray in the same manner as I did in Russia. I did not say to the Devil that I would take him on and defeat him. Rather, I prayed for the liberation of China from the clutches of evil and of Satan. Obviously, Satan's presence could be felt in China.

I also noticed that there were very few children in a country where they have a population of 1.9 billion people. The policy of China is one child per family. Most Chinese people want a boy as the first born. If the first born is not a boy, the Chinese people would usually abort the girl. This policy is a direct violation on life and discriminates against women. I found that there was about one girl to every four boys. Unfortunately, China no longer has the respect it once had in regards to family life. Many of us felt the tension among the Chinese people, especially when it came to trust. We saw many young people constantly begging for food, money and anything that they could get. Even though we could not help them much, many of them fought over the little they received. As a result, the stronger people prevailed while the others often went away without anything.

When we finally left China, we encountered a lot of stress. The problem was that the Communists deliberately delayed us so that we were not able to get out of the country on time. However, they finally allowed us to board the plane without charging us extra. But, they did make us wait for two hours before we were able to take off.

When we got to Japan, it was very late. First, we went to Akita so that we could see the visionary, Sr. Agnes Sasagawa. The Blessed Mother appeared to her in her convent 101 times and wept tears, even tears of blood. Now, Sr. Sasagawa has the visible stigmata. She was able to greet us while she was in bed suffering. I was able to have a private audience with her because of my acquaintance with Francis Fukushima who wrote a book on Akita.

Francis Fukushima drove on the same bus as I did while going from the airport to Akita. Although I never saw a picture of him, I heard a man talking to a priest about Akita and things that I had read in his book. So, I turned to him and said, "Did you write a book?" And he said, "Yes I did." Then I asked him who published the book and he responded, "Queenship Publishing." So, I said to him, "You must be Francis Fukushima." So, I told him that I read his book and gave the permission to have it published. Then he said, "You must be Fr. Luke Zimmer."

Francis took me to see Sister Agnes Sasagawa and interpreted my conversation with her. While we were visiting, Sister said that she would pray for me and the founding of the Servants community. Then, she said she would love to have a prayer written where all the prayers would be offered in union with each Mass throughout the world. I then excitably explained to her that I wrote a prayer like that called the Mystical Mass Prayer and the Mystical Rosary. Naturally, sister was extremely happy and exclaimed, "Finally, my prayer has been answered."

So again, the Mystical Mass Prayer and the Mystical Rosary are so important for the good of the whole world. The reason, of course, is because I believe the world can be saved through the sufferings and passion of Christ and His offering, which we are privileged to celebrate and offer every day in our priesthood, and that is the Eucharistic Liturgy.

Finally, from Japan we flew to Alaska and arrived very late. Unfortunately, the personnel were not there to handle the baggage or to help us go through customs. Because of this incident, we missed our connection when we arrived in New York. We had to re-book everyone and reroute their flights, which took six hours to accomplish.

I felt that this pilgrimage was worth the many trying times, especially during the last part of our pilgrimage. We were able to offer a lot of prayers and sacrifices so as to bring about some peace in the world. Hopefully, these things will happen as we know they will because Truth, Love and Freedom always prevail. It just takes time to bring these things about and we look forward to the time when that will happen.

I. Bishop Wiegand

In December of 1994, Bishop William Wiegand of Sacramento spoke with Deacon Don De Haven and said that he would like to have a new religious community come into the diocese. The bishop said that a community would be a great blessing for the diocese. So, Deacon Don De Haven told him about the Servants of the Sacred Heart of Jesus, Mary and Joseph. Bishop Wiegand expressed his desire to have me call and set up a date to visit with him. Immediately afterwards, I called and made all the necessary arrangements so that I could see the bishop.

The meeting I had with Bishop Wiegand was wonderful; he expressed his desire to bring the Apostolate of Christian Renewal into the Sacramento Diocese. During the meeting, I was very open and honest with him. I told the bishop that Cardinal Roger Mahony did not want the religious communities to be founded in the Archdiocese of Los Angeles or any other diocese. I told Bishop Wiegand that I did not know the whole reason for the Cardinal's objection and that I could not give him very much information in regards to the Cardinal's objection. Yet, Bishop Wiegand said that he would try to find a way to bring me to the Diocese of Sacramento without causing any problems with the Cardinal.

Over the course of the next year, 1995, Bishop Wiegand tried many different ways to bring me into the diocese. He expressed various thoughts and offered different ideas, which would allow me to come into the Diocese of Sacramento, such as becoming involved in different activities throughout the diocese. However, something always seemed to hinder my transfer. There was opposition from the Bishop's Personnel Board or opposition from the priests of his diocese. I felt that the main reason my transfer was so difficult was because the priests were afraid of me coming into the diocese for some unknown reason.

At one time, the bishop wanted me to take care of a parish. However, the priests complained that I would draw people from other parishes. They said that they needed to have their own people to stay in their own Churches, especially on Sundays and Holy Days of Obligation. Well, I don't know if this would have happened, but certainly this was not my intention. Rather, I feel that people need to belong to their own parishes and be a part of the services on Sunday and other occasions.

CHAPTER 21

1995

A. *Oil of gladness brings joy to the heart*

During Holy Week, the Church is not permitted to keep the Blessed Sacrament in the tabernacle. Rather, the Church puts the Blessed Sacrament in a repository after the Mass on Holy Thursday until after the Vigil Mass on Holy Saturday.

I attended the Holy Week services at St. Francis of Assisi, in Fillmore, during April 13th-15th, 1995. After the service, I came home on Holy Thursday and took the large Host from the lunette and put it into a ciborium which held two smaller consecrated Hosts. Then I took the ciborium and put it in the repository. On April 15th, I took the ciborium from the repository and put it back in the tabernacle after the Vigil Mass on Saturday evening. As I was putting the ciborium back into the tabernacle, I decided to offer a prayer because I wanted to make a novena to surrender myself more fully to the Lord. In my novena, I prayed so that God could use me according to His will and in any way that He wished. (I have been surrendering myself daily for a number of years, but this year I wanted to make it very special. That is why I made a novena of surrender during the Holy Week.)

As I put the ciborium into the tabernacle, I paused and said this prayer: *Lord, if I have done anything wrong that I should not have done or I have not done something that I should have done, I am very sorry. People have been accusing me over the years that I was doing my own thing, that I was building a cult around myself, that I was doing everything for my honor and glory and not Your honor and glory. I've always wanted and tried to do everything for Your honor and glory and since they are saying these things, I do not know how to change their attitude. But, I surrender to You: my body, my mind, my soul, my spirit and my whole being. I surrender to You the Servants; that is the priests and brothers who You wish to live in a religious community. I surrender to You the Handmaids, who are already sisters and I ask Your blessings upon that community, especially for an increase in vocations. I offer You the lay Servants and Handmaids and I ask that You spread this work throughout the world. I surrender to You the properties that have been given in order to foster this work. I give to You the Servants and Handmaids of the Sacred Heart of Jesus, Mary and Joseph. I give You everything. I don't know how You are going to convince others. I don't know what You are going to do, but You've got to do something.* With this prayer, I closed the tabernacle and went to bed.

The next day, I invited people that I knew for a long time for Easter morning Mass. They were going to celebrate their twenty-fifth wedding anniversary in a few days, so I thought it would be a very beautiful opportunity to have them come and participate in the Easter Eucharistic celebration. The family was Chuck and Rosalie Zwicker with their daughter Dawn and son Eric. Don Tesmer was also with us in the Chapel. When it came time to receive Holy Communion, I took the ciborium from the tabernacle. When I opened the ciborium, I found that the Eucharist was exuding oil, and I expressed my amazement by saying, "What happened?" Then I took the large Host, and I felt the oil on my fingers. Then I turned to our painting of Divine Mercy and said to Jesus, "What am I going to do with You?" I put the Host back into the ciborium and placed it in the tabernacle.

Later in the day, I called my spiritual director Monsignor John Rohde. I told him what happened and I said, "What should I do?" He told me that since I was going to Sacramento to give a Renewal at St. Elizabeth's Parish, I should report to him upon my return, which was on May 6th.

When I was at St. Elizabeth's Parish, I received a phone call on May 1st, the person said that Msgr. Rohde just died from cardiac arrest. Naturally, I was shocked and surprised at the suddenness of his death. When I returned to Fillmore, I went to see Fr.

Norman Supancheck, who is the pastor of St. Francis of Assisi Parish. I told him everything that had happened in regards to the Eucharist. Fr. Norman seemed to be surprised, excited and supportive. Later, I talked with the regional bishop, Bishop Thomas Curry and told him as well. His reaction was one of caution and rightly so. He said that we should never put our trust in signs and wonders. He made the observation that many locutionists, visionaries and people who claim to have things from God are not from God at all. Rather, he said, we need to talk about the teachings of the faith and build up the Church. I agreed with him wholeheartedly. I asked him, "Should I have the oil tested?" He said, "Why? You will only find oil." So I said to him, "What should I do?" He said, "You can do anything that you want."

I had another spiritual director for many years and he always gave me the same advice as Msgr. Rohde. Neither of the spiritual directors knew of each other, yet, they always said the same things. This gave me a lot of confidence and trust that what I was doing was really from the Lord. After the death of Msgr. Rohde, I chose another spiritual director, whom I've known for many years. He is very wise, solid and has his feet on the ground. In fact, he is a "no nonsense" priest. So, I feel very comfortable in following any direction that he might give me in regards to this Eucharistic miracle. It is he who told me to write this testimony. He also said that this is necessary so that people will not distort what really took place.

In the Old Testament, there are various references to the "Oil of Gladness," which brings joy to a person's heart. We also read that oil was used for the anointing of a priest, a king and a prophet. The oil of gladness is referred to as the working of the Holy Spirit, and so in this Eucharistic miracle, from the Body of Christ, the Holy Spirit is being manifested.

Oil is very precious in religion and in our faith. We use oil during four different sacraments. The first sacrament is the Sacrament of Baptism. When a person is baptized, the priest takes the oil of chrism and seals the crown of the person's head. At that moment, the person being baptized is given the gift of priesthood, prophet and king. Jesus himself was anointed priest, prophet and king when He was anointed at His Baptism. Christ means the anointed one. When we are anointed with the oil of chrism, we too are called Christians, that is, followers of Christ. We also need to receive the Baptism in the Holy Spirit besides the Baptism of water in the Name of the Father, the Son and the Holy Spirit. Scripture states (John 1: 30-33) that Jesus is the person who baptizes in the Spirit.

When we are baptized with water in the name of the Father, Son and Holy Spirit, Original Sin is taken from our whole being. God then infuses Sanctifying Grace into the person. This means that we participate in the very life of God. The Holy Spirit seals us as a Child of God and as a member of the Church, the Mystical Body of Christ. We also become the temple of the Holy Spirit. The Triune God lives within us: the Father, the Son and the Holy Spirit. We are also given the gifts of faith, hope and charity. We receive the moral virtues as well: justice, fortitude, temperance and prudence. We are also given the Seven Fold Gifts of the Holy Spirit: wisdom, understanding, knowledge, counsel, fortitude, piety and fear of the Lord. We receive all these things that are needed in order to be saved and sanctified. We are not always aware of what takes place at our Baptism. We need to accept and believe everything on faith. In order to grow in grace, a person needs to surrender and cooperate with God throughout his or her life. This means that we are to keep sin out of our lives. In order to do this, a person should be baptized in the Holy Spirit.

The Baptism in the Holy Spirit is different from the Baptism with water. However, when a person is baptized in the Holy Spirit, it should make the person aware of what took place at Baptism with water in the name of the Father, Son and Holy Spirit. When we receive the Baptism in the Holy Spirit, we become transformed. We also become aware that God is within us. We are aware of the presence of the Lord and we want to know, love and serve Him. And so, we become truly alive in the Lord. Christ lives in us and we in Christ. It seems that when a person is baptized in the Spirit, he or she wishes to share this joyous experience with others. It is necessary to remember that a person should have prudent zeal. It is easy to come across too strong and turn people off in wanting others to have the gift that has been received. The Holy Spirit also gives various charismatic gifts that should be used correctly. A person must remember that the charismatic gifts are given to serve others and never for one's own honor and glory.

Oil is used in the Sacrament of Confirmation, where the one being confirmed becomes a disciple of the Lord. To be a disciple of the Lord, each person has the responsibility and privilege of sharing the Good News. I would say the best way to find out more about the teachings of Jesus is to learn what is in the new *Catechism of the Catholic Church*. This catechism is a real treasure and a gift given to us by God. The new *Catechism of the Catholic Church* is also the fruit of Vatican Council II. We should be familiar with Scripture, the teachings of the Fathers of the Church and the Magisterium of the Church. Then we can be a true disciple of the Lord. We are also able to teach others. However, we do not need to know everything before we begin to catechize and evangelize.

Oil is used in the Sacrament of Holy Orders. The priest is anointed so that he can act in the person of Jesus, while he is celebrating the Eucharistic Liturgy, hearing Confessions, preaching, administering the sacraments and carrying out the work of the Lord. The ministerial priest is different from the common priesthood. The ministerial priest is given the command by the Lord to do what He did. Jesus gave this command at the Last Supper. When we are offering the Mass, we are doing what the Lord did and what He commanded us to do.

Oil is used in the Sacrament of the Sick. When someone receives the Sacrament of the Sick, it is possible that the person will be healed, given special graces and gifts to suffer in a proper manner. Suffering may help a person to either become a saint or lead a person to Satan. When suffering is accepted with a proper attitude, this allows and helps a person to want to do God's Will. Suffering should be used for the good of others. Another effect of the Sacrament of the Sick is to help a person prepare for life after death. Death is a passing from this world into the next. This is a very important sacrament of the Lord.

Any person can use blessed oil to bless people. This is an ordinary blessing given while praying for the person who is sick. If the person is sick, it is also necessary to remember that this is not the Sacrament of the Sick. The Sacrament of the Sick must be administered by a priest or a bishop. No one else can do this. It would be good too if parents would bless their children as was the custom in the Old Testament.

While I was praying on July 10th, I received infused knowledge that God gave this Eucharistic miracle mainly for those who are ministerial priests. Priests are to come and be blessed with this Eucharist. They are to offer the Eucharistic Liturgy and to spend some time with the Lord renewing their commitment to Him as a priest. They are to go forth and renew the faith of the people that Jesus is present in the Blessed Sacrament. I also had the opportunity to see priests who came to receive a blessing from the Eucharistic miracle. In fact, many of the priests were transformed in their attitude and whole being because they received many great blessings, graces and gifts. I have seen this take place at our Center in Fillmore.

Our Lord said that He was going to give His Flesh to eat and His Blood to drink. He told this to His disciples, the Apostles and to other people who were in Capernaum. When the disciples heard this, they said it was a hard saying. They walked away and never came back. Jesus turned to the Apostles and said, "Will you go too?" Simon Peter answered, "To whom shall we go? You have the words of everlasting life." In other words, He was making an act of faith and we too need to make an act of faith. We are able to show that this is not against reason. We cannot understand Jesus' presence in the Eucharist thoroughly because it is a mystery. We have to accept it because Jesus said so. We are able to believe because Jesus is the God-man. We know that Jesus cannot deceive us and what He says is true. We accept wholeheartedly that Jesus is truly present: Body, Blood, Soul and Divinity in the Eucharist after the Consecration of the Host and wine by a validly ordained ministerial priest.

On October 26th, God let me understand that the Eucharistic miracle was not given just for the ministerial priest. Rather, the Eucharistic miracle was also given for those who are baptized and have received the common priesthood. Each person is to exercise the common priesthood by participating in the Eucharistic Liturgy. The Eucharistic Liturgy is a sacrifice, sacrament, banquet and memorial of Jesus that is offered to the Heavenly Father. Whenever a person offers any prayer, suffering or daily living, the person exercises his or her common priesthood. We should be very grateful that God has given the great gift of the priesthood to all people.

There is a great difference between a ministerial priesthood and a common priesthood. A ministerial priest differs in essence from the common priesthood of the faithful because it is a sacrament that confers a sacred power to be used for giving service to the faithful. This is stated in Article 1592 in the *Catechism of the Catholic Church*. In other words, it is the priest who offers the Mass in the person of Jesus Christ for the whole assembly of all the people present. When the priest takes the Host and says, "This is my Body," it becomes the Body, Blood, Soul and Divinity of Jesus Christ. When he takes the chalice with the wine and says, "This is My Blood," it becomes the Body, Blood, Soul and Divinity of Jesus Christ. Even though it appears to be like bread, tastes like bread and feels like bread, it is the Body, Blood, Soul and Divinity of Jesus. The same is true with the Precious Blood. It has the appearance of wine; it tastes like wine, has the effects of wine, but it is not wine. It is the Body, Blood, Soul and Divinity of Jesus Christ. Through transubstantiation, there is no bread, there is no wine, only Jesus is present. The common priesthood, on the other hand, carries out its role by fulfilling what God wants them to do in offering the Eucharistic Liturgy to the Heavenly Father.

1. From the Jerusalem Catechesis (Office of Readings-Saturday within the Octave of Easter)

"On the night he was betrayed our Lord Jesus Christ took bread, and when he had given thanks, he broke it and gave it to his disciples and said, 'Take, eat: this is my body.' He took the cup, gave thanks and said: 'Take, drink: this is my blood.' Since Christ himself has declared the bread to be his body, who can have any further doubt? Since he himself has said quite categorically, 'This is my blood,' who can dare to question it and say that it is not his blood?

"Therefore, it is with complete assurance that we receive the bread and wine as the body and blood of Christ. His body is given to us under the symbol of bread and His blood is given to us under the symbol of wine, in order to make us by receiving them one body and blood with him. Having his body and blood in our members, we become bearers of Christ and sharers, as St. Peter says, in the Divine nature.

"Once when speaking to the Jews, Christ said: 'Unless you eat my flesh and drink my blood you shall have no life in you.' This horrified them and they left him. Not understanding his words in a spiritual way, they thought the Savior wished them to practice cannibalism.

"Under the old covenant, there was show bread, but it came to an end with the old dispensation to which it belonged. Under the new covenant, there is bread from Heaven and the cup of salvation. They sanctify both the body and the soul, the bread being adapted to the sanctification of the body, the Word, to the sanctification of the soul.

"Do not, then, regard the Eucharistic elements as ordinary bread and wine: they are in fact the body and blood of the Lord, as he himself has declared. Whatever your senses may tell you, be strong in faith.

"You have been taught and you are firmly convinced that what looks and tastes like bread and wine is not bread and wine, but the body and blood of Christ. You know also how David referred to this long ago when he sang: 'Bread gives strength to man's heart and makes his face shine with the oil of gladness. Strengthen your heart, then, by receiving this as spiritual bread, and bring joy to the face of your soul.'

"May purity of conscience remove the veil from the face of your soul so that by contemplating the glory of the Lord, as in a mirror, you may be transformed from glory to glory in Christ Our Lord."

a.   Different Eucharistic miracles

We have different Eucharistic miracles that have happened throughout the world. I've seen some of them and participated in Masses that honor Jesus present in the Blessed Sacrament. In Lanciano, Italy, a priest had a doubt whether Jesus was truly present in the Blessed Sacrament after he said the words of the Consecration. He agonized tremendously each time he offered Mass. One day, when he said the words of Consecration, he saw Jesus in the host and in the Precious Blood in the Chalice. The Host and Precious Blood are kept in the shrine at Lanciano. In 1967, Pope Paul VI ordered a scientific experiment to be made on the Host and Precious Blood. They took a little piece of the Host and discovered that it was a tissue from the heart of a human person. They tested the Precious Blood and found out it was fresh blood and is still alive. We know that when blood is exposed, it deteriorates within twelve to twenty-four hours. This blood has not. From the scientific experiment, no one can say it is Jesus. We, however, know it is Jesus because it was the Host used during the Eucharistic Liturgy. The words of Consecration were pronounced by a valid ordained priest. Therefore, we believe Jesus is present in the Host. We believe the same to be true in regard to the Blood. Jesus is present in the chalice. We are able to accept this fact by faith because Jesus said that He would give His Flesh to eat and His Blood to drink.

Another Eucharistic miracle happened in Santarem, Portugal. A woman there had marital problems. Her husband was very rude toward her and she did not know what to do. She just wanted happiness. She then went to a sorcerer, who asked the woman to bring back a consecrated Host and her troubles would be over. She went to Church and received Holy Communion. She pretended to take the Host, but instead, she hid the Host in her handkerchief. As she was leaving the Church, blood began to flow from her hand. People noticed it and said, "Why are you bleeding? What happened to your hand?" She became so frightened that she ran home and she hid the Host in a trunk. In the middle of the night, the Host lit up the house with a bright light. The husband wanted to know what happened and she explained everything to him. They both knelt down and adored Jesus present in the trunk. They took the Host and gave it to a priest, who put it in the tabernacle. He then was going to take the Host to the bishop, but when he went to get it, he found it encased in plastic. In those days, there was no such thing as plastic. I have seen this Eucharistic miracle. I offered Mass there and gave the people a blessing with the Monstrance that holds the Host.

There are other Eucharistic miracles all over the world. There are Eucharistic miracles in Belgium and Germany. I have also gone there and have seen them. But there is never any instance that I know of that the Eucharist exuded oil. This is something new. It is mysterious; yet, it is believable because of the oil spoken of in the Old Testament, is a manifestation of the Holy Spirit.

The Eucharistic miracle that happened in Fillmore is still exuding oil. It is Jesus who baptizes in the Holy Spirit (Cf. John 1: 32-33). Hopefully, this will happen to many people as they come to witness this miracle. Also, I'm praying that it will move many people to have their sins forgiven in the Sacrament of Reconciliation. Every person needs the Sacrament of Mercy, the sacrament of Love, the sacrament of Compassion and the sacrament of Forgiveness. Having received forgiveness, the person is worthy to receive Jesus in the Blessed Sacrament. We know that anyone who has committed a mortal sin is unworthy to receive Holy Communion. He or she needs to make peace with God and then one is able to worthily receive Jesus in Holy Communion.

It is not really necessary to visit a shrine where a Eucharistic miracle has taken place or where something miraculous has happened. We should know and believe that Jesus is truly present in the Blessed Sacrament in every Catholic Church, Chapel, Religious community and Catholic Shrine. If a person does not visit a shrine, then he or she should spend time with Jesus in the Blessed Sacrament. It would be great if every person did visit Jesus in the Blessed Sacrament in his or her own parish at least once a week or even daily.

2. From the Jerusalem Catechesis (Office of Readings - Friday within the Octave of Easter)

"When we were baptized into Christ and clothed ourselves in him, we were transformed into the likeness of the Son of God. Having destined us to be his adopted sons, God gave us a likeness to Christ in his glory and living as we do in communion with Christ. God's anointed, we ourselves are rightly called 'the anointed ones.' When he said: 'Do not touch my anointed ones,' He was speaking of us.

"We became 'the anointed ones' when we received the sign of the Holy Spirit. Indeed, everything took place in us by means of images, because we ourselves are images of Christ. Christ bathed in the Jordan river, imparting to its waters the fragrance of his divinity, and when he came up from the sacred waters, the Holy Spirit descended upon him, like resting upon like. So we also, after coming up from the sacred waters of Baptism, were anointed with chrism, which signifies the Holy Spirit, by whom Christ was anointed and of whom blessed Isaiah prophesied in the name of the Lord: 'The Spirit of the Lord is upon me, because he has anointed me. He has sent me to preach good news to the poor.'

"Christ's anointing was not with human hands, nor was it with ordinary oil. On the contrary, having destined him to be the Savior of the whole world, the Father himself anointed him with the Holy Spirit. The words of Peter bear witness to this: Jesus of Nazareth, whom God anointed with the Holy Spirit. And David the prophet proclaimed: 'Your throne, O God, shall endure forever; your royal scepter is a scepter of justice. You have loved righteousness and hated iniquity; therefore God, your God, has anointed you with the oil of gladness above all your fellows.'

"The oil of gladness with which Christ was anointed was a spiritual oil; it was in fact the Holy Spirit himself, who is called the oil of gladness because he is the source of spiritual joy. But we too have been anointed with oil, and by this anointing we have entered into fellowship with Christ and have received a share in his life. Beware of thinking this holy oil is simply ordinary oil and nothing else. After the invocation of the Spirit, it is no longer ordinary oil but the gift of Christ, and by the presence of his divinity, it becomes the instrument through which we receive the Holy Spirit. While symbolically, on our foreheads and senses, our bodies are anointed with this oil that we see, our souls are sanctified by the holy and life-giving Spirit."

a.   Invitation to the Diocese of Sacramento

Finally, on the Feast of Christ the King in November 1995, Bishop William Wiegand invited me to the Sacramento diocese. I then asked Father Provincial and the Council if I could have permission to go to the diocese to establish the Apostolate of Christina Renewal. The Provincial and the Council gave me permission. However, the Provincial was not too happy because nothing was done in writing and there was no contact with the Provincial on the part of the bishop.

Father Provincial then had a meeting with me and said that he wanted everything to be brought into the open and to let the Cardinal know that I was going to go to Sacramento. The reason why the Provincial wanted this to be done was so that the Bishop of Sacramento would have the opportunity to know everything. This would also allow me to be accepted in Sacramento wholeheartedly and that there would be no possibility of me being asked to leave the diocese.

I did not realize the problems that were in Sacramento at the time. Some priests were opposed to things that were going on in the diocese. I just took for granted that everything would be all right. Thus, I moved from Fillmore to Sacramento in the early part of January, 1996.

When I got to Sacramento, I was able to obtain a place that was very adequate for me and for those who would join me. The location was close to the Chancery Office and to the residence of the bishop. In fact, I lived by some of my close friends who lived in the area.

B. Opposition

While I was in the Sacramento Diocese, I received a lot of opposition from some of the priests in this diocese. I also learned that there was another priest who found himself in a very similar situation. The bishop brought this priest into his diocese in the same manner that he did with me. However, the Personnel Board, the Priests' Senate and the Priests' Council were more or less against this priest and what he was doing. Yet, this priest was very solid in his theology and was a tremendous preacher. Unfortunately, some of the lay people in flocking to him and participating in his days of teaching the *Catechism of the Catholic Church* made the remark that they had to go to him to receive the truth. Thus, the priests of the diocese were insulted by the way the laity were reacting. So, there seemed to be an uproar continuously in the diocese over this priest. I was very surprised when I found out that the people were saying the same thing about me.

C. Mom appearing to me

In November, 1995, I was very concerned about future of the Apostolate of Christian Renewal and the Servants and Handmaids of the Sacred Heart of Jesus, Mary and Joseph. Then Mom appeared to me with a radiant simile and said, "Don't worry, everything will be worked out." From this experience, I received a lot of joy and peace because of Mom's assurance.

D. Eucharistic miracle

I was invited to celebrate a Peace Mass in Sacramento. The sponsors asked me to bring the Eucharistic miracle so that I could bless people. Unfortunately, while they were spreading the publicity for this Mass, they mentioned that I would bless people with the Eucharist. Regrettably, they made the statement that oil being exuded from the Host was a proof that Jesus Christ is indeed present in the Eucharist. Well, this is not the whole truth. Even though Jesus is indeed present in the Eucharist, it is not because oil is being exuded. Rather, Jesus is present in the Eucharist because these hosts were consecrated by a validly ordained priest.

As a result, the priests were up in arms when they read this in the publicity statement sent by the sponsors of the Peace Mass. I was quite stunned to say the least when I saw this statement. Naturally, I had no idea how to defend myself. In fact, I tried to be low-keyed and did not say a word, but the bishop said that the priests were protesting against this. It seems that if there is anything extraordinary or if something is not just according to the teachings of the faith or if it cannot be explained properly, then it's not acceptable. So, I found myself added to the unaccepted list with a constant bombardment of protest against my being in Sacramento.

After this occasion, Bishop Wiegand expressed that I should take the Host to the Trappist Monastery and have the monks observe and investigate the Host so as to see whether anything like this has ever happened before. I then took the Eucharistic miracle to the Trappists in Vina, California and left the Eucharist there. The bishop said I should leave the Host there for a week, but I left the Host there for a whole month. Later, I decided to make my annual retreat during Holy Week at the Trappist Monastery.

A Journey Through Life: Chosen

CHAPTER 22

1996

A. Annual retreat at the monastery

While I was on my annual retreat, I talked to the Abbot about the Eucharistic miracle. I also talked to a monk, who was considered to be a very spiritual man and who understood mystical theology. This monk said to me, "The Eucharistic miracle is a consecrated host, therefore Jesus is present body, blood, soul and divinity. Regarding the oil coming from the Eucharist, this is God's secret and is a true mystery. We will just have to wait until God reveals what He wants and what it is all about."

1. After my retreat

When I came back from my retreat, Bishop Wiegand called me into his office and said that the opposition continued so strenuously that he felt it was better that I returned to Fillmore. The bishop said that he made this decision because I could continue to work for the Apostolate in the Archdiocese of Los Angeles.

This surprising event was both shocking and humiliating because I had to return and tell my superiors that I was no longer welcome in Sacramento. I then wrote to Cardinal Roger Mahony asking again for priestly faculties so that I could return to the Archdiocese of Los Angeles.

B. In regards to my death

1. Stopping in Santa Maria on my way home from Sacramento

On my way home from Sacramento to Fillmore, I stopped in Santa Maria, California, to celebrate a Baptism on May 11th, 1996. This Baptism was very beautiful. I also stayed overnight because the Baptism was late in the evening.

I attended an apparition on that day as well as the next with Barbara Matthias. The first day's apparition was special because only one other person and myself were present. While the Blessed Mother was appearing to Barbara Matthias in ecstasy, Barbara invited me to come forward. She then blessed me as our Mother Mary, Jesus and St. Joseph directed.

I have been in attendance at Barbara's apparitions from time to time over the past few years. Those experiences have always been a real blessing to me because every time I was asked to come up, the Blessed Mother directed that my priesthood, my ministry and prayer life be blessed. At times, the Blessed Mother would also bless my Rosary and crucifix. Sometimes, Mary would bless various areas on my body where I was experiencing pain or an illness.

On the next day, I was again invited to come forward during the apparition. During the apparition on May 12th, Barbara spent some time blessing my side where my pancreas, liver and gallbladder are located. She blessed this area over and over and over. After that, she pointed to my former spiritual director, Msgr. John Rohde's funeral Mass leaflet with his picture. Barbara kept pointing to his picture and then pointing to me and pointing back to his picture. I then said, "She wants to have the picture of Msgr. John Rohde." Then, she opened the funeral Mass leaflet and pointed to the words, "Sing with all the saints of glory. Sing with all the saints of glory." Again, she did this repeatedly. Finally, she went down to the last line of that song in which it said, "In God's likeness we awaken, knowing everlasting Peace." Then, the next line up says, "Clouds are breaking soon, the storms of time shall cease." At that moment, I said that she was speaking about my death. Of course, the others who were there disagreed and laughed at me when I made this remark. Barbara continued to go through the funeral Mass and pointed to the second reading which was I Cor. 12, 12-14, 27-31, which said, "For just as the body is one and has many members, and for all the members of the body, though many, are one body, so it is with Christ. For in the one Spirit we were baptized into one body, Jews or Greeks, slaves or free, and we were all made to drink of the one Spirit. Indeed, the body does not consist of one member but of many. Now, you are the body of Christ and, individually, members of it. And God has appointed in the Church first Apostles, second prophets, third teachers, then deeds of prayer, then gifts of healing, forms of assistants, forms of leadership, various kinds of tongues. Are all Apostles? Are all prophets? Are all teachers? Do all work miracles? Do all possess gifts of healing? Do all speak in tongues? Do all interpret? Aspire for the greater gift, and I will show you a more excellent way... Naturally, the excellent way is love. Only love remains when we die, while faith, gives way to sight and hope, gives way to possession. So, we posses God, we see God, we are with God and we love God. So, love is what remains."

Then, Barbara pointed to the first reading, which is a reading from Ruth 1, 15-19. Here, Ruth responds to her mother-in-law that she will go where she goes and that she will not be separated from her and will not abandon her. And then, the reading explains the loyalty of Ruth to her mother-in-law, Naomi, and also states "your God will be my God."

Next, Barbara went over to the next page and pointed out the words, "Holy, Holy, Holy." She pointed out the Liturgy of the Eucharist and then went down to the "Great Amen." She then turned to the last page and pointed to the words, "Amazing Grace" and then to the word, "Silence." Finally, she pointed to the Final Commendation, "The Song of Farewell." Then to the procession to the place of committal. As she kept pointing to all these different places, I again stated that God was calling me home.

2. Cardinal refuses faculties

When I returned to Fillmore, my Provincial called me and said that the Cardinal refused to give me faculties as long as I stayed in Fillmore. Naturally, I was quite shocked because I could not understand the reasoning why the Cardinal would not allow me to exercise the priestly faculties in the diocese. Especially since all that I wanted to do was just carry on my work as I did in the past. But this time, the Cardinal was quite adamant.

Next, I met with the Provincial and the Council. They decided not to plead with the Cardinal for me to stay in Fillmore. Rather, they decided that I would be assigned to St. Paul the Apostle Parish in Chino Hills, California. Thus, I would be in a house where the Sacred Heart Fathers were stationed. They would also seek faculties for me from the San Bernadino Diocese. In this parish, they said that I could be an associate pastor and continue the work of the Apostolate for the rest of 1996. Then in January, 1997, I would become a full-time associate.

3. Receiving a new assignment

After this whole experience, I spoke with the Provincial and the Council and they gave me my new assignment. Yet, my death was in the forefront on my mind. I thought, "Perhaps I may not even get to my new assignment." The reason is because I had to finish up a few Renewal Weeks and other previous commitments.

4. Neskoro, Wisconsin

One of these Renewal Weeks was in Neskoro, WI. On my way to Wisconsin, I was thinking on the plane about all the various events that had transpired, but especially the experience I had with Barbara Matthias in Santa Maria. I also thought about those days that followed when Barbara came to visit me in Fillmore on May 25th-26th, 1996. During these apparitions, it was evident that, "The great work of the Apostolate must continue and that I must abase myself." In other words, I must be humble and obedient. I also had to remember everything that I was taught by my spiritual director. These were some of my thoughts on the plane until the Lord said to me, "Have no fear, I go before you. Come, follow me and I will give you rest." Immediately, I knew that I was being called home to Heaven. However, I still did not know when and I wondered if I would ever be able to go to my new assignment.

During the Renewal Week in Neskoro, I got diarrhea and felt tired. However, I never felt any real pain, especially in the area which Barbara blessed.

5. Owensboro, Kentucky

After Neskoro, I went to Owensboro, Kentucky to give three days of recollection to the Carmelites and all the people who came for that time of God's grace. During these talks, I felt the Lord's Spirit working very powerfully. On the third day, Thursday, I noticed that my hands were a little yellow, but I thought I was imagining this. On the next day, Friday, I went to the Passionist sisters and celebrated Mass and spoke with the sisters. Again, I felt a little tired, but I thought it came from preaching in Neskoro and the talks with the Carmelites. But, I again noticed that I was getting more yellow in other parts of my body, especially around my neck. I really did not know what was happening. I thought maybe I contracted hepatitis because I was with some people in Sacramento who had hepatitis and I visited and ate with them. So, I thought that maybe I had hepatitis. The next day, Saturday, I was to perform a wedding so I thought I would wait until after the wedding to get this checked out.

It was the wedding of Bob Adams and Jenny Lilly. I performed the wedding in the afternoon and went to the reception afterwards, but I wasn't feeling too well. Again, I felt more tired than anything else, except I noticed that the yellowness started to cover my whole body.

The very next day, Sunday, July 7th, I had Mass with the sisters at the Carmel Home. After the Mass, I asked Sr. Francis Theresa if she noticed that I was yellow. She said, "Well yes, you are very yellow and I was going to say something to you." So, I asked if I could see a nurse so that I could talk with her. The nurse then told me that I needed to be checked by a doctor.

a. Dr. O'Neil

She looked up the phone number of Dr. O'Neil. She called him and he said that I needed to go to the emergency room and get some blood tests. When I got to the emergency room, the doctor told me that they would have the results on Tuesday. Because of this delay, he thought I should go to the hospital. And so, he called Dr. O'Neil and they both agreed. I was admitted to the hospital that very evening. I was put in isolation because they were not sure if I had hepatitis or not.

On Tuesday, the results came back negative. So, they had to find out what was really causing the jaundice. Dr. O'Neil asked Dr. Davis to see me. Next, they prescribed a sonogram and discovered that I had an enlarged liver. Because the liver seemed to be stretched, Dr. O'Neil and Dr. Davis decided that I should have a CAT scan done.

The next morning during the CAT scan, they found that I had blockage in my bile duct. They thought they would be unable to remove whatever it was because it was too enmeshed and too hard to extract. The Doctors suspected that I had a tumor in my bile duct. As a result, the doctors consulted with a surgeon, Dr. McCoy, who went over my chart and without any further tests, he said that I had cancer and did not have much time to live. Dr. McCoy did not tell me this, rather he told Martha and Bob Lilly, who were visiting with me and helping me while I was in Kentucky. I sincerely thank Martha and Bob for all their help. I felt very comfortable during my time with them. After Dr. McCoy left Martha and Bob, they told me what he said. Naturally, my reaction was that "we will see what we will see."

The next day, the doctors administered an arteriogram. In this test, they again found blockage in my bile duct. One of the arteries was not functioning. Even though they did not know exactly what this meant, they thought the cancer had spread to the arteries and beyond.

The surgeon, Dr. McCoy came in and drew a picture showing where the liver, gall bladder, pancreas and stomach were located. He said that he would operate and that if he could, he would remove the tumor from the bile duct. He planned to take part of the pancreas and part of the stomach, remove the bile duct and then reconstruct whatever was needed so that I would be able to function properly. If he was not able to remove the tumor from the bile duct, he would then take a piece of the intestines and connect it with the gall bladder so that the bile from the liver could go through the gall bladder and through the intestines so that I would get rid of the yellow jaundice.

Dr. McCoy said that the operation could last eight hours and that he wanted to devote his whole day for my operation. So, he wanted to wait for three days before the operation. I also decided to stay in the hospital because my diabetes was acting erratically. I hoped that the surgery would be able to correct my condition, but I didn't realize the extent of the damage that would be found. As a result, the pancreas would never function again properly. I would also have to take insulin for the rest of my life so as to keep my diabetes under control.

b. Operation

Before my operation, I surrendered everything to God and was willing to go through this operation. On July 18th, at 7 o'clock in the morning, I was wheeled down to the operating room. After that, I was totally oblivious to whatever they did because they had to put me under.

During the operation, they found that the cancer and tumor had spread. The tumor blocked the bile duct, where the cancer spread from my pancreas around one artery. Since they thought that it was too dangerous to operate any further, for fear that I might die right there on the table, they just connected the intestines to the gall bladder so that the bile could be drained from my liver.

I was then taken to my own room where I awoke from the anesthesia. Since I woke up at nine o'clock at night, I thought they did an extensive surgery rather than just the minimal surgery. However, I was told that the surgery was only minimal and that they couldn't do anything. Dr. McCoy said that there was no need to give me chemotherapy or radiation because my condition was beyond treatment. He also said that I had three to six months to live.

Dr. Davis said that sometimes science can only go so far, can only do so much, and that they had tried their best. They wished that they could have done more, but that they were unable to do so. This was the prognosis and when I heard it, I totally surrendered to God because of what Jesus told me on the plane, "Be not afraid. I walk before you, come follow me, and I will give you rest." So, I was at total peace and a certain joy filled my heart. I realized that this is what the Little Flower went through when she discovered she was bleeding from her sickness of tuberculosis. This was the first warning and sign that God was calling her home. Like the Little Flower, I felt that this was the confirmation that God has been revealing to me since May. In other words, God is calling me Home.

c.   While I was at the Carmel Home.

I stayed in the hospital from July 7th-28th, until I was able to walk around and regain some of my strength. People suggested that I should go to the Carmel Home for recovery until the staples on my stomach healed. So, I went to the Caramel Home and stayed there for two weeks in a section for those who are ill and need special care.

The incision was very long and went from one hip to the top of my stomach and down to the other hip. There were sixty staples used to close the incision. Twice, everyday, the incision had to be dressed and sterilized so as to minimize the risk of an infection. The Carmel Home is dedicated to helping the aged. The nurses and every other person at the Carmel Home treated me wonderfully and they were all very dedicated. I am sincerely grateful that they were able to take care of me.

While I was at the Caramel Home, I was moved to read the life of the Little Flower again. This time, *The Story of a Soul* touched me tremendously. The book had so much more meaning to me because of her sufferings and what she went through before she died. I knew that she was with me because I received a steady stream of roses.

d.   Don't pray for a miracle

During this time, I was hoping that people would not pray for a miracle, although praying for a miracle is quite natural. But, most people do not realize that a person does not need to be living to carry out the work of God. Rather, a person can carry out God's work from Heaven as well. And I believe that this is my time to go

Home because there is a time for everything, especially when it comes to fulfilling God's plan.

In reference to my pancreatic cancer, God's Will must be done and a person does not have to use extraordinary means to prolong life. Rather, a person must use reasonable means so that nature can takes its course. Only in using natural means is there real dignity in death, especially when there is no possibility of getting well. In other words, true dignity is not suicide or assisted suicide because God is the author of life and not man. God is the One Who calls us Home. Therefore, we must wait on God and accept all sufferings no matter what that may be. However, when there is hope of being cured, a person needs to use proper means to be healed.

Presently, I don't feel any pain. Although I have lost quite a bit of weight through this whole ordeal. But now, I am starting to level off and I am regaining my strength. However, I know this strength will not last long because eventually I will lose some more weight and go through some suffering. Yet, I'm willing to do whatever God wants.

Pancreatic cancer is called the silent killer. The cancer grows silently within a person. If a person is lucky enough and the doctors discover the cancer before it has progressed too far, it is possible to treat the cancer. However, after discovering the cancer after a particular stage, then there is nothing that can be done.

6. Poem

In His Presence

Bright yellow sun
ball, red encircling, sitting
together on
the western horizon.

Corn,
no longer the green
of August,
but dry
and you would think
fragile,

holds itself erect
in the field,
as does the man
faded now
and close to the end.

Life funnels into
the unknown
for infinitely less than
the blink of
an eye, is made
whole again
in His presence.

M. Ptacek

7. Surrender to God

Jesus surrendered to the Will of His Father through His sufferings and death on the Cross, He won salvation for everyone who wishes to accept this great gift. Jesus became our Lord and Savior. Mary surrendered to the Will of God the Father. In doing His Will, she became the Virgin Mother of Jesus, the wife of Joseph, the mother of all humankind and the Mother of the Church. Joseph surrendered to the plan of God the Father. In doing His Will, he became the husband of Mary, a father to Jesus and the head of the Holy Family. He is also the protector and provider of the Church. Jesus said that when we surrender to the Will of our Heavenly Father, He will do all things for us. When our will is in union with the Will of God, we belong to God. We are His adopted children and all that He has belongs to us.

One day, while praying the Rosary, the following thoughts came to my mind. I was meditating on the Fifth Joyful Mystery. When Jesus was found in the temple by Joseph and Mary, He told them that He had to be about His Father's business. Mary kept these things in her heart and pondered about what He said to her. Then Scripture tells us that He went home with them and was obedient to them for the next eighteen years.

At Baptism, we become the temple of God. God lives in us and we are His home. The thought that struck me very forcefully was Jesus is obedient to us. Being in union with the Will of God, we are able to ask anything in the name of Jesus and He obediently grants whatever we ask. This is what Jesus tells us in the Bible. We need to believe, trust and accept what Jesus said. It is an awesome thought to realize that Jesus and the Triune God is obedient to us. It is really a humbling experience to understand this great reality in spiritual living. God grants these free gifts because He is a loving God.

Fr. Robert Faricy, S.J., who teaches theology at the Gregorian University in Rome, came to visit me. I told him about my thoughts about God being obedient to us. He confirmed that this was theologically correct.

8. Being grateful

I am very grateful to God because He has given me this time to prepare for eternal life. As a person comes closer to death, the more there is a need to let go of all that is earthly and to ponder on the real values of life. A person needs to let go and let God as well as to die more to self and become more like God each day. This is a great gift and opportunity. When a person lives for eternal life, he or she never needs to fear death.

a. Terminal cancer

When I found out that I had terminal cancer, I wanted to contact Sr. Belane so that she would know about my cancer and pray for me. When we finally got in contact, she told me that she too had cancer and that she had been in the hospital for three weeks.

Sr. Belane told me in 1946 that I would join the Congregation of the Sacred Hearts and that my religious name would be Luke. Ever since then, she has been praying for my priesthood and my ministry. She is ninty-two years old and we have remained very close over the years. In fact, I always remember her during Mass so that she would be blessed and benefit for everything she has ever done for me.

Sr. Belane is very different from me in regards to the spiritual life. She doesn't receive insights, revelations or locutions. In fact, I have a great danger of falling into pride because of all the gifts God has given me. This is how the Devil works against me, even though he has never been successful in leading me away from God. Hopefully with God's grace, I will persevere to the end. I believe that if I remain faithful to prayer and penance, God will give me His grace to live a sanctifying life. As I always say, God's grace is sufficient. As for Sr. Belane, her spiritual life calls for heroic faith. In other words, because she doesn't receive these gifts, she has to live a life of love by her example and commitment to her fellow sisters. Her way of life entails great faith and dedication so that she would never be led astray. The only danger is that the Devil can attack her and make her feel depressed, worthless and abandoned. As a result, she could feel that she might not go to Heaven. However, this is further from the truth. Because of her heroic faith, she has been a tremendous witness to those who know her. Personally, I believe that Sr. Belane is a very saintly person and has always been a source of inspiration.

9. Hales Corners, Wisconsin

When it was time to leave the Carmel Home, I decided that I should stay with my brother, Dr. James Zimmer, who lives in Hales Corners, Wisconsin. My brothers, Jim and Larry rented a vehicle that was specially equipped to have me transferred from Kentucky to Wisconsin on August 10th. When I saw this vehicle, I thought that I could sit in the back seat where I was able to recline. However, after the first stop, I just put a pillow under me and another behind my neck because this was much more comfortable. The trip was very long and tiring. Naturally, I was extremely happy to arrive in Hales Corners. Since then, I have been living with Dr. Jim and slowly regaining my strength. However, I'm still losing weight and I beginning not to sleep too well. But, the doctors said that this is all a part of having cancer.

a. Fr. Provincial

Fr. Provincial decided to visit with me for a few days at the end of August. During the visit, he said that I should stay with Dr. Jim and his family until my death. I agreed because Dr. Jim is a surgeon and he will be able to provide professional care. Strangely, after my diagnosis, I could no longer picture myself moving back to California because the Cardinal did not want me to live in Fillmore and as a result, I would have to live in a parish. The real problem to this whole picture after my diagnosis was that I would become a burden to them. So, I was very pleased that Father Provincial allowed me to stay with my family in Hales Corners.

Fr. Provincial also said that I should be buried in Wisconsin. Naturally, I was a little shocked because I always thought I would be buried with my brother priests in my Congregation. However, this is God's Will and I am happy to do God's Will. I am also grateful that I will be able to be buried in the parish where I attended Mass as a little boy. I also find being buried next to my Mom and Dad in the parish family cemetery to be very comforting.

10. The Eucharistic miracle was disolved

When my Provincial visited me, I asked him if he would bring the Eucharist that was exuding oil so that I could be blessed and adore Jesus in the remaining days of my life. Fr. Provincial then told me that the Eucharist was dissolved. Naturally, I was upset because I did not understand why this was done. So, I wrote to the Cardinal and told him that someone told me about the Eucharist. I stated that I didn't need to know why this was done, but that it would be nice to know the reason. When the Cardinal wrote back, he confirmed that the Eucharistic miracle no longer existed. He also said that when he found out about my terminal cancer and that I wasn't coming back to California that he consulted with some theologians from Sacramento. They advised him that the Eucharistic miracle or consecrated hosts should not be moved from place to place around the country. Rather, they advised him that the Eucharistic miracle should be dissolved, and this is what the Cardinal decided to do.

From this experience, I realized that the Cardinal and other people who have received authority are responsible for many decisions. Even though we may not understand various decisions, we are not in the position to make these decisions. Rather, we need to be obedient, respectful and loving towards people with authority. That's why we should always pray to the Holy Spirit so that He can guide these people. However, we have the right to know why things are done. We can even express our opinion and disagree as long as we use prudence, respect and love. Likewise, we should always be willing to forgive those who may do us wrong because this is what Jesus would do.

As for the Cardinal and others who I have disagreed with from time to time, I have nothing but the greatest respect and highest esteem for them because they are my brothers and sisters in Christ. Hopefully, they will realize that I pray and love them as true friends. I always pray for their sanctity and with God's grace, I will see all of them in Heaven.

a.   Letter received from Ann Holcomb

On September 8th, 1996 I received the following letter from Ann Holcomb:

Dear Fr. Luke,

The following letter was sent to me by Marge Beitz, sister of Frances Uzarski. Another sister, Helena Johnson called me from Oregon in August. She inquired about the state of your health. It was then when she told me about the dream of Frances' daughter, Maureen Uzarski Sikora had about you. I received the following letter on August 15th, 1996.

"In March 1996, I had a dream of my mother Frances Uzarski, and all my family being in Medjugorje. Mom was glowing and showing us pictures. The pictures were of places never seen before on earth. We asked where we could go to see these places. Mom answered, 'These are pictures I brought from Heaven.' She also said, 'God will be taking another great person from this earth soon.' Then I saw an alter covered with roses. There was a picture of Father Luke Zimmer circled in red. The Church was half sheltered. Children were everywhere dressed in long white gowns. One child was holding a Crucifix, which was covered with roses. Everyone was holding roses. The moment Father Luke's picture was shown all of the roses shriveled and died. In July, 1996, I went to visit my aunt Margaret. At that time, I told aunt Margaret about the dream. She then revealed to me that Father Luke had three to six months to live and that he had cancer."

Sincerely,
Marleen Uzarski Sikora

b. The details of funeral

Now that I have some time on my hands, I will be able to plan my funeral Mass at St. Columba's Church in Lake Five, Wisconsin. I decided that my nephew, Fr. Tony Zimmer will be the main celebrant. Hopefully, my cousin Fr. Bill Zimmer will also be present. As for my homily, Fr. Tony will give the eulogy, while Father Provincial, Fr. Mike Sears and Fr. Scott Adams will also speak.

I hope and desire that Memorial Masses would be held at various places across the country so that all lay Servants and Handmaids of the Sacred Heart of Jesus, Mary and Joseph will be able to attend. I hope that during this time, these people will make a commitment to continue the work so as to spread the Apostolate far and wide.

11. Apostolate of Christian Renewal is proposing

The Apostolate of Christian Renewal is trying to bring about happiness, peace and joy in other people's lives. However, many people put their trust in material things as seen on TV and other advertisements. These material and temporal things do not bring peace or happiness. Rather, the only thing that gives true peace and joy is a personal love-relationship with the Blessed Trinity. This is what we are dedicated to and hope will be brought about. No matter what happens to me, the Apostolate of Christian Renewal will continue because it is the Will of God.

a.   All for God's honor and glory

I believe that each person should have the proper attitude of doing everything for God's honor and glory. I hope that anyone who becomes a Servant or Handmaid will ask God for this grace so as to live for Him alone. I believe that if the Servants and Handmaids have this proper attitude, then any obstacle can be overcome. As a result, a person will be full of peace and joy because they are in union with God's Will. When we are in love with God, He gives us the gift of peace and nobody can ever take away or destroy this gift no matter what they say or do.

b.   After my death

I hope that after I die, the work of the Apostolate of Christian Renewal will spread far and wide. In order to bring this about, I hope that lay Servants and Handmaids will financially support the Apostolate. I hope these Servants and Handmaids will be committed and be filled with prudent zeal so as to share the charism, spirituality and purpose. I also hope that after I die, the Servants' community of priests and brothers will be founded as well as an outgrowth of the Handmaid's community of sisters.

c.   The Apostolate of Christian Renewal

The Apostolate of Christian Renewal has been around for over twenty-five years. Even though the Apostolate will eventually dissolve after the Servants are founded, I believe that the Apostolate of Christian Renewal will be an important element in the founding of the Servants. Until then, the Apostolate needs to continue to carry out the work of the Lord. The Apostolate of Christian Renewal invites every person to learn more fully the charism, spirituality and purpose of the Servants and Handmaids of the Sacred Heart of Jesus, Mary and Joseph. People can learn more about the Apostolate by reading our books, listening to our audio and video tapes and reading the *Christian Renewal News*.

The *Christian Renewal News* is a newspaper that we send to people four times a year. Even though we give the newspaper away for free, I think we should have sold subscriptions. The reason is because the newspaper costs so much money. In fact, each time the Apostolate sends out a newspaper, it costs about $14,000 an issue. Usually, the only way the Apostolate was able to pay for the *Christian Renewal News* was from the money I received during Renewal Weeks. The money came from the sale of my books, tapes, pictures and donations that were requested at the end of each Renewal Week. Nevertheless, I think that the *Christian Renewal News* is extremely helpful and insightful in spreading the work of the Lord. Hopefully, many people will respond with a generous donation so that the *Christian Renewal News* can continue to help thousands of people in the future.

Unfortunately, the majority of our Catholic people are not accustomed to giving a lot of money. Thank God, the Apostolate received other donations so that we were able to meet all of our other expenses. Another tremendous expense of the Apostolate of Christian Renewal is running the Center so that young men have a place to discern their vocation in life. Along with the expenses of the Center, insurance and taxes, I also gave a yearly contribution to my Congregation.

In the future, I hope that many people will be generous so that the Apostolate does not have to worry about finances. In this way, the Apostolate can begin to save money so as to build other Centers and pay for the seminarians' expenses when they go to school.

Even though the Apostolate was unable to accumulate a lot of money, we certainly could not have come as far as we are without doing God's Will. In the future, people will have to take the initiative and be generous with the blessings, graces and gifts that God has given them.

d. Spreading the Apostolate after I die

One way to spread the work of the Apostolate of Christian Renewal is to speak with another person on a one-to-one basis. On this basis, a person should explain the charism, spirituality and purpose. Another way to spread the Apostolate is having small groups come together so as to pray the Mystical Mass Prayer, the Mystical Rosary and to study the charism, spirituality and purpose.

I think that these groups should meet at least once a week in order to be vital and vibrant. As these groups grow, this movement can be spread to other small groups and be carried out in a similar way.

Remember, the Servants and Handmaids of the Sacred Heart of Jesus, Mary and Joseph is to be a movement, not an organization. These groups should not get bogged down and stifle the Spirit. However, I believe certain people need to be trained as leaders so that they can guide others to continue to carry out the work. This is why we need to build spiritual centers.

These spiritual centers will cost a lot of money, time and energy on the part of the people. There will be many sacrifices that need to be made. But this is explained in the booklet, *A Way of Life: Be a Saint.*

Each person can spread this work of the Lord in many ways, but each person needs to be committed. So I say to you, do not lose courage when a person does not accept, believe or practice this way of life. The world is big and there are many people thirsty for a new way of life. Do not be too adamant if people do not accept this way of life. Rather, be accepting and loving so that God's Holy Spirit can work through you. Let God touch your heart and illuminate your mind so that you are truly an instrument of God in carrying out His work that He has called me to begin, and for you to continue and spread across the world. Remember, each person has a free will and allow the person to learn from your example. Be like Jesus so that others can be touched so as to live a holy way of life. May God bless each of you in a very special way for anything that you do in living this way of life and sharing this with others.

EPILOGUE

During the last six months of Fr. Luke's life, God gave Fr. Luke many blessings, graces and gifts. The greatest gift, of course, was the gift to offer all his sufferings with Jesus in each Eucharistic Liturgy throughout the world and throughout all time. Fr. Luke also continued to keep his rigorous schedule until the last few days of his life. This means that Fr. Luke continued to offer the Eucharistic Liturgy, pray the Liturgy of the Hours as well as pray the fifteen-decade Rosary three times a day. He also continued to answer letters and phone calls. During this time, he never complained about being overwhelmed by pain, work or anything else. For many of those people who were with him during this time, Fr. Luke was a source of inspiration by his natural acts of virtue.

During the last month of Fr. Luke's life, he slowly lost the taste for meat as well as for other foods. In fact, he said that eating was becoming more of a penance each day. Along with the loss of taste, he began to feel nausea, vomit blood and lose his strength. Over the course of his last month, there were many times when he was extremely weak. However, after a few days, Fr. Luke seemed to recover and regain some of his strength. Eventually, these periods of weakness became longer and longer.

On Saturday morning, January 3rd, 1997, most of Fr. Luke's immediate family came to say good-bye because he started to lose consciousness. During this time, his nephew, Fr. Tony Zimmer, said the prayers for the dying along with the Mystical Rosary. Shortly after the Rosary, Fr. Luke slowly lost consciousness. However, he regained consciousness for one last time and asked the score between the Green Bay Packers and the San Francisco Forty-niners. Naturally, all those who were present thought this was pretty funny considering that he did not have much time left. In fact, those words were Fr. Luke's last because he then became comatose.

On Tuesday, January 7th, Fr. Luke's breathing became very irregular and his fingernails began to turn blue. These were signs that he was near death because his lungs were filling up with water. At 8:10 PM, Fr. Tony Zimmer arrived to say the prayers for the dying. Shortly after Fr. Tony finished, Fr. Luke took his last breath and left behind one last tear. Fr. Luke died at 8:22 PM, January 7, 1997.

After Fr. Luke's death, he was buried on the following Saturday, January 11, 1997. Fr. Luke was buried next to his Mom and Dad at St. Columba's Parish, Lake Five, Wisconsin.

APPENDIX

On November 27th, 1996, Cardinal Roger Mahony gave Fr. Michael Sears verbal permission to start the Confraternity of Priests of the Sacred Heart of Jesus, Mary and Joseph. On December 5th, 1996, Fr. Michael Sears received a formal letter confirming the approval for the Confraternity of Priests. The following letter is the eloquent document Fr. Michael wrote to the Cardinal:

CONFRATERNITY OF PRIESTS OF THE SACRED HEART OF JESUS, MARY AND JOSEPH

Charism

Jesus prayer of unity at the Last Supper:
Father, may they all be one, even as you, Father, are in me, and I in you, that they also may be one in us, so that the world may believe that you sent me. (Jn. 17:21)

- This charism is given for priests to unite themselves more intimately to Jesus Christ in the Eucharistic Liturgy. This unity brings a greater awareness of the union that exists in the Trinity. The great love in the Godhead is manifested most perfectly in the Son who became human and offered Himself for us in the Paschal Mystery - His life, death, resurrection, ascension, and giving of the Holy Spirit. The gift of the Holy Spirit vivifies the Church to perpetuate these saving events in the life of the Mystical Body of Christ, especially in the Eucharistic Liturgy. The unity in the Father, Son, and Holy Spirit extends to all creation. This is experienced in the angels and saints in heaven, the souls in purgatory, the Church on earth, and all who seek God with a sincere heart. All prayers offered to God need to be consciously united to the summit, source, and focal point of all history and in every person, Jesus Christ.

- This charism can be manifested by unity in prayer with all the angels, saints, suffering souls, every person in the body of Christ and the family of God, offering all acts of praise and adoration, thanksgiving, sorrow for sins, and intercessory prayer in union with each Mass celebrated each day throughout all time. These *prayers* become the *one prayer* of Christ the High Priest who has offered Himself once for all, for all time.

- This charism brings a more profound awareness of the Trinitarian unity. A Trinitarian unity that exists as family. The clearest reflection of this unity of the Father, Son, and Spirit is the Holy Family. The love that was present in Jesus, Mary, and Joseph at Nazareth was so intense and pure that they became one; one heart in the Son, Jesus Christ. The expression of redemption by the Father, carried out by the Son, and applied by the Holy Spirit is realized in the communion of saints, the body of Christ, which was most perfectly lived by the Blessed Virgin Mary and St. Joseph. Thus, we invoke the Holy Family under the title Sacred Heart of Jesus, Mary, and Joseph to bring unity to us as individuals with the Lord but also with all in heaven, purgatory, and on earth. This incarnational unity in Christ exists and is preeminent in the Eucharist.

Spirituality

The gift of the Holy Family gives us the example of how the Holy Spirit can bring unity to one another when the object of one's love is Jesus. Chosen by God to reflect and initiate the unity of the Triune God who is Love, the Holy Family entrusted their lives to the will of the Father and movement of the Holy Spirit:

> *And Mary said, "...Let it be done according to your word."* (Lk 1:38)

> *When Joseph awoke, he did as the angel of the Lord had directed him.* (Mt 1:24)

> *And he (Jesus) went down with them (Mary and Joseph) and came to Nazareth, and was obedient to them.* (Lk 2:51)

> *And Jesus said, "...Not my will but yours be done."* (Lk 22:42)

Meditation on their life on earth is but part. The reality of the mission of the Holy Family that continues needs to be realized as substantial. The Holy Family can become active in everyday life, especially in the priest, who carries the presence of Christ, in a unique way, in his very person. Each person of the Holy Family can be reflected in the life and ministry of the priest:

> *Jesus* - As the One chosen to be the High Priest, the life, death and resurrection of Jesus is the acceptable sacrifice that is offered to bring to fruition the unity of all humanity. The ministry of Jesus is unity, *Father, may they all be one, even as you, Father, are in me, and I in you, that they also may be one in us, so that the world may believe that you sent me* (Jn. 17: 21). This ministry of unity is given to the Church to be the instrument of unity in Christ. This is manifested most perfectly in the Eucharisitc Liturgy. This offering is made present *through* the gift of priesthood given in holy orders. But the Catholic priest carries this presence *in* his very person. The increased awareness of the presence of Christ will allow a clearer vision of unity lived out in the life of the priest. The priest has a special calling to not only reflect Jesus but is called *to be* Jesus *for* and *to* others. This can be seen in the relationship that Jesus had with Mary and Joseph. The vulnerability of Jesus and his reliance on his mother and foster-father, who are valuable instruments in the mission of Christ, provides an example of unity through humility and trust. The humanity of Jesus that is offered as the perfect sacrifice *flows* from the Holy Family. This presence of Jesus,

human and divine, in the priest transforms him into an instrument of unity for the people of God.

Mary - As the one chosen to carry the Son of God in her person, Mary becomes the perfect created instrument of unity in Jesus. The ministry of Mary, as God-bearer, is reflected in the vocation of the priest as the one who brings Jesus to others and brings others to her Divine Son. The active role of the Virgin Mary in the life of the priest *teaches* him to love Jesus personally, *nurtures* him in the spiritual life, *stands* with him in times of trial, and is *mystically present* with the priest in the sacramental ministry, especially in the Eucharist.

Joseph - As the one chosen to be the spouse and father of the Holy Family, Joseph becomes the model of unity in Jesus. The ministry of Joseph, as Patron and Guardian of Christ, is reflected in the ministry of the priest as a *type of priest* through his fatherly privilege of receiving and presenting Jesus to all. The presence of St. Joseph in the life of the priest teaches him to *honor and reverence* the body of Christ, in the Church and especially in the Eucharist, provides a profound meditation on the presence of Jesus in *everyday life*, brings *confidence and assurance* in difficult times, and establishes a true sense of *fatherhood* in ministry.

The Holy Family is unified in the Heart of Jesus. Inspired by the divine love of the Father, the center of love flows to and from the presence of God in the Christ and unites Jesus, Mary and Joseph to each other as one. The sacredness of this divinely inspired human love is recognized in the unity of hearts in the Holy Family. The priest can tap into this source of love by uniting himself to the Sacred Heart of Jesus, Mary and Joseph and become a more profound instrument of the unity that is present in the Trinity.